English Victorian Churches

Architecture, Faith, & Revival

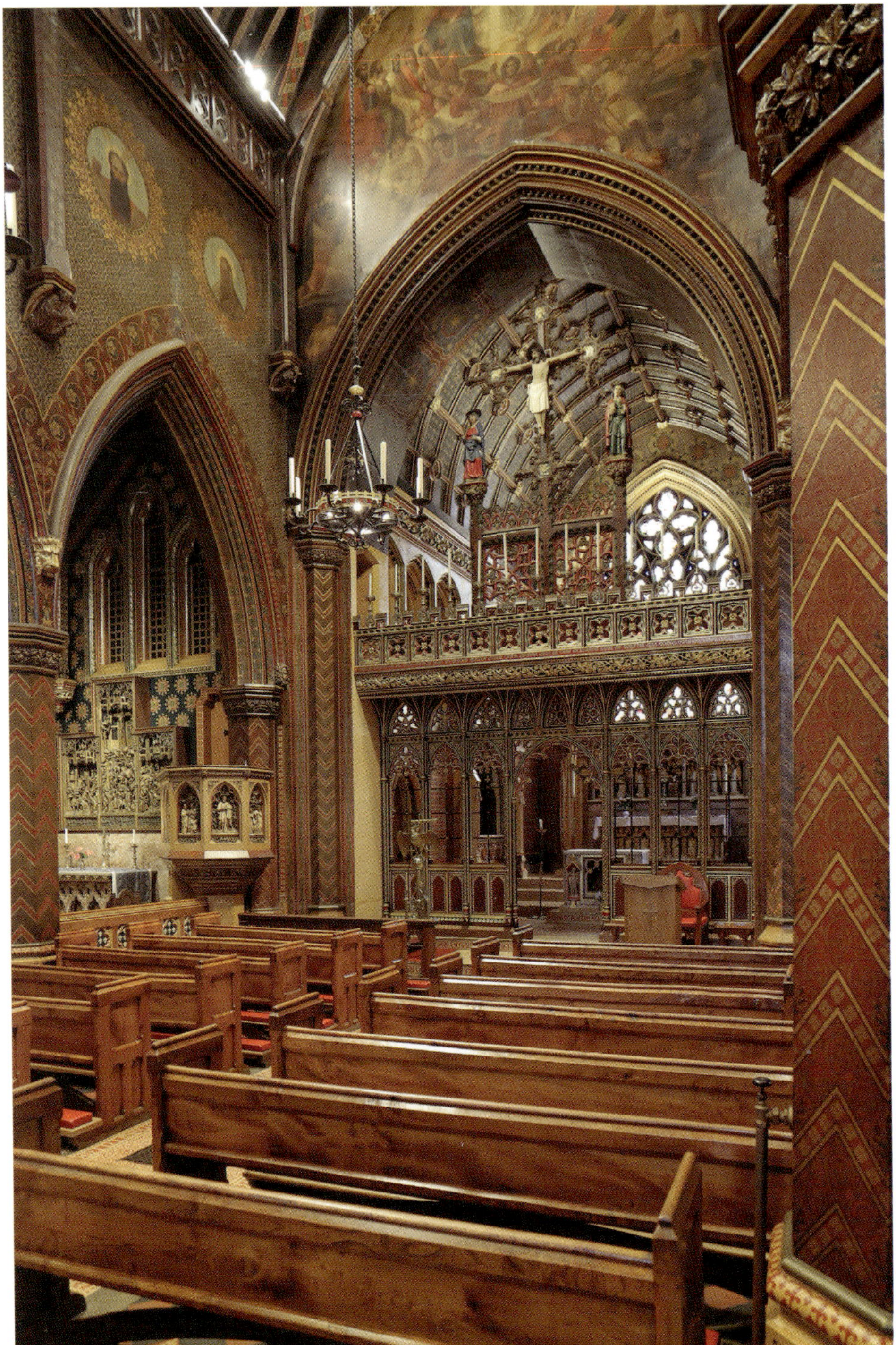

Frontispiece St Giles's R.C. Church, Cheadle, Staffordshire (1841–6), by A.W.N. Pugin. The style is Second Pointed throughout, and the interior is sumptuously coloured. The chancel is divided from the nave by a chancel arch, below which is an exquisite screen, with coving, loft, and rood (MK [2019]).

English Victorian Churches

Architecture, Faith, & Revival

JAMES STEVENS CURL

with numerous photographs by
Geoff Brandwood and others
and a Foreword by Barry Orford

I find I never weary of great churches...

ROBERT LOUIS BALFOUR STEVENSON (1850–94):
'Noyon Cathedral' in *An Inland Voyage* **xvii** in the
Tusitala Edition (London: William Heinemann Ltd, 1924), 80.

John Hudson
Publishing

Published by

John Hudson Publishing
22 Stratford Grove
London SW15 1NU

First published 2022

ISBN 978-1-7398229-3-4 (hardback)
ISBN 978-1-7398229-4-1 (ebook)

British Library Cataloguing in Publication data
A CIP catalogue for this book is available from the British Library.

Edited by Sarah Enticknap
Indexed by Auriol Griffith-Jones
Design and layout by Nicola Willmot (info@twoplusgeorge.co.uk)
Typeset in Kings Caslon
Printed and bound in the United Kingdom by Short Run Press, Exeter

Front cover Church of St Leonard, Scorborough, Yorkshire (ER) (1857–9), by John Loughborough Pearson, built 'as a thank-offering for many blessings' at the expense of James Hall, Lord Hotham's land agent and tenant at Scorborough Hall, showing the extraordinarily inventive steeple in which the huge angle-pinnacles and steeply gabled elements disguise the shift from square to octagonal plan (© Geoff Brandwood [2021]).

Back cover Rood screen and loft by J.N. Comper – designed from 1898, made by John Parsons of St Teath and decorated under the supervision of H.A. Bernard Smith, with rood and figures carved by W.D. Gough of London, completed 1908 – in the Church of St Petroc Minor, Little Petherick, Cornwall, rebuilt by William White in 1858 (© James Stevens Curl [2021]).

In Memoriam

Geoffrey ('Geoff') Kenneth Brandwood (1945–2021)
Friend, Colleague, Scholar, Enthusiast, Ecclesiologist,
and Architectural Photographer with a Discerning Eye

Nam idem velle atque idem nolle,
ea demum firma amicitia est
(to like and dislike the same things, that is truly real friendship).

GAIUS SALLUSTIUS CRISPUS (86–35 BC):
Bellum Catilinæ **xx**.

Namque tu solebas
Meas esse aliquid putare nugas
(for you used to think my trifles were worth something).

GAIUS VALERIUS CATULLUS (*c*.84–*c*.54 BC):
Carmina **i**.

Some other published writings by James Stevens Curl

St Michael's Kirkyard, Dumfries: A Presbyterian Valhalla with a Foreword by Roger Bowdler and an Epilogue by Robert L.D. Cooper (Holywood: Nerfl Press, 2021)

Introductory Essay and Bibliography in a fine, enlarged, numbered, limited, facsimile edition of *On the Laying Out, Planting, and Managing of Cemeteries; and on the Improvement of Churchyards* by John Claudius Loudon (originally published 1843) with a Foreword by Ian Dungavell and an Index by Auriol Griffith-Jones (Holywood: Nerfl Press, 2019)

Making Dystopia: The Strange Rise and Survival of Architectural Barbarism with a Prolegomenon by Timothy Brittain-Catlin (Oxford: Oxford University Press, 2018, 2019)

'A Short History of the Cemetery Movement' in *The Art of Memory: Sculpture in the Cemeteries of London* by Richard Barnes (Kirstead, Norfolk: Frontier Publishing, 2016)

The Oxford Dictionary of Architecture (with Susan Wilson) (Oxford: Oxford University Press, 2015, 2016)

Funerary Monuments & Memorials in the Church of Ireland (Anglican) Cathedral of St Patrick, Armagh with an Introit by The Most Reverend A.E.T. Harper, Archbishop of Armagh and Primate of All Ireland 2007–12, and a Foreword by Professor Janet Myles Spencer (Whitstable: Historical Publications, 2013)

Georgian Architecture in the British Isles 1714–1830 (Swindon: English Heritage, 2011)

Freemasonry & the Enlightenment: Architecture, Symbols, & Influences with a Preface by Professor Andrew Prescott (London: Historical Publications, 2011)

Spas, Wells, & Pleasure-Gardens of London (London: Historical Publications, 2010)

Victorian Architecture: Diversity & Invention (Reading: Spire Books, 2007)

The Egyptian Revival: Ancient Egypt as the Inspiration for Design Motifs in the West with a Foreword by Peter Clayton (London & New York: Routledge, 2005)

The Victorian Celebration of Death (Thrupp, Stroud: Sutton Publishing, 2004)

'A Short History of the Cemetery Movement in Europe' in *Italian Memorial Sculpture 1820–1940: A Legacy of Love* by Sandra Berresford, with contributions by Fred S. Licht, Francesca Bregoli, Franco Sborgi, Robert W. Fichter, and Robert Freidus (London: Frances Lincoln, 2004)

Kensal Green Cemetery: The Origins & Development of the General Cemetery of All Souls, Kensal Green, London, 1824–2001 (ed., with contributions from several scholars) (Chichester: Phillimore, 2001)

The Honourable The Irish Society 1608–2000 and the Plantation of Ulster. The City of London and the Colonisation of County Londonderry in the Province of Ulster in Ireland. A History and Critique (Chichester: Phillimore, 2000)

The Londonderry Plantation 1609–1914. The History, Architecture, and Planning of the Estates of the City of London and its Livery Companies in Ulster (Chichester: Phillimore, 1986)

The Life and Work of Henry Roberts, 1803–76, Architect: The Evangelical Conscience and the Campaign for Model Housing and Healthy Nations (Chichester: Phillimore, 1983)

A Celebration of Death. An Introduction to Some of the Buildings, Monuments, and Settings of Funerary Architecture in the Western European Tradition (London: Constable, 1980)

The Erosion of Oxford (Oxford: Oxford Illustrated Press, 1977)

Contents

Foreword

'Oh, a horrible pompous thing,' [the Vicar] said; 'it was behind the altar – most pagan and unsuitable ... The first moment I entered the church, I said to myself, "that must go," and I have succeeded, though it was hard enough to collect the money, and actually some of the old people here objected.'

Arthur Christopher Benson (1862–1925):
The Upton Letters (London: Smith, Elder, & Co., 1906), 60.

English churches have frequently been unfortunate. They have endured the attacks of foreign foes, from the Vikings to the Luftwaffe, and have suffered the ravages of home-grown destroyers. The tales of post-Reformation vandals fervidly obliterating signs of 'superstition' are painful, and the Puritans' religious fanaticism wreaked further damage. Ignorant zeal has greatly harmed our ecclesiastical inheritance, and, in the 20th and 21st centuries, Victorian buildings have been particular targets for misguided adaptation or demolition.

It must be admitted that the Victorians, riding a wave of confident, mission-minded enthusiasm, built an excessively large number of places of worship. Many could not foresee that the forces which would remove the Church from its central place in society were growing even as they built, although some, more perspicacious, were acutely aware that great changes lay ahead. Superfluous to requirements today, these forlorn shells invite a superficial view that Victorian work is dispensable.

This book provides the material for preventing such continuing disregard for the surviving fabric entrusted to us. Professor Curl helps us to understand both why and how the Victorians built as they did. He charts the remarkable stylistic shifts characterising ecclesiastical architecture of the time, and suggests why great designers and restorers such as G.G. Scott, Butterfield, Burges, Street, Pearson, Bodley, and Temple Moore really *are* great, and why their works, and those of lesser-known names, deserve our care, appreciation, and gratitude. Readers of this fine book will have their eyes opened to the glories (sometimes extravagant ones) which await attention even in small buildings in out-of-the-way locations.

The story of Victorian ecclesiastical architecture is inseparable from that of the Oxford Movement, which awakened the Church of England to an awareness of its Catholic roots. Professor Curl is right to remind us of the honour due to generous benefactors, inspired by Tractarian ideals, who paid for new churches, especially those which brought faith, hope, and colour to some of the worst areas of burgeoning Victorian cities.

As the 19th century progressed, houses of God were designed to accommodate the ritual developments fostered by the Oxford Movement's disciples. It is an irony that recent liturgical changes have been the cause of much ill-considered damage to what Victorian architects so carefully planned. This need not happen if clergy and congregations understand what those architects intended, and work sensitively *with*, rather than *against*, their buildings.

Victorian church builders knew that beauty enriches the worship of God: this splendidly illustrated book is a reminder of that fact to a generation which is inclined to forget it.

Barry A. Orford
Emeritus Fellow, St Cross College, Oxford
October 2021

Preface and Acknowledgements

I have a good eye, uncle: I can see a church by daylight.

WILLIAM SHAKESPEARE (1564–1616):
Much Ado About Nothing (1598–9), Act 2, Scene 1, line 86.

Gratia pro rebus merito debetur inemptis
(thanks are justly due for things unbought).

PUBLIUS OVIDIUS NASO (OVID) (43 BC–*c.* AD 17):
Amores, **i**, Elegy 10, 43.

More than six decades have passed since my earliest observations on under-appreciated and often threatened Victorian architecture were published, and half a century ago my first book on the period appeared; since then, problems of neglect, inner-city decay, vandalism (official and unofficial), and the march of time have further eroded a rich 19th-century legacy. Yet we could learn much from the Victorians concerning architecture that often rose to its occasion, and of all Victorian building types, none is as fascinating as that designed for Christian worship. Into their churches Victorians poured creative genius, and the finest exemplars stand comparison with the best mediæval work, often surpassing it in quality.

I have long been interested in ecclesiastical buildings, and have travelled in every English county to study them. Mention of counties prompts an explanation: throughout, I have used the names of old counties to describe locations because, first, they are still widely recognised despite subsequent changes; second, the *Buildings of England* series is arranged county by county; and, third, the old county boundaries were related to diocesan boundaries, and had profound historical associations. Yorkshire is presently divided into West, South, and North Yorkshire, and, bizarrely, the East Riding (which I identify as ER): I have retained the former North and West Ridings, using abbreviations NR and WR as appropriate. Cumbria (created 1974) I have had to accept: it embraces Cumberland, Westmorland, the Furness district of northern Lancashire, and Sedbergh district, formerly within Yorkshire's West Riding.

As we move into the third decade of the 21st century, it becomes more difficult to explore churches. Often the finest works of architecture in an area, they are terra incognita to a largely uninterested population: there are even indications that any building that can be considered as real architecture will be an object of loathing for the visually desensitised, while anything connected with the Middle Ages, especially 'Gothic', is dismissed as 'irrelevant'. All this has brought responses from the Churches: 'redundant plant' is a label ecclesiastical authorities apply to buildings of which they wish to be rid, while increasing numbers of abandoned buildings fall to vandalism or demolition. Many Victorian churches in inner cities or towns have been destroyed, or are under threat, yet most are not mere copies of mediæval styles (ignorantly termed 'pastiches' by modernists): indeed they are often marvellously original; not a few display craftsmanship second to none; and several are among the first architectural ranks of any period. Another problem is that 21st-century English society is largely secular: few people understand churches, feel easy in them, or know how they once were used. I say 'once were used' because what goes on in most of them bears little resemblance to the forms of service for which they were designed. Both the Anglican and Roman Catholic Churches (the latter referred to hereafter as R.C.) have embraced such radical changes to their liturgies that the buildings no longer make sense.

At the end of Queen Victoria's reign (1901), the Church of England was alive, well, and vigorous: it was central to national life; everywhere there were Anglican churches; and it had over 20,000 clergymen. It possessed a great tradition of church music; it was effective in providing education, and its influence pervaded countless institutions; it was a dignified, civilised, tolerant, and fundamentally decent presence throughout the land; and its buildings, new and old, for the most part were the best and the finest the genius of the nation could create.

Old churches were tombs of dead generations (often commemorated on mural tablets or funerary monuments, but today even those are under threat), and churchyards were packed with bones of parishioners interred over the centuries, so communities were physically and spiritually connected with their history, collective memories, and antecedents. The mellifluous texts of the Prayer Book were familiar, laying foundations of feelings for the English tongue and the seemly dignity of ceremonial and worship. Our language owes much to the King James Bible, yet few now read it: the disappearance of elementary Christian knowledge has eroded aspects of English identity, and there can be no doubting resultant linguistic impoverishment. Mystery and numinousness have been discarded in favour of fatuous virtue signalling, absurd attempts to introduce a language akin to street argot in order to 'reach out' to the masses (clearly it does no such thing), and tenth-rate 'music' that lowers rather than elevates the spirits. When many are seeking spirituality, the Church appears unable to provide it: some senior clergy have even attempted to curry favour with mobs by concurring with demands for iconoclasm, notably concerning the removal or destruction of funerary monuments commemorating historical figures currently out of fashion.

There is another factor, usually avoided or ignored: recent demographic changes in many English towns and cities have been phenomenal. Many areas are now occupied by non-Christians, so churches in such areas have lost their congregations. Furthermore, the ascendancy of the Evangelical party within the Anglican Church (for which buildings, designed for ritualistic use, are no longer regarded as appropriate for worship) has led to either the abandonment of large numbers of unloved churches or drastic alterations to their physical fabric, destroying their æsthetic and architectural integrity.

Why write a book on Victorian religious buildings in 2022, and how does it fit a climate that is inimical to history (especially to England's history), favouring a *tabula rasa* owing nothing to the past? My objectives include a desire to show how rich is England's 19th-century church architecture; to describe its various styles; and to give a flavour of the backgrounds that prompted its designs and realisations. Some ecclesiastical buildings are wonderful repositories of the very best exemplars produced by craftsmen of genius; others are quirky, not necessarily things of beauty; and others are included for different reasons, but always in order to make a point. Yet I am aware that in some respects this book has an elegiac quality, for not a few of my chosen works face an uncertain future.

Restricted space precludes a discussion of tradesmen who worked on the buildings (a vast subject in itself), although a few important interior fittings and their creators are identified. The story of Victorian churches does not begin with the Queen's accession to the throne in 1837 any more than it ends with her death in 1901: this book therefore takes into account the historical background stretching back to the reigns of Anne, the first four Georges, and William IV, and ends in the Edwardian era a few years before the 1914–18 war.

Students of Victorian churches should travel with the *Buildings of England* volumes, and try to recognise the main architectural styles (although Pevsner's judgements, largely formed when peering through Bauhaus-tinted spectacles, should not be uncritically accepted). To get the most out of visits to churches, some preliminary study of styles is desirable, together with an acquaintance with their recurring elements. In the interests of brevity in what is intended as an introduction to the subject, this book does not include a detailed glossary of architectural terms, which would only duplicate material already available. Readers are advised to refer to *The Oxford Dictionary of Architecture* by James Stevens Curl and Susan Wilson, published by Oxford University Press, 2015, 2016, and available in print form and online, which has the fullest entries, including biographies of architects and descriptions of styles. A glossary of specialised architectural, ecclesiological, liturgiological, and theological terms is included on pages 187-208 of the present volume.

I owe much to my understanding of Victorian churches to the years 1970–3, during which I was architectural editor of *The Survey of London*: by a happy chance the area on which I worked was the parish of Kensington, and I studied every ecclesiastical building within it, organising drawings and photographic records as well as writing the descriptions. As most Kensington churches are Victorian, I absorbed a generous range of 19th-century responses to the problems of designing them, an invaluable experience for which I shall always be grateful.

This book's conception began in the early 1990s, when Tim Auger, then Batsford's commissioning editor, suggested I should take on one of the series then being published for English Heritage. I was aware that omissions would attract criticism, while inclusions would bring opprobrium: I tried to give as wide a stylistic and chronological range of buildings as possible within the limitations of my brief, for the volume was neither a gazetteer nor a catalogue. It was decided to eschew footnotes (and endnotes, which I regard as an unhelpful abomination). I was also somewhat restricted to black-and-white images, the few colour plates (mostly taken by Martin Charles) being bunched together rather than integrated within the text (which itself was printed in two columns on each rather cramped page). The finished tome came out (1995) as *English Heritage Book of Victorian Churches*. In the spirit of that earlier book, this one again confines itself to churches in England, and on the Anglican tradition, although buildings of other denominations and faiths are included within Chapters 4 and 9.

Limitations regarding illustrations, length, etc., imposed on me made me realise that there were many things that could have been improved, not least coverage of the later Victorian period. When I worked with the Gothic Design Practice, my colleagues made valuable suggestions, triggering memories of conversations I had had some years previously with Stephen Dykes Bower, who noted that the 'period when architects endowed their buildings with a recognisable style, predominantly Gothic, but in which horizons gradually expanded to embrace much that was not Gothic' could be belatedly admired, if not envied. It was 'after this broadening tendency had begun that the greatest perfection in Gothic itself was attained ... The chief significance of an epoch that extended well into [the 20th] century ... lay in the persisting ability to find inspiration in style and handle it with originality'.

Quite so, and this volume attempts to include an appreciation of the late Gothic Revival, putting it firmly within the social and liturgical context without which it cannot make sense. Pevsnerian bias against the later Goths is, at least in part, redressed, for the masters who created some of the very best churches and fittings (and whose influence continued through the work of Dykes Bower and his pupils) were not afraid of talking about, and creating, *Beauty* in architecture. Twenty years ago John Richardson brought out an improved version of the original book under the unfortunate title of *Piety Proclaimed*, a label which scuppered its chances, and it did not make much of an impression, despite considerable improvements and a general upgrading of what was essentially the same book. Since that time I have had ample opportunities to cogitate further about the subject, absorbing remarks made by those colleagues of years ago.

I was fortunate to meet John Hudson, of the publishing arm of English Heritage, when he worked with me on my *Georgian Architecture in the British Isles 1714–1830* (2011). When the publishing side of EH (which had become Historic England by then) was transferred to Liverpool University Press, he established his own publishing house in London. We renewed contact, and decided that giving *Victorian Churches* a new start would offer a suitable vehicle for collaboration. However, the Covid-19 pandemic was over a year old by then, and we recognised there would be difficulties in obtaining material, but made several decisions anyway: we would again save space by avoiding footnotes or endnotes, aiming for a general readership; dates of individuals would be given in the Index rather than litter the text; because of exorbitant charges now levied by photographic archives, we would replace most, if not all, existing illustrations, and, in any case, we should have colour when possible; we would acknowledge important publications published since the 1995 book came out; and we would revise the text.

Then my good friend and colleague, Geoff Brandwood, discussed illustrations with me, and started providing new and very fine images from late 2020, many specially taken for this book. I am extremely grateful to him for his expertise, not only for his own splendid work, but for helpful suggestions, advice, introductions, and his considerable skills in tweaking photographs, including mine. His sudden and unexpected death in November 2021 was a terrible shock and a huge loss: his name, therefore, appears on the dedication page of this book, but I shall miss his conviviality, his enthusiasms, his sound judgements, and his generosity in reading my texts and making invaluable suggestions for improvements.

Martin Charles's collection of photographs was deposited after his untimely death with the RIBA: Jonathan Makepeace, Imaging Services Manager, informed me that the RIBA would be 'happy to honour the previous arrangement' I had had with him, and granted permission to re-use images. Further help with illustrations and other matters came from individuals, including David Abitbol, Sophie Andreae, Eli

Ballon, Tom Bilson (Head of Digital Media, The Courtauld Institute of Art), Alan Brooks, James Crowley, James O. Davies, Sonia Deadman, Andrew Derrick, the Revd Henry Everett, Andrew Foyle, Alex Hamilton, Charles Hind, Angelo Hornak, Mark Kirby, Timothy Knox (Director, The Royal Collection), Beccy Lane, Carole Laverick, Karen Lawson (Picture Library Manager, Royal Collections Trust), Kevin Lowe, Rosemary Lyons, Keith Ovenden (Archivist, Record Office for Leicestershire, Leicester, and Rutland), Daniel Partridge (Digital Images, Royal Collections Trust, St James's Palace), Mark Pearce, Patrick Pearce, Chris J. Pickford, Steve Pilcher, Alex Ramsay, Chris W. Redgrave, John Roberts, Peter Rogan, John Salmon, David Scott, the Revd Gerard Skinner, Brian Thornley, Mark Watson, Christopher Webster, and Susan Wilson. I am most grateful to all of them.

The compiler of a volume such as this incurs many obligations, not least to fellow scholars, archivists, librarians, and many others. Among those who helped in one way or another (many no longer with us) were Gordon Barnes, Richard Barnes, A.H. Buck, Eric Cartwright, Sir Howard Colvin, S.E. Dykes Bower, Edmund Esdaile, S.L. Evans, Jennifer Freeman, John Gloag, John Greenacombe, the Revd David Haddon-Reece, Basil Handford, Mark Haworth-Booth, Hermione Hobhouse, Mike Huxley, Dame Penelope Jessel, Stephen Johnson, Barry Ketchum, Hugh Mathew, William Murray, Kit and Lisa Norbury, Janet Perry, Warwick Pethers, John Physick, Anthony W. Pullan, Timothy Richards, Anthony Rossi, John Sambrook, Richard Sidwell, Gavin Stamp, Christopher Stell, Sir John Summerson, Peter Swallow, the Revd Anthony Symondson, Trevor Todd, and David Watkin.

I have drawn upon numerous collections including the Royal Archives, Windsor Castle; the Bodleian Library, University of Oxford; the British Library; Lambeth Palace Library; and the University of Leicester Library. Those who rendered especial assistance included Ann Perry, Roger Towe, Mary Weston, and Kay Woollen (Kimberlin Library, De Montfort University); Karen Latimer, Dan Holden, and Michael Smallman (The Queen's University of Belfast); Simon Edwards, Malcolm Green, Dawn Humm, Peter Kent, Claudia Mernick, and Cathy Wilson (RIBA Library and Information Service); Jill Palmer, Martyn Everett, and Alan Stevens (Saffron Walden Public Library); Colin Clarkson and Lucas Elkin (University of Cambridge Library); and John Fisher, Ralph Hyde, and Jeremy Smith (of what was Prints and Maps, Guildhall Library, Corporation of London). Jeremy Smith latterly has been with what is now known as the London Metropolitan Archives, and has generously helped.

The structure of the original book was sketched during one of my Visiting Fellowships at Peterhouse, University of Cambridge, and I thank the Governing Body of that venerable college for enabling me to work happily in agreeable surroundings. That book was prepared by Margaret Eborall, who has my gratitude for providing an electronic version of the original typescript which I was able to use as the skeleton on which the present work is based, and then for standardising the numbering system of my chaotic additions. Ingrid Curl, Barry Orford, and the late Geoff Brandwood kindly read the texts and made invaluable suggestions: their generosity is humbly acknowledged. My wife, Dorota, accompanied me in search of Yorkshire exemplars by Burges, Butterfield, Temple Moore, Pearson, and Street, so has my gratitude for that and much else: our journeys were always interesting and rewarding, and we gained much pleasure from them. Inevitably, in a work of this nature, some quotations are necessary. The Select Bibliography contains works in which readers can follow up the points made in the present book, and texts from which this volume has drawn information have been acknowledged in this way.

For access to buildings I record here my appreciation of countless clergymen, caretakers, churchwardens, and others who have enabled me to see what lies (almost inevitably these days) behind locked doors. To those incumbents, individuals, and archivists who allowed me access to buildings or records, and are too numerous to record individually here, I give thanks: without them this book could never have been written.

Finally, I thank John Hudson for publishing the book, Nicola Willmot for designing and setting it, Auriol Griffith-Jones for compiling the index, Sarah Enticknap for her painstaking editing skills, the Revd Barry Orford, for writing the elegant foreword, and I recall with affection and gratitude my friend, Geoff Brandwood, to the memory of whom this book is dedicated.

JAMES STEVENS CURL

Burley-on-the-Hill, Rutland; Peterhouse, Cambridge; Broadfans, Dunmow; Saffron Walden, Essex; and Holywood, County Down, 1992–2022

Note on Illustrations

Throughout, captions refer to the liturgical orientation of churches, whether or not the sanctuary is placed at the east end. Sources of illustrations are given in parentheses after each caption, with the year in which the picture was taken (where known) in square brackets. Abbreviations used are:

AH	© Angelo Hornak, London
AR	© Alex Ramsay
CJP	© C.J. Pickford
coll.	collection
CW	© Christopher Webster, or from his collection
CWR	© Chris W. Redgrave
DA	© David Abitbol, '*Quelles sont belles tes demeures ô Israel*'
DNS	© David N. Scott
GB	© Geoff Brandwood
GS	© Revd Gerard Skinner
HEA	© Historic England Archive
JE	© John Elliott
JOD	© James O. Davies
JR	© John Roberts
JS	© John Salmon
JSC	© James Stevens Curl
MC/RIBAC	© Martin Charles/Royal Institute of British Architects Collections
MK	© Mark Kirby
MW	© Mark Watson
PP	© Patrick Pearce
RIBAC	© Royal Institute of British Architects Collections
ROL&R	© Record Office for Leicestershire & Rutland
RU	© Robin Utracik of Northern Studios, Preston, Lancashire

The age in which we live is a most eventful period for English art. We are just emerging from a state which might be termed the dark ages of architecture. After a gradual decay of four centuries, the style, – for style there was, – became so execrably bad, that the cup of degradation was filled to the brim; and as taste had fallen to its lowest depth, a favourable re-action commenced.

AUGUSTUS WELBY NORTHMORE PUGIN (1812–52):
An Apology for The Revival of Christian Architecture in England
(London: John Weale, 1843), 1.

1

An Introduction to Denominations and Victorian Churches

'What is a church?' – Our honest sexton tells,
''Tis a tall building, with a tower and bells.'

GEORGE CRABBE (1754–1832):
The Borough (1810), Letter 2, 'The Church', line 11.

For commonly, wheresoever God buildeth a church, the devil will build a chapel just by.

THOMAS BECON (1512–67) edited by JOHN AYRE (1801–69):
The Catechism of Thomas Becon, STP, Chaplain to Archbishop Cranmer, … etc.
(Cambridge: Cambridge University Press for The Parker Society, 1844), 361.

Preliminary Remarks

It is as well to remind ourselves what is meant by the Victorian Age. It began when Princess Alexandrina Victoria of Kent (b. 24 May 1819) succeeded to the throne on the death of William IV on 20 June 1837: it was to end on 22 January 1901. Her reign is often perceived as the period when the Industrial Revolution, the railways, urban slums, and much else came into being; yet the Industrial Revolution began some 80 years before 1837, and the first railways were operational in the reigns of her uncles, George IV (1820–30) and William IV (1830–7).

The most spectacular changes to Victorian England involved urbanisation: it was the first truly urbanised modern society, and by 1890 London was a major world metropolis. The 1901 Census showed that more than three-quarters of the population lived in urban areas: towns became magnets for rural labourers, offering opportunities for personal advancement unthinkable in the countryside, and in the course of the Queen's reign there was a shift from high to low birth and death rates in urban areas. Gross National Product dramatically increased; income per head more than doubled between 1850 and 1900; and the Victorian legacy was one of unparalleled achievement and unimaginable wealth creation by the standards of a century before. Even more remarkable was the civilising of the urban masses through education, sanitary reform, housing provision, and the stabilisation of society. Urban Man became literate and numerate; for the most part was far better housed than was the case in 1801; was less inclined to riot as part of a gin-soaked mob; and paid greater attention to hygiene, in the process becoming, as it were, potty-trained. And the parts the Churches played in all this must be stressed, for without them it is doubtful if anything like stability would have been achieved at all, let alone the extraordinary advances in adult literacy, conditions of housing, and general cleanliness: the great numbers of surviving Victorian churches and chapels are reminders of those heroic efforts.

The Established Church

In the third decade of the 21st century the majority of the populace of England knows little of what goes on in churches, and lacks understanding of the denominational animosities that loomed large in Victorian times. Church leaders have admitted that Christianity has almost been eliminated from any relevance in the United Kingdom. In *Dover Beach* (1867), Matthew Arnold referred to the 'Sea of Faith' that

> Was once ... at the full, and round earth's shore
> Lay like the folds of a bright girdle furled.

However, even then, when Victorian church building was everywhere apparent, he could only hear

> Its melancholy, long, withdrawing roar,
> Retreating, to the breath
> Of the night-wind, down the vast edges drear
> And naked shingles of the world.

That ebbing of faith has not been reversed, and so it is probably helpful to outline the main religious groups.

Undoubtedly the finest and most numerous legacy of Victorian ecclesiastical buildings in England is that of the Anglican Church. The Anglican Communion of the Reformed Church of England (known until the disestablishment of the Anglican Church of Ireland in 1869 as the United Church of England and Ireland) claimed to be a fellowship within the One Holy, Catholic, and Apostolic Church of those constituted dioceses, provinces, or regional Churches in communion with the See of Canterbury: it claimed (and claims) to be part of the Catholic (Universal) Church, the authority of which stemmed from a supposed uninterrupted consecration of bishops from the time of St Augustine, Archbishop of Canterbury and Apostle of the English. However, the supreme authority of the Pope ceased to be acknowledged when the monarch was declared to be Supreme Head of the Church of England in 1534. So the Anglican Church, or the Church of England (otherwise known as The Established Church, the clergy, upholders, or members of which were and are known as Churchmen), was and is the State Church, headed by the reigning monarch, and is subject in part to Parliament (a fact that has caused disquiet among not a few Churchmen).

Within the Anglican Church was a broad sweep of opinion and practice, from the 'High Church', 'Anglo-Catholic', 'Ritualistic', 'Tractarian', or 'Puseyite' groups (which sought to emphasise the 'Catholic' character of Church, exalted the authority of the episcopate and the priesthood, believed in the saving Grace of the Sacraments, and regarded the Church of England as being in full continuity with the pre-Reformation Church in England) to the Low Church or Evangelical wing (which was more inclined to the Protestant view that repudiated papal authority).

A Protestant was the name given to those who separated from the R.C. Communion in the 16th century in the Declaration of Dissent (essentially a protest) from the decision of the Diet of Speier (1529), which reaffirmed the Edict of the Diet of Worms denouncing the Reformation. However, the term 'Protestant' in relation to the Anglican Church has varied: in the 17th century it was applied to the Established Churches of England and Ireland, but in the 19th century the nomenclature began to fall from favour among those Churchmen who laid stress on the claims of Anglicans to be equally 'Catholic' with the R.C. Church. Curiously, in the 17th century, Presbyterians, Quakers, or Separatists (those [also called 'Dissenters'] who withdrew from, or advocated separation from, the Established Church) were differentiated from 'Protestants' (primarily Anglicans, opposed to 'papists').

The Evangelical party was equated more closely with Protestant opinion, which maintained that the essence of the Gospels was the doctrine of salvation by faith in the Atoning Death of Christ, and tended to deny that Good Works or the Sacraments had any saving efficacy. Nineteenth-century Evangelicalism, in the words of 'George Eliot' (Mary Ann Evans), in *Middlemarch* (1871–2), 'cast a certain suspicion as of plague-infection over the few amusements which survived in the provinces': in short, it tended towards Sabbatarianism (the view of Sunday as a 'Sabbath', in which the Fourth Commandment is strictly and joylessly observed), was very restrictive, and emphasised 'The Word' of the Gospels rather than rituals or Sacramentalism.

A Sacrament is the common name for certain visible solemn ceremonies or religious acts (also called 'efficacious signs'): before the Reformation there were Seven Sacraments (Baptism, Confirmation, the Eucharist, Penance, Holy Orders, Matrimony, and Extreme Unction), but Protestants generally only recognised Baptism and Holy Communion (the Eucharist or the Lord's Supper). The pre-Reformation view was that the Sacraments differed from other rites because they were channels by which supernatural Grace (the divine influence which operates in Man to regenerate and sanctify, to inspire virtuous impulses, and to grant strength to endure temptation or tribulation) is imparted. The Protestant historical view of two Sacraments was based on the signs ordained by Christ, but neither was seen as conveying supernatural Grace. The Seven Sacraments, however, remained, and remain, part of R.C. belief.

Somewhere between the High and Low wings of Anglicanism was Broad Church, favouring a wide, liberal interpretation of dogmatic definitions and subscription to the Creed, and which emphasised the comprehensive and tolerant nature of the Church in order to admit a variety of opinion relating to belief, practice, and ritual. Unlike the High or Low Church parties, Broad Church devotees were not organised for proselytising purposes.

In architecture, Evangelicals required what was essentially an auditorium with excellent acoustics and sightlines so that the preacher of The Word could be seen and heard: chancels were not given emphasis, while the altar was a 'Communion table', used on occasion, but not on a daily basis. Thus Anglican churches built for Low Church or Evangelical services had plenty of accommodation, small chancels, wide, auditorium-like naves, and if there were transepts these would be occupied by seats, not chapels. In such churches the Gothic style of architecture was sometimes uneasily applied to the building, for nave piers had to be slender (for visibility), and often supported galleries, so they were frequently made of cast iron. Architectural results were sometimes startling, rather than scholarly, and buildings not infrequently somewhat ham-fistedly composed.

Churches for Anglo-Catholic, High Church, or Ritualist parties, on the other hand, were more impressive, colourful, and often scholarly and imaginative. Naves, aisles, and chancels were usually separated visibly from each other, and chancels were large, often richly furnished, and fitted out. Emphasis was on a setting for ritualistic ceremony rather than on static congregational worship. Chapels with altars were rare until around the 1870s, when they were sometimes called 'morning chapels', and Lady chapels were unusual until the 20th century, when chapels for the Reserved Sacrament (where part of the consecrated Host of the Eucharist is kept) and distinct baptistries also came into use. Anglican churches were usually orientated west–east, with the altar at the east end.

Nonconformity

Non-Anglican places of worship were mostly for Nonconformists: indeed, there were far more church buildings erected for Nonconformists than for Anglicans in the 19th century, and those were generally known as 'chapels'. Nonconformists suffered grave disadvantages (as did Roman Catholics) under historical parliamentary enactments, but in 1828 these restrictions were repealed, and Nonconformists (in the widest sense) could vote and hold office. Further disadvantages imposed on Roman Catholics were lifted ('Catholic Emancipation') in the following year. Nevertheless, a certain social stigma attached to Nonconformists and Roman Catholics (whose places of worship were also referred to as 'chapels') until almost the end of Victoria's reign, although Roman Catholics succeeded in achieving a fashionable status in certain instances and areas, especially when several distinguished Anglican clerics, eminent aristocratic families, or wealthy individuals converted to Rome. However, it was a feature of 19th-century Dissent that differences of opinion led to secessions: many branches, sects, and minorities often broke away from the main groups to found their own congregations. This led to the erection of many more buildings, usually quite small structures, but sometimes with pretensions to grandeur in order to cock a snook at the parent body.

Now all these groups of Nonconformist (in the sense, originally, of one who refused to conform to the discipline and ceremonies of the Church of England, and, later, of those who refused to conform or to subscribe to the Act of Uniformity of 1662) Protestant Dissenters had to raise funds to build their places of worship without State aid. The erection of chapels was therefore much more of local concern than was the case in the Anglican Church: Nonconformists and their ministers would form a committee to plan and erect the building, money being raised by donations, collections, borrowing, and, in some cases, the renting of pews (which led critics to declare that Dissent was mercantile in spirit, and preached the Gospel only to those who could pay for the privilege). In the mid-19th century, however, some Nonconformist national bodies were set up to organise finance and to establish guidelines for the design and management of chapels. Sometimes, chapels were private speculations by ambitious preachers or their supporters, but, more often, they were erected by groups of the like-minded of a particular denomination (or seceders from a denomination).

Many chapels foundered through lack of support, internal wrangles, or other problems, while some preachers misjudged the responses their performances would bring. Certain milleniarists, for example, misjudged the date of the Second Coming, which failed to occur: it would appear that support for those who miscalculated dwindled at once.

In terms of basic architectural requirements, the several denominations of Nonconformists differed little from each other. As preaching was the central element in Nonconformist observance, the minister had to be seen and heard by the whole congregation, which, because of the static nature of the services, had to be seated in relative comfort (a similar demand for comfortable seating developed in Anglican churches of the Broad and Evangelical type, and reflected a desire to demonstrate improving social position and clout). The provision of galleries enabled a congregation to be housed within a smaller ground area, and these galleries were usually placed on three sides of the building, supported on slender cast-iron columns, while the fourth side (opposite the entrance doors) was occupied by a large arrangement including the pulpit, a platform or a rostrum, and (if prosperity permitted) the organ (*see* Fig. 9.6). Orientation was unimportant in Nonconformist architecture, so there was no requirement for the pulpit end to be at the east: this had the advantage that Nonconformist chapels could be slotted into street frontages, and any architectural show confined to the main façade. In a great many early Nonconformist chapels, the street fronts often betrayed the two-storey arrangement behind. Simple pitched roofs terminated in pediments, and façades were of brick, stone, or stucco faced. In the cases of Wesleyan Methodists and Presbyterians, there was a certain emphasis on the 'Communion table', but even it would be set below the pulpit and the architectural ensemble incorporating organ, platform, and, sometimes, choir. In this design, The Word was given visible precedence, and the Communion rite was reduced in importance to a memorial or an allegory. However, this Nonconformist arrangement was really only a derivation of 18th-century Low Church Anglican church interiors before the Anglican Tractarian and Ritualist reforms obliterated so many of them (a few survive). Indeed, many features of early 19th-century chapels were essentially a continuation of the Classical Georgian tradition.

At this point a few outline notes on the most important groups among Nonconformists will not be out of place. Methodists, for example, only became known as Nonconformists in the 19th century: originally (in the Protestant sense), a Methodist was a member of a religious society, established at Oxford in 1729 by John and Charles Wesley, to promote piety and morality, but the term subsequently became associated with an adherent of those evangelistic religious bodies that originated from the work of the Wesleys and of George Whitefield, the leader of the Calvinistic branch of Methodism. Wesleyans, as Methodists were known, originally saw themselves as part of the Anglican Church, but became an independent sect, as their 'enthusiasm' did not go down well among rational, decorous, Georgian Churchmen. Furthermore, Charles Wesley disapproved of his brother John's actions, which broke with the Church of England: Charles was clear that he remained a priest of the Anglican Church until his death. The Whitefield-led groups tended to be more severely Calvinistic, and the Wesleyans themselves evolved seceding groups which became known as Primitive Methodists (almost completely a working-class denomination with numbers of small and unpretentious chapels), the United Methodist Free Church, and others accepting in the main the Arminian theology of Wesley (so called after Jacobus Arminius, who denied the Calvinistic doctrine of absolute predestination and irresistible Grace). Methodist chapels will often have the words WESLEYAN CHAPEL and a date displayed on the entrance front.

Another significant group of Nonconformists was the Unitarian persuasion, which affirmed the unipersonality of the Godhead (as opposed to the Trinitarian view), and ascribed divinity to God the Father only. Unitarianism grew out of a protest by Theophilus Lindsey, Vicar of Catterick, against the imposition of Anglican orthodoxies as tests of belief in general. Unitarians believed that each congregation should have independent authority, that God was Unity, and that there should be freedom for (and tolerance of) different religious beliefs. Unitarians were essentially liberal, tolerant monotheists who, although not numerous, were significant in municipal and political terms, and erected some important buildings that reflected their influence and power. In fact, Nonconformists generally had considerable strength in the provincial manufacturing towns, and certainly wielded clout in municipal affairs in places such as Birmingham, Bradford, Leeds, Leicester, Manchester, Newcastle, Oldham, Salford, Sheffield, and Wolverhampton: in Liverpool, Churchmen and Dissenters were openly hostile to each other, and this reflected the growing influence and success of Nonconformists in business and commerce. So powerful were the Unitarians in Leicester (and produced so many mayors) that the Unitarian chapel there was known as the 'mares' nest'. In Birmingham, a spectacular example of Geometrical Gothic, adapted to Nonconformist use, was the Church of the Messiah, a Unitarian centre built in 1860 on arches over the Birmingham Canal: its sheer size indicated the importance of Unitarianism in Birmingham under the leadership of the powerful Chamberlain and Nettlefold families. It was demolished in 1978.

Baptists formed another dissenting sect, which held that Baptism by immersion should only be administered to believers (and so required the unusual feature of very large fonts in their chapels): this group was also called the Anabaptists, and its members were often successful in commerce. Also significant were Congregationalists, who took their name from the substitution of 'Congregation' for 'Church' by 16th-century English Reformers: in the Congregational system the whole local body of worshippers was distinguished from 'the Church', or company of communicants, and each congregation was independent in managing its own affairs. Congregationalists were also called Independents, so 'Independent Chapel' was a self-governing Nonconformist group. They also carried considerable influence in municipal and political life, and were particularly strong in cities such as Bradford, Halifax, and London.

Presbyterianism was conceived as a kind of democratic church organisation, based on biblical authority, rejecting the episcopal hierarchies of Catholicism and Anglicanism. In individual Presbyterian congregations no higher order that that of elder is recognised, all being of equal rank, and each congregation is governed by its kirk session, composed of the minister and elders. Sessions are answerable to the presbytery (a kind of judiciary); that, in turn, is subordinate to the synod; and the synod could be overruled by the General Assembly of the Presbyterian Church. Although such an organisation was intended to give equal status to individuals, in practice it sometimes resulted in disputes and the formation of seceding congregations.

Quakers, or members of the Religious Society of Friends, founded by Leicestershire-born George Fox in 1648–50, had meeting houses with no architectural pretensions whatsoever, and indeed Quaker buildings often adopted a modest domestic air. The Friends, however, had considerable influence, economically and politically, and seven of Birmingham's 19th-century mayors were Quakers.

One sect of Nonconformists managed to produce a few distinguished works of architecture. Annan-born Edward Irving arrived in London in 1822, and was soon lionised by the capital's society. Some likened the suddenness with which Irving leapt to fame with Byron 'finding himself famous' in 1812 on the publication of *Childe Harold*: his oratory was pronounced worthy of his melodious and resonant voice, swarthy features, long hair, noble presence, commanding stature, and 'handsome features ... marred only by a slight obliquity of vision'. His eloquence transformed his small and poor congregation into a large and rich one, and he was able to move to a new church in Regent Square, regarded as one of the handsomest in London. A congregation of a thousand gluttons for punishment flocked thither Sunday after Sunday to hear him preach for three hours at a time. In 1828, he became convinced of the imminence of the Second Coming, and in 1830 the first instance of a woman speaking in 'unknown tongues' occurred. Soon these outbursts became habitual, and the Regent Square church witnessed several public outbreaks of unintelligible gibberish in which Irving rejoiced, observing that the 'bridal jewels of the church' had been recovered. Irving was removed from the pulpit at Regent Square in 1832, and broke with Presbyterianism. His flock followed him, and so was founded the 'Holy Catholic Apostolic Church', otherwise known as the 'Irvingites', which survived for a time, claiming Irving's relationship to it was rather like that of John the Baptist to the early Christian Church, thus he was the prophet of the coming dispensation. The services adopted (1842) were potpourris based on Anglican, R.C., and Greek Orthodox liturgies, with Presbyterian seasoning, and ceremonial was best observed in the impressive First Pointed church in Gordon Square, Bloomsbury, London (1850–5), designed by John Raphael Brandon and his then partner (from *c.* 1849), Robert Ritchie. Known as Christ the King, Gordon Square, the building is now (2022) the University of London Anglican Chaplaincy.

There were other Dissenting chapels run by small sects, or even by individual preachers, which might have had names such as Enon or Elim Chapel, Bethesda, or even gloried in the nomenclature of 'Tabernacle' in order to emphasise the temporary nature of such humble buildings (as opposed to the grander, more permanent churches of Anglicans, Roman Catholics, and some Nonconformists), and to make a connection with the Old Testament and the idea of the Chosen People.

Roman Catholicism

As mentioned above, Roman Catholics (referred to in the past as, variously, 'Romanists', 'Romans', 'Catholics', or 'papists', and meaning those recognising the spiritual supremacy of the Bishop of Rome as Pope, who are members of the R.C. Church) were also lumped with Nonconformists in the early 19th century. English Roman Catholics were known as recusants (those who refused to attend Church of England services when it was legally compulsory to do so) and were regarded therefore as types of Dissenters. Early 19th-century R.C. churches tended to be poor and architecturally unpretentious (not least so as not to be conspicuous), but, after 'Catholic Emancipation' (1829), and, especially after the restoration of the episcopal hierarchy in England (1850), an undoubted triumphalism could be detected. However, although some R.C. churches are impressive buildings, the numbers of the faithful were often too small to justify the building of a great church, except in the north-western parts of England (where many members of the landed gentry were recusants and so set an example to their tenants and employees) and London, and, in any case, funds were all too often lacking (except when wealthy Roman Catholics stepped in). When there was plentiful money, the results were often outstanding, as at Brompton Oratory, London, St Giles's, Cheadle, Staffordshire, or Westminster Cathedral, London. High Anglican and R.C. churches had many things in common, but generally speaking there was a refinement in the fittings in Anglican churches that was often missing in many R.C. church interiors. Roman Catholic churches erected from the 1850s onwards tended to draw heavily on Continental (especially French) models, and often sported canted apsidal chancels: they might have one or more chapels (one of which was, almost inevitably, the Lady chapel), decked out with lavish finery. Unlike the majority of Anglican churches, however, they were infrequently orientated west–east because, since the Counter Reformation, such orientation ceased to be regarded as important, while new churches squeezed within awkward urban sites made the west–east arrangement impossible.

Need for New Churches

French Revolutionary excesses had caused revulsion in late Georgian England. The rabid anti-clericalism of the 1790s and early 1800s in France was perceived as extremely dangerous, and authorities in England realised new Anglican churches were few, notably where there were large, growing populations. It was calculated that the population exceeded the seating available in Anglican churches by about two and a half million. Godlessness and revolution were seen as connected, so the provision of new churches became imperative. After all, Nonconformity had been instrumental in the overthrow and death of King Charles I, had been intimately concerned in the American Revolution, and, more recently, was closely involved in the dangerous rebellion in Ireland in 1798. The Established religion was perceived as a way of stemming the tides of violence.

In the early 19th century, then, religion (and especially its Anglican manifestation) was seen as providing the framework by which the lower orders might be civilised. Anglican Churchmen also saw the building of churches as a bulwark against the growth of Nonconformity or Dissent. Contrary to popular belief, churchgoing was not universal in the Victorian period. The Anglican Church had experienced moves away from it; there was a growth of indifference to religion; Nonconformist sects attracted an enormous following (especially in northern and midland towns); and there was a new and growing challenge from the R.C. Church. The Established Church was also hampered because in the rapidly growing urban areas its traditional diocesan and parish organisations were ill equipped to cope with new conditions, and, in any case, could only minister to, and seat, a tiny proportion of the population.

In rural districts the influence of the Established Church was still strong in a social hierarchy where people 'knew their place', but in the urban milieu those hierarchies tended to break down, and the notion of 'social place' was diluted. In the 1851 Census it was demonstrated in Birmingham that something like 75 per cent of the population regularly 'abstained' from public worship, and the Churches began to talk openly of missionary activities at home rather than abroad. The call to public worship in areas like London's East End or the teeming streets of Lambeth was largely ignored, while there were considerable numbers of working men who were openly hostile towards religion. The scent of moral danger lay heavy on the smoky urban air.

The Fabric

So the Victorians and their predecessors were mightily concerned for the future of religion in urban areas, and much capital was to go into church building. For example, some 43 churches and chapels were erected in the newly expanded suburb of Kensington in around 20 years. Now this is phenomenal, but such patterns were not unusual: this extraordinary activity on the part of Anglicans, Nonconformists, and Roman Catholics deserves our closest attention.

Much of the urban fabric of Victorian England is Sublime, in the sense of that 18th-century æsthetic category associated with vastness, ruggedness, power, terror, and the ability to stimulate the imagination and the emotions. Victorian built fabric could astonish, and its huge size could overawe, impress, and subdue. In short, there appears to have been a relationship between religious rhetoric and Sublime architecture: this is amply demonstrated by the vast urban citadels of faith built by Tractarian Ritualists of the Church of England; in the larger, grandiose, Classical and Gothic chapels for Nonconformists in the northern towns; and in the huge, dim, cavernous Byzantinesque gloomths of the mighty R.C. cathedral in Westminster. Rhetoric was firmly embedded in Victorian culture (as should be clear from any readings of the outpourings of religious harangues, published sermons, and tracts that appeared during that period), and was realised in an architecture for posterity as a permanent reminder, a monumental warning, and a symbolic presence. That permanence has been abandoned in the early 21st century. A church is no longer regarded as essential to the success of a speculative housing development (as it was in Victorian England), or as a beacon of hope, bringing consolation, education, morality, and faith to the urban masses: indeed, many religious buildings have been abandoned by the very organisations that created them.

Anyone familiar with the towns and cities of England must be aware of the very great numbers of churches and chapels that are scattered through them. Apart from mediæval churches and cathedrals, there will be some impressive 18th-century structures, but throughout those urban areas developed during the Victorian period are many ecclesiastical buildings, often presenting a varied stylistic kaleidoscope of 19th-century taste in both architectural and denominational terms. There are tall towers, often with spires, attached to large, bulky structures (frequently and impressively faced with stone), still dominating residential areas; huge brick churches like massive citadels rising up above the rooftops of London's Victorian suburbs; Gothic churches that look as though they had strayed from the countryside and become marooned in the morass of decaying houses or waste ground; plain chapels (often simple Classical preaching boxes); buildings drawing on Byzantine, Romanesque, and Lombardic round-arched precedents; and strange stylistic hybrids that almost defy description. Many ecclesiastical buildings in urban areas today are in a poor state of repair, fall into the category of 'redundant plant', or have been adapted for uses that are wholly incompatible with their architecture or with the purpose for which they were built. To stand in the abandoned nave of a great Victorian polychrome Gothic church, where the dust and dirt lie thickly and soddenly on the floors and surfaces, the wind blows through the vandalised stained-glass windows, the rain drips through the damaged roof from which the lead has been stripped, and the once lovely and finely crafted fittings are smashed and overturned, can be a profoundly disturbing experience, for such places were built to resist the ravages of time: they were the products of faith, they were there to bring that faith to the people, and they were profoundly wonderful buildings for the very large part. And if their rhetoric resounded, and even resounds today, they are none the worse for that.

All in all, then, there was a considerable variety of religious buildings erected in the Victorian Age for large numbers of religious groups. This brief survey will describe the main themes and types, and will illustrate some outstanding examples.

2

Architecture, Antiquarianism, and Styles

Tous les genres sont bons hors le genre ennuyeux.
(All styles are good, except the boring kind).

FRANÇOIS-MARIE AROUET (Voltaire) (1694–1778):
Preface to *L'Enfant prodigue* (1736).

Pointed architecture came into existence, not in the weakness of infancy, but like a new and heaven-born principle; it proceeded through a surprisingly rapid course, constantly assuming new forms, each in perfect consistency with its exalted principles, and ever throwing aside those which had been once developed and made use of, till it attained the highest pitch of beauty and glory.

GEORGE GILBERT SCOTT (1811–78):
A Plea for the Faithful Restoration of our Ancient Churches
(Oxford: John Henry Parker, 1850), 24–5.

Introduction

Architecture once had profound resonances: one only has to consider how the style, miscalled 'Gothic', has been perceived, used, and evolved, to realise that meaning in architecture was at one time significant in terms of culture, politics, continuity, and much else. Surviving English mediæval parish churches are generally Gothic, and were created for R.C. religious observance. They are familiar aspects of villages, towns, and landscapes, and have been eloquent witnesses to a millennium or more of history: in some extraordinary way they represent what was the collective memory (now being rapidly eroded) of the English people.

Victorian churches came in a variety of styles. By far the most numerous were Gothic, often freely treated in original ways, with exquisite craftsmanship, and showing evidence of impressive scholarship. This phenomenon, known as the 'Gothic Revival', produced many of England's greatest works of architecture, and forms the kernel of this study, so explanations of its origins and widespread adoption need to be outlined.

The Residue of a National Architecture

Long before the Victorian Age, a sophisticated European ecclesiastical architecture had evolved, and post-mediæval Europe inherited many Gothic buildings. Yet Italian Renaissance architects despised Gothic as German, accursed, and irrational, invented by Teutonic invaders who had sacked Imperial Rome in 410 (thus destroying the Antique Classical culture Renaissance architects and patrons were trying to recover), but by then the mediæval systems that invented Gothic had largely collapsed, for Teutons led a more revolutionary attack on mediævalism after Luther posted his theses against the abuse of indulgences in 1517. Ensuing theologies led to the establishment of Protestantism and a rejection of papal authority in Northern Europe. In England, Wales, and Ireland, the dissolution of the monasteries under Henry VIII from the late 1530s, one of the largest land-grabs in history, dotted the countryside with ruins, many impressive and extensive. Some monastic churches remained as cathedrals of the reformed Established Church, and others, either whole or part, as parish churches, though stripped of 'papist' paraphernalia to ensure destruction of the visible expressions of R.C. systems of belief. Yet even where Roman Catholicism remained dominant elsewhere in Europe, mediæval architecture was passé: many churches were recased in Baroque finery or completely rebuilt. Thus the Protestant Reformation, the R.C. Counter Reformation, and the Renaissance damaged, destroyed, or obscured much Gothic fabric.

However, in England, much did escape complete obliteration: that is important for any consideration of 19th-century architecture, for the country was spared the ferocious destruction of the Thirty Years' War and the French Revolution, even though it lost much through Henrician, Edwardine, Elizabethan, and later upheavals. By the 17th century, the term 'Gothic' was being employed to describe mediæval buildings, and it was then that a revival of Gothic began, for differing reasons, many of them contradictory.

17th-Century Gothic

The colleges of Oxford and Cambridge universities were mediæval foundations: they also provided clergy to serve the Established Anglican Church. Significantly, nearly all their new early 17th-century buildings were Gothic. So why, when Renaissance elements had been present in Elizabethan and Jacobean prodigy houses, and Inigo Jones had created Palladian buildings for the Jacobean and Caroline Courts, were so many 17th-century buildings in a Gothic style? After the Church of England had been severed from the papacy, ecclesiastical hierarchies, parishes, forms of worship, and buildings (albeit stripped bare) remained. Most importantly, however, the English Church, at once reformed and part of the one 'Catholick and Apostolick Church', claimed it owed its authority to historical continuity traced back to the Apostles, but that it always had an identity distinct from the R.C. Church in other European countries. The use of Gothic, consciously employed, therefore, was hugely significant in matters of religious authenticity, continuity, legitimacy, and even national identity, in times when England was partly isolated from Europe, and there were questions regarding the monarchy itself, for Queen Elizabeth's position had been internationally insecure, and it was essential to emphasise, by all means possible, her legitimate claims to the throne. The high drama of houses such as Wollaton Hall, Nottingham (1580–8), although clothed in Renaissance garments, suggests something of mediæval castles in massing, and the Keep, Bolsover Castle, Derbyshire (completed *c.*1621), has mediævalising vaulting and arrow loops. Architecture, pageantry, heraldry, and mythology were necessary (in dangerous times) to create a sense of nationhood and to establish a sense of continuity with a mediæval past.

If 'Gothic Revival' at Oxford and Cambridge had been employed, apparently as a conscious choice, Gothic also survived elsewhere. Plenty of English churches or parts of churches were still being erected in the Gothic style, such as the massive tower of St Mary's, Goudhurst, Kent (1638–40). In London and the Home Counties the Gothic tradition was largely maintained by The Worshipful Company of Masons: the City of London turned to that Company to build St Columb's cathedral church (consecrated 1633) in its new city of Londonderry, Ireland. It was Gothic because that is the way the Company of Masons did things, and also made English settlers feel comfortable through a reassuringly mediævalising building. Holy Trinity, Staunton Harold, Leicestershire (1653–65), erected by Sir Thomas Shirley, Bt, was Gothic for different reasons, as a protest against Puritanism, Presbyterianism, and Republicanism. The Republican Commonwealth (1649–60) abolished the Anglican Establishment, so Shirley's church was a visible expression of resistance to the new regime: the use of Gothic demonstrated that a mediæval past actually mattered, inducing emotional and intellectual responses unthinkable today.

There were further complications, for Gothic resonances were also connected with constitutional liberty and nationhood. Renaissance authors had identified Pointed architecture with 'Gothic barbarians', but to Northern Europeans the invaders of *their* territories were Romans. Sixteenth-century reformers were influenced by the 6th-century work of Jordanes, historian of those Goths who had brought about the downfall of Rome: they could see analogies between liberty-loving Teutons toppling a Roman tyranny, and German Protestants rejecting papal oppression. In England, Parliamentarians realised that ideas floated during the German Reformation were important in creating precedents, including the right of Parliament to curtail the power of monarchy. If 17th-century Gothic architecture could suggest historical continuity and legitimacy as far as monarchy and Church were concerned, so history could be called upon to legitimise the authority of Parliament. The antiquary Verstegen demonstrated that English reverence for liberty reflected virtues the Roman historian Cornelius Tacitus had noted in the Germans; Saxon kings, it was claimed, were elected by the successors to tribal councils, so 17th-century Parliamentarians perceived themselves as heirs of that system. The Puritan, Nathaniel Bacon, claimed no nation preserved 'so much of the ancient Gothique law' as did England.

With the restoration of the monarchy (1660), however, French Classicism became fashionable, and after the Great Fire of London (1666) the monopoly of the Company of Masons was undermined: artisans (not associated with the Company) had to be employed for extensive new works, labouring under the direction of Wren and his team using an architectural language imported from Europe. There were a few exceptions, though, for St Mary Aldermary (1679–82 and 1701–4) and St Dunstan-in-the-East (1668–71) were firmly Gothic.

After 1666 anyone wishing to build in Gothic would not have sought a mason in London. Gothic, however, survived in areas where it was kept alive by masons working on repairs to old ecclesiastical fabric. It was not the break with Rome, Protestantism, or Henry VIII that put an end to Gothic, which survived as a living tradition well into the 18th century: it was the fact that masons lost ground to architects, who promoted new-fangled Classicism from the Continent (some parts of which did not adhere to Protestantism). Indeed, when architects turned to Gothic, the results were often curious.

By various enactments, following the deposition of James II and VII, not only was the Protestant succession through the Hanoverian line secured, but a constitutional monarchy limited in its powers by Parliament was established, and numerous publications argued that those changes in the governance of Britain were based on historical precedents: English liberty, with its origins in Gothic councils, had matured and reached its apogee in the post-1689 settlement. Anglicans generally accepted the overhauled Establishment under William and Mary II, but, like others, had to call upon scholars to provide suitable evidence to legitimise new positions. The ecclesiastical historian Inett, for example, argued that the Reformation had restored ancient religious and political rights curtailed or usurped under 'popery'.

And the glue for many, wearied by strife throughout the 17th century, was Gothic.

Goths in Gardens

Gothic ideas, then, were deeply embedded in the Establishment, and this partly explains why, ever since the 16th-century break with Rome, Gothic architecture remained an important part of national awareness. The new, post-1689 settlement claimed continuity, not only with the mediæval Church and State, but with the 'freedoms' of Gothic history.

Thus researchers assumed a position of immense importance. One of the most outstanding was Sir William Dugdale: with Roger Dodsworth he compiled *Monasticon Anglicanum* (1655–73), probably the finest antiquarian publication of the 17th century. The title-page (by Wenceslaus Hollar) made Dugdale's position clear: Henry VIII stands before wrecked monastic buildings, while, on the opposite panel, a mediæval English king is seen at his devotions in a great church, a symbol of social order and peace. Hollar's plates in some ways anticipate illustrations in A.W.N. Pugin's *Contrasts* (1836, 1841). In addition, the title page suggests the English Church was independent of State control, drew its authority not from the Crown but from the pre-Reformation Catholic Church, and traced its history back to Sts Augustine of Canterbury and Gregory the Great, and even to Joseph of Arimathea, supposedly founder of Glastonbury Abbey. To Dugdale, Gothic was the indigenous English language of architecture: his great book, enlarged, was brought out in a magnificent new edition (1817–30), and this is significant, for in the post-Waterloo period, everything Dugdale had stood for (which, despite batterings, had never really evaporated) once more became of paramount importance as the Anglican Church came under sustained attack, civil unrest was rife, religious divisions fuelled fears of social collapse, Nonconformist and Catholic 'Emancipation' challenged the established order, and even milleniarism was widespread.

We associate the Georgian period (1714–1830) with Classical understatement and elegance. Yet the Georgians built in other styles too, notably in their new, carefully contrived gardens. The first 18th-century Gothic garden building was erected (1716–17) at Shotover Park, Oxfordshire, for James Tyrrell. The dates are significant, for in 1714 the Prince-Elector (*Kurfürst*) of Hanover became King George I, although there were still supporters of the House of Stuart, known as Tories, who had to be pacified; indeed, there was armed insurrection in 1715 on behalf of the deposed Stuarts, but this failed. Tyrrell's 'Gothic Temple' commemorated Whig victory and the success of the post-1689 settlement: it celebrated 'Gothic Liberty', yet suggested an origin far back in time, and begat generations of Gothic *fabriques* in gardens. Such so-called follies were of ideological importance.

James Gibbs also turned his hand to Gothic, as in the 'Temple of Liberty', Stowe, Buckinghamshire (1741–4), built for the Whig grandee, Richard Temple, 1st Viscount Cobham. So we have here a peculiarly English muddle: a Scots R.C. Tory, with powerful Tory patrons, designing a Gothic monument to English liberty for an English Whig. The 'Temple' alluded to freedoms which Tacitus had claimed for the Germans, and was inscribed 'I THANK GOD THAT I AM NOT A ROMAN', suggesting that Roman Catholicism had been abjured, that the building was subject to neither ecclesiastical nor imperial Rome, but was a statement of 'Gothic freedom'. Gothic increasingly came to be associated with nationhood, and, because it was used in so many garden buildings, led directly to a greater appreciation of Gothic, and the way began to be cleared for the remains of a mediæval past to be viewed at first with delicious shivers of apprehension, and then with altogether kindlier eyes.

A rather more serious Jacobite attempt to regain the throne occurred in 1745–6, but ended at Culloden. Again Gothic was invoked to mark the Hanoverian victory, notably in the Culloden Tower, Richmond, Yorkshire NR (*c.*1746), and the Gothic Banqueting House, Gibside, Co. Durham (1751), set on an axis leading the eye to a 'Column of British Liberty' (begun 1750, 'a splendid symbol of British Whiggery'). In the aftermath of 1745–6 several manifestations of Gothic became reality. Sanderson Miller erected a castellated tower at Edgehill, Warwickshire (1745–7), designed to resemble the mediæval Guy's Tower of Warwick Castle, so his 'folly' was probably one of the very first Gothic eye-catchers/belvederes to derive from real mediæval precedents. That tower affords a view over the site of the first battle of the English Civil War (1642), and the allusion to Warwick Castle was a nod to earlier wars, those of the Roses (1455–87), and the power behind the throne, Richard Neville, Earl of Warwick and Salisbury, known as the 'Kingmaker'. As Chris Brooks perceptively observed, Miller's tower invites contemplation of the drama of the 'making and unmaking of kings and constitutions, played out within the terms of gothic and feudal principles, from the Wars of the Roses, to the Civil War, to the tragedy of Culloden. And the mode of historical engagement it offers is reflective, not triumphalist: it takes no sides'. Quite so, and Miller's structure suggested that it was once part of something bigger, now partly ruined, and so could have strayed from a landscape painting, where depictions of ruins could often be found. A built 'sham' ruin could give additional *gravitas* to a landscape, and therefore to an estate, and could even allow a squire to create a past (and thus give a necessary sense of historical continuity to ownership). Like heraldry and documentation, ruins could suggest legitimacy, a history, and respectability: Georgian Gothic was no laughing matter.

An example was Miller's Hagley Castle, Worcestershire (1747–8); erected for Sir George Lyttelton, Bt, Horace Walpole declared it had 'the true rust of the Barons' Wars', a remark that is not as innocently connected with æsthetics as it might seem, for the Lytteltons were major players during the Middle Ages, especially in 1263–7. Furthermore, Miller's client had close political connections with Cobham of Stowe, so, by a process of association, familiar then but not now, Miller's Gothic 'ruin' linked notions of Whig liberty with mediæval history, with the 13th-century Barons' Wars, and with the wider post-Culloden political climate; in addition, the cunningly contrived 'castle' transformed its site into 'historical ground', in the words of William Shenstone. Furthermore, where substantial real mediæval ruins survived, they could become useful elements in newly designed landscaped parks (e.g. Fountains Abbey in relation to Studley Royal, Yorkshire WR).

It was a short step from ruins and follies to inhabitable buildings. Roger Morris had designed Clearwell Court (later Castle), Gloucestershire (*c.*1725–8 – the earliest Gothic Revival castellated house in England), for Thomas Wyndham, but his masterpiece is Inveraray Castle, Argyll (1745–60), a symmetrically disposed Gothic house with massive towers at the corners. Built for Archibald Campbell, 3rd Duke of Argyll, who supported the Hanoverian cause, it makes a powerful political statement, a Sublime fortress of Whiggery in a land where there had been significant Jacobite support to threaten the Hanoverian succession. Inveraray has a central hall illuminated from a mighty crenellated clerestorey, so Morris was also looking back to prodigy houses like Wollaton Hall.

Gothic, or rather 'Gothick' (in the sense of an artificial 18th-century style that owed little to historical precedent), was promoted by the pattern books of Batty Langley, William Halfpenny, et al., and the Abbé Marc-Antoine Laugier's influential *Observations sur l'Architecture* (1765) recognised the grace of Gothic. So, as the 18th century drew to its close, an array of architectural styles was available, but Gothic began to be subject to studious investigations, not least because it was intertwined with ideas concerning English nationhood, history, governance, freedom, and much else.

Why was there a revived interest in mediæval buildings in the 1790s? A major factor was the isolation of the British Isles during the French Wars. Denied the broad educational possibilities of the 18th-century grand tour, scholars, led by the Society of Antiquaries, turned to a consideration of the Middle Ages. Horace Walpole noted that, as isolation grew, the nation sought 'lustre' from its past: that seeking increased after 1789.

The 19th century saw an explosion of scholarly architectural investigation of Gothic exemplars, and it is to that period that we now turn.

Gothic and the Nation: The Beginnings of Gothic Scholarship

James Wyatt made his name with the Pantheon, Oxford Street, London (1769–72 – with his elder brother Samuel), but his ensuing fashionable success led to his appointments as Surveyor to the Fabric of several mediæval buildings, where he made controversial alterations to several English cathedrals (his work at Salisbury, Wiltshire [1789–92], and Hereford [1786–96] earned him the nickname 'The Destroyer'). At Durham Cathedral his proposals to demolish the Galilee and commit other acts of vandalism aroused ferocious opposition led by the antiquary and Gothic protagonist, John Carter.

Carter had produced numerous survey drawings for several publications, notably Gough's *Sepulchral Monuments* (1786); his own *Ancient Architecture of England*

(1795–1814) was his major work, remarkable for its accurately observed detail. Thus archæological and scholarly studies of Gothic started to appear, prompted, in part, by a perceived necessity to counter ignorant architectural interventions such as those of Wyatt: just as Classicism needed its scholarly texts, so did Gothic, and this was now becoming extremely urgent. Carter was one of the first to take on the architectural establishment, and his weapons included linking patriotism and æsthetics, a formidable combination. He advocated a study of home-grown English architecture instead of an acceptance of 'the contagion' of 'unwholesome' influences from abroad. With 'The Destroyer' in his sights, he denounced architects who were contaminated with 'prejudices' and incapable of designing in Gothic: their enthusiasm for 'foreign modes' prevented them from being 'true to the ancient architecture of their native land'. Carter detested the contemporary fashion for 'improvement', seeing it as secular 'progress' inappropriately applied to architecture: '*Improvement*, like *Reformation*, is a big sounding word and oftentimes alike – mischievous in its consequences', an explosive statement for the time. Perceptively, he saw that both Batty Langley and Wyatt thought in terms of Classicism, even when attempting to design in Gothic (a term Carter hated): the architectural establishment was dominated by 'barbarous innovators' and 'illiterate mechanicks', from whom he had to endure 'envenomed malice' and 'poisonous calumny' from the 'destroyers of our ancient arts'. Carter, J. Mordaunt Crook has sagely observed, 'almost as much as Pugin', turned the Gothic Revival from a 'cult into a crusade': he played a large part in changing the sensibilities of a whole generation. Carter's publications set new standards in the accurate representation of Gothic architecture.

It was Carter too, anticipating A.W.N. Pugin, who argued that 14th-century English Gothic was the 'finest specimen of the pointed style that has ever adorned this country'. His copious writings were acknowledged by figures including William Burges as catalysts for the Gothic Revival, and others noted it would be 'difficult to overestimate the value of Carter's elaborate illustrations of Gothic detail in keeping alive [mediæval] sentiment'. Crook has gone further, and startlingly observed that 'Carter played John the Baptist to Pugin's Christ'.

Another figure, often underestimated, who should be mentioned here, is Dr John Milner, R.C. Bishop of Castabala *in partibus Infidelium* (because the R.C. episcopal hierarchy had not then been restored, such exotic titles were given to senior clerics in England), antiquary, Carter's ally, and author of an important work of English topography, *The History, Civil and Ecclesiastical, and Survey of the Antiquities of Winchester* (1798–1801). He also wrote a dissertation on the 'Modern Style' of 'Altering Ancient Cathedrals', as 'exemplified in the Cathedral Church of Salisbury', in which he attacked crass interventions by Wyatt and others. Carter, in 1792, designed St Peter's R.C. chapel, Winchester, for Milner, and was branded as a 'popish architect' for his pains. The Roman Catholic Relief Act had become law in 1791, thus St Peter's, a little-known but nevertheless significant exemplar, was one of the first R.C. places of worship to be erected in its aftermath, and was Perpendicular in style, six and a half crenellated bays long. Inside, the building (now called Milner Hall) consisted of one space, and there was no screen, the sanctuary being simply demarcated by means of a railing. The chapel was superseded (1924–6) by St Peter's Church, Jewry Street, in a late Decorated style.

By the mid-1790s, then, scholars were taking Gothic seriously. Several publications came out to improve knowledge, including *The Antiquities of England and Wales* (1783–97 and other dates) by Francis Grose. Such widespread interest in mediæval architecture received a further boost from France, where secular antiquarianism developed in reaction to destruction carried out during the Revolution. Alexandre-Marie Lenoir was appointed (1791) garde du dépôt des Petits Augustins, and in 1796 director of the Musée des Monuments Français, where mediæval artefacts from buildings looted by revolutionaries were given asylum, yet in their translation lost much of their resonances, so much so that A.-C. Quatremère de Quincy bravely demanded that they should be returned to their original homes. In Rouen, too, E.-H. Langlois established another collection of mediæval antiquities in the former Convent of the Visitation of Mary. So French scholars appear to have influenced English antiquaries, and spurred them to celebrate and treasure native mediæval architecture. It must be emphasised that appreciation of archæologically correct Gothic had its origins among scholars, who in turn influenced architects: if left to their own devices, architects, fashionable or otherwise, could do untold damage.

Early decades of the 19th century experienced an upsurge of publications concerning mediæval architecture: some had especial influence, e.g. those of Britton (1801–38), offering 'correct delineation' and 'scrupulous accuracy' in the recording of Gothic buildings. In 1798 Milner had suggested that the term 'Gothic' should be dropped in favour of 'the Pointed Order', so cleansing mediæval architecture of associations with barbarity, and even with some varieties of political extremism. The word was also associated with so-called Gothic novels, puerile tales of the supernatural, like Walpole's *Castle of Otranto* (1764), and also had connections with the 'gloomths' of the 'Graveyard Poets' Blair, Gray, and Young. Evocations of the mediæval period were common in Romantic writings, as in Southey's *Joan of Arc* (1795), Coleridge's *Christabel* (1797–1800), and hundreds of lesser-known poems and other writings peppered with allusions to the Middle Ages, ruins, and Gothic architecture. As Ernest Short observed in his *A History of Religious Architecture*, the Gothic Revival had its literary and historical side as well as its architectural aspect.

Sir Walter Scott's novels enjoyed widespread international fame, popularising the idea of Gothic architecture in the English-speaking world and, in translation, throughout Europe. Scott's works are shot through with mediævalisms, and he employed ideas of chivalry to ennoble his work and raise it above supernatural Gothick horrors. But his evocation of mediæval chivalry had more to it than mere fictional dreamings: it offered a kind of framework on which a world that had been severely threatened by the French Revolution and by political trends at home could be restored and reimagined. An emerging, modern, industrialising 19th-century Britain drew upon powerful precedents: mediæval history, with its chivalrous aristocracy, Gothic architecture, and appeals to honour could offer modern times nobler models than the ghastliness of the blood-soaked iconoclastic French Revolution which, in its excesses and mob rule, had destroyed so much. Nineteenth-century (and especially Victorian) backward glances to the Middle Ages (and therefore to Gothic architecture) were not extraordinary, reactionary, or even unduly Romantic: they were part of a deeply felt necessity in the Establishment to repair colossal damage, for the safety, prosperity, and future of the United Kingdom were perceived as being dependent upon the nation's history and sense of chivalry. All those evolved from the Middle Ages, so it is small wonder Gothic architecture became so important.

Milner tentatively proposed a chronological progression, and in 1811 published his *Treatise on the Ecclesiastical Architecture of England* in which he suggested a First Order of the Pointed Style (*c.*1175), a Second Order (*c.*1300), and a Third Order (early 16th century). He also sowed the poisonous seeds of moral judgement, claiming that the First Order had developed into the 'chaste grandeur' of the Second, and then, in the Third Order, decayed into dubious 'ingenuity' and excessive 'depression'. Perception of the so-called Perpendicular style as degenerate was to be part of that ever-present enemy of objective observation, Received Opinion. Although Milner's rise-and-fall musings remained firmly embedded for many years, his work as an antiquary was superseded by Thomas Rickman's *An Attempt to Discriminate the Styles of English Architecture from the Conquest to the Reformation*, which appeared in the first of many editions in 1817. This was the first systematic treatise on Gothic architecture in England, and its importance cannot be overemphasised. Substantially, beautifully, and accurately illustrated, it identified Norman architecture (1066–*c.*1189) and was able to date Early English First Pointed (*c.*1189–*c.*1307), Decorated Second Pointed (*c.*1307–77), and Perpendicular Third Pointed (*c.*1377–*c.*1547), though nowadays we would put Perpendicular a bit earlier for its starting date (*c.*1335), and Early English ending *c.*1250, when Geometrical Middle Pointed tracery came in.

Rickman's identification of Gothic with Englishness, however, was a shade too chauvinistic, for George Downing Whittington had already classified it (1809) as a French 12th-century invention. Whittington was correct, but in the climate of the time, when all things French were suspect, his work was either pooh-poohed (by Milner) or ignored (by almost everyone else). However, Rickman's *Attempt* enabled critics and creators to look at Gothic buildings with more informed eyes. Correctness, in the archæological sense, became important, and further publications aided the Gothic cause. Accurate illustrations of real mediæval Gothic details were essential when architects, prompted by the Romantic spirit of the times and more especially by pressure from antiquarians, were beginning to work in a scholarly and archæological rather than Langleyesque manner. Among the most significant books to record Gothic correctly were A.C. Pugin's *Specimens of Gothic Architecture... at Oxford* (with F. Mackenzie, 1816), *Specimens of Gothic Architecture* (1821–3, with descriptions by Edward James Willson [a Roman Catholic]), and *Examples of Gothic Architecture* (1828–30, 1831–4, and 1836, with texts by Willson and Thomas Larkins Walker).

For some of his later books, e.g. *Examples*, Pugin was assisted by his son, Augustus Welby Northmore Pugin. Willson collaborated with Britton on *Architectural Antiquities of Great Britain* (1807–26), *Cathedral Antiquities* (1814–35), and *Picturesque Antiquities of the English Cities* (1830), and proposed (1831) amending Britton's 'Christian' to 'Catholic' in the Introduction to A.C. Pugin's *Examples*, a suggestion that was not taken up, although it impressed the younger Pugin. 'Christian' (meaning Gothic) seems to have been lifted from Arcisse de Caumont, leading French antiquarian and friend of the elder Pugin. De Caumont argued that 13th-century Gothic had reached something very like perfection, a notion that seems to have rubbed off on English scholars, who began to appreciate 'Middle Pointed' (i.e. late 13th-century Gothic, or early Second Pointed of the Geometrical variety). Pugin, his son, and members of his drawing school knew not only de Caumont, but E.-H. Langlois, mentioned earlier. French antiquaries, then, began to influence their English counterparts during the debates of the 1820s and 1830s concerning nomenclature. Even more importantly, around the beginning of the 19th century, despite the Revolution and the Napoleonic Empire, there was a profound reaction in certain quarters of French society against the anti-clericalism and iconoclasm of the destroyers which had parallels with English regrets concerning post-Reformation and Puritan damage to mediæval buildings. Gothic architecture began to be appreciated for its association with the spiritual life of the mediæval period, and the beauties of Gothic artefacts were invoked to point to an age of religious devotion and rich creativity. Christianity began to come back into fashion, and with it Gothic, spurred by influential publications such as those of Châteaubriand.

There were, at the time, many questions in the air, not least those casting doubts on the official, received versions of history, especially religious history. There were many R.C. refugees (some members of religious Orders) in Britain who had fled from the French revolutionaries to escape persecution or death, and the anti-revolutionary patriotism of many English recusant families could not be doubted any more, so there grew a new sympathy for Roman Catholics, a complete reversal of the hatred and mob violence (resulting in the sacking of several R.C. chapels in London) revoltingly obvious in the riots of 1780 instigated by Lord George Gordon. Indeed, William Cobbett, an English Anglican, was to perceive the Reformation as a 'devastation of England' by 'brutal barbarians', who had pillaged religious houses and destroyed their remains for fear they might be reminders of the 'rapacity and cruelty of their tyrant and his fellow-plunderers'.

Such a view, calling into question much that had resulted from the break with Rome and the Reformation, was unusual for the 1820s, and stemmed from Cobbett's hatred of injustice, yet there can be no doubting his patriotism, his love of England. But he saw much in contemporary England that was disturbing: growing utilitarian attitudes; money-grubbing and greed; ruthlessness and exploitation; and a terrible ugliness, among much else that was far-removed from his vision of a kindly, religious, rural England, where hospitality, beauty, and justice could be found in the 'happiest country, perhaps, that the world has ever seen'. The myth of 'Merrie England' was really fathered by Cobbett, who, although responding instinctively to indignation and melancholy engendered by a contemplation of monastic ruins, was undoubtedly partly correct in his diagnosis.

The modern R.C. Irish-born historian, Eamon Duffy, has painstakingly revealed much about English popular religion in the 15th and 16th centuries, and his researches bear out much that Cobbett had felt.

3

The Religious Atmosphere in the 1830s and 1840s

On Sunday July 14, 1833, Mr Keble preached the assize sermon in the University pulpit. It was published under the title of National Apostasy. I have ever considered and kept the day as the start of the religious movement of 1833.

JOHN HENRY NEWMAN (1801–90):
Apologia Pro Vita Sua: Being a History of his Religious Opinions,
MARTIN JAMES SVAGLIC (1916–98) (ed.) (Oxford: Clarendon Press, 1967), 43.

What is called the Oxford or Tractarian movement began ... in a vigorous effort for the immediate defence of the Church against serious dangers, arising from the threatening temper of the days of the Reform Bill.

RICHARD WILLIAM CHURCH (1815–90):
The Oxford Movement: Twelve Years, 1833–1845, i
(London: Macmillan & Co., 1891), 1.

Introduction

Upheavals of the 1790s profoundly affected the nation, for the French Revolution, radical ideas, subsequent wars, and the Irish Rebellion of 1798 threatened national security and the established order, leading to several momentous changes. In order to bring Ireland more under control, Great Britain and Ireland were united by enactments passed by both parliaments, which became law on 1 January 1801. Through those Acts the Churches of England and Ireland were also joined, and despite hopes of strengthening Anglicanism, in that union there lay profound dangers, soon all too apparent, that threatened the very survival of the Church.

However, those shoal waters lay ahead, for at the start of the 19th century patriotism, stirred by the great victories at Trafalgar (1805) and Waterloo (1815), was very much alive. There was an upsurge of Anglican activity: promotion of Anglicanism, and the creation of a visible Anglican presence in towns and cities, were primary concerns of constitutional loyalists.

Evangelicals and High Churchmen: The Clapham Sect and the Hackney Phalanx

Evangelicals in London within the Established Church, prompted by the teachings of John Wesley, became influential: they believed in teaching by example, supporting temperance, performing good works, and observing the 'Sabbath' (Sunday, in Evangelical Sabbatarian terms) to invigorate the nation's spiritual life, stability, and moral well-being. In parallel was the emergence of the 'High and Dry' party of Sacramentarians which perceived the Anglican Church as having a powerful role in raising the tone of society as a whole. Sydney Smith identified these two groups (consisting mostly of laymen, merchants, and intellectuals) as the 'Clapham Sect' (Evangelical) and the 'Hackney Phalanx' (High Church), after the (then well-heeled) eponymous London suburbs.

At Clapham, John Venn, rector from 1792 until his death, was at the centre of a group of philanthropists exerting an influence far greater than its numbers might indicate: it was a prime mover in the slave trade's abolition; it promoted exemplary housing and adequate schooling for the labouring classes; and helped to bring literacy, hygiene, and sobriety to populations of growing urban areas. It was the single most significant factor in creating the conscience of the Victorian Age.

The Hackney Phalanx, under the leadership of Joshua Watson (brother of the rector, John James Watson) and Henry Handley Norris (Perpetual Curate and later Rector of St John of Jerusalem, the parish church of South Hackney [Clapton]) became an active promoter of religious and philanthropic projects of the High Church party. Through its influence with Lord Liverpool, prime minister (1812–27), it secured the passing of the Act for Promoting the Building of Additional Churches in Populous Parishes (1818).

As early as 1803, An Act to Promote the Building, Repairing, or Otherwise Providing of Churches and Chapels and of Houses for the Residence of Ministers, and the Providing of Church Yards and Glebes had become law, amended (1811) as Gifts for Churches, by which lands could be vested in any person for building or repairing a church or house for the residence of a parson, and allowing persons owning land to grant five acres for ecclesiastical purposes, but the Act of 1818 was an important catalyst for the creation of Anglican churches. The Phalanx supported the formation of the Church Building Society (1818 – incorporated in 1828), the Royal Commission for Church Building (1818), and, ultimately, the Ecclesiastical Commissioners (1836), which provided the administrative structure within which the Anglican Church functioned during the Victorian period.

The 1818 Act allowed £1 million of State finance to be made available for the erection of churches: the buildings put up as a result were known as Waterloo or Commissioners' churches, because they came into being under the ægis of the Commissioners for Building New Churches appointed under the Act in the years following Waterloo (1815). More than 200 such churches were erected, and most were capacious to hold static congregations: some were Classical (especially the then fashionable Greek Revival) in style, but others (the majority) were 'Pointed', many being thin travesties of Gothic consisting of rectangular preaching boxes that could just as easily have been Classical late Georgian auditory churches, but that paid lip-service to Gothic by acquiring pointed windows and insubstantial, unconvincing buttresses. Soon, however, Gothic gradually replaced Classicism as a favoured style for other reasons. An Act to Make Further Provision and to Amend and Render More Effectual Three Acts ... for Building and Promoting the Building of Additional Churches in Populous Parishes was passed in 1824, consolidating earlier enactments, and providing another £500,000 of State funding.

During the later Hanoverian period (1800–37), religious and secular administrations were closely intertwined. However, very often (especially in booming, expanding London), where more accommodation for worshippers was required, this took the form of proprietary chapels, erected by owners of land and/or developers (sometimes clergymen were active in creating such chapels) in areas where new houses were built within existing parish boundaries. Intended to increase the desirability of a residential district (and so ensure that rents could be kept at a satisfactory level), such chapels were supported by pew rents (as was the case with all new church buildings), but their effectiveness depended largely on the charisma of the incumbent. Nevertheless, the very existence of proprietary chapels (often drab, basic buildings) could inhibit the erection of new parish churches because of vested interests of proprietors and preachers.

Tory post-Waterloo legislation eased matters by providing public funds for new Anglican churches, long overdue where there had been urban expansion. However, those various Acts were passed against a background of fear: social unrest was endemic, and it was hoped that a programme of church building would help to bring a modicum of stability; Dissent was increasing, and was seen by Anglicans as disloyal and schismatic; the upheavals and new ideas of revolutionary France had removed the old order in Europe and had destroyed much Continental ecclesiastical fabric and organisation; and all the time the towns and cities inexorably grew as a result of migration from the land and the demands of commerce and industry. Even before Queen Victoria's accession in 1837, the position of constitutional loyalists, the links between Anglicanism and the State, and, indeed, the basis of the Union were being undermined.

Threats to the Established Order

Secularism (the belief that the State, morals, and education should be independent of religion), utilitarianism (the theory evolved by Jeremy Bentham that found the basis of moral distinctions in the usefulness of actions, and only actions which bring happiness to the greatest numbers have moral worth), Nonconformity, and religious expediency were fast advancing in the 1820s, along with other very real threats to Anglican pre-eminence.

First (1828) came 'Nonconformist Emancipation', when most restrictions on Dissenters were removed. Not for the first or last time was Ireland to play a significant role in English affairs, in this instance as a direct result of the union of the two parliaments, for the voters of County Clare had obstinately insisted on electing Daniel O'Connell – a Roman Catholic, and therefore disbarred from Parliament – as their MP at Westminster. This forced Parliament's hand, and so 'Catholic Emancipation' became a reality in the Roman Catholic Relief Act (1829), which abolished similar disadvantages to Roman Catholics in public life.

Many were appalled at the time and later by these events. John Ruskin declared that the 1829 Act was a crime for which the Deity would require vengeance. However, when Ruskin, in the late 1840s and early 1850s, was denouncing the Parliament of the 1820s, 'Catholic Emancipation' had already led to a demand for new R.C. churches, and in 1850 Pope Pius IX (*Pio Nono*), in a brief widely regarded as 'papal aggression', re-established the R.C. episcopal hierarchy in England and Wales. Set against widespread controversy over Ritualism in the Anglican Church, secessions to Rome, and the influx of destitute Irish fleeing from the Great Hunger occasioned by potato blight during the 1840s, this caused uproar, and Parliament in 1851 passed the Ecclesiastical Titles Act prohibiting assumption of territorial titles by R.C. archbishops, bishops, and deans: this Act, however, never enforced, was repealed in 1871.

During the last years of the reign of King George IV, many Anglican churches were built under the relevant Acts, and were run by the vicars, vestries, and churchwardens of parishes. These churches did not have the obvious commercial stigma of proprietary chapels (which they largely made redundant). Furthermore, they had free seats as well as rented pews, so answered some criticisms. Nevertheless, a profound and growing sense of unease prevailed in Church circles, for reasons that can only be outlined here. Although some State-supported works of church building and extension were carried out (though most church building was not funded by the State), the relationship between Anglicanism and the State was showing signs of stress. Apart from the 'emancipation' of Nonconformists and Roman Catholics, certain groups (e.g. Dissenters, radicals, utilitarians, and certain Whigs) were shrill in their demands for an end to payments to the Established Church (including church rates and burial fees), having succeeded, in any case, in virtually abolishing the secular powers of parish organisations. Then came the huge upheavals of Whig 'reform' and events followed rapidly in what was to be, in fact, partial disestablishment of the Anglican Church.

Unrest in Ireland over, the collection of tithes, among other things, led to the passing of an Act (1832) by the Whig government to facilitate the recovery of tithes in Ireland and for the relief of the clergy of the Established Anglican Church there (the Church of Ireland). Galvanised by fears that revolution would break out in the British Isles (as it had done in several countries in 1830), the government passed (1832) the momentous Representation of the People Act (otherwise known as the Great Reform), which increased the number of parliamentary seats (105 were Irish) as well as the numbers allowed to vote: it also gave political power to groups who cared nothing for the delicate balance between Church and State that had prevailed ever since 1689.

There followed legislation concerning finance and the Church, although the anomaly of a minority Church in Ireland supported by a tax on the entire agricultural system remained a source of trouble, so the Irish Tithe Composition Act began the process of commutation. In 1833 the Church Temporalities (Ireland) Act was passed: it reduced two of the four archbishoprics (Tuam and Cashel) to bishoprics; united 10 of the 20 existing bishoprics to adjacent sees; revoked the rights of churchwardens to levy church cess (an exaction) for the upkeep of ecclesiastical buildings; and permitted tenants on episcopal lands to purchase their holdings at a fixed annual rent. Purchase sums and reserved rents, along with income from the suppressed sees, tax on ecclesiastical livings, levies on the wealthier dioceses (e.g. Armagh and Derry), and income and functions of the Board of First Fruits (the body set up in the 18th century to fund the building and repair of churches and glebes) were vested in the new Ecclesiastical Commissioners, who were empowered to use them for the building, upkeep, repair, and improvement of churches and other buildings. Shortly after the Church Temporalities (Ireland) Act was passed, under the Irish Tithe Arrears Act, £1 million was advanced for the relief of tithe owners on the security of arrears.

Although from an administrative/utilitarian point of view the Acts provided for more efficient allocation of resources, they fatally weakened the Church of Ireland's position, and led to de facto disestablishment in 1869 under the Irish Church Act, passed by the Liberal government led by Gladstone, whose lofty ambition was to 'pacify Ireland'. Another Liberal administration, under Asquith, in which Lloyd George was a prime mover, disestablished the Anglican Church in Wales (1914), but this did not take effect until after the 1914–18 war.

Ecclesiastical matters (especially in Ireland) might not seem significant to Anglocentric minds, but a general assault on the established order extended far into other areas. There had long been Poor Laws, but under legislation in William IV's reign, parishes were united under Boards of Guardians for their administration: a sub-district so formed was called a Union, and the Union Workhouses, a new and particularly grim building type, came into being. Regimes in those (often terrible) places were so draconian that the poor would do all they could to avoid them. Then the Poor Law Amendment Act of 1834 was passed, which had a further sinister side to it, for it and the 1832 Act for Regulating Schools of Anatomy in effect criminalised paupers by making corpses of unfortunates who died penniless in workhouses available for dissection: this was perceived as further punishment, because until then the only legal supply of dead bodies for anatomists had been from the gallows (i.e. cadavers of executed felons). There must have been a residue of traditional religious belief among early 19th-century labouring classes, for there was a huge growth in burial clubs, as the poor tried to ensure there were sufficient funds available for decent burial to avoid dissection. Certainly those offensive and cruel enactments cut across all traditional Tory concerns, such as *noblesse oblige*, by which the deserving poor were supported by a high-minded aristocracy and landed gentry. Then, in 1835, came the Municipal Corporations Act, which virtually removed all remaining secular authority held by the Established Church.

To claim that secular and other threats to the Anglican Church were harbingers of disestablishment is no exaggeration, for the Irish legislation was writing on the wall writ large. The destruction of the Church's secular authority and the erosion of Anglicanism in Ireland (culminating in the Acts of 1833 and 1869) for what seemed to be reasons of political expediency were powerful stimuli to the Oxford Movement and to the huge upsurge of spiritual, theological, and architectural revival. The cumulative effects of these enactments were to alarm and enrage Churchmen, something that is usually interpreted as a reaction to loss of power, influence, and prestige: the main problem for Churchmen, however, was none of those, but a perception that a collection of politicians had no right to interfere in or legislate for a body that was Catholic and bound by divine laws and orders. The Anglican Church, for so long as one with the State, was being sundered from that State, and its destinies were being increasingly controlled by a Parliament in which radicalism, Whiggery, utilitarianism, and Nonconformity were overwhelming Anglican Tory constitutional loyalism. Thereafter, the systematic erosion of the powers and status of the Anglican Church was to continue, and secular/political control over the Church drove many Churchmen to convert to Roman Catholicism or Nonconformity: some gave up on the Christian Churches and became non-attenders or agnostic. Those who seceded to Rome found the authority of the papacy and the certainty of dogmas more congenial than seeing the State Church being humbled and dictated to by Whiggish politicians.

Although 'pacification' of Ireland clearly was behind the two important Acts that spelled disestablishment, this did not happen: attempts (significantly for the running of Parliament) to placate anti-Union MPs did not work. As many predicted, disestablishment sent out clear messages, and the Government of Ireland Act of 1914 (the 'Home Rule Act') signalled the beginning of the end of the Union. However, 26 counties of Ireland disowned constitutional nationalism after 1918, so that the only part of Ireland that got 'Home Rule' (six of the nine counties of the province of Ulster, called 'Northern Ireland') was the part that did not want it.

Counter-Attack, Liturgical Studies, Tractarianism, and the Newman Crisis

Many were deeply disturbed by these matters, not least William Cobbett, whose *History of the Protestant 'Reformation' in England and Ireland* (1824–6) and *Rural Rides* made clear his indignation at the state of rural England as well as his perception that events in the 1820s and 1830s were potentially just as destructive as the devastation of Henrician, Edwardine, and Elizabethen times. Enactments of the 1830s, therefore, cannot be overestimated in their long-term effects. It appeared that the towel was being thrown in as far as the Anglican Church was concerned, and that the process of dismantling it had begun.

Outraged by the passing of the Church Temporalities (Ireland) Act, John Keble was prompted to preach his celebrated sermon on 'National Apostasy' from the university pulpit. Like other dons at Oxford, Keble had been profoundly affected by Nonconformist and Catholic Emancipation, and by the 'Great Reform' Bill: his famous sermon was a call to action, and stimulated leading Oxford Churchmen to begin a systematic campaign to revive High Church principles and patristic theology (scholarship based on the doctrines, writings, and opinions of the Fathers of the Church). J.H. Newman, in his *Apologia pro vita sua* (1864), was emphatic in his assertion that Keble was the 'true and primary author' of the impressive and great revival of Anglicanism known as The Oxford Movement. R.W. Church was quite clear: he recognised that the Oxford or Tractarian movement began in defence of the Church against many hostile assaults in the reign of William IV.

Keble's well-aimed attack on Erastianism and Whiggery was therefore of great importance, but although it was a catalyst in the revival of Anglicanism (and therefore a major factor in the revivals of ecclesiology, liturgiology, and Gothic architecture), foundations had already been laid. When Charles Lloyd was appointed (1822) Regius Professor of Divinity at Oxford, he disseminated his views that the Anglican Prayer Book was essentially derived from early Christian and mediæval devotions (still at that time to be found in their Latin forms in R.C. service books), and, when many Anglicans were starting to perceive the Church of England in historical terms of continuity with the pre-Reformation Church, Lloyd's teachings were significant. Among those he influenced were J.R. Bloxam, R.H. Froude, Frederick Oakeley, and E.B. Pusey, all of whom became powers in the Oxford Movement. Lloyd clarified the aspects of Anglican texts and practices that were early, mediæval, or post-Reformation.

Lloyd (consecrated Bishop of Oxford in 1827) left copious notes and annotated works: these were collected, edited, and published (1832), with new research, by

William Palmer, as *Origines Liturgicæ*, the year before Keble's sermon. Palmer's book came out in a revised edition (1845), and there can be no doubting its importance in Anglican circles, any more than the impact of Lloyd's teachings on what was to become the Oxford Movement can be questioned, though this has received limited recognition.

Thus, in the 1820s and 1830s, many questions were in the air. Robert Southey, like Cobbett, queried achievements of the Reformation, and doubted if the spirit that had built and endowed the monasteries had been superseded for the better by the builders of steam engines and cotton mills. Sir Francis Palgrave, distinguished archivist and historian, even suggested that the humbler echelons of society might in some ways have been treated more humanely under Norman feudal systems than was the case in the reign of William IV.

In 1832 Hugh James Rose founded a journal to propagate High Church views on the restoration of ancient Anglican doctrines and practices. Described as the 'Cambridge originator of the Oxford Movement', Rose established connections with Newman and other Oxford luminaries, and in July 1833 Froude, Palmer, and A.P. Perceval visited Rose at his rectory in Hadleigh, Suffolk, to discuss the worrying ecclesiastical-political situation: soon afterwards Froude and Palmer founded the Association of Friends of the Church. The 'Hadleigh Conference' is regarded as an important landmark in the history of Tractarianism.

The first of the *Tracts for the Times*, by members of the University of Oxford, appeared in 1833, and the last in 1841. Authors included Froude, Keble, Newman, and Pusey: the *Tracts* were issued with the intention (among others) of reviving doctrines and historical connections that had become clouded or submerged. Pusey, Regius Professor of Hebrew at Oxford from 1828, gave the Oxford Movement cohesion, respectability, and fame – so much so that the Tractarians and adherents of the Oxford Movement became known as 'Puseyites' (though Tractarianism was also referred to, irreverently, as 'Newmania'). Under Pusey's influence the *Tracts* became solid, scholarly, doctrinal treatises, and his own contributions drew the attention of Churchmen to the almost forgotten sacrificial aspects of the Eucharist, as well as to the profound significance of the Sacrament of Baptism. Tractarianism aimed to secure for Anglicanism a base of doctrine and discipline in the event of the very real threat of disestablishment, or the equally real and unsettling possibility that High Churchmen might secede. Questions about the Reformation were causing unease: the Oxford Movement came under fire after the publication (1838) of the *Literary Remains* of Hurrell Froude, edited by Newman and Keble, for that work further criticised the Reformation, encouraging Evangelicals and others in their suspicions that Tractarians were crypto-'papists' or worse. In the same year a project was floated by Evangelicals to erect a memorial to three 'Protestant martyrs' (Cranmer [Archbishop of Canterbury], Latimer [Bishop of Worcester], and Ridley [Bishop of London]) burned at the stake in Oxford in the reign of the R.C. Queen Mary I. This proposal led many to examine the theological, moral, and ecclesiastical positions of the 'martyrs', and not all were convinced of their soundness. In the event, the Martyrs' Memorial, based on one of the mediæval 'Eleanor Crosses' was erected (1841–3) in St Giles', Oxford, to designs by George Gilbert ('Great') Scott.

Then a real crisis developed. In 1841 was published Newman's *Tract xc*, dealing, inter alia, with the compatibility of the Church of England's 16th-century Thirty-Nine Articles of Religion with Roman Catholicism, and the storm broke. Not only was publication of the *Tracts* ended, but Newman's decidedly shaky arguments were demolished by Dr Nicholas Wiseman, president of the R.C. Oscott College (with which A.W.N. Pugin was connected, as Professor of Ecclesiastical Antiquities), Bishop of Melipotamus *in partibus Infidelium* (from 1840), later (1850) created Cardinal Archbishop of Westminster by *Pio Nono*. Wiseman contributed several articles to the *Dublin Review* (collected and published [1841] as *High-Church Claims*) exposing the Tractarians' illogical positions. Newman's *Tract* was also attacked by Evangelicals, most effectively by Archibald Campbell Tait, then a tutor at Balliol College, Oxford (later Bishop of London [1856] and Archbishop of Canterbury [1869]), who felt that the limits of honest interpretation had been transgressed by Newman's over-zealous attempts to interpret the Articles in a sense favourable to the 'Romanist' practices which they (the Articles) had been framed to condemn, and argued that the reputation of the teaching body at Oxford would be impaired if no protest were made. By the end of 1841 Newman's allegiance to Anglicanism was broken: in 1845 he was received into the R.C. Church and was created cardinal in 1871. Disraeli and Gladstone, for once of similar mind, opined that Newman's 'calamitous' secession was a blow under which the Church of England still reeled years afterwards.

Tractarian attempts to revive an almost lost belief in the historical continuity and liturgy of the Anglican Church had been very badly dented, and the Oxford Movement attracted opprobrium. However, aspects of the Movement's ethos survived, both in the Church of England in general, and in the infant Anglo-Catholic party within the Church in particular. Clergy began to take their responsibilities more seriously, and the dignity of their calling was given greater emphasis: High Church clergy carried out rubrical directions, and introduced changes into the forms of Divine Service that excited Protestant opposition and the condemnation of several bishops. In the 1830s, all forms of Ritualism were suspect, chancels had often been abandoned or (in post-Reformation churches) were virtually non-existent, while vestments and even the cross were unthinkable: clergymen wore severe black gowns, and congregations were of the static, non-participatory kind.

However, the Oxford Movement had begun with several express aims, one of which was to uphold the Church against growing secularism and political interference. Despite the Newman case (which was by no means unique, as many followed him to Rome), Tractarian ideals did not fade away, for in reality liturgical and æsthetic debate became more vociferous. The High Church movement did not collapse either: on the contrary, Newman's secession concentrated minds and led to a remarkable flowering of Ritualism, with all that it implied in the way of architecture and artefacts, giving rise to an Anglo-Catholicism that drew on English mediæval liturgical traditions influenced by such works as the *Directorium Anglicanum* (1858).

By the end of the century, despite attempts to curb Ritualism by means such as the Public Worship Regulation Act (1874), 'Bells and Smells', and with them a beautiful ritual carried out in appropriate architectural settings, were established in many churches in England (and especially in London).

The Rise of Ecclesiology

So 1833 was a significant year for the future of Anglicanism in many ways, not least because the supreme jurisdiction in ecclesiastical matters within the Church of England was passed to the Judicial Committee of the Privy Council, and alarm bells rang ever more loudly. Soon afterwards, influential architectural societies were established at the universities of Oxford and Cambridge: the Oxford Society for Promoting the Study of Gothic Architecture (later called The Oxford Architectural Society); and The Cambridge Camden Society (named after the antiquary and historian William Camden). The latter promoted the study of ecclesiastical architecture and of mutilated architectural remains through visits to churches, collections of brass rubbings, and published articles, criticisms, and illustrations. From its beginnings (it was formally constituted in 1839), it was far more than an antiquarian society: it was a pressure group and a proselytising body that set out to encourage a study of mediæval art and architecture in order to promote the restoration of decayed churches and the building of new ones that would be scholarly, structurally excellent, and provide appropriate settings for revived liturgical practices. Its ideals were set out in various publications, but in 1841 appeared the first issue of *The Ecclesiologist*, one of the most important Victorian architectural journals long influential after its cessation in 1868.

Ecclesiology is essentially the study of church forms and traditions, and of church building and decorations: the Cambridge Camden Society (CCS hereafter) provided a framework and a stimulus for the study of the arts, architecture, and liturgy of the Christian Church. Very quickly, it became identified with Tractarianism, and got into hot water as a result: by 1843 several branches of the Oxford and Cambridge architectural societies began to sever their ties with the CCS, and in 1844 Dr Francis Close, Dean of Carlisle, an Evangelical, lambasted the two societies, claiming that 'Romanism' was taught analytically at Oxford, that *The Ecclesiologist* promoted doctrines identical to those in *Tracts for the Times*, and that restoration of churches not only tended to encourage, but actually was, 'popery'. One of the problems was that supporters of the two societies (members of which became known as Ecclesiologists) not only studied and published mediæval architecture, but explained to a nominally 'Protestant' population (that knew nothing, or very little, about such matters) what details, furnishings, and parts of churches were for and meant, and how they had been used. Some were suspicious of such studies and explanations, fearing they might have dire consequences. The CCS refuted these suggestions, but Close's accusations came at the time of Newman's secession to Rome, so there seemed to be something in Protestant fears. Close's 1844 book was based on a sermon he delivered in the parish church of Cheltenham, Gloucestershire, on 5 November 1844. Taking II Kings xviii, 4, as his text, he justified iconoclasm, and argued against reconstruction, restoration, the use of incense, and the whole philosophy of Ecclesiology. A reading of his sermon today leaves one wondering what all the fuss was about, for its relationship to the biblical text is highly contrived, and the sermon, as a whole, fails to impress.

Some influential persons distanced themselves from the CCS, and in 1845 it was proposed that the society should be wound up: in fact, it changed its name to The Ecclesiological Society, continued to publish *The Ecclesiologist*, but ceased to be associated with Cambridge, and became a national body based in London. Taking its cues from Milner, Pugin, and others, it began (dangerously) to equate morality with architecture, and exhorted architects, masons, carpenters, bricklayers, and all persons involved in church building and restoration to live holy and serious lives. *The Ecclesiologist* became a powerful organ for architectural criticism, and could make or break reputations.

The Anglican Response after 1833: A Church-Building Age

Many Churchmen, dismayed by events in the early 1830s, had prophesied the end of Anglicanism, but, apart from the activities in Oxford and Cambridge associated with leading High Church personalities and with Tractarianism, Evangelicalism was by no means moribund.

Abolitionists of slavery led by William Wilberforce, the Clapham Sect, the Church Missionary Society, and the Religious Tract Society were all active in promoting Evangelical activities, and were conspicuously successful in their efforts. In addition, the important figure of Charles Simeon, incumbent of Holy Trinity, Cambridge, Fellow of King's College, one of the founders (1797) of the Church Missionary Society, and friend of John Venn, brought the influence of the Clapham Sect to the university and town. Simeon's 'tenacious grasp of distinctive principles made him known beyond Cambridge, and he became an acknowledged leader' among Evangelical Churchmen. Indeed, in later life he became an object of something like veneration, and exerted at Cambridge an influence still recognised more than a century after his death.

Thus both Evangelical and Ecclesiological influences were strong in Cambridge, and Simeon had a considerable following of young men – larger and no less devoted than Newman had at Oxford (where Tractarian High Churchmen were dominant) – and for a much longer time. Firmly attached to the Church of England, to her doctrines, and to her liturgy, he was a good example of a Churchman who believed in the efficacy of good works, and who eschewed controversies aroused by Tractarianism. However, despite reactions occasioned by hostile legislation, some observers feared the Church of England was set to become just one denomination among others, some of which had made considerable strides, and appeared as aggressive and threatening to the Established Church. Many Churchmen, therefore, fired with Tractarian zeal or Evangelical fervour, determined to bring new life to Anglicanism.

One of the key figures in the Anglican response to secularisation was Charles James Blomfield, Bishop of London from 1828: he recognised that if the Church were to survive, it would require major reorganisation. Given the concessions made to Dissenters and Roman Catholics, and realising that it was impossible for Anglicanism to go on as it had done, Blomfield craftily gained the ear of Sir Robert Peel, who helped him to achieve several objectives by lobbying and other means. Having prepared the political ground, as it were, the bishop introduced proposals in the House of Lords in 1836 'for the creation of a fund to be applied to the building and endowment of additional churches in the metropolis'. He was behind the establishment of the Ecclesiastical Commission (also 1836), and was especially concerned with 'the better distribution of ecclesiastical revenues and duties, the prevention or diminution of pluralities and non-residence, and the augmentation of poor benefices and endowment of new ones'. His energetic efforts were successful in remedying the inadequate provision of churches, schools, and clergymen for the rapidly increasing population. Soon money was to flood into the bishop's 'Metropolitan Churches Extension Fund', and several local associations for church extensions were set up, benefiting districts such as Bethnal Green, Islington, St Pancras, Paddington, and Westminster. The Fund was subsumed into the London Diocesan Church Building Society in 1854.

Blomfield's initiative in targeting Bethnal Green was important, for it was probably the first constructive programme of intervention to improve the moral and social conditions of the East End, though it was eventually not to prove really successful because there were too many churches and parishes in a district where churchgoing was not ingrained, and the habit did not noticeably increase: parishes that succeeded were the ones with lively schools, suggesting that churches were probably not what were really needed in working-class areas, and should have been built after parish life had been established by other means.

In places such as the parish of Kensington, however, which experienced a phenomenal amount of new building in the Victorian period, churches were deemed necessary to raise or set the tone of an urban neighbourhood, and small ecclesiastical parishes were thereby created. The earliest church accommodation to be provided (in addition to the existing parish church of St Mary Abbots – soon to be grandly rebuilt by 'Great' Scott in 1869–79) was a proprietary chapel, erected, without any charge to the parish, by private individuals as a commercial enterprise. However, *The Christian Observer*, the main publication of the Evangelical party, condemned proprietary chapels without reservation, mostly because of their commercial associations. Some church building followed, supported by the government under the post-Waterloo Acts, and the Kensington vestry obtained grants, facilitating the erection of the 'Commissioners' churches' of St Barnabas, Addison Road (in the late Perpendicular style of Gothic, erected 1826–9 to designs by Lewis Vulliamy) and Holy Trinity, Brompton (in the baldest First Pointed Lancet style [but subsequently altered], also erected 1826–9, this time to designs by T.L. Donaldson). The way in which the 'Commissioners' churches' were realised resembled the provision of public housing later: the government provided grants on certain conditions; the vestries raised the balance (often by borrowing); and pew rents were set to support and maintain the churches. As a benefit, the presence of the new churches would help to bring respectability to the immediate areas around them, and provide a reassuring visible presence of the Established Church.

Blomfield campaigned for funding from private sources for church building, and stated it was the duty of landowners and property-owners either to build churches or contribute towards their costs. Furthermore, he created patterns of small ecclesiastical districts, each of 'manageable size', and each with its church, schools, and charities. Thus, in the large parish of St Mary Abbots, Kensington, the vicar from 1845, John Sinclair, followed Blomfield's policies in creating new ecclesiastical districts within the parish, and, in turn, those districts were further subdivided, each new division requiring its own church. As they were created, they acquired parochial rights and duties, and each was subdivided as soon as it was necessary to do so.

In the case of Kensington, new Anglican churches built under Sinclair's ægis consisted of two basic types: there were the estate churches erected or promoted by landowners to make their speculative housing developments more attractive to leaseholders (an important factor when, in many conventional households, churchgoing was obligatory, even for servants), and the 'private' churches promoted by clergymen in order to foster a type of Churchmanship, be it 'High', 'Low', or 'Broad'. Generally, estate churches tended to be of the Low Church type, built to accommodate as many people in the new district as possible, and were therefore unritualistic, often with galleries, and with small chancels. Private churches tended to be more High Church, promoted by clergymen and their supporters in order to foster Ritualism and Tractarianism. In Kensington there were animosities between the High Church Tractarian and Low Church Evangelical parties, but the national and diocesan funding (so important in poorer parts of London) was relatively insignificant because the parish on the whole was wealthy. Some estate churches were erected by landowners or developers, who paid the entire cost, but more usually the landowner presented the sites for church building or sold them for much less than market value, leaving vicar-designates and church-building committees to raise the money for the fabric itself. In some cases, temporary prefabricated churches (often of iron) were erected while funds were being raised and plans drawn up, and once their usefulness had passed, the temporary structures were sold to other districts or parishes. Private ventures usually had to find the money to pay for the site as well as the building.

This over-provision of churches was a recipe for future disaster: there was an assumption that Anglican clergymen would always come from the higher, well-heeled echelons of society, and would therefore have substantial (or sufficient) private incomes; and it was also hoped, optimistically, that Kensington residents would always be prosperous, disposed to attend church, and able to put plenty of cash in the collection plates. In almost all cases, however, the churches were under-endowed, and by the end of the century it became clear that some districts were too small to support their churches in the future. In later years it was generally true that most vicars no longer had comfortable private incomes. Multiple occupation of houses originally intended for family occupation, and the exodus of families from Kensington, led to dramatic declines in church attendance, although celebrated centres of Anglo-Catholicism such as St Cuthbert, Philbeach Gardens, continued to flourish because they drew their congregations from a very wide area rather than from parish or district alone.

As for the parish church of St Mary Abbots, Kensington, the old church (completed in 1704) was declared unsafe in 1866, but it is likely that the desire of Archdeacon Sinclair to build a new church 'on a scale proportioned to the opulence and importance' of a great metropolitan parish had more to do with the decision to demolish and provide a new structure in the Gothic Revival style. Such a desire for importance, show, and status enshrined in a building was common throughout the country, and was intimately connected with the ambitions of Churchmen to match their rhetoric with architectural grandeur.

Nonconformists (never very influential in places like Kensington) often came to grief when enthusiastic pastors imagined they would attract larger congregations than they actually achieved, and there was much financial over-extension. Nonconformists generally, throughout the country, remained faithful to Classicism until they became infected with the Gothic bug in the 1850s.

Afterword

Nevertheless, Anglicanism experienced a revival within itself, Evangelical in nature, that partly stemmed from outside criticism, and partly grew as an attempt to counteract charismatic preaching of Nonconformist pastors. The Established Church attempted to demonstrate it was capable of servicing the new England, so the parish, the parson's freehold, private patronage, and the training of ministers all had to come under scrutiny, and, ultimately, had to change. After all, the parochial system was predominantly rural (and had served the countryside well), but it was difficult to translate it to new urban conditions. In short, the Anglican Church was not well prepared to deal with the changing structure of the nation, so it responded by developing systems of urban parishes in order to retrieve the situation. The parochial system, expanded and adapted for contemporary conditions, was seen by Churchmen as a means of rescuing society from its parlous state, but parochial systems needed churches, clergy houses, and other buildings, and these cost money. Furthermore, the system of pew rents might work in well-heeled places like Kensington, but would not be popular in poorer manufacturing districts, so many new churches were obliged to provide free pews, which placed an added burden on over-stretched finances. Obviously, new churches should have as many sittings as possible, but this aim clashed with the established institution of the family pew. In the 18th century the high-backed, well-cushioned, and carpeted 'box pew' was a feature of many churches, and ensured a modicum of comfort for the 'owner' who paid a 'rent' for the privilege of having it. But such pews took up space, and disadvantaged those who could not afford them. At the beginning of the 19th century the idea of sitting on plain benches wherever a seat could be found, with no concepts of proprietorship, would have been unthinkable. As Eastlake (1872) put it:

> to sit on uncovered wooden benches as congregations do now in half the modern churches of London – to make, in short, no distinction between the rich and poor assembled in common worship – would have been considered something altogether incompatible with the requirements of a genteel congregation. In this dilemma it was obvious that the only expedient by which a certain number of sittings could be obtained without doubling the size and cost of the church was the erection of galleries, and these were freely adopted, without the slightest reference either to ancient precedent or to architectural effect.

Provincial church-building societies were unable to keep pace, year by year, with increasing populations, and the percentage of persons that could be accommodated in Anglican churches in urban areas was small. Evangelical Churchmen set up trusts in a number of cases to ensure a succession of devoted and like-minded ministers, thus replacing the patronage of a living with committees. Historically, the right of bestowing church benefices lay with a variety of groups and individuals, including Oxbridge colleges and private patrons (often aristocrats or at least landed gentry), so the change was remarkable. Evangelicals were deeply serious, provided more services, emphasised preaching, insisted that rectors should live permanently in their rectories, encouraged the development of religious societies, and conscientiously carried out their official duties. The demands of long sermons, static congregations, and finance ensured that churches should be large, should have good acoustics to enable The Word to be heard, should have comfortable seating so as not to distract the congregation from The Word, and should have good visibility so that the minister could be seen from all parts of the church. There were also the questions of maintaining standards of comfort in seating for those who were used to it, and of providing adequate heating during inclement weather.

One of the great problems was that incumbents of parishes were grossly overworked, for everything in parochial life centred on them, including the running of schools, the chairing of meetings, the directing of visiting, the conducting of services, and (even more time-consuming and exhausting) the raising of funds. Unfortunately, the incumbent was left with virtually no time in which to study, or to have much of a social life, with the result that he very frequently had little or no knowledge or appreciation of contemporary life.

There was another difficulty. In spite of its energetic activities and undoubted influence on national life, the Evangelical Movement within the Church of England was in a weak position in that it lacked coherent arguments in upholding historical ecclesiastical principles, and, like many of the Nonconformist groups, tended to be overdependent on charismatic preachers rather than on tradition, on the legitimacy of Apostolic Succession, and on ritual (all things the High Church Tractarians valued): for Evangelicals the major emphasis was on the Bible and on direct experience.

Evangelicals (much given to abstinence from alcohol) were keen to condemn worldliness and the study of secular matters, with the result that they relied on denunciations rather than on intelligent analyses of important issues, and so were regarded by many as 'unclubbable' bores. Critics complained of the commonplace abuse heaped upon scepticism, other branches of Christianity, and non-Christians, and noted that clergy might be more effective if they could dispute points and win them in fair debate. But Evangelicals were ill equipped to do this, for their intellectual bases were no match for the arguments of their enemies (secular and non-secular).

Scolding was of little avail against scepticism, and after Darwin's *On the Origin of Species* appeared (1859) the scolding became a rant.

4

Recusants, Goths, Converts, Ultramontanes, and Controversies

The waste of time, of energy, and printer's ink, involved by endless discussions on the respective merits of Mediæval and Renaissance architecture during twenty years, can only be realised by those who have studied the current art literature of that period.

CHARLES LOCKE EASTLAKE (1836–1906):
A History of the Gothic Revival
(London: Longmans, Green, & Co., 1872), 333.

Vitruvius would spew if he beheld the works of those who glory in calling him master.

AUGUSTUS WELBY NORTHMORE PUGIN (1812–52):
An Apology for the Revival of Christian Architecture in England
(London: John Weale, 1843), 5.

Introduction

English mediæval parish churches and cathedrals were largely Gothic, and Roman Catholicism had been practised therein, but since the 16th-century break with Rome, adherents to the old faith had had a very difficult time in these islands. Several plots, from those against Queen Elizabeth to the 1798 Irish Rebellion, all caused Roman Catholicism to be viewed with suspicion by a largely 'Protestant' nation. As the years passed, however, the Gothic connection with Roman Catholicism passed from common memory.

Gothic had enjoyed a certain notoriety in the 18th century, but began to be more fashionable when it was given the royal imprimatur at Carlton House (1807) and Windsor Castle (from 1824). As far as an appreciation of it as a serious style was concerned, the foundations had already been laid by writers such as Milner, Carter, Britton, A.C. Pugin, and Rickman, and as the 19th century progressed, publications based on meticulous surveys and analyses of real mediæval work appeared, completely superseding 18th-century whimsical, fanciful Gothick.

Then John Keble, defender of Anglicanism by recovering its historical links with the pre-Reformation Church, the Caroline High Churchmen, and Sacramentalism, in his *Lectures on Poetry*, given 1832–41, later (1844) published in Oxford by J.H. Parker as *De Poeticæ vi Medica*, described Gothic as the most beautiful of all architectural styles, and by far the most in harmony with the mysteries of religion (Lecture 3).

In October 1834 the old Palace of Westminster was destroyed by fire, and with it the work of 'The Destroyer' Wyatt. Young Pugin was overjoyed. With this momentous conflagration the principles of Georgian Picturesque also went up in smoke, and on the site arose the new, Gothic Revival Palace of Westminster, won in competition by Charles Barry with whom A.W.N. Pugin was to collaborate on much of the detail.

Pugin's *Contrasts* and After

A.W.N. Pugin converted to Roman Catholicism in 1835, and the following year he brought out *Contrasts; or, A Parallel between the Noble Edifices of the Fourteenth and Fifteenth Centuries, and Similar Buildings of the Present Day; Shewing the Present Decay of Taste*, published by himself. A second edition, with a slightly amended title, was published in 1841.

Contrasts did not contain an original message, for many of its themes had been aired before: what was new was the series of drawings contrasting works of some well-known architects of the day with selected mediæval buildings, and finding the former wanting. Pugin claimed that English 'Pointed Architecture', produced by 'the Catholic faith', was destroyed by Protestantism. Classical architecture was 'pagan', and religious reformers were 'Church plunderers and crafty political intriguers'. Mediæval 'Catholic' architecture had a 'wonderful superiority' over Classical buildings, for in it, and in it alone, 'the faith of Christianity was embodied'.

Some of the architects Pugin named had occupied positions of distinction: for a young man in his twenties to ridicule them was a brave (or foolhardy) thing to do. Pugin stressed that art is intimately connected with the state of the society that produces it, and argued that only when the piety and communal spirit of the mediæval period had been re-established could a true and noble Christian architecture re-arise.

When the 1841 edition of *Contrasts* came out, considerable changes had taken place. The Palace of Westminster was under construction, and Pugin, who from 1844 until his death worked with Barry, had a major hand in it. Consequently, he altered the tone of *Contrasts*: he watered down his attacks on Protestantism, seeing its rise as more a product of 'Catholic degeneracy'; he was more scathing about 'pagan' architecture; and he appeared to be optimistic that Gothic architecture would be revived in England rather than in R.C. countries like Italy where 'pagan' architecture was deeply entrenched.

Although *Contrasts* named and shamed a few top architects of the time, it was aimed at the revival of a Roman Catholic mediæval England, yet struck all sorts of chords among Anglicans, and, as G.G. 'Great' Scott admitted, Pugin was the decisive influence on many Anglican Gothic Revivalists. 'The thunder of Pugin's writings' awakened Scott from his 'slumbers'. Pugin's articles in *The Dublin Review* (no. 20, of May 1841, and no. 23, of February 1842) seem to be the texts that fired him up. Perhaps *Contrasts* has been given too much credit as an influence on early Victorian architecture: Benjamin Webb, for example, did not study *Contrasts* until 1842, which makes one wonder what the print run of the 1836 edition actually was. The 1841 edition appears to have made the greater impact, with *The Dublin Review* adding mightily to the conflagration.

Contrasts claimed superiority for 14th-century 'Catholic' architecture: everything good or noble in architecture was only possible through the beneficent influence of the R.C. Church; destruction, vandalism, irreverence, and loss of sensitive perception were the direct results of the Renaissance and the Reformation; and the degraded state of architecture was due to an absence of 'Catholic' feeling. *Contrasts* was followed by *The True Principles of Pointed or Christian Architecture set forth in Two Lectures delivered at St Marie's, Oscott* (1841), *The Present State of Ecclesiastical Architecture in England* (1843), and *An Apology for the Revival of Christian Architecture in England* (1843). In all of these the message was loud and clear: Classical architecture was pagan, earth-bound, and no more sophisticated than Stonehenge in the essence of its structural system; while Gothic was not a style, but a principle, a moral crusade, and the only mode of building possible for a Christian nation.

Pugin warned against the contemporary tendency to ransack sourcebooks of Gothic and apply the pieces to a design. Scott, in his *A Plea for the Faithful Restoration of our Ancient Churches* (1850) referred to capricious 'restorers' who were glad to lose an ancient detail as an excuse to introduce a 'favourite morsel' of Gothic from one of the many illustrated tomes then available. Pugin seemed to suggest that architectural volumes of this type in the hands of practitioners were as dangerous as the Bible in the hands of Evangelicals.

To Pugin a revival of mediæval architecture would herald a regeneration of English Roman Catholicism. Furthermore, he claimed Gothic was more suited to the times than was Classicism: Classical buildings put elevations first, but in Gothic architecture elevations were dependent upon, and subservient to, plans. He further argued that the revival of mediæval architecture would be a 'perfect expression of all we should hold sacred, honourable, and national, and connected with the holiest and dearest associations', from the monarchy downwards. He stated that England was ideally placed to 'revive ancient excellence and solemnity', for it had 'immense power, vast wealth, and great though often misdirected zeal'. England, while the last to abandon 'Christian' architecture, was foremost in 'hailing and aiding its revival', using 'perfect models for imitation', and, in any case, its institutions were essentially those of the Middle Ages.

One of Pugin's aims was to establish a continuity between the R.C. Church in 19th-century England and the legacy of surviving 14th- and 15th-century buildings and artefacts. To him great art and Catholicism were intimately connected, and he sought a revival of *English* Gothic, partly to emphasise that continuity. Such a programme required a revival of liturgical scholarship, the father of which (in the R.C. Church) was Daniel Rock, recusant priest and chaplain to John Talbot, 16th Earl of Shrewsbury, one of England's leading R.C. peers. Born in the year of the Roman Catholic Relief Act (1791), Talbot was one of the first sons of English R.C. gentlemen able, in the early 19th century, to benefit from a solid R.C. education in Britain. Rock's *Hierurgia* came out in 1833, based on researches he had carried out at Shrewsbury's instigation: his work connected the early Church with modern times, thus demonstrating continuity from the Roman catacombs to R.C. liturgical practice in the 1830s.

Ultramontanism

However, there was a problem. Pugin and his allies longed to restore mediæval English Catholicism, not embrace modern Ultramontanism (the principles and practice of absolute papal supremacy outside Italy, north of the Alps) with its love of Baroque splendour. While Anglicans were beginning to rediscover the meaning of the Sacraments, Pugin sought to provide settings and artefacts to beautify R.C. worship. He gave Ecclesiology, intimately associated with his love of ritual, symbols, and detail, an important role, and one that was hugely significant outside the R.C. Church. This was because his pro-Gothic zeal did not find favour with all that many clergy of his own (recently acquired) faith, who would have been more familiar with Continental, especially Roman, ecclesiastical architecture, where the Pointed style was not predominant. Indeed, Pugin received most of his support from the old recusant aristocracy and land-owning classes of England, and his influence was strongest among those Oxbridge-educated young men who were to serve both Church and State in the years to come.

Pressurised by Emperor Charles V, the Council of Trent was convened (1545–63) to clarify and restate doctrine in the face of Evangelical assaults; it was also concerned with setting down frameworks for worship, codifying what became known as the Tridentine Mass, which remained in use for the following four centuries. A key figure in this was the nephew of Pope Pius IV, Carlo Borromeo, created cardinal in 1560, Archbishop of Milan in 1564, and who, from the age of 22, was de facto the leading statesman of the Papal Court. Borromeo (canonised 1610) drew up (1577) a manual for church building and furnishing, *Instructiones Fabricæ et Supellectilis Ecclesiasticæ*, subsequently adopted on an almost universal scale. It was published (1857) by Dolman in an English translation by G.J. Wigley, with illustrations by S.J. Nicholl. Now Borromeo, contrary to widely held beliefs, did not say very much about screens, except to advocate erecting them down the centres of naves to separate the sexes. However, affirmation of the importance of the Sacraments, and especially of the Eucharist and the Real Presence, meant that there was an architectural emphasis on the high altar with its tabernacle clearly visible from the single space of the church interior, the model being Il Gesù, Rome, erected (1568–84) to designs by Vignola and della Porta for the Society of Jesus, with later embellishments throughout the 17th century. Thus aisles, with nave arcades blocking the visibility of the high altar, separate long chancels with screens, and everything associated with typical mediæval churches, were unsatisfactory for post-Tridentine liturgical requirements, and although there were no formal proscriptions, it was clear that screens were really incompatible with the visibility desired during the Counter Reformation, which created a climate hostile to Pointed architecture and all that went with it. So the R.C. Church, by the time Pugin was passionately arguing in favour of Gothic, rood screens, and a general revival of English mediæval church architecture and furnishings, had moved far away from such things.

Pugin's vision of what he wished to restore was based on what had developed in churches since the 4th Lateran Council (1215) under Pope Innocent III: it required that a separate space had to be created for the positioning and protection of the Blessed Sacrament, so screens were erected between that space and the main body of the church. Some chancel screens were of stone (e.g. that in St Mary's church, Westwell, Kent [13th century], but it would seem that such a feature was by no means unfamiliar in that part of England, for the 7th-century Saxon church at Reculver had a stone screen, and there seems to have been something similar in the contemporary St Pancras's, Canterbury). There were, of course, massive screens in larger churches, such as the pulpitum (*c.*1320–40) in Southwell Minster, Nottinghamshire, but the more usual chancel screen was of timber, and in England (where the predominant order of Divine Service from the 11th century until the Reformation was the Sarum Rite or Use) screens increasingly incorporated a rood loft. So Pugin's architectural ideas, and those he passionately held regarding rood screens and church furnishings generally, envisaged settings appropriate for the Sarum Use rather than the Roman Breviary, which had only been introduced following the deliberations of the Council of Trent. Pugin's thinking, therefore, was not unlike that of many Anglican High Churchmen and numerous English old Catholic families, who longed for some kind of understanding between Rome and Canterbury.

Ultramontanes, convinced of claims that the R.C. Church was pre-eminent, would have no truck with links to pre-Reformation English Catholicism, and so were antipathetic not only to screens, with or without roods, but indeed to Gothic architecture. This explains, to some extent, why, for many early (and some later) churches and chapels, Roman Catholics eschewed Gothic, and embraced Classicism, Baroque, and other non-Gothic styles.

Some Roman Catholic Churches

In 1786–7 was built the R.C. Chapel of St Mary in the grounds of Lulworth Castle, Wareham, Dorset, to designs by John Tasker, for Thomas Weld (a friend of Milner), of an old recusant family. The first free-standing R.C. chapel to be erected in England since the Reformation, its outward appearance was tactfully unlike a church: it is essentially a rotunda with four apses, forming a quatrefoil on plan, three of the lobes containing galleries, and the fourth the altar. But the elegant Classical building is also a mausoleum: the vaulted crypt is the Weld family tomb.

Mention was made earlier of the small R.C. chapel which Carter designed for Dr John Milner in Winchester. Although it was Perpendicular Gothic, it had no screen, and there were no provisions for screens in buildings used for public R.C. worship until the 1840s. It appears, however, that the first post-Reformation chancel screen erected for an R.C. place of worship in England was that designed by William Railton for the chapel (1833–7) at Grace-Dieu Manor, Leicestershire, for Ambrose Lisle March Phillipps (later de Lisle), a Cambridge man who had been converted to Roman Catholicism in the 1820s, and who admired Continental R.C. art and architecture. Phillipps was introduced into his novel *Coningsby* (1844) by Benjamin Disraeli, thinly disguised as 'Eustace Lyle'. Railton's screen was replaced to new designs by A.W.N. Pugin not long after it was erected. Screens, thereafter, were to loom large in Pugin's short life, and disputes about them would cause him considerable grief.

Pugin's work for Barry's Palace of Westminster was in the 'Third Pointed', or 'Perpendicular' (an unfortunate term), style which, by the 1840s, tended to be regarded as too much associated with the despised Tudor period. In *True Principles* he opined that 'the moment the *flat* or *four-centred arch* was introduced, the spirit of Christian architecture was on the wane. *Height* or the *vertical principle*, emblematic of the resurrection, is the very essence of Christian architecture'. Scott, in his *Plea for the Faithful Restoration of our Ancient Churches*, took his cue from Pugin, stating that few could 'fail to perceive' in Perpendicular a want of 'that warmth of religious feeling

... found in the works of earlier periods' (a dubious conclusion, as all students of Perpendicular will agree). Morality, religion, and architecture were now thoroughly joined in an unholy *ménage-à-trois*.

To Pugin, the Gothic style was not just a wholly integrated system of architecture, but symbolised a society that was at peace with itself and serene in its history. In 1837 he made his first visit to Alton Towers, Staffordshire, seat of the Earl of Shrewsbury, who became his patron, and for whom he was to carry out extensive works. Shrewsbury was one of a relatively small group of powerful, well-connected (not only in England) aristocrats and landed gentry, sometimes referred to as 'Romantic Catholics', who had an influence far greater than their numbers might suggest: it was they who really launched Pugin's career.

Nevertheless, Pugin's early church buildings, such as St Mary's (or Marie's), Derby (1837–9) (Fig. 4.1) and St Alban's, Macclesfield (1838–41) (Fig. 4.2), are both in the Perpendicular style, with western towers (that of St Alban's was never completed), large traceried windows, and small chancels, so resemble some of the better Commissioners' churches for Anglicans. St Wilfrid's, Hulme, Manchester, of 1839–42, is First Pointed, or Early English, in style, that is with lancets, which was cheaper than providing large traceried windows. He also used First Pointed at Mount St Bernard Abbey, Leicestershire, founded in 1835 for a community of Cistercian monks by Phillipps (a friend of Lord Shrewsbury), who was convinced that only monasticism would Christianise places like Manchester, and worked tirelessly for the reunion of the R.C. and Anglican Churches. For this he had more support from Tractarians than from the R.C. authorities, and indeed Phillipps believed Anglican Orders were valid and Anglican theology (because pre-Tridentine) was more authentically 'Catholic' than that prevailing in his own Church, a poisonous view to Ultramontanes.

At St Chad's Cathedral, Birmingham (1839–41 – the first English R.C. cathedral to be built since mediæval times), Pugin chose brick as his material, and the twin western towers with spires look back to the *Backsteingotik* of 14th-century northern Germany (especially the Baltic towns): tracery and other details were based on 14th-century Second Pointed precedents, associated by Pugin with the period in England when R.C. observance was at its strongest. There is, however, evidence that this view is erroneous, and that it was at its most impressive in the period immediately before the Henrician and Edwardine iconoclasm of the 16th century. For St Chad's, Pugin designed another screen, and this time he encountered resistance from the Church authorities, notably from the then co-adjutor to the vicar apostolic of the Midland District, N.P.S. Wiseman, who had little sympathy with the notion of reviving a pre-Reformation English Church with all its Gothic settings: his parents were both Irish, after all; he had been born in Seville; and he had studied for the priesthood in Rome from 1818. It was only the double threats of Pugin's resignation and, perhaps more important, the withdrawal of funding, that enabled the rood screen to be installed (Fig. 4.3). Pugin began to realise that opposition to his work was most likely to come from the Ultramontane tendency of the Roman Church. In his *Treatise on Chancel Screens and Rood Lofts* (1851), an increasingly embittered Pugin denounced four types of what he called 'ambonoclasts': Protestant Calvinists; 'pagans'; revolutionaries; and R.C. modernists. The ambonoclasts eventually got their way, and St Chad's screen was removed as part of the reordering (1966–8).

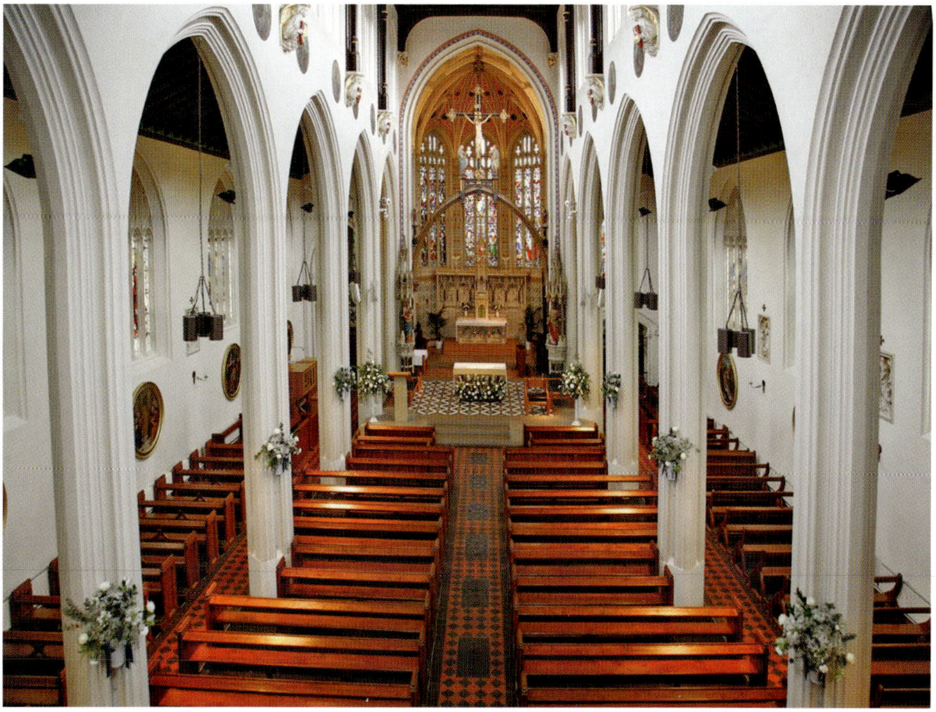

Fig. 4.1 St Mary's (or Marie's), Derby (1837–9), A.W.N. Pugin's first large R.C. parish church, in the Perpendicular style, one of several financed by Lord Shrewsbury. Although similar to St Alban's, Macclesfield, Cheshire (*see* Fig. 4.2), here the nave arcades eschew capitals. A beam surmounted by a rood was installed at the chancel arch, giving an unobstructed view of the altar, and the sanctuary was separated from the nave by low altar rails (GB [2013]).

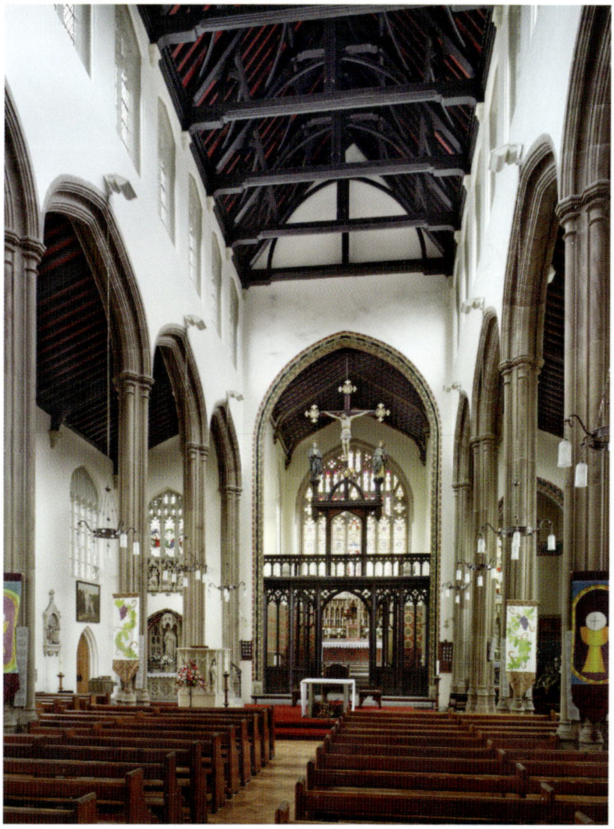

Fig. 4.2 St Alban's R.C. Church, Macclesfield, Cheshire (1838–41), by A.W.N. Pugin, partly financed by Lord Shrewsbury. Entirely Perpendicular, it has extraordinarily slender piers, this time with capitals. Both St Mary's, Derby (*see* Fig. 4.1), and St Alban's were designed before Pugin turned to Second Pointed as his preferred style. The screen was one of Pugin's first for a church where public worship took place, and is surmounted by a 16th-century German rood donated by him (AH [2011]).

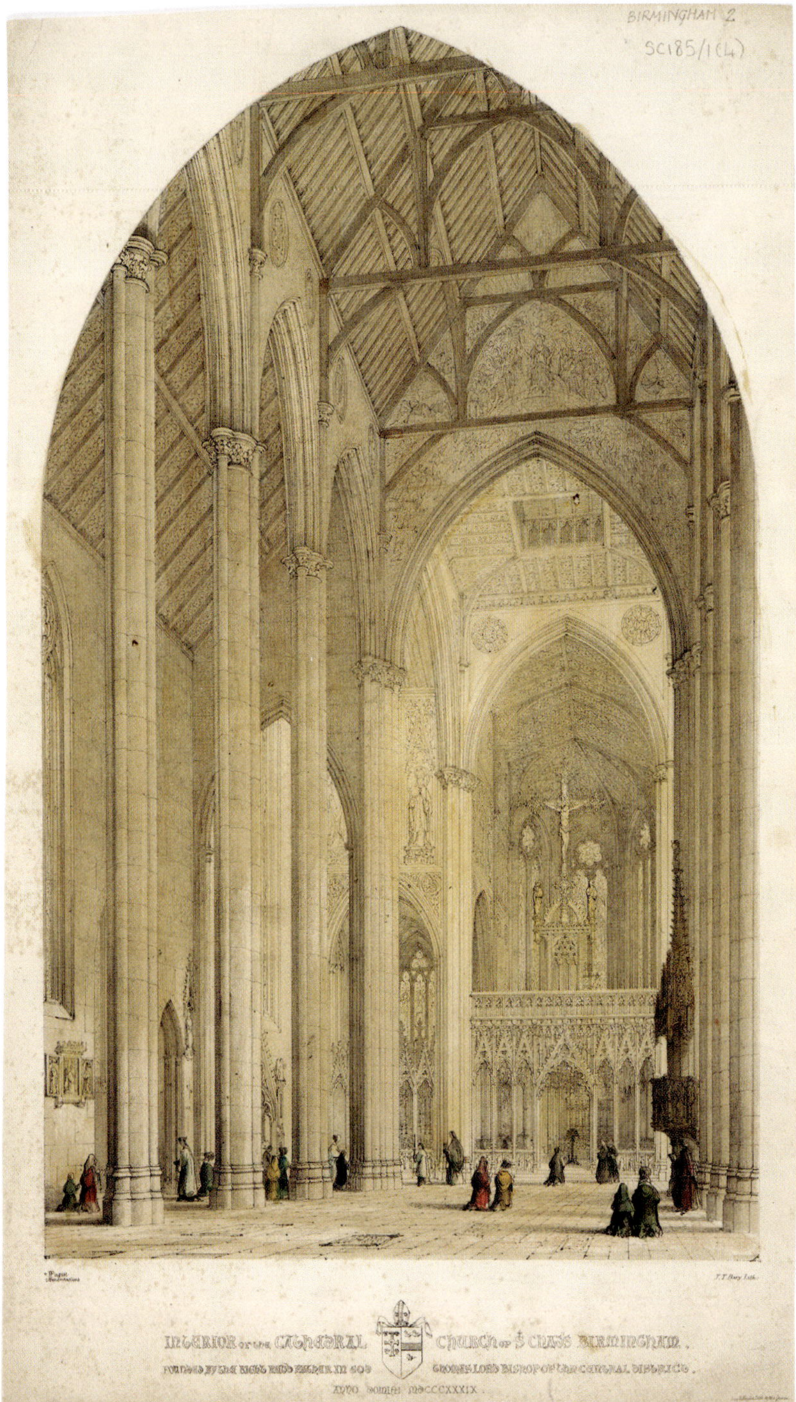

Fig. 4.3 The Second Pointed R.C. Cathedral of St Chad, Birmingham (1839–41), drawn to a slightly inflated scale by A.W.N. Pugin, showing the chancel screen and rood before removal (1966–8). Pugin signs himself *cœmentarius*, meaning a mason who measures, weighs, and has the knowledge to erect harmonious compositions (lithographed by Thomas Talbot Bury for the firm established by William Day and Louis Haghe [1839] RIBAC SC185/13).

By 1841, when his *True Principles* appeared, Pugin's growing confidence was apparent. There he set out practical examples of mediæval design, while also ridiculing Neo-Classical buildings. In the same year he brought out his revised edition of *Contrasts* in which he changed his earlier admiration for Perpendicular Gothic to 14th-century Second Pointed, and also shifted something of the blame for the decline of taste away from Protestantism and towards the Renaissance. Significantly, he expressed his belief in the superiority of mediæval 'Catholic' society (*c.*1440) when contrasted with conditions in 1840 by showing views of the same town as it appeared in the 15th and 19th centuries. The addition of the famous 'Contrasted Residences for the Poor' displayed his hatred of Benthamite utilitarian ideas, and of the Anatomy and Poor Law Amendment Acts of the 1830s. Pugin's shift of preference towards Second Pointed followed the views of earlier commentators (as noted previously), but the main catalyst for his changes of perspective may have been Charles-Forbes-René, Comte de Montalambert, who provided a hefty appendix to the 1841 edition of *Contrasts* entitled 'Account of the Destructive and Revised Pagan Principle in France'. There was also a second appendix on the abbey of St Wandrille, Normandy, by Eustache-Hyacinthe Langlois (keeper of the Gothic antiquities he had collected and housed in Rouen, writer, and friend of the Pugins).

At this time Pugin carried out numerous R.C. commissions: they include St George's Cathedral, Southwark (1841–8 – badly damaged in the 1939–45 war and rebuilt [1953–63] in a desiccated style by Romilly Craze); St Mary's Cathedral, Newcastle upon Tyne (1841–4); and the cathedrals at Killarney, Co. Kerry (1842–50), and Enniscorthy, Co. Wexford (1843–50). These, together with over 20 other church buildings, built or under construction, are delineated in the frontispiece of Pugin's *An Apology for the Revival of Christian Architecture in England*, and represent a phenomenal workload, even though many of the buildings are shown with towers and spires that were never realised.

From 1843 he began work on his own house, The Grange, Ramsgate, Kent, which, with the adjoining Church of St Augustine (1845–52), was an example of his 'True Picturesque' style, irregularly composed, and freely grouped. He considered

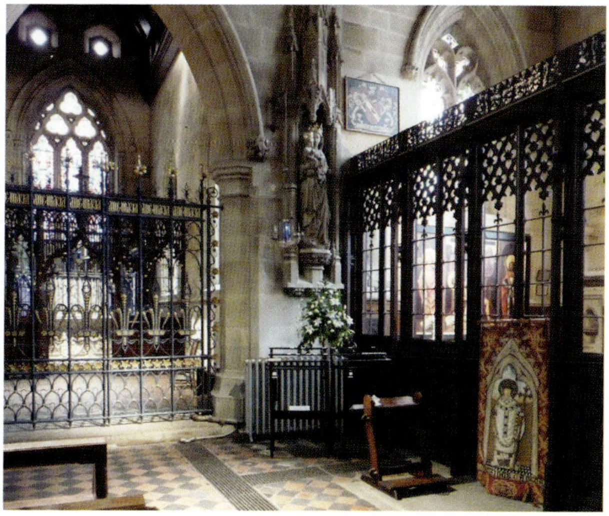

Fig. 4.4 St Augustine's Second Pointed R.C. church, Ramsgate, Kent (1845–51), by A.W.N. Pugin, sumptuously fitted out with screens (GB [2011]).

it to be one of his finest achievements: St Augustine's contains screens (recently restored) (Fig. 4.4). Within the chantry chapel of Sts Lawrence and Stephen in the south transept is Pugin's tomb-chest and effigy designed by E.W. Pugin (1852).

Pugin's most beautiful church, St Giles's, Cheadle, Staffordshire (1841–6), was firmly in the English Second Pointed Curvilinear style (later than Geometrical Middle Pointed, the style favoured by 'Great' Scott), built of local red sandstone, and was designed for Lord Shrewsbury as a model parish church (Fig. 4.5). 'Perfect Cheadle', as its architect described it, was, without question, Pugin's masterpiece, and, thanks to Shrewsbury, he was able to lavish his skills on it without penny-pinching. The interior, glowing with colour (Fig. 4.6 and *see* frontispiece), is based on scholarly studies of mediæval precedents, and influenced, to a certain extent, by the restoration of Sainte-Chapelle, Paris (from 1837), by Viollet-le-Duc, Félix-Louis-Jacques Duban, and Jean-Baptiste-Antoine Lassus, which Pugin, in 1844, hailed as 'glorious'. Newman described the Cheadle church as the 'gate of heaven' when he saw it shortly before it opened, and called it the 'most splendid building' he had ever seen. But Newman was to change his attitudes to Pugin, becoming opposed to the architect's enthusiasm for screens in particular and English Gothic Revival in general. As Andrew Derrick has noted, the 'apogee of Pugin's ambonophilia' was at St Giles's, but soon Pugin was to fall out with the Oratorians, a post-Reformation Order, of which Newman was a member (he founded [1849] its house in Birmingham), and one that was particularly noted for its *Romanità*.

However, apart from his great achievements at Cheadle and Ramsgate, Pugin's ecclesiastical work is, on the whole, disappointing: usually there was a

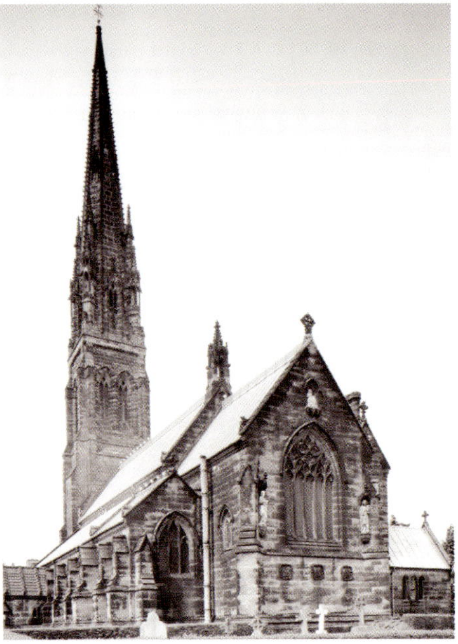

Fig. 4.5 St Giles's R.C. Church, Cheadle, Staffordshire (1841–6), by A.W.N. Pugin: revival of a type of English parish church dating from the time of Edward I. The steeple is one of the most perfect of the Gothic Revival. Over the chancel arch is a bell- or sancte-cote (MC/RIBAC F260494 [1994]).

Fig. 4.6 Baptistry in St Giles's, Cheadle, with font, font cover, and scholarly, polychrome decoration (MK [2019]).

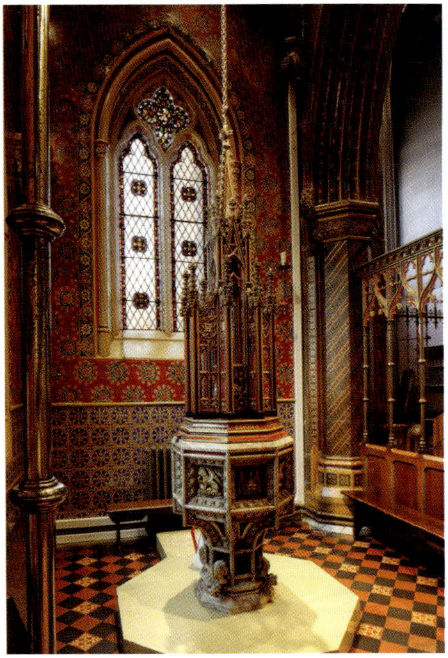

shortage of money, and Pugin's prickly, fanatical personality cannot have made relations with his patrons easy. In any case, the R.C. Church in England was a minority institution, with æsthetic and stylistic leanings (if it had any at all) towards Roman exemplars: Classical, Italianate, and Baroque architectural styles were more suited to its post-Tridentine ethos than was Gothic, which, in any case, was associated in the minds of most with Anglicanism. Furthermore, to be told by a fairly recent convert that English Gothic was the only style fit for a Christian or Catholic country must have been hard to swallow, and, besides, many priests were Irish. Pugin himself noted that there was 'no country in Europe where the externals of religion' presented 'so distressing an aspect as Ireland': in the larger towns there was 'a lavish display of the vilest trash about the altars', and clergy were all too often 'filled with the most anti-Christian ideas of art'. Such views would not have endeared Pugin to certain R.C. clergy.

Four Classical Exemplars

A fine example of a Neo-Classical chapel erected at the expense of R.C. landed gentry (in this case William Constable-Maxwell), shortly after the passing of 'Catholic Emancipation' (1829), can be found at Everingham, Yorkshire ER, where the delightful Sts Mary and Everilda's (1836–9) is as far removed from Puginian ideals as is possible. Designed by Agostino Giorgioli, and built under the direction of John Harper of York, its interior, one of the most impressive evocations of Rome in all England, is spectacular (Fig. 4.7). A similar arrangement (this time a full-blown basilica with aisles) is found in St Bartholomew's, Rainhill Stoops, Lancashire (1836–40), paid for by Bartholomew Bretherton, who sent the architect, Joshua Dawson of Preston, to Rome to study ecclesiastical exemplars. It should be emphasised that this was a deliberate link with Rome, eschewing all Gothic influences.

Another such R.C. place of worship can be found at Prior Park, Bath, where a chapel was added next to the west wing of the Palladian mansion. Begun in 1844, it was not completed until 1882. It is again a Neo-Classical basilica with a coffered barrel vault springing from the entablature of the Corinthian Order, and the east end is again apsidal with a hemi-dome carried over the entablature, which is supported on engaged

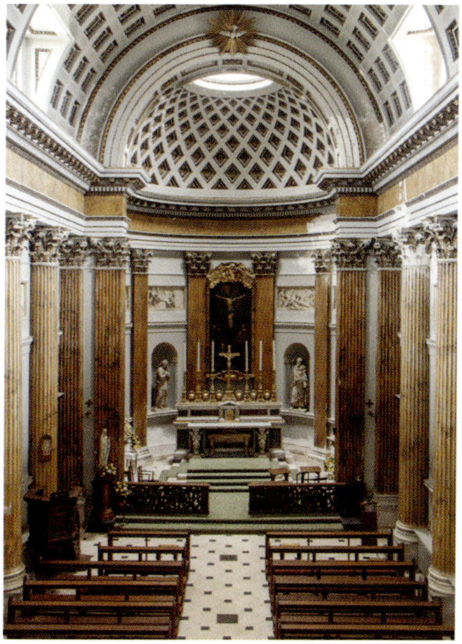

Fig. 4.7 R.C. Chapel of Sts Mary and Everilda, Everingham, Yorkshire (ER) (1836–9), lined with engaged Corinthian columns and pilasters (all with scagliola shafts) supporting an entablature from which springs a coffered tunnel vault with penetrations for high-level lighting: the coffered apse has a glazed skylight. A pronounced Classicism contrasts with Pugin's English mediævalisms (AR [2005]).

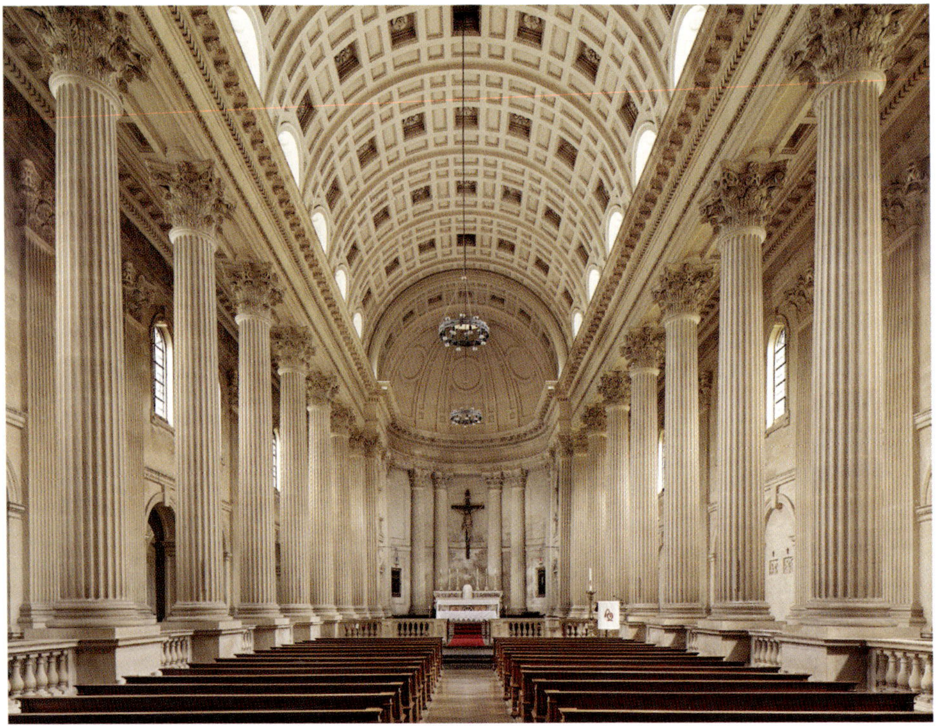

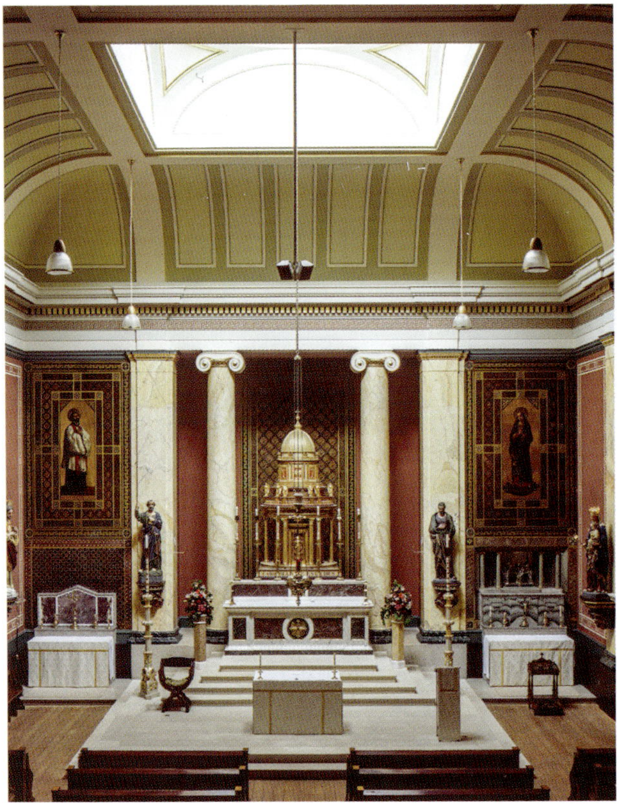

Fig. 4.8 R.C. chapel at Prior Park, Bath (1844–82), by J.J. Scoles, a refined Neo-Classical basilica influenced by French 18th-century examplars, notably Chalgrin's church of St-Philippe-du-Roule, Paris (JOD [2021]).

Fig. 4.9 St Francis Xavier's R.C. Church, Hereford (1837–9), by Charles Day, showing the Bernini-inspired tabernacle (c.1850) by J.J. Scoles between *in antis* Ionic columns. The building was rescued from ruin under the direction of Brownhill Hayward Brown of Lichfield (1997–2003) (AR [2005]).

paired columns: the refined architectural style is overwhelmingly French, of the 18th century (Fig. 4.8).

An outstanding example of the Greek Revival applied to an R.C. church is in Broad Street, Hereford: St Francis Xavier's (1837–8) was erected at the beginning of the Victorian period. The façade features a Greek Doric portico, distyle *in antis*, vaguely based on the treasury at Delphi, but tightened up, and more powerful as a result, and the interior is one large top-lit space (Fig. 4.9). Pugin hated it, denouncing it as 'a pagan temple' and a 'Catholic concert hall', remarks deplored by Peter Augustine Baines (vicar apostolic of the Western District in succession to Milner, and Bishop Assistant to the Pontifical Throne) in *The Catholic Directory* (1840) as an 'unauthorised and virulent attack'. Baines was a stout champion of Classical architecture, and had little time for Gothic revivalists of the Puginian kind.

An Uneasy Stylistic Brew

Before Victoria came to the throne, R.C. Masses at the Bavarian and Sardinian Embassy chapels in London would be attended by those who were willing to pay considerable sums to hear the operatically inspired services, but such splendours could not be found in the average urban R.C. church.

Early 19th-century R.C. churches took their cues from Anglican proprietary chapels, for they had class exclusiveness (enshrined in the seating arrangements) combined with the barely devotional atmosphere of a Dissenters' chapel. Churches were generally locked; weekday services were rare; altars and decorations were dismal and meagre (statues were virtually unknown); and seats were let out for fees. Curiously, many R.C. services bore all the hallmarks of Protestant revivalism, and indeed Evangelicals and Ultramontanes shared much, winning souls in the spiritual deserts of teeming English cities. Many R.C. divines felt the refined gentility of the Church of England was no way to reclaim souls: more effective were admonitory batterings to bring the sinful to repentance, and the exploitation of any means to bring sinners under the sanctifying drip of The Precious Blood. By the 1860s, however, after the restoration of the R.C. episcopal hierarchy, devotion to The Blessed Sacrament was on the increase, while Communions on common Sundays were numerous. Services were many, were accessible to the people, and most were free. Along aisles altars were set up, and devotion to Our Lady became usual. Churches became more lavishly furnished, and took on a distinctly R.C. appearance.

Much of Pugin's *œuvre* is exquisite, but his importance does not lie solely in his skills as a designer but as a proselytiser. However, by the time Victoria ascended the throne, the Pointed style was becoming the preferred choice for Anglicans, and even 'Gothic authenticity' was being sought, so Pugin was really kicking at a half-opened door. His single-mindedness and phenomenal energy were undoubted major catalysts in the Gothic Revival, and his own designs, notably at St Giles's, Cheadle, were of a quality to attract admiration and emulation.

When Pugin died, worn out and insane, in 1852, there were a few distinguished R.C. architects who followed his theories and architectural language, but most R.C. churches erected in the 1850s were dull. An exception was the R.C. Cathedral of St John at Salford, Manchester (1844–55), by J.G. Weightman and M.E. Hadfield: this

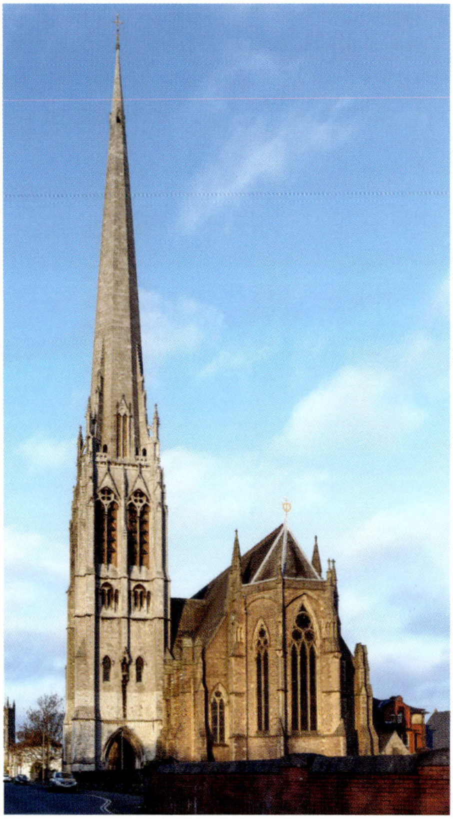

Fig. 4.10 St Walburge's R.C. Church, Preston, Lancashire, by J.A. Hansom (1850–4, tower c.1857, prodigious spire 1867, apse by S.J. Nicholl, 1872) (AR [2018]).

represents the eclectic and 'archæological' approach to architecture, embracing quotations from St Mary Magdalene's, Newark, Nottinghamshire (13th and 14th centuries); St Peter's, Howden, Yorkshire ER; and the Abbey Church of Sts Mary and Germain, Selby, Yorkshire WR. Also eclectic was the architecture of J.A. Hansom, whose Holy Name of Jesus, Manchester (1869), and St Philip Neri (now the Cathedral Church of Our Lady and St Philip Howard), Arundel, West Sussex (1870–3) – the last for the 15th Duke of Norfolk – are of particular distinction. Both reflect a mid-19th-century interest in and study of Continental Gothic, in this case French. Yet (especially at Arundel) the detail tends to be mechanical, while the figure sculpture is sentimentally vapid.

Hansom's St Walburge's, Preston, Lancashire (1850–4), for the Jesuits, however, is a particularly interesting example of the difficulties inherent in reconciling Tridentine principles of visibility with the Gothic Revival. It is a building of architectural extremes, with an unforgettably tall, slender steeple (Fig. 4.10), but the interior is almost shocking (Fig. 4.11). *The Ecclesiologist* (**lxxxix** [April 1852], 109) put its critical finger on the problem: the church was the 'flaunting offspring of the unhappy nuptials of Oratorianism and true Christian ecclesiology', and difficulties of meeting Counter Reformation requirements using the architectural language of Gothic are here made overt.

Preston in the 19th century had a large R.C. population, and indeed recusants were numerous throughout Lancashire, where many families had remained true to the old faith. In 1793 the town acquired the barnlike St Wilfrid's in Chapel Street, but it proved too small for a swelling population by 1870. The barn was magnificently replaced by a basilica (1878–80), and the exterior was recased (1890s) in brick-and-terracotta North Italian Renaissance garb. The Italian-inspired interior has a barrel-vaulted ceiling, the entablature is carried on Corinthian columns with shafts of polished Shap granite on tall Belgian black-marble bases, and the apsidal sanctuary has a hemi-dome with hexagonal and lozenge-shaped coffers. Marble, alabaster, mosaics, and gilding enhance the opulence of a superb monument to Ultramontane church architecture (Fig. 4.12), a far cry from anything advocated by Pugin.

A major problem was that from the 1830s Pugin's ideas about Gothic as the only proper style for church buildings were already and independently becoming common

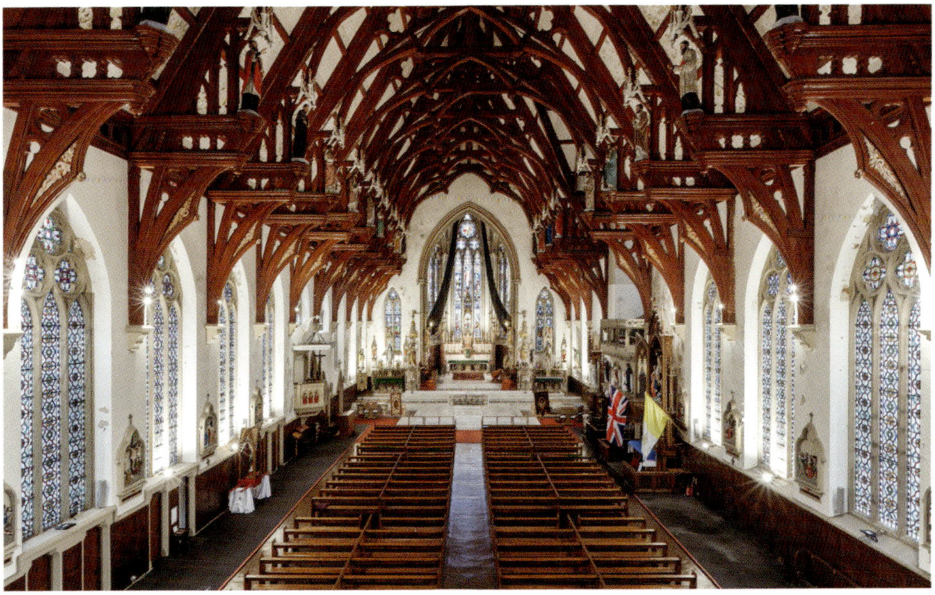

Fig. 4.11 St Walburge's, Preston, more like a secular aisleless hall than a church, the space covered by a vast steeply pitched hammer-beam roof, made more frantic by means of connecting elements of tracery, with statues of saints on the beam-ends. The chancel arch before the apse with two openings on either side was suggested, perhaps, by Girona Cathedral, Spain (AR [2018]).

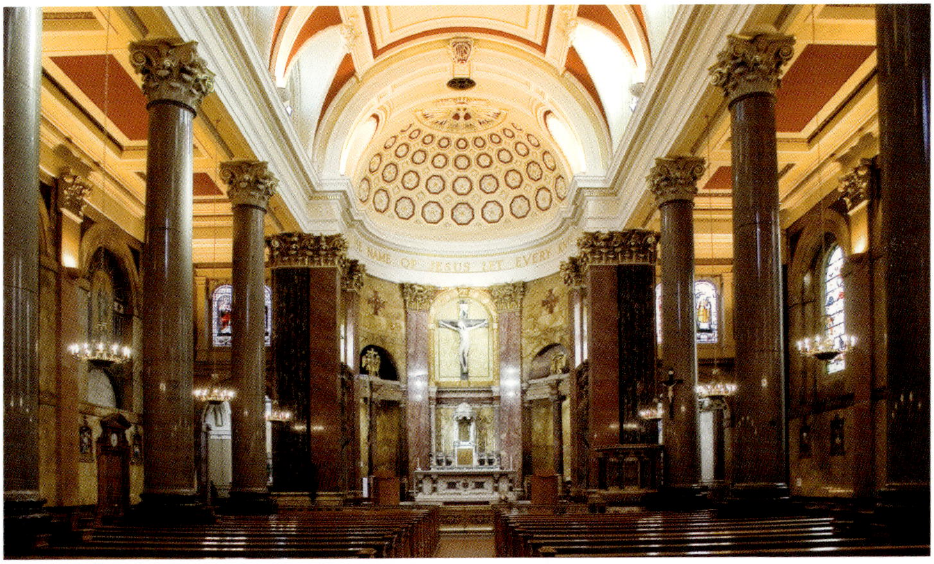

Fig. 4.12 St Wilfrid's R.C. Church, Preston (1878–80), by the Revd Ignatius Scoles and S.J. Nicholl. An exceptionally rich interior, heavily influenced by Italian exemplars (RU [2010]).

currency among Anglicans, something that would be cemented by the fervent advocacy of Ecclesiologists. However, G.J. Wigley, in the Preface to his translation of Borromeo's *Instructions*, hoped to remove from 'English Catholic architecture ... the Anglican tendency with which it is threatened', and reminded his readers that 'we [i.e. English Roman Catholics] are but a branch (and almost a *new* shoot) from the ever prolific Roman stem'. So Puginism was by the 1850s perceived as a 'threat', to be avoided by R.C. interests, and Wigley went on to clarify the position regarding screens: 'the image of the Cross, and of Christ our Lord affixed thereon, ... should be set up and aptly placed in every church ... under the very arch of the high chapel ... or it may be placed ... on top of the gate of the railing enclosure of the chapel'. He added that St Charles Borromeo described the great rood or crucifix without 'in the least alluding to Rood screens': indeed he emphasised that any barrier defining the sanctuary should resemble the low cancelli of Early Christian churches in Rome.

Given these controversies, it is not surprising that some R.C. architects, Goths in spite of Ultramontane tendencies in Church circles, turned to the Continental (especially French) early Second Pointed style for their models, rather than to English exemplars, for, after all, French churches of around 1300 were tall, impressive, had apsidal chancels (most English ones were square), and had few associations with Anglicanism. Pugin's son, Edward Welby Pugin, was spectacularly successful in suggesting triumphalism in his buildings, notably the former Franciscan Church and Friary of St Francis, Gorton, Manchester of 1864–72, an essay in the style of the late 13th century: this large and impressive church was built of brick, with very generous and robustly detailed stone dressings. Its west front was a showpiece of Continental Gothic Revival, and it certainly did not look at all like an Anglican church (Fig. 4.13).

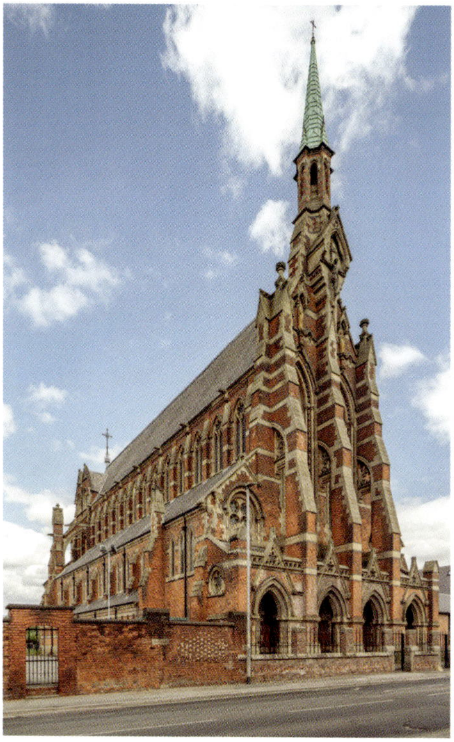

Fig. 4.13 The former R.C. Friary Church of St Francis, Gorton, Manchester (1864–72), with tall, striped bell turret set over a Crucifixus rising from the middle buttress between two enormous traceried windows (MW [2021]).

Nevertheless, Gothic remained the favoured style for the majority of churches throughout the Victorian period: among distinguished designs in that style for the Roman Catholics are the Jesuit Church of The Immaculate Conception, Farm Street, London, by J.J. Scoles, of 1844–9 (in careful late Decorated Gothic); St John the Baptist, St Giles's Gate, Norwich (it became a cathedral in 1976), a splendid, noble, yet sombre essay in Early English Gothic (Figs 4.14 and 4.15), for taste had moved away from early Middle Pointed to First Pointed and even to more 'primitive' early Burgundian Gothic of the late 12th or early 13th centuries; and St James's, Spanish Place, Westminster, by Edward Goldie, of 1885–1918 (a scholarly and serious interior, vaulted throughout, in a mixture of early French and English Gothic, with some remnants of decorations by J.F. Bentley of 1891).

As the century progressed, many architects of distinction produced impressive work for the R.C. Church. In 1878 a competition was announced for the design (to be 'Italian Renaissance')

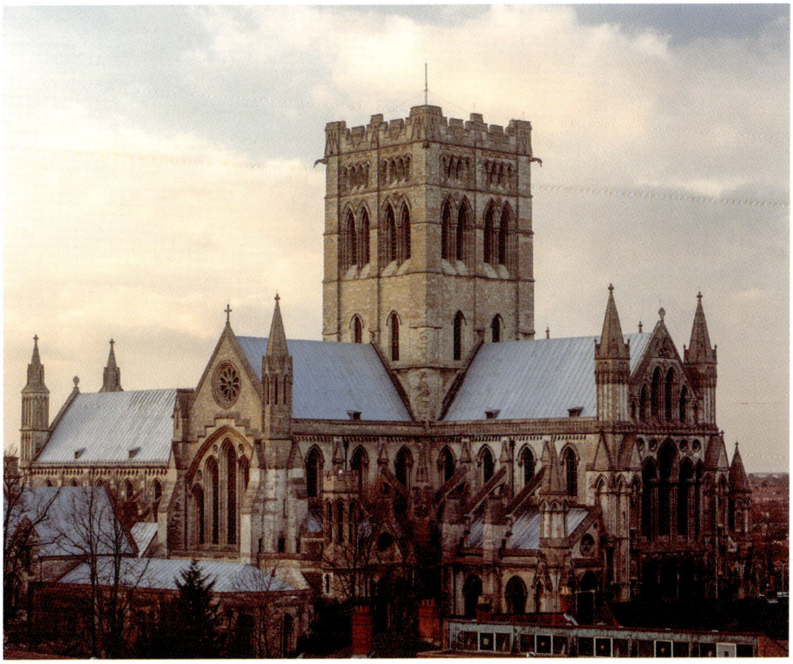

Fig. 4.14 St John the Baptist (since 1976 the R.C. cathedral), Norwich (1884–1910), by G.G. 'Middle' Scott and J.O. Scott, funded by the 15th Duke of Norfolk, who requested the predominantly English First Pointed style, with lancets much in evidence. When consecrated it was the grandest parish church in England (AR [2005]).

of a new church for the London Oratory of St Philip Neri and the Church of the Immaculate Heart of Mary at Brompton, and the winner was H.A.K. Gribble, a pupil of J.A. Hansom, who had worked on the Manchester and Arundel churches: an essay in Roman Baroque, modelled on Santa Maria in Vallicella, the Chiesa Nuova (1575–1606), mother church of the Oratorians in Rome, it has a sumptuous interior of the Gesù type (Figs 4.16 and 4.17). As previously noted, to Ultramontanes the desirable architectural style in which to build churches was essentially Classical, with some Baroque flourishes; and, in any case, the associations of Gothic with Anglicanism were too strong to be ignored.

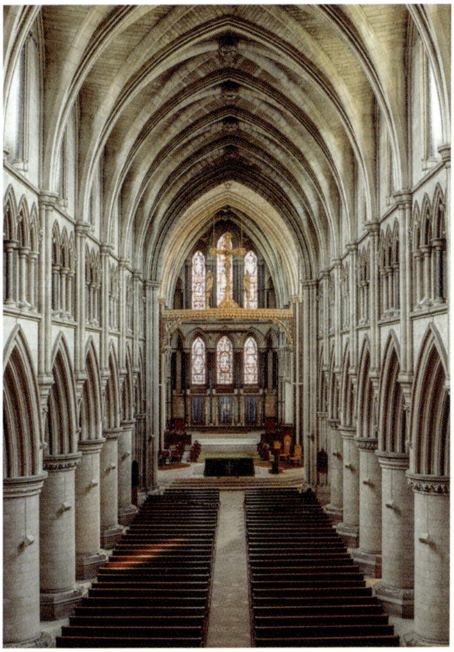

Fig. 4.15 The vaulted nave, R.C. Cathedral of St John the Baptist, Norwich: a scholarly revival of 13th-century English Gothic, but the overall impression is one of melancholy, perhaps because the optimism concerning the future of religion in England that was behind the whole concept faded long ago. The beam with rood, carved by Peter Rendl of Oberammergau, was erected 1910–11 (AR [2005]).

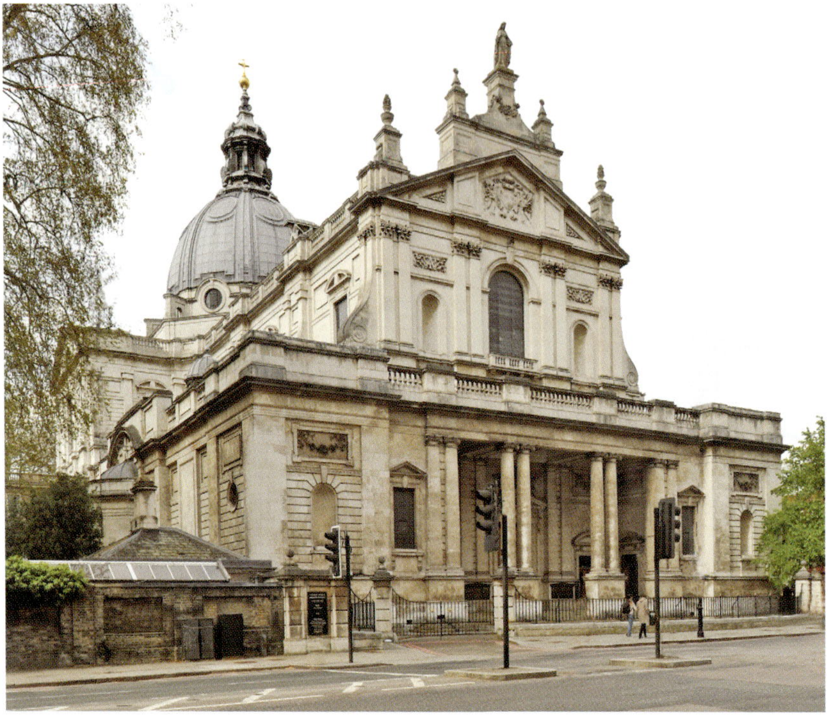

Fig. 4.16 The London Oratory of St Philip Neri and the Church of the Immaculate Heart of Mary, Brompton, London (designed from 1878), a fine essay in Roman Baroque, with a steel-framed dome (1896) over the crossing by George Sherrin (GB [2021]).

Fig. 4.17 The London Oratory of St Philip Neri and the Church of the Immaculate Heart of Mary, Brompton, showing the Baroque style, with massive piers separating the chapels on either side, a plan derived from Il Gesù in Rome. Decorations (mostly 1927–32) were largely by Commendatore C.T.G. Formilli (GB [2021]).

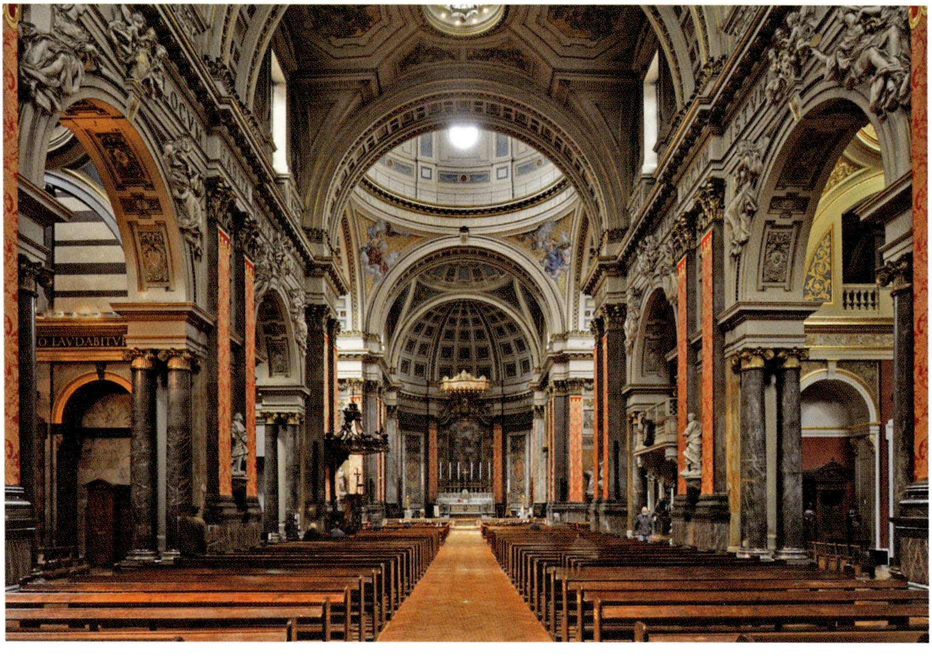

The Contribution of John Francis Bentley

John Bentley was born in Doncaster, Yorkshire WR, and despite objections from his wine-merchant father, showed great interest in buildings from an early age. After St George's, Doncaster, burned down in 1853, George Gilbert 'Great' Scott was entrusted with its rebuilding, and young Bentley rendered assistance to the clerk of works (*see* Fig. 6.25). Not until 1857, however, after his father's death, was Bentley able to become an assistant in Henry Clutton's office, and his life was to change utterly as a result.

The Oblates of St Charles Borromeo, a small community of priests founded (1857) at Bayswater by Dr Henry Edward Manning (who had converted from Anglicanism [1851] as a direct result of the Gorham case [*see* Chapter 6]) at the behest of Cardinal Wiseman to carry out missionary and educational work in north-west London, appointed Henry Augustus Rawes (another convert) to take charge of the Notting Hill District, and acquired a tight wedge-shaped site in the poor area known as The Potteries, Notting Dale. Clutton was appointed to design the church, presbytery, and schools of St Francis of Assisi, erected on that site in 1859–60 at the expense of

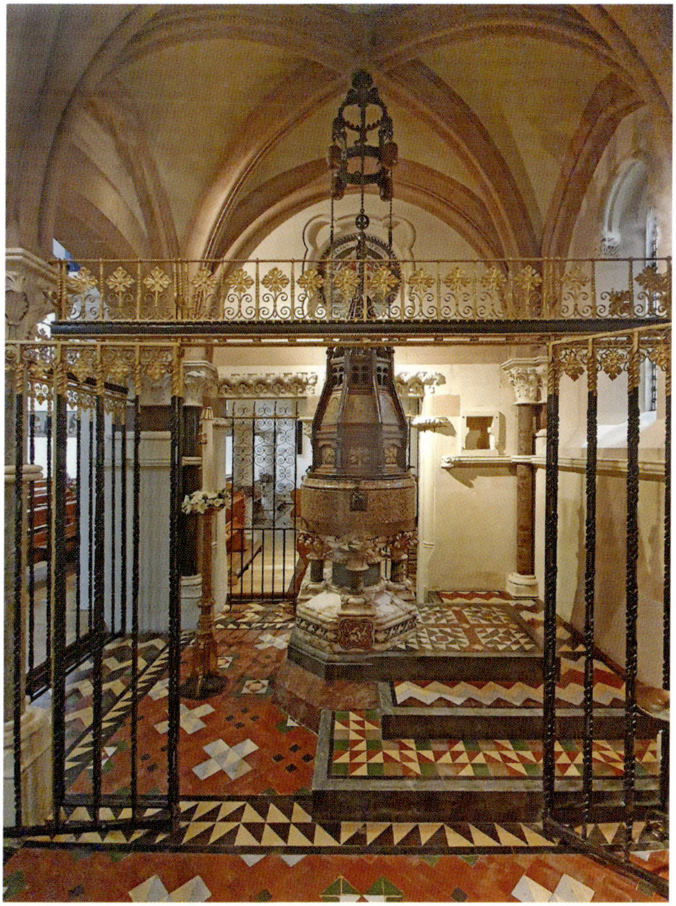

Fig. 4.18 Baptistry, R.C. Church of St Francis of Assisi, Notting Hill, London, by J.F. Bentley, of 1861–3, an exquisite, scholarly revival of early French Gothic (GS [2021]).

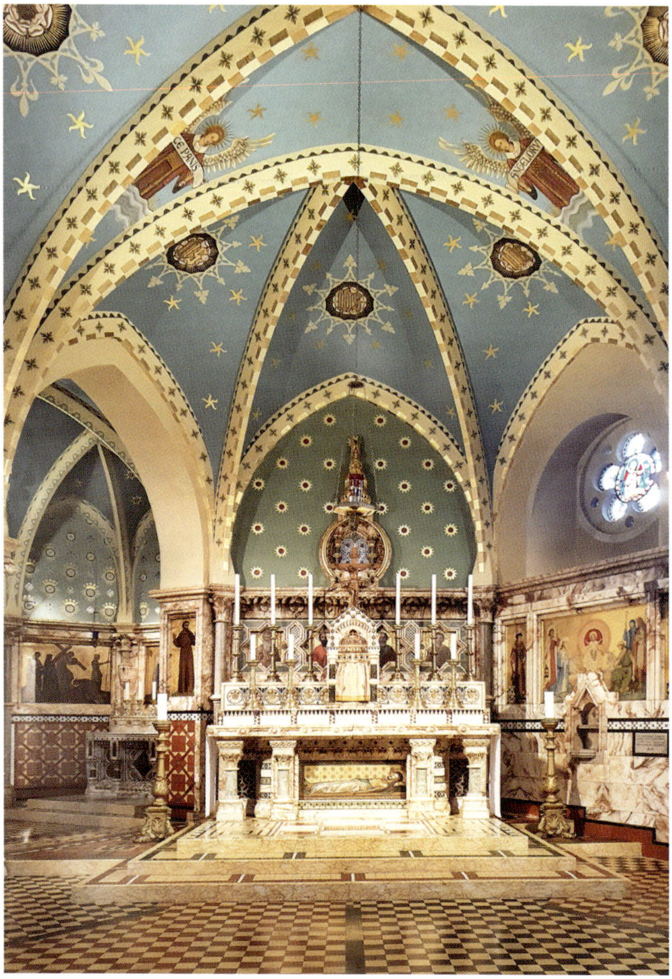

Fig. 4.19 High altar, R.C. Church of St Francis of Assisi, Notting Hill (1863), by Bentley. Of alabaster, it is richly inlaid with marble and mosaic. The altar frontal has short marble colonnettes with capitals supporting the slab (mensa): the central panel is painted. The first super-altar is inlaid with patterns of dark and light marbles, and the second super-altar has circular panels separated from each other by inlays of black foliate patterns of proto-art nouveau style. The reredos itself is surmounted by a leaf-cornice, and by four panels each containing a painted figure. A corbel carries a throne above with a vesica piscis or mandorla shape and the Pelican in Piety surmounts the gilded canopy. On the left can be seen part of the altar in the Chapel of Our Lady of the Seven Dolours (GS [2020]).

Father Rawes. The church is a tiny building of stock brick relieved by bands of black bricks forming part of a brilliantly designed compact group, and is in a severely simple French-provincial Pointed style based on 13th-century examples: its construction was supervised by young Bentley, who became entirely responsible for the design of the furnishings and fittings from 1861.

The baptistry is an impressive work (Fig. 4.18), and Bentley himself was received into the R.C. Church there (1862), taking as his middle name that of the patron saint of the new building. Both the sumptuous high altar and reredos (Fig. 4.19) and the chapel of the Seven Dolours are wonderful things. It was in 1862 also that Bentley left Clutton's office and established his own practice.

Bentley designed a new apse and other details for what is now known as Our Lady of the Assumption and St Gregory, Soho, London, a plain 18th-century building originally built 1730, but wrecked during the Gordon Riots (1780), rebuilt under Joseph Bonomi, and reconsecrated (1789) as the Royal Bavarian Embassy Chapel. By the 1870s it still looked rather like a Georgian Nonconformist meeting house, and there were proposals to completely rebuild, but Bentley's interventions were more modest, including the glorious apse, subsequently redecorated to a revised scheme also by him (Fig. 4.20). Thus Bentley, even in the 1870s, demonstrated skills unrestricted by narrow stylistic parameters.

Bentley's finest Gothic church is Holy Rood, Watford, Hertfordshire: had he not gone on to produce Westminster Cathedral, the Holy Rood would have secured his reputation, for it is one of the best later Gothic Revival churches in England, and the style is late Decorated/early Perpendicular, but handled unpedantically, freely, with assured panache, and with a strong seasoning of Arts and Crafts quirkiness. The project was funded, as a thank-offering for his conversion, by S.T. Holland (of a well-known firm of London building contractors with which Bentley had been connected

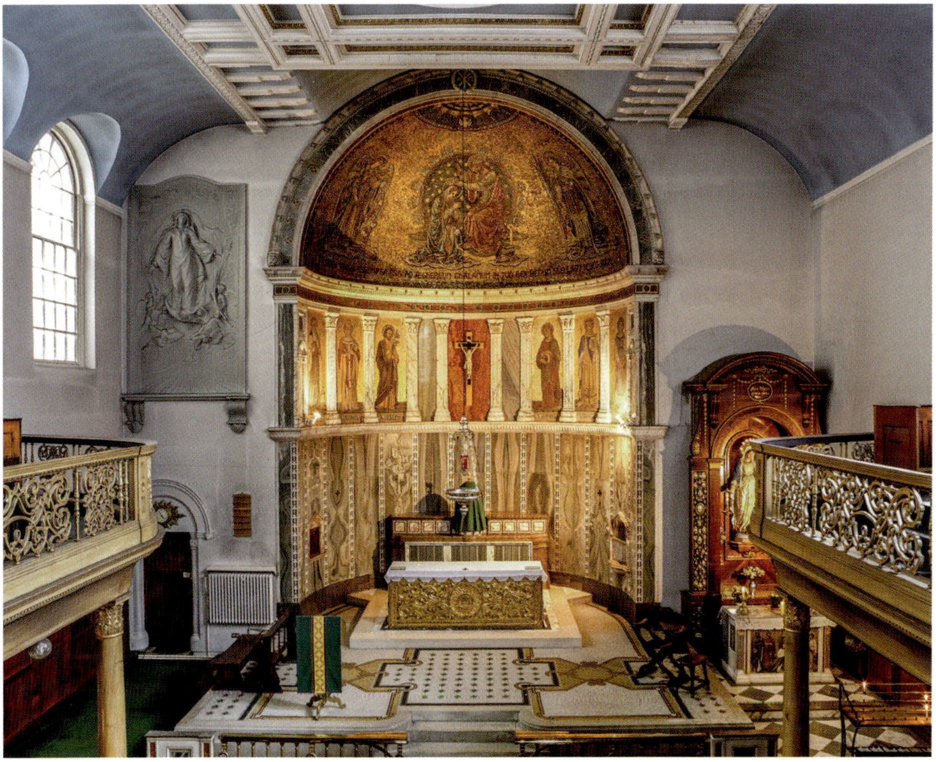

Fig. 4.20 J.F. Bentley's Veneto-Byzantine apse (1874–5), R.C. Church of Our Lady of the Assumption, Soho, London. Bentley redesigned (1900) the decorations, executed with variations after his death under John A. Marshall: the overall effect is, astonishingly, almost Sezessionist, realised by George Bridge and his assistants. The Assumption relief on the left is by J.E. Carew (1853), taken from the earlier high altar (AR [2005]).

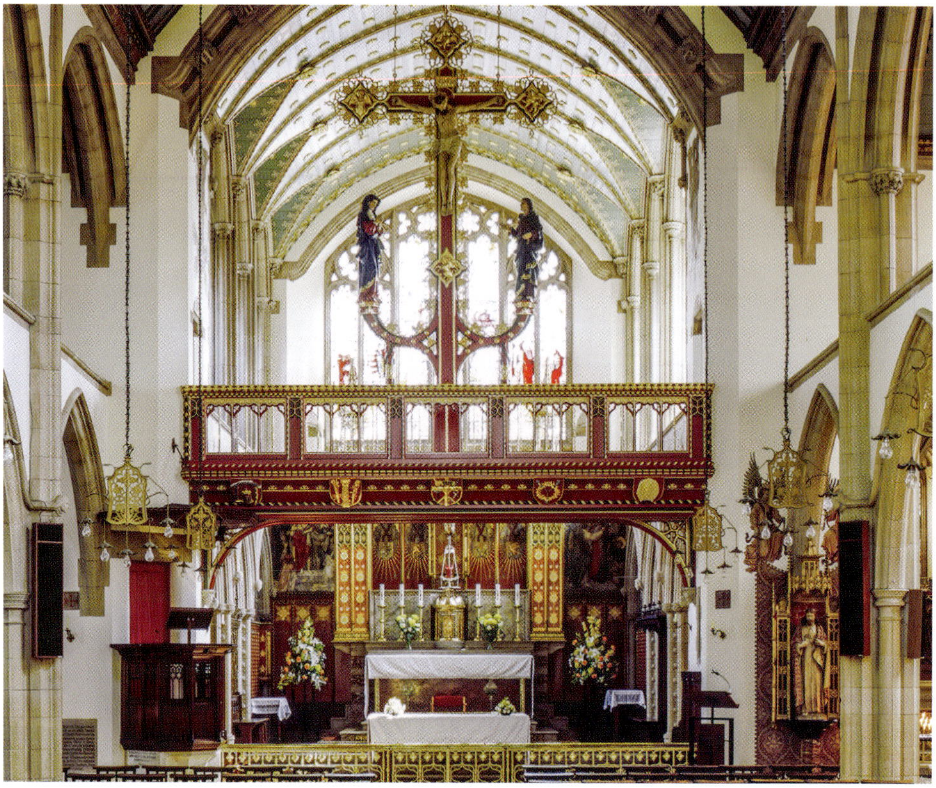

Fig. 4.21 R.C. Church of the Holy Rood, Watford, Hertfordshire (1889–1900), by J.F. Bentley, with what its architect claimed was the largest rood erected in England since the widespread destruction during the reign of Edward VI (AR [2005]).

when young). The beautiful rood in no way impedes visibility, for the altar is not obscured by a screen (Fig. 4.21).

Manning (who became Archbishop of Westminster in 1865, and cardinal in 1875), had long hoped to build a large cathedral church in Westminster, and Clutton was commissioned to design it: a Gothic building would have been the result, though it appears Manning had hoped for something based on the Constantinian basilica of San Pietro in Rome (destroyed when the present church was erected in the 16th century). Then Sir Tatton Sykes II, Bt, who had a passion for church building (among other enthusiasms), proposed (1882) that the Austrian architect, Heinrich, Freiherr von Ferstel, should be employed to build a version of his Gothic Revival *Votivkirche*, Vienna (1856–82), in London, but the baron's death in the following year put paid to that. Things moved forward in 1892 when H.A.H.J.T. Vaughan was appointed Archbishop of Westminster by Pope Leo XIII: Vaughan received the pallium in Brompton Oratory (the first time it had been conferred in England since Cardinal Pole's time [1556]), and acquired his red hat in 1893. The new cardinal-archbishop, who had been one of Manning's original oblates of St Charles Borromeo, saw the construction of Westminster Cathedral as a symbol of the coming of age of the restored R.C. hierarchy as well as a memorial to Wiseman, and in 1894 Bentley (who abhorred architectural competitions, and was not too keen on the RIBA either) was appointed architect.

Bentley had made his reputation as a Goth, albeit a very inventive one, but by the time a new cathedral at Westminster was mooted there were many changes in the air, and one of the catalysts for change was provided by 'Middle' Scott (yet another convert to Catholicism), who made a great contribution to liturgiology as well as church design. He brought out *An Essay on the History of English Church Architecture prior to the Separation of England from the Roman Obedience* (1881) in which he set English ecclesiastical architecture within an historic context, relating it back to early Roman basilicas. The *Essay* contained illustrations of early altars (many covered by baldacchini) and churches: in the text Scott argued that liturgical use must therefore influence (and even dictate) plans and internal volumes of churches (something that should have been obvious). This was not the only influential text.

One outstanding R.C. ecclesiologist (or liturgiologist) was Edmund Bishop, who was an expert on the development of church architecture, and who gave an important paper (1881) on the baldachin (or baldacchino), which he insisted was a necessary part of any Christian altar. When F.A. Walters designed the Jesuit church of the Sacred Heart, Edge Hill, Wimbledon (1886–1901), he provided a baldacchino over the high altar, and the building acquired furnishings and stained glass by members of the Guild of St Gregory and St Luke (of which Walters was a member), a body founded to promote the study of Christian antiquities and to disseminate the principles of Christian art.

L.A.S. Stokes, also a member of the Guild, and a former pupil of Street and Bodley, designed St Clare's R.C. Church, Sefton Park, Liverpool (1888–90), but the handling of Gothic, though dependent to a certain extent on the *Wandpfeiler* (wall-pier) arrangement of the Dominican church in Gent, is ingenious, and the triforium gallery also pierces the wall-piers as well as the aisle passage. Stokes's wide nave enables the congregation to have good views of the altar.

So by the time Westminster Cathedral began to look as though it might become reality, there were precedents aplenty, many of which were anything but Gothic. Vaughan insisted on three basic essentials: a broad nave so that the congegation could always see the altar; a building that could be erected first and internally decorated later; and a structure stylistically un-Gothic, preferably Italian or Byzantine. Such a stylistic choice was prompted by a growing interest in Byzantine forms at the time, but it also seems that the Church hierarchy was anxious to create a distinctive building which would emphasise historical and Roman connections, which would be a dignified and suitable cathedral – impressive, modern, yet joined to the great traditions from the time of St Peter the Apostle, and which could not be confused with the Anglican abbey down the road.

Bentley set off on a Continental study-tour, and formed a dim opinion of St Peter's Basilica in Rome because of its confusing scale, a criticism with which there can be no argument. That was not all: he perceived Rome as a city largely dating from the 16th century, and considered Italian detail the most thoughtless, heartless stuff he had ever seen. Vaughan's ambition to have a church resembling a basilica such as San Paolo fuori le Mura was strongly resisted by Bentley (it had been virtually reconstructed anyway after a disastrous fire of 1823), so brought powerful arguments to bear against the adoption of a style for which he could feel neither interest nor admiration. Indeed, Bentley had originally wanted to design Westminster Cathedral

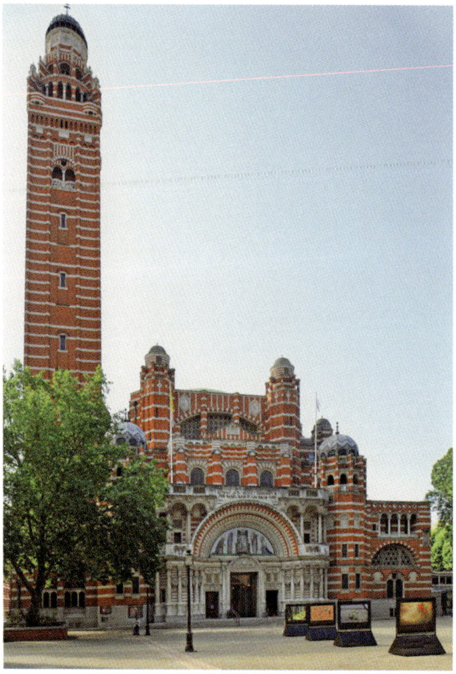

Fig. 4.22 R.C. Metropolitan Cathedral Church of The Most Precious Blood of Our Lord Jesus Christ at Westminster, designed from 1894 by J.F. Bentley. It features variations on the Diocletian window in the clerestorey, and is an inventive mixture of styles derived from Byzantine Ravenna, Romanesque Pisa, Bologna, Milan, Padua, Siena, Torcello, Venice, the architecture of Louis-Joseph Duc, the so-called 'Free Style', and much more, an assured virtuoso performance in scholarly eclecticism (GB [2018])

in Gothic, so was obliged to rethink his whole approach to ecclesiastical design because of Vaughan's brief.

What Vaughan got was an eclectic building constructed of brick, stone, and concrete (containing an aggregate of broken brick), but there was no metal reinforcing, although some rolled-steel ties were employed in divisions in the transepts. Stylistically, Westminster Cathedral is a fusion of Byzantine and Romanesque elements, with a red-and-white striped exterior infuenced partly by Norman Shaw's New Scotland Yard (1887–90): other precedents were San Marco, Venice; Hagia Sophia, Constantinople; Sant' Ambrogio, Milan; San Vitale, Ravenna; the Duomo, Pisa; the Domkirche, Speier; and the Certosa, Pavia (Fig. 4.22). Although Bentley had not managed to visit the former Hagia Sophia, he derived great benefit from Lethaby and Swainson's study of Byzantine architecture (1894).

Bentley drew on many sources. First, there is the vast nave covered with saucer-domes recalling the structure of St-Front, Périgueux, and high passage aisles running through gigantic wall-piers supporting transverse barrel vaults ending in Diocletian windows: those aisles have chapels beyond them. There is also a Baroque second element taken from the plan of the mother church of the Society of Jesus in Rome, Il Gesù. The third precedent is the desire for spatial clarity that grew from the Gothic Revival, and Bentley's cathedral incorporates many of the planning and structural systems that had been discussed and experimented with at length by ecclesiologists, liturgiologists, and Goths: Westminster Cathedral could be gothicised and still have the same plan.

Bentley was another member of the Guild of St Gregory and St Luke, and Bishop's influence on Westminster Cathedral is clear. Not only is the building a Byzantinised development of the wall-pier system of Albi and Gent, but, based on the precedent in Sant' Ambrogio, Milan, there is a splendid baldacchino (1905–6, designed 1901) over the high altar that was entirely due to Bishop's badgering of a reluctant Bentley. Vaughan's vision was brilliantly realised, and the broad nave gives an unimpeded view of the high altar (Fig. 4.23). Visibility is enhanced by the fact that the sanctuary rises in a series of platforms set over a crypt. Bentley also designed (1901) the mighty rood, set on high. The marble finishes are splendid, their colours and patterns deriving from over a hundred different stones: much of this work was by Farmer & Brindley.

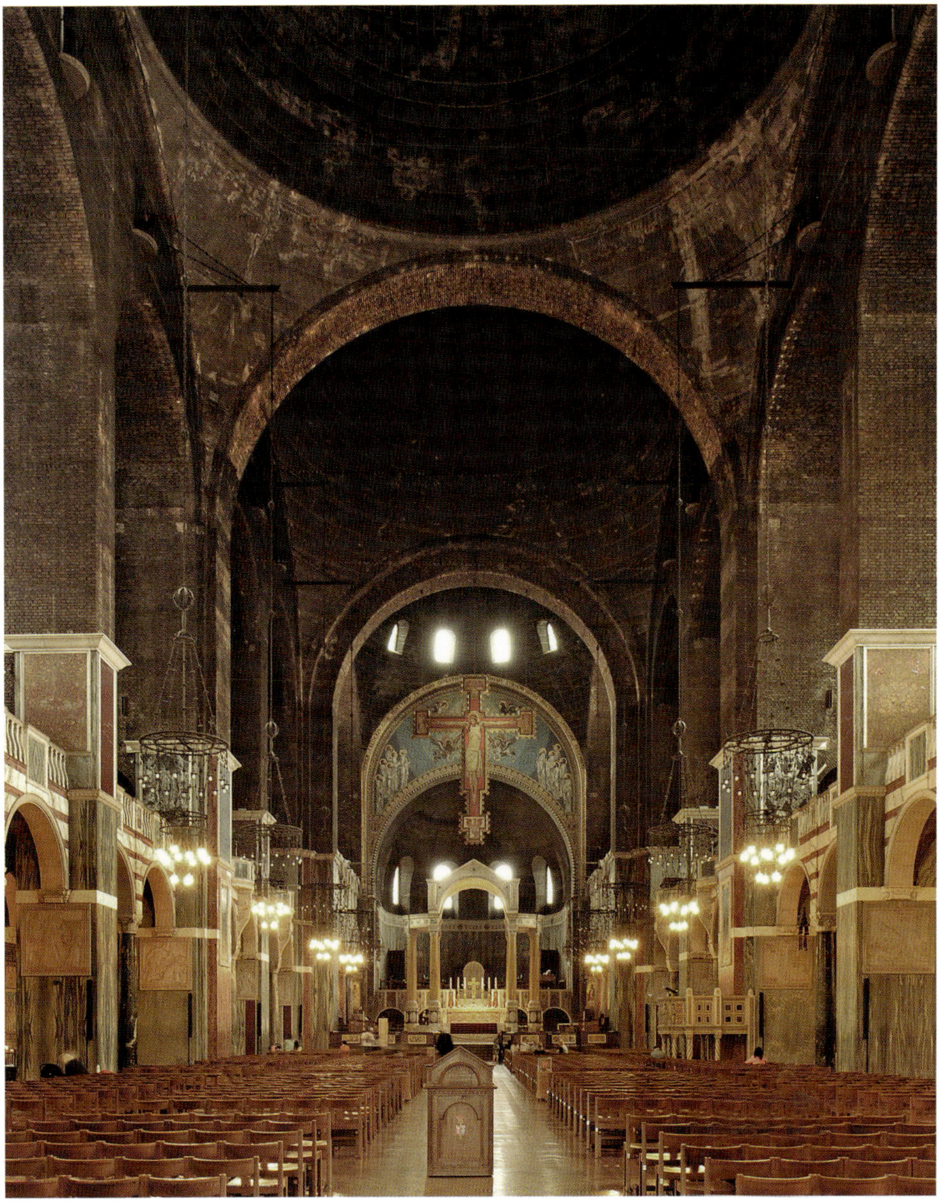

Fig. 4.23 Westminster Cathedral, with the high altar and baldacchino in the distance. This longitudinal domed space is a clever Byzantinesque variation on the 16th-century elements of Il Gesù, Rome. Bentley intended the walls to be covered in coloured marbles, and the upper walls and vaults with mosiacs. The enormous suspended rood, designed (1896–1901) by Bentley, was made (1902) by Charles Beyaert in Brugge, Belgium, and painted by William Christian Symons (1903). The mighty baldacchino over the high altar, designed (1901) by Bentley, and made 1905–6, is based on the exemplar in Sant' Ambrogio, Milan (GB [2018]).

Some idea of how Vaughan envisaged the whole interior may be gained from the numerous chapels (each contained between what are essentially internal buttresses): that of the Holy Souls (1902–6) is exceptionally beautiful and very rich (Fig. 4.24). However, in the nave the intended mosaics above the marble finishes were not carried out on the upper parts of the walls, piers, and vaults. Some regret this, but the bare

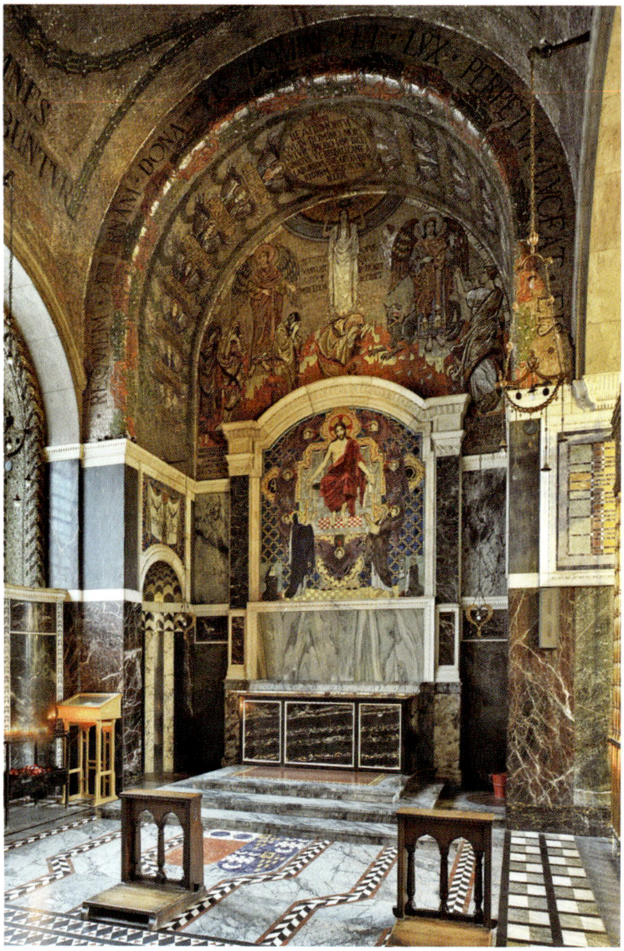

Fig. 4.24 Chapel of the Holy Souls, Westminster Cathedral (1902–6), by Bentley and W.C. Symons, with mosaics by George Bridge and others. It is indicative of what Bentley intended for the rest of the cathedral's interior (GB [2018]).

brick and concrete surfaces enable us to appreciate the grandeur of the clear, uncomplicated geometries in one of London's greatest ecclesiastical buildings. Norman Shaw thought Westminster Cathedral 'the finest church that has been built for centuries', and that it was 'impossible to overrate the magnificence of this design'. I would not dissent from this assessment: it is a stunning achievement in which scholarship, intelligence, invention, and superb craftsmanship and understanding of detail combine to realise an Ultramontane ideal.

Another convert to Roman Catholicism, Coventry Patmore, an extraordinarily perceptive Victorian architectural critic, said of Bentley that he was the only architect who knew more about architecture than he (Patmore) did, high praise from someone who thought most contemporary critics (including Ruskin) were hopelessly askew.

I fully endorse both those opinions.

5

The Anglican Revival

I am afraid he has not been in the inside of a church for many years; but he never passes a church without pulling off his hat. This shows that he has good principles.

SAMUEL JOHNSON (1709–84):
quoted in JAMES BOSWELL (1740–95): *The Life of Samuel Johnson*
(on DR JOHN CAMPBELL [1708–75], 1 July 1763).

The renewal, in this country, of a taste for Mediæval architecture, and the reapplication of those principles which regulate its design, represent one of the most interesting and remarkable phases in the history of art.

CHARLES LOCKE EASTLAKE (1836–1906):
A History of the Gothic Revival (London: Longmans, Green, & Co., 1872), 1.

Introduction

The late 1820s and the 1830s were tumultuous times. Thomas Mozley, divine, journalist, friend, and brother-in-law of Newman, recorded that the 'whole fabric of English ... society, was trembling to the foundations ... a thousand projectors were screaming from a thousand platforms ... all England was dinned with philanthropy and revolution'. Quite so, and Mozley's *Reminiscences, Chiefly of Oriel College and the Oxford Movement*, published in 1882, is a very full account, and, with Newman's *Apologia pro Vita Sua*, is essential reading for any student of Tractarianism. Things looked very rocky for the established order of things: there was a disturbing growth of various sects; the Anglican Church and the monarchy were under attack; utilitarianism and unfeeling attitudes towards the less fortunate members of society were causing concern; power was about to shift away from a landed aristocracy and gentry; and a mainly country-dwelling nation was to become urbanised.

Yet during a time of momentous change (1830–7) reigned a king who deserves more credit than he is usually given: supported by his gentle, intelligent consort, Adelaide, William IV steered the British monarchy through a difficult time, leaving it more secure than it had been on the death of his dissipated brother, George IV. Eccentric, bluff, dutiful, and fundamentally decent, known as the 'Sailor-King', William deserved the accolades of those who called out as he passed by, 'Well done, old boy!'

When Victoria was born, her appellation had a foreign sound, exciting some insular prejudice, but gradually it acquired an appropriateness to her reign during which the United Kingdom of Great Britain and Ireland enjoyed unprecedented prestige, and became what is now known as a superpower. In some ways the Victorian Age, with its certainties and doubts, its order and frenetic change, its values and its questionings, was to linger on after the Queen's death, but ended in the catastrophe of the

1914–18 war, when even the dynastic ties between Britain's royals and their German relatives were denied.

Although Lytton Strachey's *Eminent Victorians* was permeated with judgements inimical to the personalities of the age, he was deferential towards the Queen herself. When she died, he wrote, the 'majority of her subjects had never known a time when [she] had not been reigning over them. She had become an indissoluble part of their whole scheme of things'. Yet 'Victorian' came to mean hypocritical, mealy-mouthed, and prudish. But, as the compilers of the *Oxford Dictionary of National Biography* observed, 'earnestness can ... look like cant' to the unsympathetic; and 'moral certitude' can look like hypocrisy. 'In her sincerity, her enthusiasms, her effort to do her duty, Victoria was truly Victorian: the age rightly bears her name.'

There is nothing to quarrel with in that judgement. The Victorian Age cannot be understood as an isolated phenomenon, but only when some of the historical background, forces, concerns, events, movements, legislation, and much else that came before it and informed it have begun to be understood. This is why the previous centuries have been discussed above: things do not happen in a vacuum.

The Revival of the Anglican Liturgy

During the 19th century the Church of England enjoyed a ceremonial revival that was remarkable for its beauty, its scholarship, its impact, and its integrity. Its influence was immense, and it led to the creation of much fine architecture as well as to the making of countless beautiful artefacts. The regeneration of Anglican ceremonial worship was one of the most extraordinary phenomena ever to occur in England. It gained momentum thanks to the efforts of many individuals and texts, but its true progenitor was John Rouse Bloxam, clergyman, learned ecclesiologist, meticulous scholar, member of the Oxford Society for Promoting the Study of Gothic Architecture, and brother of Matthew Holbeche Bloxam. He was for a time (1837–40) curate at Littlemore, near Oxford, and remained on good terms with Newman until the latter's death. He had known Rock, and was Pugin's chief link with the Oxford Movement. He became friendly with Ambrose Lisle March Phillipps de Lisle, with whom he corresponded on a possible reunion of the Anglican and R.C. Churches. He collected much material on customs, liturgies, and rites, abstracting it from many sources (printed and otherwise), and published this privately as *The Book of Fragments* (1842), although it was an incomplete account, being overtaken by events. The scholar and friend of both Newman and Hurrell Froude, Frederic Rogers, called Bloxam the 'Grandfather of the Ritualists'.

Under the ægis of the Cambridge Camden Society, an even larger antiquarian collection, describing the survival of pre-Reformation ornaments, artefacts, and customs, the practices of the Caroline Church, and details of parish and cathedral ceremonies that owed their origins to earlier (even pre-Tridentine) times, appeared in 1848. Published as *Hierurgia Anglicana: Documents and Extracts Illustrative of the Ritual of the Church of England after the Reformation* (1848), it gave a very broad picture of Anglican liturgical customs from the 16th century, and was scholarly as well as intended to have practical application. In addition, it claimed lawful authority for ceremonial and decorations, and so became a catalyst for what was to become known as Ritualism. It provided the basis for the restoration of daily prayer, regular

Communion, archæologically and liturgically correct Eucharistic vestments, appropriately decorated altars (with candles), the revival of church music (including ancient forms), seemly celebration of ecclesiastical feasts and festivals, and much else that was required (apparently to the surprise of many) by ecclesiastical statutes.

It is odd that the Bloxam brothers have not been granted the credit they deserve by many later writers, although Eastlake gave M.H. Bloxam a cursory nod in his *A History of the Gothic Revival* (1872); the Revd Anthony Symondson recognised the importance of J.R. Bloxam as an influence on ceremonial revival, but M.H. Bloxam was unquestionably of great significance in architectural history. Influenced by his friend, Thomas Rickman, he brought out the first edition of *The Principles of Gothic Ecclesiastical Architecture*, published in 1829, a remarkable achievement for a young man then in his twenties: it was a hugely important book. Bloxam's tome was several years ahead of Pugin's more celebrated publications, and earlier than those of John Henry Parker. Bloxam's *Principles* exists in many editions, including a German version of the seventh edition published in Leipzig (1847). Prompted by 'Great' Scott, Bloxam was persuaded to revise and expand the work, and the eleventh edition, in three volumes, running to 1,049 pages, including additional material on vestments and church arrangements, came out in 1882. Apart from this and other books, he wrote many scholarly essays on antiquarian and ecclesiological matters, including sepulchral monuments. However, Bloxam's great *Principles*, illustrated with numerous admirable woodcuts by T.O.S. Jewitt (who, with his brother, L.F.W. Jewitt, prepared fine illustrations for J.H. Parker's *Glossary of Terms used in Grecian, Roman, Italian, and Gothic Architecture*), must stand as one of the earliest influential texts of the whole Ecclesiological movement. Parker's *Glossary* first appeared in 1836, and went into several editions: with its copious illustrations, it still remains indispensable for any student of Gothic. It was Parker, too, who edited (from 1848) and added to Rickman's great *Attempt*, the seventh edition of which (1881) is a truly outstanding publication.

It is also curious that Parker's importance is similarly ignored or understated, for he did more to popularise a knowledge of mediæval architecture than any other Englishman of the time: Eastlake mentions him in connection with T.H. Turner's book on *Domestic Architecture in England*, the second and third volumes of which were completed and published by Parker, but neither he nor others gave him the credit that is his due. Furthermore, Parker was closely associated with the Tractarians, publishing many of their works. Among his other publications may be cited J.H. Markland's *Remarks* (1840), later expanded (1842) to become what Eastlake called a 'well known and ably written little work'. Markland, writing in the first years of Victoria's reign, noted with satisfaction that 'England ... is again a Church-Building Country: and may she so continue, until she shall have provided the means of Divine Worship for every son and daughter of her immense population, who wish to abide in the Faith of her Apostolic Church'. Markland also regretted much of the 16th- and 17th-century destruction, and wished that many more aspects of the pre-Reformation Church had been retained.

Again, the importance of the contributions of antiquaries, rather than architects, to the rise of Gothic should be stressed: among them was E.J. Carlos, whose numerous pieces on antiquarian topics, descriptions of new churches, critical reviews of works of restoration, and reviews of books on architecture appeared in the *Gentleman's*

Magazine from 1822 to 1848. Carlos was one of the earliest impassioned conservationists, appalled by the loss of mediæval and other historical fabric (he published an account [1832] of London Bridge, with observations on its architecture during its demolition, and in the same year he was active in the campaign to rescue the Lady chapel of St Mary Overie [now Southwark Cathedral] from destruction).

So, by the beginning of Queen Victoria's reign, architects had useful sourcebooks for Gothic styles. Nevertheless, the rise in appreciation of mediæval architecture and a new architecture based on the precedent of Gothic was enhanced by complex catalysts previously outlined, as well as by concerns which were voiced in the decades before Victoria came to the throne, not least a revival of religious activity to counter destructive utilitarian, revolutionary, iconoclastic, so-called 'progressive', and 'liberal' forces, all of which had contributed to widespread damage to the fabric of both buildings and society.

The Impact of Ecclesiology

Mention has been made above of the university societies at Oxford and Cambridge which led to a phenomenal amount of study of mediæval church architecture from the 1840s. If Evangelicals had been the most significant group behind shifts in national consciousness in the first half of the 19th century, the High Church, Tractarian, or Puseyite party within the Church of England assumed an important role in the second, and certainly from the first appearance of *The Ecclesiologist*. Many Anglican churches had been shamefully neglected since the depredations of the Henrician, Edwardine, Elizabethan, and Commonwealth periods: Ecclesiologists demanded why it was that private houses were kept clean and comfortable when the House of God often had broken or blocked windows, damp walls, rotting roofs, and ancient decorative features hidden or mutilated. They also explained in their publications the arrangements and purposes of the fabric of mediæval churches to a largely ignorant, surprised, and often suspicious Protestant nation. Suggestions were made for the restoration and furnishing of naves and chancels, and moves towards rubrical reform were mooted. From the very beginning, however, Ecclesiologists cautioned against over-zealous works that might 'restore' historic buildings within inches of their lives, and 'Great' Scott noted that 'an old church is so common and so familiar an object that we are often in danger of forgetting its value, and it is only by cultivating a correct appreciation of what our churches *really are* that we shall obtain a true and earnest feeling for their conservation'. In spite of such warnings, many insensitive schemes scraped away genuine fabric that was in any way damaged, decayed, or inconvenient, and left mediæval buildings looking like dull, mechanical, half-hearted copies of old work (some were not even copies, but based on guesses approximating to what architects thought might have been appropriate, which often was nothing of the kind). One such was the removal of four semicircular arches at the east end of the nave arcades of St Wystan's, Repton, Derbyshire (1854), and their replacement with Pointed arches on hexagonal piers conforming to the rest of the 14th-century arcades: at least two of the destroyed arches were pre-Conquest work.

There is no doubting that the Oxbridge architectural societies were immensely successful in promoting the Gothic Revival. As Eastlake put it, 'graduates who left their college rooms for curates' quarters in remote parishes', or who 'settled down as doctors and attorneys in many a country town, carried with them a pleasant recollection' of field days and explorations, study visits to churches, meetings, lectures, papers, and lively discussions about mediæval architecture. The converts went forth as missionaries, with all the zeal of youth, to rescue England from its spiritual and architectural torpor. Pugin wanted to revive Gothic architecture by reviving Roman Catholicism, but Ecclesiologists wished to revive the Anglican Church by, inter alia, resurrecting the Gothic style, and resurrect it they did, for throughout the British Isles evidence of their success is clear. Again, it should be emphasised that the extraordinary ubiquity of Gothic in 19th-century church building was largely due to Oxbridge graduates, scholarly antiquarians, and clerics, rather than architects who have been given far too much credit for it. In fact, architects had to be almost bullied into having to learn Gothic, often from scratch.

However, the nation was partly indifferent to these aims, and partly anti-clerical anyway, while Dissent and Roman Catholicism were gaining ground: Anglicans knew their influence in national affairs was being reduced, and was likely to further diminish. Another problem was the Evangelical Low Church party, for which symbolism, ceremony, sacred imagery, and decoration were unacceptable: Sabbatarianism, simplicity, severity, and sermonising were more important than 'idolatrous gewgaws' and 'superstitious' practices. Chancels, with their 'popish' rood screens, sedilia, piscinæ, aumbries, and credence tables, were regarded almost as survivals from the Dark Ages. Altars were a 'scandal and a stumbling-block': as for Easter sepulchres and other features, the chances were that the average Evangelical had no idea what they were, what they were for, or why they were there. Evangelicals, in short, saw Ecclesiologists and the Gothic Revival (with their connections with Tractarianism) as a threat to the needs of society, arguing that two or three plain utilitarian brick preaching-boxes with plaster ceilings could be erected for the price of one stone church with groined vaulted ceiling (or elaborate timber-trussed roof), chancel fitted out with crypto-'papist' paraphernalia, stained-glass windows with images, and all the rest of it. An ideal Evangelical church building was freed from any 'semblance of religious superstition', and innocent of 'artistic attractions' which could ensnare the unwary and lead them to Rome: it was, in essence, cheap and utilitarian, without any appeal to æsthetic sensibilities.

Against such views Ecclesiologists, Tractarians, and the High Church party could marshal many serious charges: Evangelicals, as heirs of iconoclasts of earlier times, had permitted building fabric to fall into decay; church services had become slovenly; children were permitted to grow up uninformed as to the nature and significance of the English liturgy and the Sacraments; Baptism had degenerated into a mere naming ceremony frequently performed in the house of the parents instead of in a church; Confirmation was often dispensed with; the observance of saints' days was confined to the denizens of the cathedral close; many undergraduates only learned for the first time about Lent and Advent when at university; and the long sermons (often badly constructed and argued, and devoid of scholarship) were a signal for general somnolence.

A transformation of Anglican services from conventional and scarcely revered meetings into picturesque rites, with a corresponding revival of rubrical usage, sacred music, art, and architecture, was a remarkable achievement, and there is no doubt that the High Church party won a great deal in the space of only a generation.

Parochial clergy with Tractarian High Church leanings brought Christianity, literacy, and morality to the poorer quarters of London and many other towns and cities: the parochial buildings and splendid churches of the Victorian Gothic Revival must have seemed like oases of civilisation and hope, as citadels of faith and Anglicanism, within the urban built fabric. Charles Kingsley, in *Alton Locke, Tailor and Poet* (1850), described a new Anglican church being built in a poor quarter of a town:

> month after month I had watched it growing; I had seen one window after another filled with tracery, one buttress after another finished off with its carved pinnacle; then I had watched the skeleton of the roof gradually clothed in tiling; and then the glazing of the windows – some of them painted ... Were they going to finish that handsome tower? No; it was left with its wooden cap, I supposed, for further funds. But the nave, and the deep chancel behind it, were all finished, and surmounted by a cross; and beautiful enough the little sanctuary looked, in the virgin purity of its spotless freestone ...
>
> And then there was a grand procession of surplices and lawn sleeves; ... the bell rang to morning and evening prayers – for there were daily services there, and Saints' day services, and Lent services, and three services on a Sunday, and six or seven on Good Friday and Easter Day. The little musical bell above the chancel-arch seemed always ringing; ... And then a Gothic school-house rose at the churchyard end, and troops of children poured in and out, and women came daily for alms; and when the frosts came on, every morning I saw a crowd, and soup carried away in pitchers, and clothes and blankets given away; the giving seemed endless, boundless; ... And yet it was a pleasant sight, as every new church is to the healthy-minded man, let his religious opinions be what they may – a fresh centre of civilization, mercy, comfort for weary hearts, relief from frost and hunger; a fresh centre of instruction, humanizing, disciplining, ... to hundreds of little savage spirits; altogether a pleasant sight.

Now tracery, buttresses with carved pinnacles, tiled roofs, and glazing were only one aspect, but the deep chancel, cross over it, many services, and sancte-bell above the chancel arch were another, and unthinkable in Protestant-Evangelical terms. Gothic church architecture had roots in the rich panoply of mediæval religion, far removed from Sabbatarianism of the Dissenting or Protestant variety, Evangelical ideals, or the tradition of sermonising to packed static congregations. The Gothic Revival was a reminder of the Christian Revival, and, although at first associated with the Tractarians and with the Roman Catholics (via Pugin's arguments), began to be adopted by Evangelicals and Dissenters (often with ludicrous results, for the style had no historical connections with Evangelical or Dissenting practice).

However, such a profound change had an immense impact on the building trades as well as on architecture. Demand was created for encaustic tiles, stained-glass windows, elaborate metalwork, quality church furnishings, vestments, and anything connected with a full and scholarly revival of mediæval forms of worship and architecture. Architects, artists, and craftsmen had to learn Gothic, with its details, mouldings, and styles, while the construction industries were turned upside-down. Architectural design, freed from the tyrannies of symmetry demanded by Classicism, could blossom anew in the climate of the Gothic Revival, for architects could experiment with asymmetrical compositions, with façades pierced with openings only where they were needed, and with the breaking up of larger masses to provide cunningly detailed buildings with a prominent series of vertical emphases. Pugin's 'True Picturesque', derived from logical planning and disposition of volumes where needed, began to be employed on a nationwide basis, but it must be remembered that the architectural phenomena had their roots in scholarly antiquarianism, largely in the hands of clergy and interested laymen.

Ecclesiologists embraced Pugin's ideas about architecture, editing them for Anglican use, and soon Second Pointed Anglican churches, complete with screens, sedilia, and all the marvellous riches of Decorated Gothic were being built by High Churchmen. There was another point to all this: the Gothic Revival was a visible expression of the revival of Sacramentalism, and an affirmation of the continuity of the Catholic tradition within the Church of England. But Second Pointed was not only the approved liturgical and functional style for Ecclesiologists: it was often brutally imposed upon real mediæval churches so that they lost their Perpendicular and Early English fabric to an invasion of Victorian Middle and Second Pointed.

The period of greatest influence of Ecclesiologists also coincided with an astonishing amount of English church building by Anglicans: by 1873 about a third of all parish churches had been restored, while between the accession of William IV in 1830 and the death of the Prince Consort in 1861 about 1,500 new churches had been built. From around 1840 to the end of the century about 100 churches were erected each year, and almost every existing church was restored (with varying degrees of sensitivity and success). There was another side to the coin, however, and that was the tyranny exercised by Ecclesiologists in the reviews and criticisms of new churches or restorations. *The Ecclesiologist* had a party line that had to be adhered to in matters of style; the provision of certain elements was closely watched; and the 'correctness' of the architecture was carefully (even pedantically) monitored. Indeed, *The Ecclesiologist* must not be underestimated as an architectural journal of immense power and influence. When English Second Pointed Gothic was de rigueur, Ecclesiologists encouraged the copying of bits of real mediæval buildings on the grounds that architects had to learn the alphabet, grammar, and syntax of Gothic before they could even begin to attempt to create original compositions. To this end they selected buildings, parts of buildings, and details which they regarded as worthy of emulation, and made them familiar in publications. But this was only a beginning.

The Gothic Revival in the 1840s

It began to be regarded as essential, when developing new residential areas, to provide a church convenient for the inhabitants. St James's, Norlands, in Northern Kensington, was such an example, and was constructed of white Suffolk bricks with minimal stone dressings in a thin, unconvincing First Pointed Lancet style, with Geometrical tracery in the tower above the door (Fig. 5.1). Interior piers and trusses are impossibly spindly, but there were galleries in 1850 which would have made the interior less fragile looking. St James's was very much Gothic 'on the cheap' (it cost £4,941), and was uncomfortably like the Inwoods' St Mary's, Eversholt Street, London (1824–7), in style – a starved, bare, and papery piece of stock-brick Gothic lampooned by Pugin in *Contrasts*.

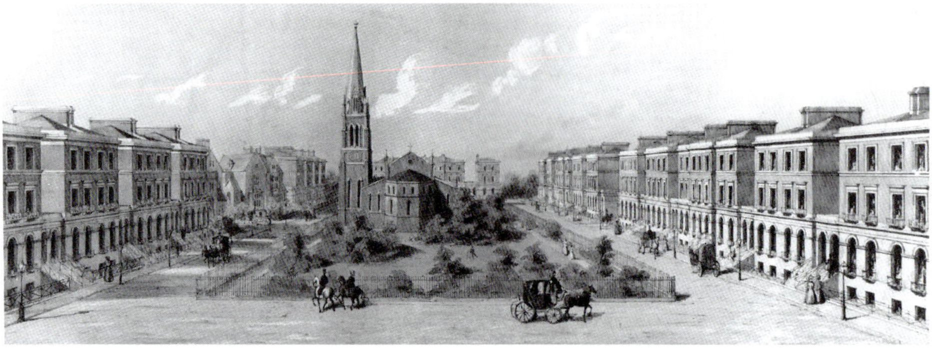

Fig. 5.1 St James's Gardens (formerly Square), Norland Estate, Kensington, with houses by John Barnett, and Church of St James, Norlands (1844–5), by Lewis Vulliamy, with spire (never realised). The commercial and social success of housing estates in London in the Victorian period often depended on the proximity of a church (coll. JSC).

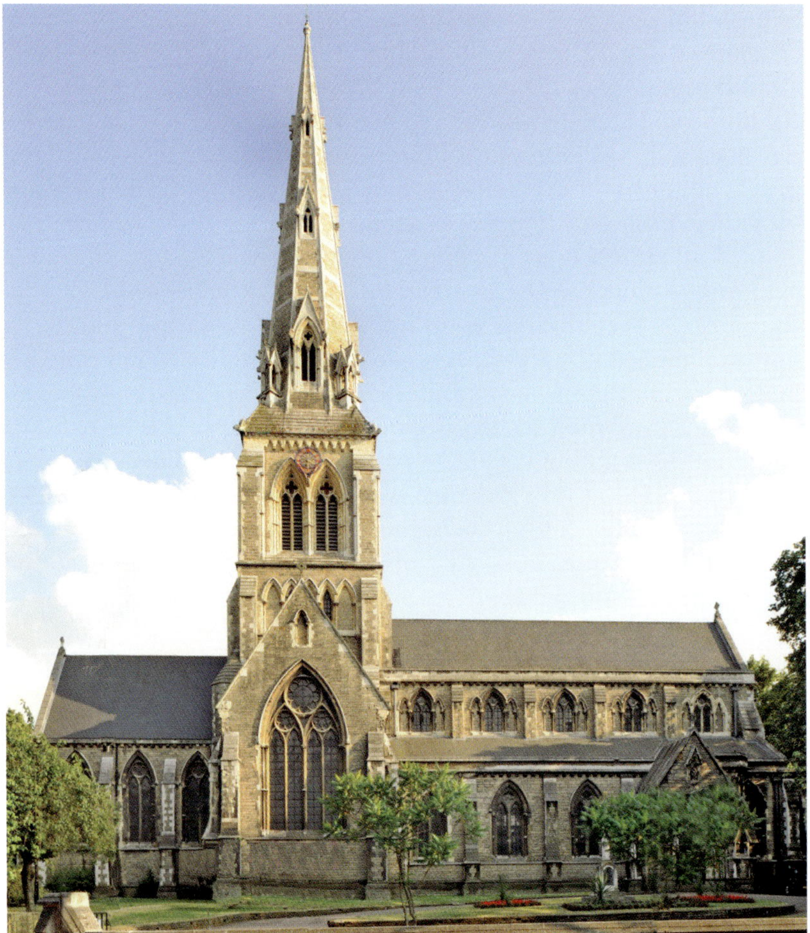

Fig. 5.2 St Giles's, Camberwell, London, by 'Great' Scott, of 1841. Eastlake noted that 'in the neighbourhood of London no church of its time was considered in purer style or more orthodox in its arrangement' (GB [2011]).

Such architecture did not meet with the approval of Ecclesiologists. George Gilbert 'Great' Scott and his partner (from 1835 to 1846), William Bonython Moffatt, however, produced an important church, St Giles's, Camberwell, London (designed 1841, consecrated 1844), with a big chancel (separated from the nave by a tower with a tall spire), Geometrical (Middle Pointed) tracery, and an exterior that was tough and sturdy (Fig. 5.2): *The Ecclesiologist* pronounced it 'one of the finest' churches of 'modern days'. St Giles's is more successful than St John the Evangelist, Ladbroke Grove, London (1844–5), by J.H. Stevens and George Alexander, who planned a First Pointed cruciform building with a crossing tower and spire based on that at Witney, Oxfordshire. St John's is representative of a somewhat timid early Victorian Gothic Revival essay that depended on copies of bits and pieces culled from real mediæval buildings, but in which those fragments were assembled without elan, verve, or any startling leaps of imagination. *The Builder* and other journals were favourable in their criticisms of what is rather a dull building, but *The Ecclesiologist*, in schoolmastery mood, hoped the architects would do better in the future. Scott's church was of more interest at the time because it showed an advance in operative skills, and it was firmly early Second Pointed, which was to be the approved style for the next decade or so.

Although Scott's work attracted favourable attention, Ecclesiologists began to move towards the idea of building exemplars rather than relying on criticism alone to obtain improvements in design. One of the first attempts to provide a church erected under the supervision of learned Ecclesiologists was Christ Church, Kilndown, Kent, begun in 1839 to designs by Anthony Salvin, but transformed inside (1840–5) by Alexander James Beresford Hope, who created a proper chancel with altar by Salvin, chandeliers, tapers, and lectern by William Butterfield, and rood screen and stalls by R.C. Carpenter (Fig. 5.3). *The Ecclesiologist* in 1845 praised the chancel as a whole of colour not to be seen in any other English church, and Kilndown can be regarded as the

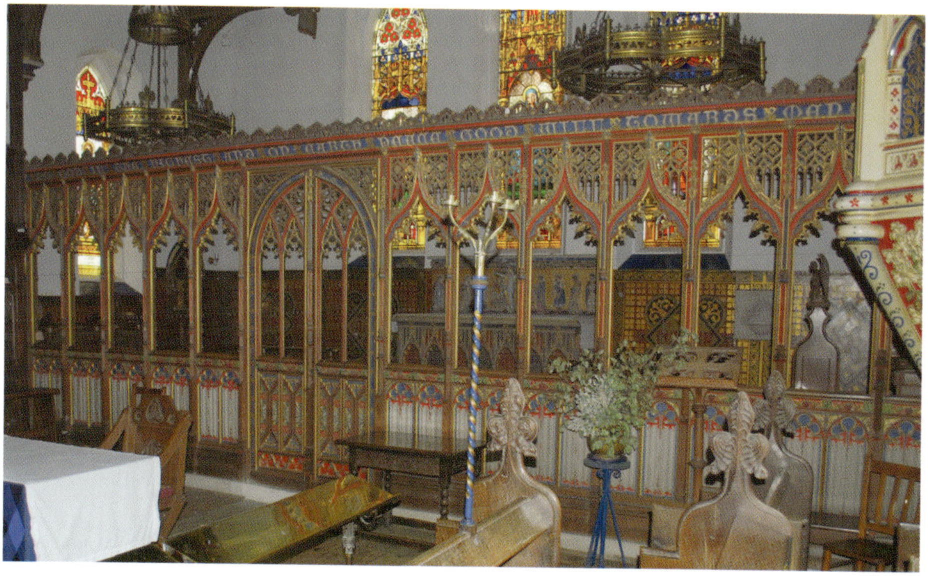

Fig. 5.3 Christ Church, Kilndown, Kent: the early Camdenian rood screen, designed by R.C. Carpenter before 1845 for Alexander Beresford Hope (JSC [2015]).

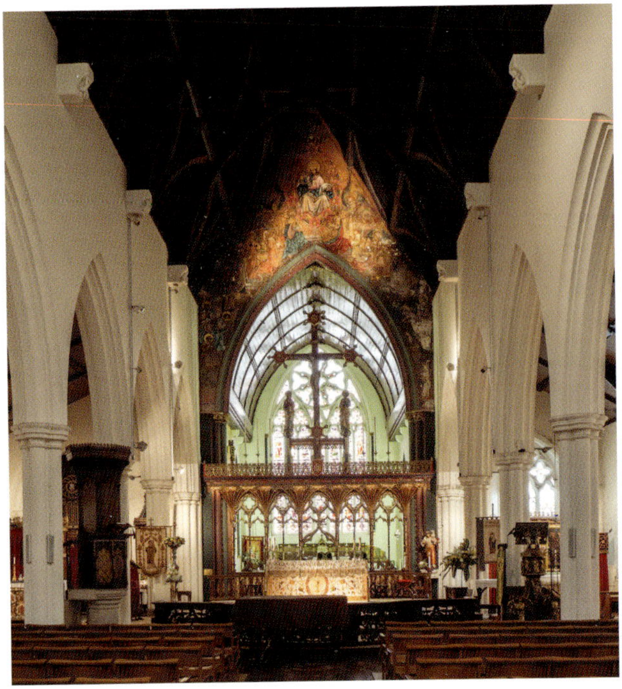

Fig. 5.4 St Paul's, Brighton, East Sussex (1846–8), by R.C. Carpenter. The loft and rood were added some years later by Bodley, with figures by John McCulloch of Kennington (JR [2018]).

first Camdenian ecclesiologically approved chancel in England. Soon Ecclesiologists began to draw up rules and principles for church design they perceived as being akin to an exact science.

Carpenter obtained the commission to build St Paul's, West Street, Brighton, Sussex, in 1846, which was Puginesque, and in the Second Pointed style (Fig. 5.4). This was his first major town church, paid for by the Revd Henry Michell Wagner, Vicar of Brighton and West Blatchington from 1824, who intended that his son, Arthur Douglas Wagner, should serve as curate at the new church from 1850. H.M. Wagner was a pre-Tractarian High Churchman, but A.D. Wagner himself was strongly influenced by the Tractarian movement. St Paul's was the first Anglican church in Brighton in which an advanced ritual, eventually with vestments and incense, was adopted: the building was praised by *The Ecclesiologist*, which rejoiced that at last Brighton had 'its proper place in the revival of church architecture, and its hideous chapels are to be shamed by a real church'. Built of brick, faced externally with knapped flint and Caen-stone dressings, the interior was later enriched with a painted chancel ceiling by G.F. Bodley, who also added the fan vaulting and rood to Carpenter's chancel screen.

Another, even more important, church by Carpenter was St Mary Magdalene, Munster Square, St Pancras, Camden, London (1849–52), also in the Second Pointed style, and built of Kentish ragstone, a material ill-suited to the capital. The interior, however, with its broad aisles, absence of clerestorey, high timber roof, distinct chancel, and furnishings (Fig. 5.5), was a model of Tractarian principles (*The Ecclesiologist* enthusiastically called it 'the most artistically correct new church yet consecrated in London'). St Mary's was built under the ægis of Edward Stuart, who had read for his first degree at Oxford, where he had been profoundly influenced by Pusey and others. Stuart proved to be an effective incumbent, educating the poor and their children, and

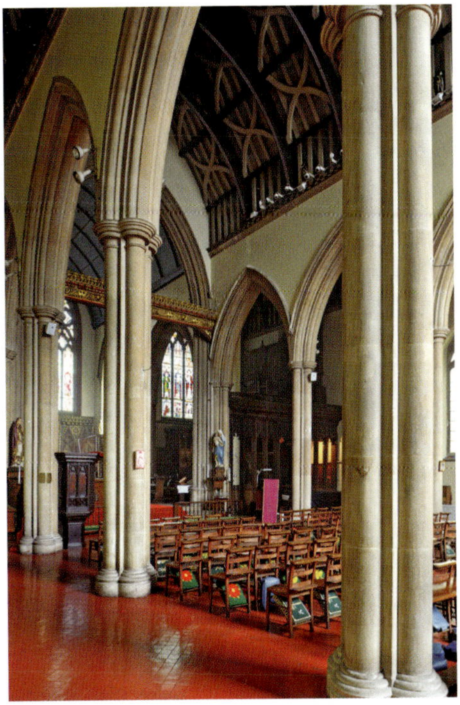

Fig. 5.5 St Mary Magdalene's, Munster Square, St Pancras, London (1849–52), by R.C. Carpenter: an essay in Second Pointed, with high arcades and steeply pitched roofs (GB [2011]).

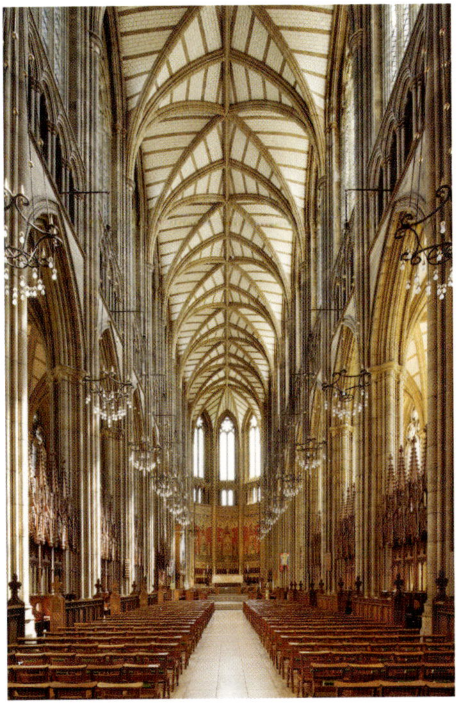

Fig. 5.6 Chapel of St Nicholas's College, Lancing, West Sussex (begun 1868, but designed in essence earlier, realised by William Slater and Richard Herbert Carpenter, but not completed until the 1970s by S.E. Dykes Bower). It is in the French 13th-century Gothic style, with tall arcades, small triforium, large clerestorey, and vaulting inspired by that of Westminster Abbey (JOD [2018]).

bringing Christianity, literacy, and decency to a deprived area. St Mary's became a model for architects in the period 1870–1900, as will be seen. However, by the mid-century there was considerable antagonism to chancel screens, and the Bishop of London, mindful of this, tried to restrain Tractarian influence. Carpenter therefore designed low walls known as cancelli separating the chancel from the nave in lieu of the screen which the bishop refused to sanction, a compromise endorsed by *The Ecclesiologist*, and one that presaged numerous similar low walls as alternatives to screens, notably in many churches by Butterfield. Tall screens, in fact, were rare in Anglican churches until the 1870s. The present rood, set high on a beam, was added later (1903–5), to designs by J.T. Micklethwaite. Carpenter was also responsible for the first designs for St Nicholas's College, Lancing, West Sussex, but the spectacular Geometrical Gothic chapel there, begun in 1868, was realised under William Slater and R.H. Carpenter (Fig. 5.6).

One of the contributors to Kilndown church, as noted above, was William Butterfield, with whom Henry Woodyer had worked in 1844. Shortly after he left Butterfield's office, Woodyer created his first independent masterpiece, Holy Innocents, Highnam, Gloucestershire (1849–51), in a robust and elaborate Second Pointed style. His patron

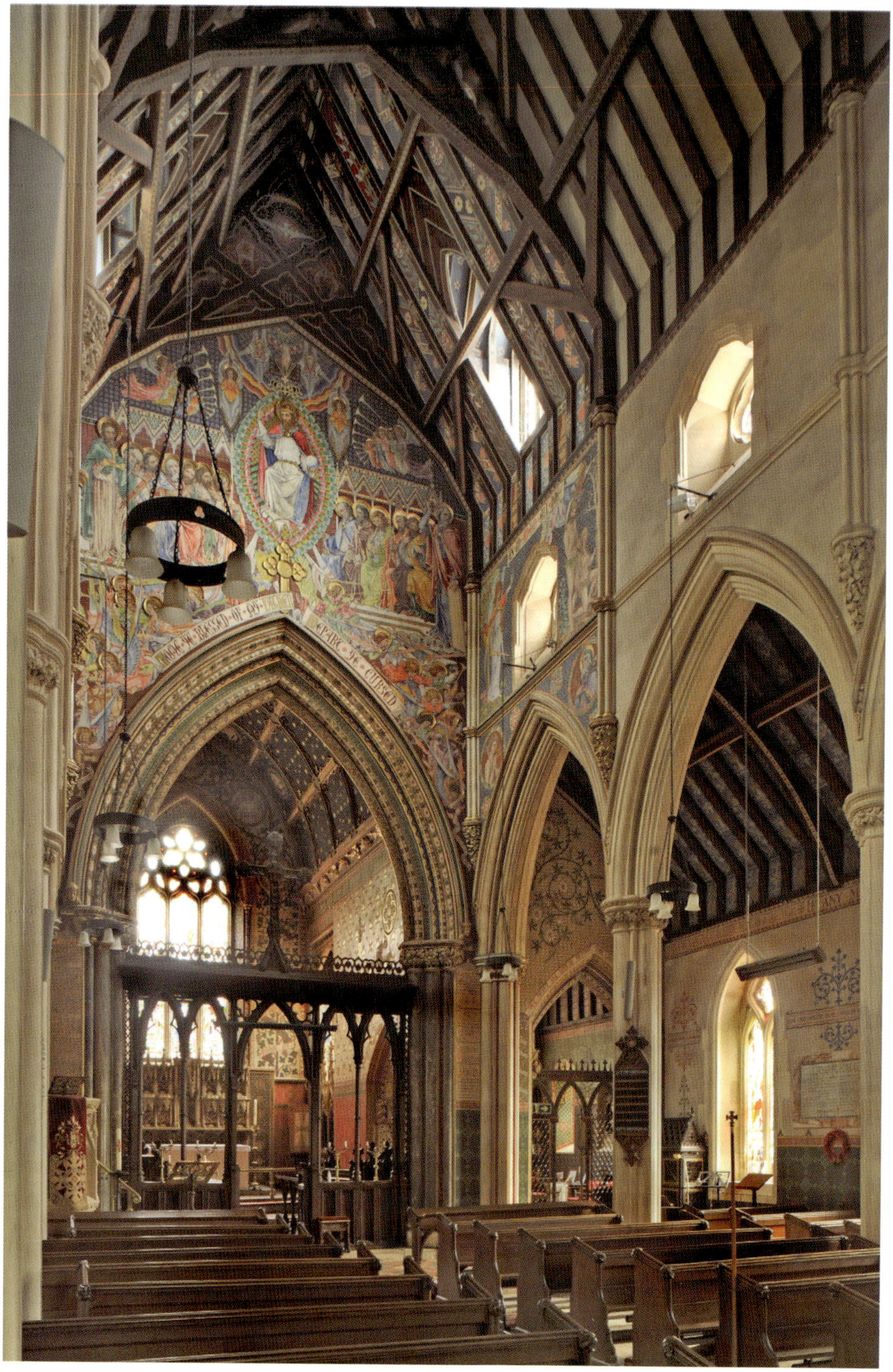

Fig. 5.7 Holy Innocents', Highnam, Gloucestershire (1849–51), by Henry Woodyer, an impressive Second Pointed ensemble, with painted polychromy: in many respects it is a fulfilment of the Puginesque ideal. The wall paintings, including the Last Judgement (1859–61) above the chancel arch, were carried out in 'spirit fresco' by Thomas Gambier Parry, restored 1987–93 by Wolfgang Gärtner and Donald Smith (GB [2021]).

was the wealthy Thomas Gambier Parry – who was responsible for the spectacular frescoes, the most important early examples of painted internal polychromy in an Anglican church following Pugin's exemplary work at Cheadle (Fig. 5.7).

Benjamin Ferrey received the imprimatur of Ecclesiological opinion with his church of St Stephen, Rochester Row, Westminster, of 1846–50, a competent essay in Second Pointed Revival, erected and endowed at the expense of Angela Georgina Burdett-Coutts in memory of her father, Sir Francis Burdett. Contemporary illustrations of this building show a crisp precision and sharpness that anticipate later interiors by Butterfield and G.E. Street. The latter architect rose to demands in *The Ecclesiologist* for a greater simplicity in the design of rural churches, and produced the robust and charming First Pointed St Mary's, at Par, Cornwall, of 1847–8, where plainness, clarity, and toughness are well to the fore.

Street was also to argue that a town church should have high, smooth walls of coloured bands, with panels; windows would be set high and would be large to admit as much light as possible without inviting vandalism; towers were to be set back from the line of the street; and a piling together of motifs, like those of a Continental town church, was to be sought. *The Ecclesiologist* was to publish appreciations of Italian Gothic architecture, and in 1848 Benjamin Webb, Secretary of the CCS, and later of the Ecclesiological Society, published his *Sketches of Continental Ecclesiology* in which he praised the brick construction of Italian churches: the emphasis of the Gothic Revival was moving away from English exemplars to the Continent.

In addition, Ecclesiologists were starting to abandon archæological correctness and copying in favour of a search for a modern style suitable for the grimy atmosphere of the Victorian urban milieu, with its thousands of coal-burning domestic fires, steam engines, and polluting industries. By the end of the 1840s it was opined that new forms and materials were essential for new developments, and, in any case, the published illustrations of buildings such as the interior of Ferrey's St Stephen's prompted what was to happen later. Italian and Continental models seemed to offer certain ways forward, because they were adapted to tight urban sites, and because, in the case of Italian exemplars, the colours of the buildings' interiors were derived from the stones and other materials used to face the walls (structural polychromy), rather than applied using paint (as Pugin had done in his interiors).

The *Rundbogenstil*

For a few years, from the 1830s, there arose a revival of interest in the round-arched styles, varying from Norman or Romanesque Revival to a more eclectic mix featuring Italianate, Lombardic, and Germanic motifs.

This originated in Germany, and it embraced the Early Christian, Byzantine, and Romanesque round-arched styles of Italy: the German word *Rundbogenstil* is applied to these styles, many of which can be traced to German enthusiasm for Italy, and the *Rundbogenstil* is related to Germanic precedents (notably in the works of Friedrich von Gärtner, Leo von Klenze, Ludwig Persius, and Karl Friedrich Schinkel); to the new interest in Italian non-Classical architecture found in the writings of Webb, Street, and others; and to the impact of the Italianate designs of Barry and his contemporaries.

Now the reader might wonder why there is a brief discussion of the round-arched styles at this point: the answer is because of polychromy. In the 1820s several young architects announced that colour was widely used in antiquity. Jakob Ignaz Hittorff, with Karl Ludwig Wilhelm von Zanth, published *Architecture Antique de la Sicile* (1827–30), which included reconstruction drawings of the colouring in Greek temples (and thereby stirred up hornets' nests of outraged objections from Received Opinion, which myopically held that Greek buildings were all white). Jules Goury with Gottfried Semper studied ancient polychromy, the results of which were published in 1834 and caused quite a stir. Goury also collected material with Owen Jones, who became an authority on colour in architecture. Hittorff's beautiful church of St-Vincent-de-Paul, Paris (1830–48), was coloured in a manner its architect insisted was a modern expression of antique polychromy.

English versions of the *Rundbogenstil* were influenced especially by buildings such as von Klenze's Allerheiligen-Hofkirche (Court Church of All Saints – 1826–37) and Alte Pinakothek (Old Picture Gallery – 1826–36, which had elements derived from the Palazzo Cancellaria and the Vatican Belvedere in Rome), and von Gärtner's Ludwigskirche (1829–40), all three in Munich. Other important precedents included Persius's beautiful Heilandskirche (Church of the Redeemer), Sacrow (1841–4), and Friedenskirche (1845–8), both in Potsdam; and August Soller's Michaelskirche (Church of St Michael), Berlin (1849–56 – partially restored after damage in the 1939–45 war). In all those buildings polychromy was employed in scholarly ways that had a wide following in Germany. Heinrich Hübsch published his important *In welchem Stil sollen wir bauen*? (In What Style Shall We Build? – 1828), which, by his championing of brick as a building material, further promoted *Rundbogenstil* experiments, not least in colour.

However, there was another important reason why polychromy became so much a part of architecture in England in the 1840s. Prince Albert himself, advised by Professor Ludwig Grüner of Dresden, did much to promote the use of colour in architecture, spurred on by his appreciation of Italian art and architecture, and especially of the Italian-influenced *Rundbogenstil* in Germany. The prince also knew of the important group of early 19th-century artists known as 'The Nazarenes', who were fascinated by the work of Dürer and Raphael, and who decorated many interiors with grand frescoes. Their ideas influenced Pugin, and were transmitted to English art through William Dyce, who had involvements with the decorations of the Palace of Westminster, a project dear to Prince Albert's heart. Furthermore, the round-arched style itself appealed to the non-sectarian instincts of the high-minded German prince, and there is no doubt that its revival and appearance in England were strongly powered by Germanic precedents.

The sometimes fierce debates about polychromy in Neo-Classical and *Rundbogenstil* structures fired further discussions about the use of colour in mediæval Gothic buildings. In England, it should be remembered, most people were used to seeing their mediæval churches with whitened walls, and were astounded to learn of coloured wall paintings (concealed under layers of whitewash), brightly coloured rood screens, coloured funerary monuments, coloured sculptures, and so on. The restoration of colour to the interior of Sainte-Chapelle in Paris (1837–43) prompted Goths to apply colour to their interiors (e.g. Pugin at Cheadle, Woodyer at Highnam, and other individuals and places).

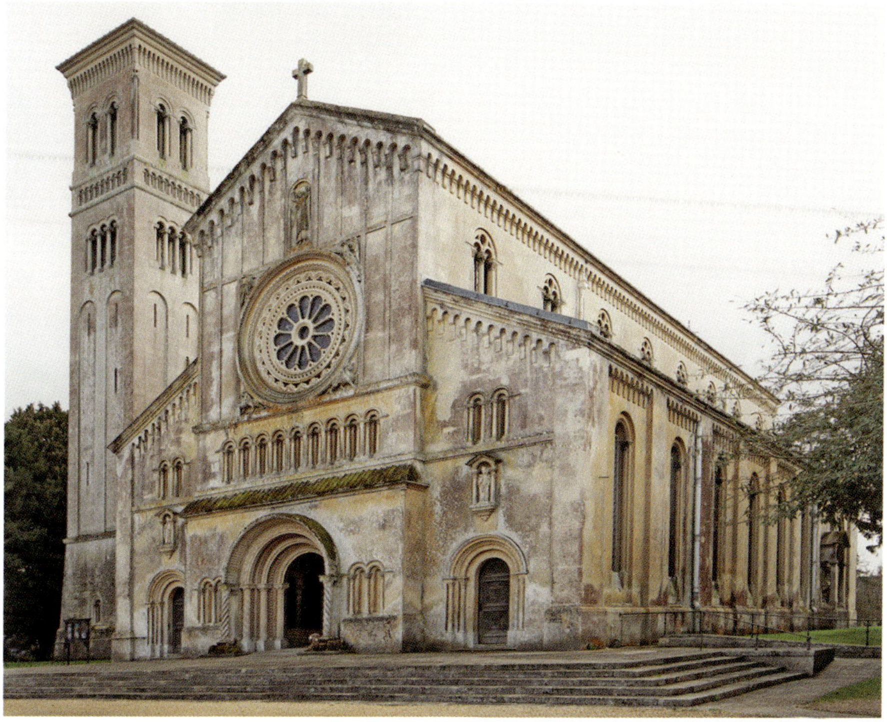

Fig. 5.8 Sts Mary and Nicholas, Wilton, Wiltshire (1840–6), by T.H. Wyatt and D. Brandon: a *Rundbogenstil* essay with a pronounced Italianate flavour derived from 11th- and 12th-century exemplars in Tuscany (JE [2021]).

Fig. 5.9 Sts Mary and Nicholas, Wilton, showing the basilican form and sumptuous apse (JE [2021]).

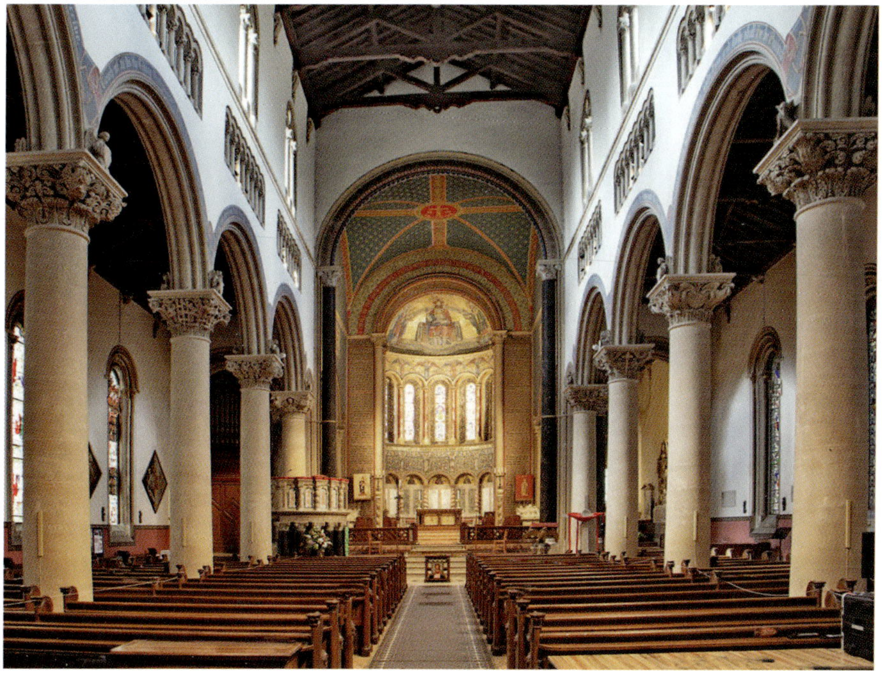

Stylistic Oddities

A convincing exercise in Italianate *Rundbogenstil*, with a tall campanile attached to it by means of a miniature gallery, is Sts Mary and Nicholas, Wilton, Wiltshire: this important (if startling) mixture of Early Christian and Lombardic Romanesque was built for the Russian-born Catherine, Countess of Pembroke, and her son, the Rt Hon Sidney Herbert, later 1st Baron Herbert of Lea (a collector of mediæval Italian art). It was recognised as a building of quality in numerous journals, even in the influential *Allgemeine Bauzeitung* of Vienna. It is predominantly Italian Romanesque in style,

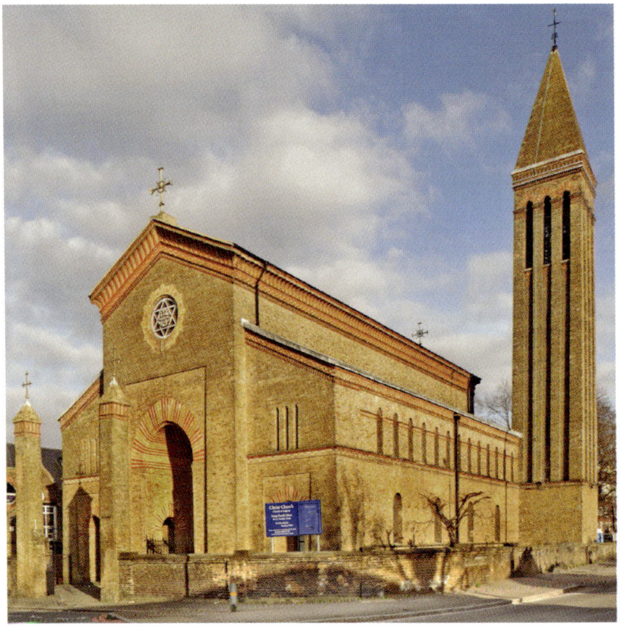

Fig. 5.10 Christ Church, Streatham Hill, London (1840–2), with fine stock-brick exterior, enlivened by voussoirs of alternating red and yellow bricks, a *Rundbogenstil* basilica with campanile (GB [2021]).

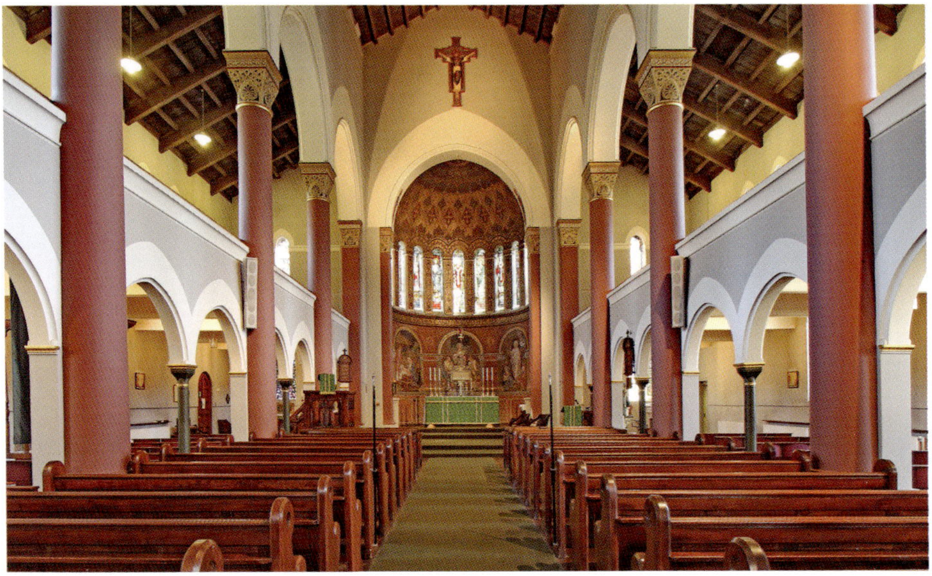

Fig. 5.11 Byzantinesque basilica with apsidal chancel based on Early Christian precedents, showing remains of decorations by Owen Jones, Christ Church, Streatham Hill, London (JS [2018]).

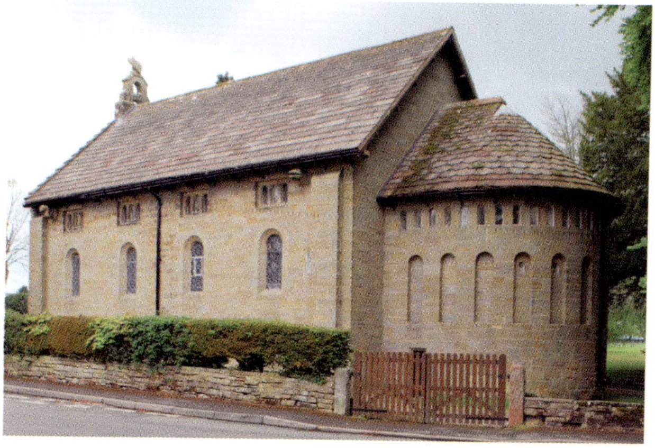

Fig. 5.12 St Mary's, Wreay, Cumbria (1840–2), showing the apsidal chancel with blank arcading and tiny windows under the eaves, and side wall with triplets of very small windows set in rectangular recesses above each of the four main windows. An eagle perches on the western bell-cote, and large carved brackets featuring emblematic monsters are set under the eaves (JSC [2021]).

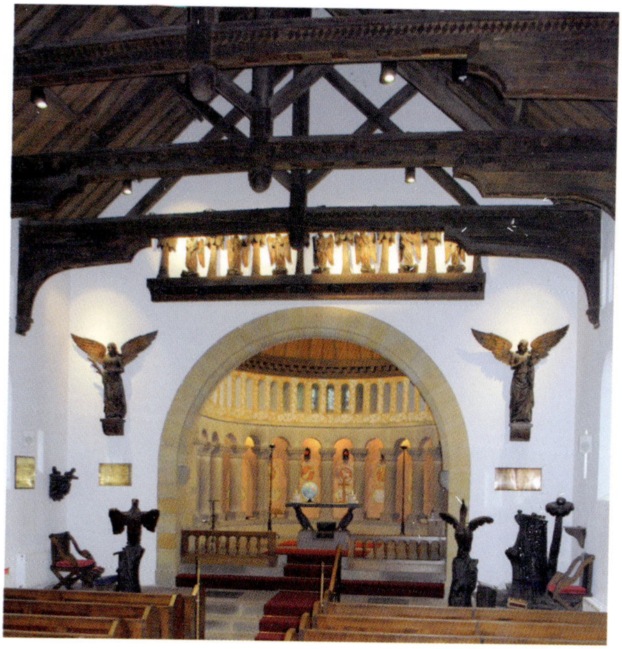

Fig. 5.13 St Mary's, Wreay: an aisleless *Rundbogenstil* church. On either side of the chancel arch is an archangel on brackets carved with images of bats and a dragon, symbolising light over darkness, and the two bog-oak lecterns represent a pelican and an eagle. Above the arch is a row of angels and palm trees set on a shelf carved with oak leaves, acorns, grasshoppers, flowers, and grapes. The altar slab is supported on eagles, set on a stone base carved with wheat ears and grapes (the Bread and Wine). Around the apse is a 13-arched arcade, suggesting the Last Supper, emphasised by symbols of Christ and the Apostles on the wall behind each seat. Small windows are deep-set, and beneath, in the arcade, are seven roundels of orange glass (the Wise Virgins' lamps, perhaps?) (JSC [2021]).

with the clear form of a basilica (that is, with clerestoreyed nave, lean-to aisles, and three eastern apses) (Figs 5.8 and 5.9).

Christ Church, Streatham, London (1840–2), by J.W. Wild, is a clear reworking of the Early Christian Italian basilican type but influenced by German precedents; nevertheless, it is stylistically eclectic. It is certainly among the most original and remarkable of all early Victorian churches: its polychrome interior (by Owen Jones) was painted over, although small patches have been reinstated (Figs 5.10 and 5.11).

Henry Roberts designed the dull Romanesque St Mary's, Elvetham Hall, Hampshire (1840–1), but St Mary's, Wreay, Cumbria (consecrated 1842), is anything but dull: it is an extraordinary mixture of French and Italian elements with a liberal dose of Rhineland Romanesque, and has a strange and wonderful apse (Figs 5.12 and 5.13). Designed by Sara Losh (whose intellect was said by Henry Lonsdale to approach in power that of 'George Eliot'), daughter of John Losh, owner of the Walker Iron Works, Newcastle upon Tyne, St Mary's was described as 'early Saxon or modified Lombardic', and the building's elaborate symbolism can probably be best explained as a kind of abstracted pantheistic celebration of Creation. Sara Losh was also responsible for the cross and primitivist mausoleum in the churchyard, built in memory of her sister, Katharine, but arrows and pine cones, which appear in several places in the church, allude to the death of her friend, Major William Thain, killed in the Afghan War in 1842. Thain sent a pine cone to Sara Losh from Afghanistan shortly before he was killed.

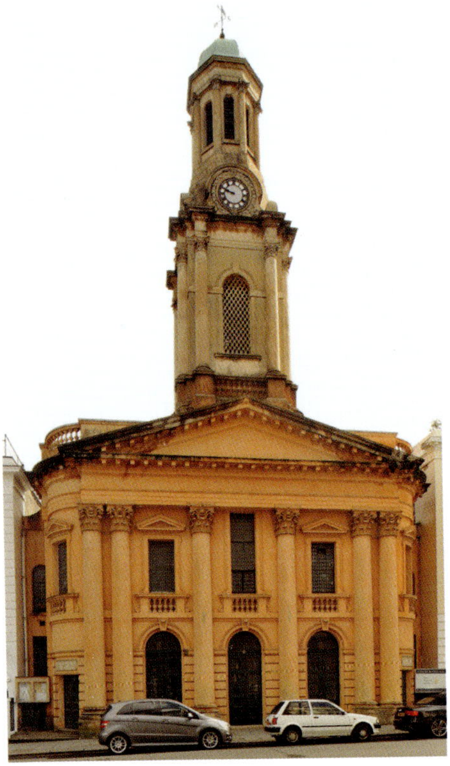

Fig. 5.14 St Peter's, main elevation to Kensington Park Road, Ladbroke Estate, London, by Thomas Allom, built 1855–7, an extraordinarily late date for a Classical Anglican church: it features an engaged Corinthian temple-front (with pediment) flanked by quadrants, with a square tower surmounted by an octagonal lantern (GB [2017]).

Among other churches featuring round arches is All Saints', Ennismore Gardens, London (1848–9 – now the Russian Orthodox Cathedral of the Dormition of the Mother of God and All Saints), by Lewis Vulliamy – a pretty basilica in the Lombardic Romanesque style, of stone with some red-brick banding (it has inside very tall columns of iron, galleries on three sides, and a small clerestorey): the campanile was completed to Vulliamy's designs by R.L. Roumieu in *c.*1860, and other works were carried out under C.H. Townsend in 1887–97, including the present west front, based on that of the great church of S. Zeno Maggiore, Verona (*c.*1123 and later).

Occasionally, there were some stylistic oddities, even for Anglican buildings. St Peter's, Kensington Park Road, London (1855–7), by Thomas Allom, was one of very few Anglican Victorian churches to be built in the Classical style (Fig. 5.14). A Classical idiom for St Peter's was no doubt dictated by the fact that this was an estate church, built in a speculative housing development on a tight site, flanked by tall terrace houses all with Italianate detailing.

The *Rundbogenstil* re-emerged in the rather odd St James's, Gerrards Cross, Buckinghamshire (1858–9), erected by the Misses Reid in memory of their brother, George Alexander Reid, MP for Windsor from 1845 until his death. The architect was William Tite, an unlikely choice as a designer of churches, but he probably got the job as a friend of the family (Fig. 5.15).

Startling though St James's is, a more distinguished example of Italianate *Rundbogenstil* is St Barnabas, Jericho, Oxford (1869–87), by (Sir) Arthur William Blomfield, a pupil of P.C. Hardwick: the building, with its handsome campanile, is rendered, with

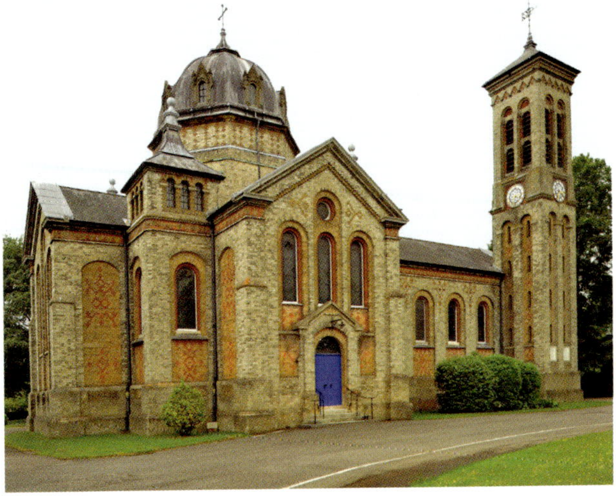

Fig. 5.15 St James's, Gerrards Cross, Buckinghamshire (1858–9), by William Tite, supposedly a modified version of the Byzantine architecture found near Venice and Padua, faced with white, red, and yellow brick (GB [2021]).

brick bands and other features (Fig. 5.16). At the east end is a large apse crowned with a hemi-dome embellished with the Pantocrator reminiscent of Sicilian Romanesque churches. The interior suggests an Early Christian basilica, a flavour reinforced by the various fittings (including the low cancelli similar to those in San Clemente, Rome), and therefore responding to tendencies apparent in R.C. churches (Fig. 5.17).

From 1874 John Pollard Seddon remodelled an 1842–3 preaching-box for William Poole, Vicar of Hoarwithy, Herefordshire, from 1854. At the splendidly sited St Catherine's, Seddon added an Italian Romanesque cloister walk that runs along the south side of the church, and a campanile that looks as though it was transplanted from a hill-top village well south of the Alps (Fig. 5.18). Seddon created a remarkable Byzantino-Romanesque ensemble at the east end of the original building, with four monolithic shafts of grey Devonshire marble carrying the structure overhead, and beyond, an apse and two half-apses completing the composition. The apse has a Pantocrator in mosaic in the Byzantine style, and the ambo features Cosmatiesque work. Decorations were by G.E. Fox; the stalls (1883) and prayer desk (1884) were carved by Harry Hems of Exeter; and the

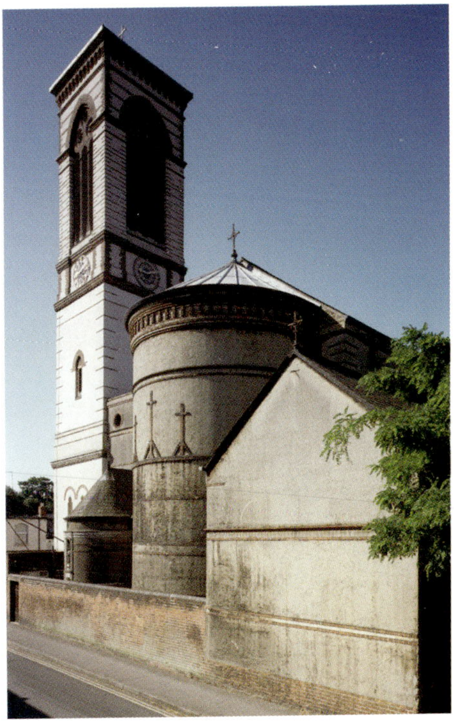

Fig. 5.16 St Barnabas's, Jericho, Oxford (1869–87), showing the Italianate campanile and apse, designed by A.W. Blomfield, built at the expense of Thomas Combe (director of the Clarendon Press) for Anglo-Catholic worship (AH [2004]).

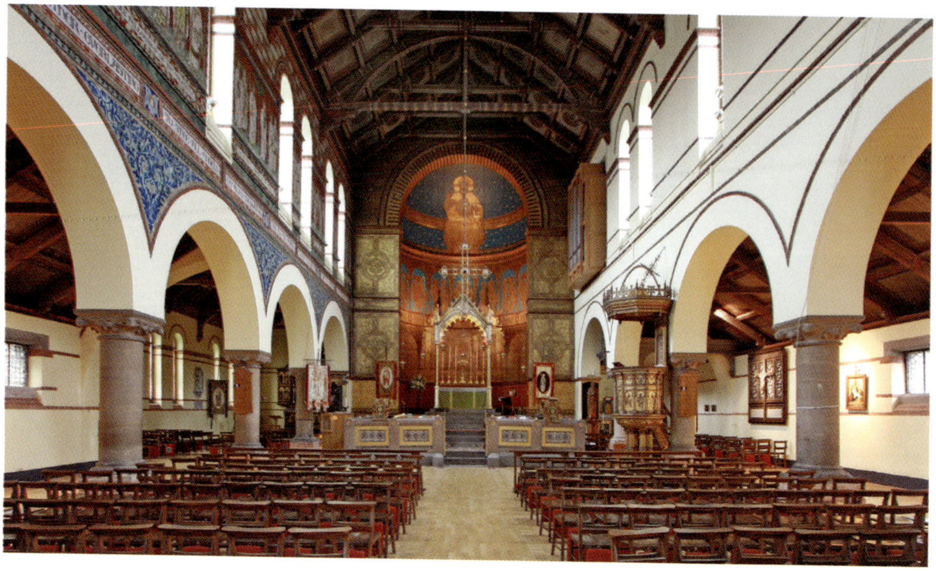

Fig. 5.17 St Barnabas's, Oxford, by Blomfield. The north aisle (1888–9), pulpit made by Heaton, Butler, & Bayne, and decorations of the east end (1893) are all by Blomfield. Stylistically, the church is an Italian Romanesque basilica, with Early Christian seasoning, but the pier capitals are French First Pointed, and the baldacchino is trecento Italian Gothic. Decorations on the north wall of the nave consist of brilliant tiles in the spandrels and rows of Christian martyrs between the clerestorey windows (derived, no doubt, from exemplars in Ravenna): they appear to have been by Powell & Sons (JS [2010]).

glass was made by S. Belham & Co. to designs by Seddon, his pupil H.A. Kennedy, and H.G. Murray (Fig. 5.19).

An undersung and extremely interesting building is St Sophia's (or The Wisdom of God), Lower Kingswood, Surrey (1890–2), an essay in a Free-Byzantine style by S.H. Barnsley for Dr Edwin Freshfield (himself a distinguished scholar) and Sir Cosmo Bonsor. Of red brick with stone dressings, it has herringbone brick friezes, and consists of a two-bay nave (with narrow passage aisles) and chancel in one volume, with an apse. Within are nine genuine Byzantine capitals, and there is an 11th-century piece of a frieze on the west wall at the north end, from the Church of the Pantocrator in Constantinople. Furnishings (also designed by Barnsley) are delightful Arts and Crafts pieces, some of which are inlaid with mother of pearl. Barnsley, W.R. Lethaby, and R. Weir Schultz all worked in Norman Shaw's office, and in 1889 Schultz and Barnsley had visited Greece together, later producing *The Monastery of St Luke of Stiris in Phocis* (1901), an important document of the Byzantine Revival: St Sophia's is one of the most distinguished examplars of that Revival, designed immediately on Barnsley's return from Greece (Fig. 5.20).

Afterword

These various themes, ideas, exemplars, experiments, styles, and trends all gradually coalesced to bring about a new direction in architecture, and the catalyst was provided by a union of Ecclesiology and Tractarianism. However, the Gothic Revival occupied at least the moral high ground, and the *Rundbogenstil* did not have associations the

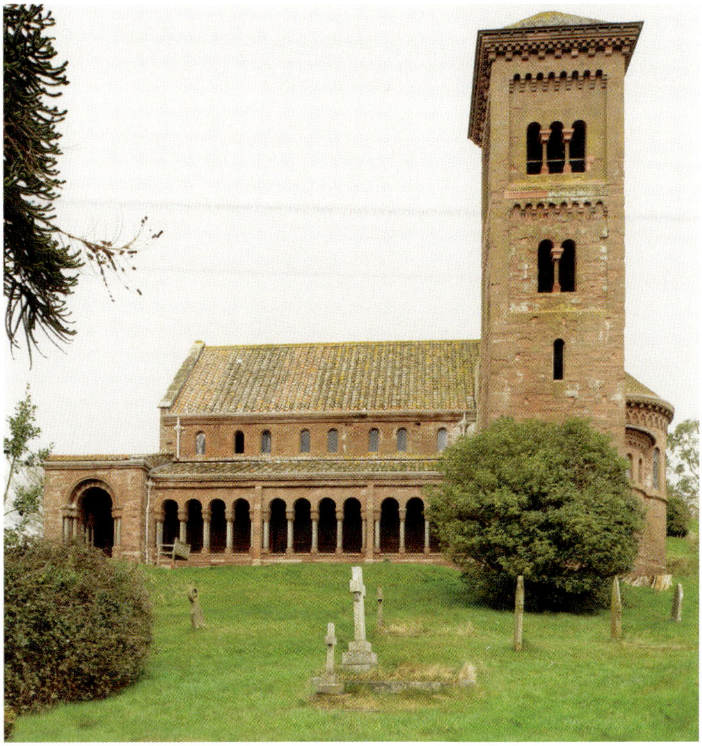

Fig. 5.18 St Catherine's, Hoarwithy, Herefordshire (1874–1903), by J.P. Seddon, showing the Italianate campanile and Romanesque loggia (GB [2018]).

Fig. 5.19 Seddon's St Catherine's, Hoarwithy, showing the Byzantine style of the architecture and the apsidal east end (GB [2018]).

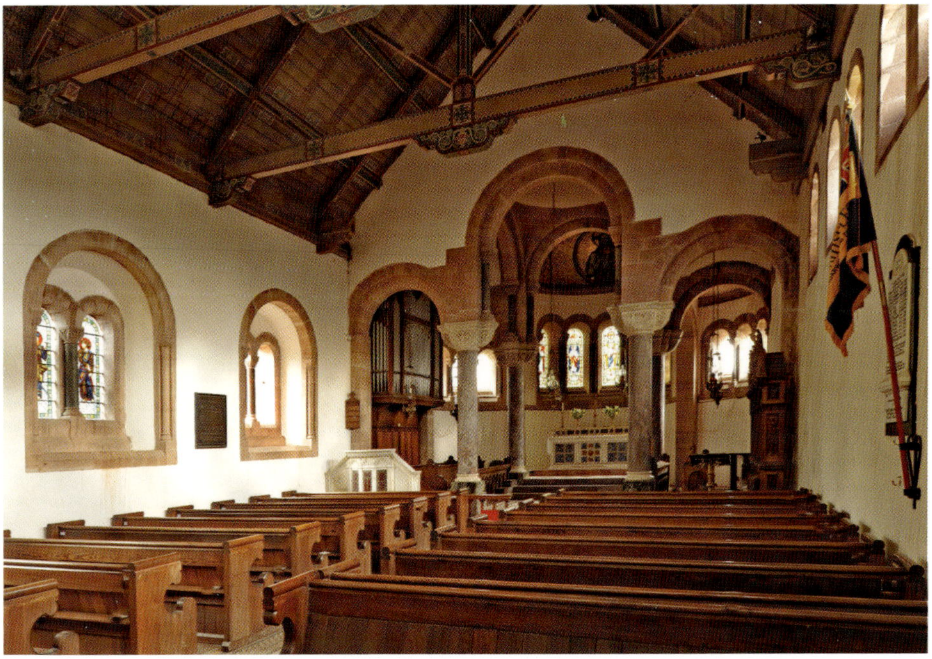

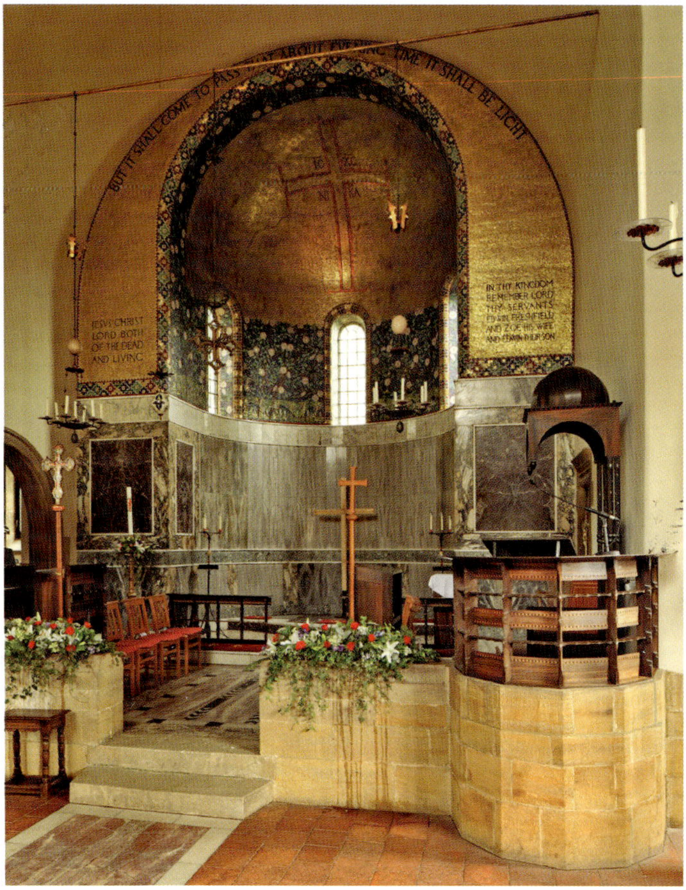

Fig. 5.20 St Sophia's, or The Wisdom of God, Lower Kingswood, Surrey (1890–2), by S.H. Barnsley, a fine example of Byzantine influenced Arts and Crafts work. Mosaics are by Powell of Whitefriars (1903) (GB [2018]).

Goths had appropriated for their own cause, largely because of Pugin (although Pugin used Romanesque for the crypt of St Chad's Cathedral, Birmingham, seemingly to suggest some notion of antiquity and a sense of slow, organic growth).

Later in the century there were to be several distinguished buildings designed using variations on a *Rundbogenstil* theme: they happened for very good reasons, and were not mere stylistic whims, so will be illustrated and described later.

6

The Search for an Ideal

It had long been a project of the Cambridge Camden Society to found a model church, which should realise in its design and internal arrangements a beau ideal of architectural beauty, and fulfil at the same time the requirements of orthodox ritual. Some years after the Society was transferred to London, an opportunity presented itself for the execution of this scheme.

CHARLES LOCKE EASTLAKE (1836–1906):
A History of the Gothic Revival (London: Longmans, Green, & Co., 1872), 251.

I believe, and sincerely hope, in spite of the opposition of the champions of the 'Classic', that a style will grow upon *the hitherto but little understood* principles *of the Mediæval style, as different as that of the fourteenth from that of the twelfth century, and as conformable to the progress of invention.*

EDWARD WILLIAM GODWIN (1833–86):
'Gothic or Classic' in *The Builder* **xv** (28 March 1857), 176.

The Anglican Crisis

The Ecclesiological Society's campaign to restore the beauty of liturgical practice in appropriate settings, aided by such works as *Hierurgia Anglicana*, was helped by clerics who began to rise to positions of eminence within the Anglican Church. William Maskell, Oxford-educated liturgical scholar, High Churchman, and mediævalist, was appointed (1842) Rector of Corscombe, Dorset, but shortly afterwards resigned his living to devote himself to detailed research into Anglican ritual. He made major contributions to liturgical studies with *The Ancient Liturgy of the Church of England, according to the uses of Sarum, York, Hereford, and Bangor, and the Roman Liturgy arranged in parallel columns, with Preface and Notes* (1844), followed by *Monumenta ritualia ecclesiæ Anglicanæ; or, Occasional offices of the Church of England according to the ancient use of Salisbury* (1846–7). Maskell's works gave impetus to the revival of Anglican ceremonial based on mediæval precedents, but, perhaps even more importantly, helped the evolution of what became known as Ritualism, in which the Eucharist was placed once again at the centre of Anglican worship. These important, scholarly publications put Maskell in the front rank of English ecclesiastical antiquaries: he was appointed domestic chaplain to Henry Phillpotts, Bishop of Exeter, and instituted (1847) Vicar of St Mary's, Torquay, Devon.

One of his first duties was to assist Phillpotts in the celebrated Gorham case.

George Cornelius Gorham was presented (1847) to the Living of Brampford Speke, near Exeter, but Phillpotts (influenced by Maskell) objected to Gorham's strongly Calvinistic views, and refused to institute him. Gorham took his case to the ecclesiastical Court of Arches, which judged (1849) in favour of the bishop, so Gorham appealed to the Privy Council's Judicial Committee, which reversed the judgement, ruling in favour of Gorham (1850), who was duly instituted into the vicarage (1851), despite all attempts by Phillpotts to prevent this. Thus the State (once again) was seen to have power to overrule the authority of the Church in matters of doctrine, and many more Tractarian-minded clergy went over to Rome, while some Anglican Evangelicals became Dissenters.

Maskell's involvement led to the publication (1848) of his work on Baptism, and in the following year a study of Absolution in which he justified the revival of Confession within the Anglican Church. But the whole business weighed heavily on Maskell's mind, and with the publication (1850) of his views on the authority of the Privy Council and other concerns of the time, it became clear his faith in his Church was faltering. Soon afterwards he consulted Newman, and was received into the R.C. Church, but never took Holy Orders, and spent the rest of his life in antiquarian pursuits, amassing a huge library of patristic literature, and occasionally indulging in theological controversy, not least over papal infallibility, which got him into trouble with Ultramontanes.

Ritualism was not an empty ceremony, with fancy theatrical goings-on for reasons only of show. As the history of Anglicanism demonstrates, many Ritualist clergymen worked in poor working-class parishes, and perceived ritual as a means of teaching ignorant congregations. Ranting about sacramental doctrine was regarded as counter-productive: what was needed was the beauty of ceremonial. Reverence, beauty, mystery, and devotion could inspire respect (earnest nagging had the opposite effect), and there is no doubt that poor parishes derived great benefit from Ritualist clergymen who taught, set examples, and, by acts of charity and educating the young, brought civilisation to poor urban areas where life was grim. It appears that such clergymen found the ground where they toiled not unreceptive, for some residual Catholic feeling seems to have survived in certain areas, notably in relation to hatred of utilitarianism, the Poor Laws, and fear of dissection, as I have noted elsewhere.

Some Ritualists based their arguments for ceremonial partly on the Ornaments Rubric of the *Book of Common Prayer*: this appeared at the beginning of the Order for Morning and Evening Prayer in 1549, was confirmed in 1604, and retained in the 1662 Prayer Book. It declared that chancels should remain as they had been, and that ornaments of the church 'and of the ministers ... at all times of their ministration' should be retained and used as they were authorised by Parliament in the second year of the reign of King Edward VI. Others, however, felt that the Rubric was out of date, and could not really provide a sound basis for 19th-century Ritualism. Better arguments had to be called upon, and scholarly investigations led to innovation.

Then *The Directorium Anglicanum ... being a manual ... for the Performance of other Rites and Ceremonies ... according to the Ancient Uses of the Church of England ...* etc., edited by John Purchas, came out in 1858. Purporting to use the Ornaments Rubric as its source, it remained a key work for Anglican ceremonial until *c.*1914, but, as Anthony Symondson has pointed out, it owed far more to the *Pontificale Romanum* (1664 edn) and to Giuseppe Baldeschi's *Esposizione delle sacre cerimonie* in Hilarius Dale's translation (1853) than it did to Anglican custom, legality, or history; thus its arguments depended largely on Roman Catholicism of the post-Reformation period.

Some clergymen, perhaps uncomfortably aware of Purchas's shaky claims, tried promoting ideas of continuity of worship with the pre-Reformation, pre-Tridentine Church, the Caroline Church, and the Church of England from the Reformation. They also tended to stick to authorised approved forms of worship, introducing 'Catholic' elements where thought appropriate. However, no matter from which stream it derived, Ritualism had a considerable effect on the design of late Victorian churches.

The Ecclesiological Society became a national body with Beresford Hope as its president in 1845, a year of crisis for the Church of England. As outlined above, Newman, alienated by Evangelical and official reactions to *Tract xc*, feeling very deeply the devastating attack on his arguments by R.C. divines (e.g. Wiseman), had gone over to Rome in that year. Under Frederick Oakeley, a proprietary chapel in London's Margaret Street had become a centre for Tractarian worship, and Oakeley was supported by Beresford Hope. The *Tract xc* ructions and other controversies led Oakeley to follow Newman to Rome, and the Evangelicals were confirmed in their worst fears: Ecclesiology and Ritualism led to Rome, crypto-'papist' mischief lurked in every Pointed niche, and heresy peeped from behind every *Ecclesiologist*-approved clustered pier.

A Church in crisis requires drastic solutions. William Upton Richards, who succeeded Oakeley in 1847, was a member of the Ecclesiological Society, and determined to build a more appropriate setting for Tractarian-inspired devotions. Architectural criticisms in *The Ecclesiologist* demonstrated that many new churches were found wanting, so the Society evolved an idea of providing an exemplar as the way forward, because architect bashing in the press was all very well, but did not invariably improve design.

For Ecclesiologists Gothic had reached its apogee in early 14th-century Second Pointed work, so that was the style agreed, because it united the best elements of Gothic, and was the common architectural language of the most cultivated nations of Europe (this was also Pugin's belief). The theory was that, once architects had become fluent in Second Pointed, a style appropriate to the 19th century would emerge, quite unlike 'decadent' Perpendicular. Of course, the 'decadent' argument does not hold water: the unbiased student of mediæval architecture must conclude that Perpendicular, unlike Gothic elsewhere in Europe, was not 'decadent'; indeed, it was probably the most original and beautiful architectural style ever to emanate from England.

The trouble with 'archæological' or 'copy-book' approaches to design in the tentative early phases of the Victorian Gothic Revival was that architectural works were often timid rehashes of bits of 'approved' buildings, lacking vitality or invention. Another problem was that stone-built churches in heavily polluted cities (notably London), often looked like scrambled pieces of church architecture from rural England placed in contexts where they weathered badly and looked inappropriate. However, contemporary illustrations of interiors, such as that of Ferrey's St Stephen's, Rochester Row, London, had a crisp, hard Second Pointed interior, like a machine-made artefact, that bore little resemblance to a real mediæval church. An appropriate image for a modern church had been found: in architectural circles, pictures matter far more than do words.

In the 1840s, Tractarians, determined to convert an indifferent and sometimes hostile urban proletariat to high-minded Anglicanism for the good of society as a whole, and perceiving that the image of a rural church was not suitable for this purpose,

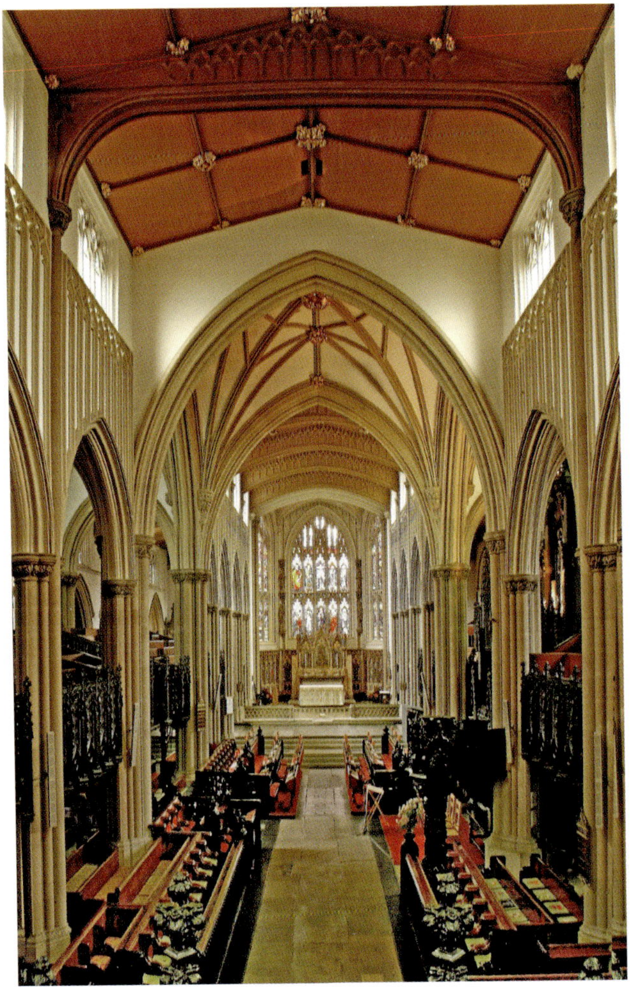

Fig. 6.1 St Peter's, Leeds, Yorkshire (WR) (1839–41), by R.D. Chantrell, showing the chancel and galleries. A scholarly mixture of Perpendicular and Second Pointed styles. The reredos was added (1872) by G.E. Street (Blacksheep Photography for CW [2009]).

decided to encourage the building of fortresses of faith, strong and tough – 'urban minsters' – with high, hard-surfaced walls, coloured bands of stone and brick, big windows and high clerestoreys out of the reach of vandals and above the surrounding buildings, towers set back from the street (but with clearly defined stages), and large chancels. This concept derives from the precedent of the slum mission, mingled with ideas culled from the writings of Pugin and others, and was to present grand and awe-inspiring services, processions, and dignified ritual to attract the urban poor.

A potent model for such an urban minster was created by Walter Farquhar Hook, Vicar of Leeds (1837–59). Hook was a High Churchman, who introduced Tractarian principles with considerable success, but was bitterly opposed by Low Church Evangelicals. His was the guiding spirit behind the rebuilding of St Peter's, Leeds (1837–41) (Fig. 6.1). This large, 'noblest among the noble' of early Victorian urban minsters, was the first attempt by the Church of England to reassert itself architecturally in an industrial town to challenge the spread of Dissent: it had a considerable influence in providing an alternative to Georgian auditory worship. Among innovations was a robed choir performing in the chancel.

Beresford Hope envisaged some other great urban minster, with schools, mechanics' institute, clergy house, and church, which, like the example described in Kingsley's *Alton Locke*, would be an exemplary presence in a rough part of London: the climate had been established and the time had come to transform Richards's Margaret Street chapel. Gradually, various threads drew together: the chapel was to be rebuilt on Tractarian lines; Ecclesiologists wanted to create an exemplary urban minster; and there was a general High Church desire to express confidence in the future of Anglicanism after all the defections to, and challenges from, Rome.

All Saints' Church, Margaret Street

By 1843 William Butterfield was regarded as an arbiter of taste regarding church fittings, from plate to pulpits. Publication of his work began with *Instrumenta Ecclesiastica* in 1844 (when he was elected a member of the Camden Society, as it was then) and continued until 1847. Through Beresford Hope he was appointed architect for the rebuilding of St Augustine's College in Canterbury, and by 1849 had designed the Tractarian College at Millport, Greater Cumbrae (the Cathedral of the Isles) for George Frederick Boyle, later (1869) 6th Earl of Glasgow.

Butterfield was chosen as architect for the Ecclesiological Society's model church, for which Beresford Hope provided not only funds, but many ideas. Several priests were to live communally on the site to keep up the daily requirements of Tractarian observance, while the musical tradition already established was to be maintained and given an appropriate setting. Thus a clergy house and a choir school were to share the cramped, almost square site with the church itself. In 1849 the area in which All Saints' was to be built consisted of dingy houses and shops: the urban minster would provide Tractarian services and a ministry, and moveable seats instead of pews were to be provided, thus destroying the undesirable social divisions of rented pews.

All Saints', designed and built 1849–59, was one of the first major Victorian buildings in which constructional colour was used, and it marks the beginning of a powerful, robust phase of the Gothic Revival. It is an experiment in encrustation with a skin of brick and tile, rather than full, deep, true structural polychromy, but it provided an admirable exemplar of permanent colour in the facing materials, and flags the start of Butterfield's polychrome style. Mindful of the incongruous and shabby appearance of ragstone in the urban setting, Butterfield chose red brick with bands, voussoirs, and diaper-work of black brick, with Bath stone dressings, for the exterior.

Butterfield placed the church on the northern part of the site, with the choir school, masters' rooms, and library in the south-west corner, and the clergy house in the south-east, both buildings joined to the church and providing a frame to the small court that is approached through an arched gateway from the street. This court, set over the common basement, is almost claustrophobic, and the effect of verticality (enhanced by the deliberately oversized buttress and pinnacle on the south face of the aisle beside the gabled porch to the church) is stupendous. High, banded, and

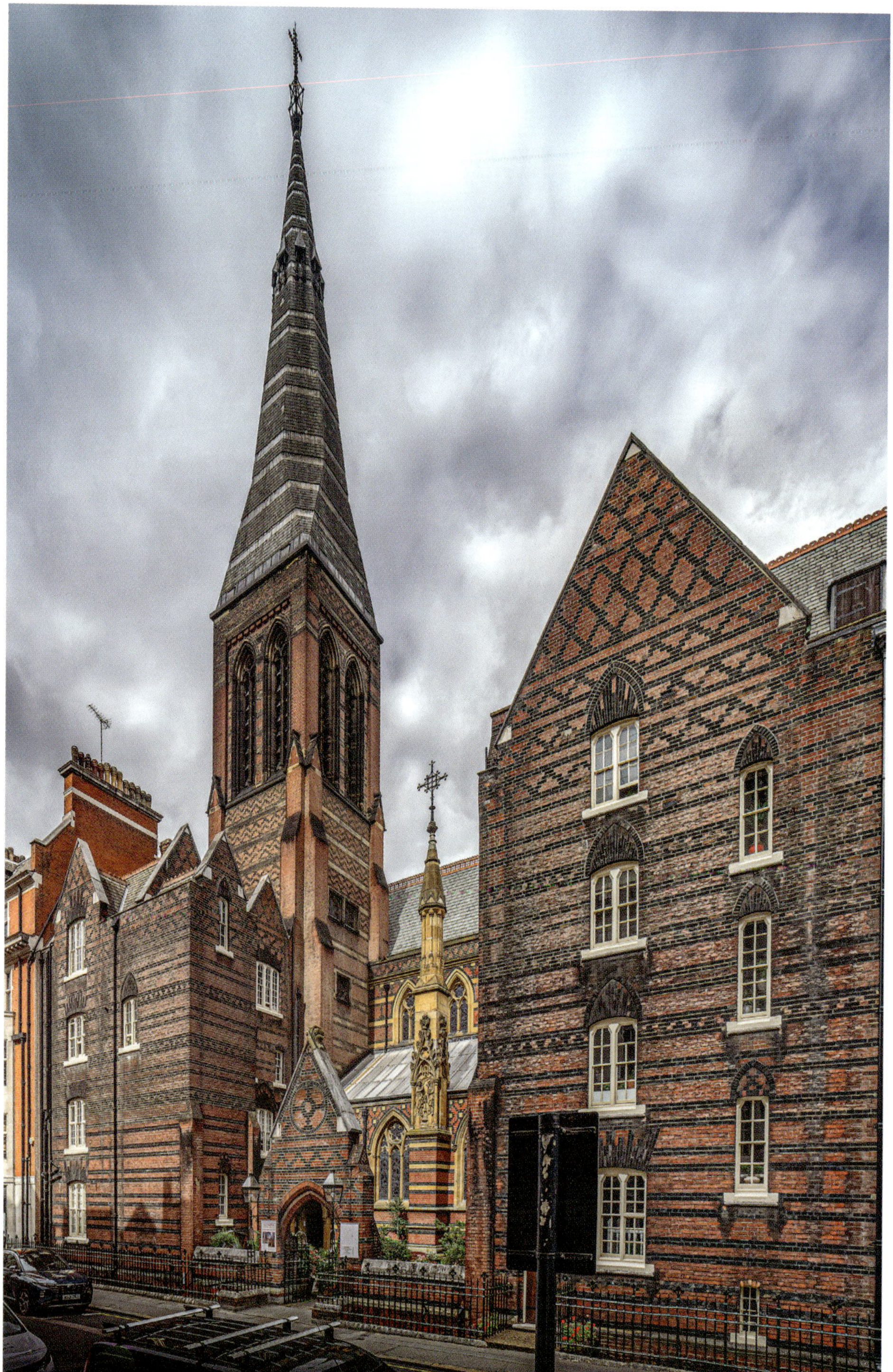

Fig. 6.2 All Saints', Margaret Street, Westminster (1849–59), an urban citadel of faith, by William Butterfield, showing the decorative brickwork, tower and broach spire, and clergy house and school on either side of the entrance court, and over-sized pinnacled buttress (CWR [2021]).

diapered walls, the steeply pitched roofs, the tough tracery of the church windows, the chunky sash window frames of the school and house, and the soaring banded broach spire enter the language of the Sublime (Fig. 6.2). Here is no feeble potpourri timidly garnered from mediæval rural churches, but a powerful, vital, tough urban design, brilliantly conceived for its position. The tightness of the site dictated a solution where the ingenious planning was also dependent upon a free type of fenestration: here was Pugin's 'True Picturesque' of his Bishop's Palace at Birmingham (1839–41) developed to new heights of invention. Here was a modern church to satisfy the demands of the revived Anglican ritual as well as the aims of architectural excellence: it was a true citadel of faith, much influenced by Continental Gothic precedents.

Yet what styles can be found at All Saints'? Certainly there is Middle Pointed work in the tracery of the church windows, the belfry stage of the tower, and the tall, pinnacled buttress (cunningly placed to draw the eye to the entrance which is approached diagonally across the court), but diaper patterns in brickwork were associated with Perpendicular or Tudor work, while the tower and the spire would not be out of place in northern Germany. At the west end there are even echoes of Monza Cathedral. So there are English, Italian, and *Backsteingotik* precedents in the composition as well, but the design as a whole was startlingly new: Butterfield created a perception of the past and invented a new and vital synthesis of styles. G.L. Hersey likened the arrival of All Saints' in the context of muted early Victorian London to that of a 'Congo chieftain' appearing in a performance of *Les Sylphides*, and although that was perhaps overstating the case, the building made a considerable impression. As Eastlake noted, the use of red brick for the external walls 'was a novelty, brick having been hitherto only used for the cheap churches' (although it had been employed by Pugin at St Chad's, Birmingham), and the 'tower and spire were of a shape and proportions which puzzled the antiquaries, scandalised the architects, and sent unprofessional critics to their wit's end with amazement. Passers-by ... asked what manner of architecture this might be ... and which could be properly referred to no century except the nineteenth.'

If the massing, colour, composition, and detail of the exterior are arresting, the interior is even more so, and can still astonish. The Tractarian arrangement is apparent: the deep, wide, high chancel with raised floor creates a visual climax, emphasising the importance of the altar (Fig. 6.3). Although the square-ended chancel is of the English type, the stepped arrangement up to the gradine is German, while the vaulted ceiling recalls the church of San Francesco in Assisi. Much of Butterfield's structural polychromy derives from northern Germany, but the interiors owe more to Italy (the circular motifs of the nave arcades are suggested by Venetian prototypes), so he achieved a stylistic mix in which Southern and Northern European Gothic precedents played their parts. Controlled polychrome patterns of strict geometrical shapes are created using granite, marbles, bricks (glazed and unglazed), tiles, and stone dressings with coloured mastic inlay. Nave arcade piers have vigorously carved alabaster capitals on shafts of polished red Peterhead granite set on black marble bases; the moulded arches are developed Second Pointed; and the spandrels are decorated with rich patterns of coloured bricks, tiles, and other materials.

From the very moment when its walls first arose, All Saints' has been recognised as a building of exceptional originality and significance. G.E. Street said of it that of

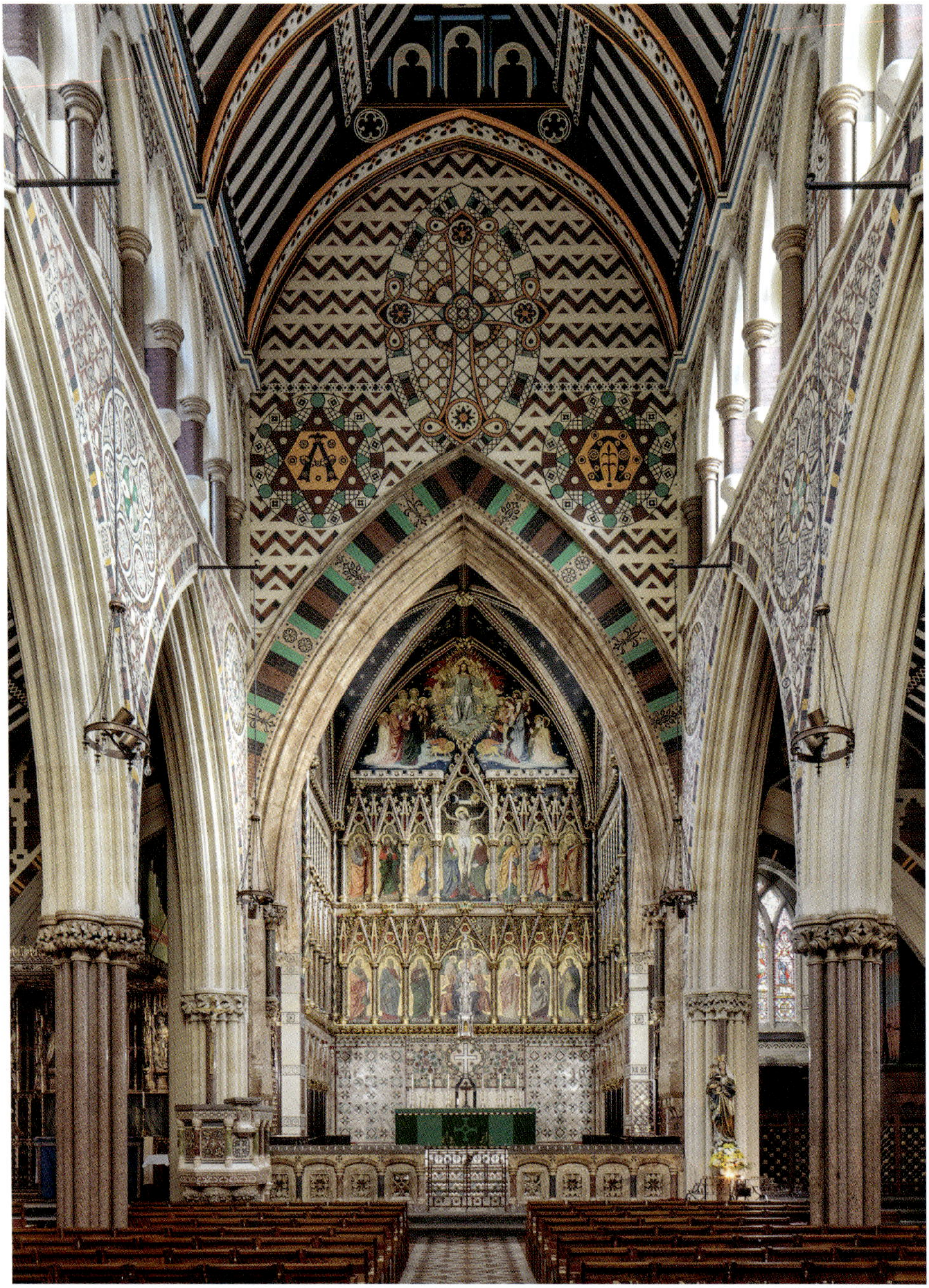

Fig. 6.3 All Saints', Margaret Street: the chancel arch enriched with glowing polychrome decorations. Note the low cancelli between the nave and chancel (an alternative to a screen) and the splendid pulpit. The vaulted chancel may have been influenced by St Francis's Church, Assisi (HEA photo CWR 1657873 [2014]).

all new churches it was 'the most beautiful, vigorous, thoughtful, and original', and H.H. Statham identified it in 1912 as 'the one Gothic revival church which is still as interesting ... as when it was built'. *The British Almanac* declared the interior of All Saints' to be 'beyond question ... the most gorgeous ... in the kingdom'. Colour and æsthetic effects were contrived to arise from 'construction' rather than from 'superaddition', and thus differ from Pugin's work at St Giles's, Cheadle, where the decorations are painted on plaster. While Webb and Ruskin probably were catalysts towards the decision to apply theories of polychromy to practical use, the actual source for the essential elements of the patterns on the internal walls was very likely *Specimens of the Geometrical Mosaic of the Middle Ages* (1848) by Matthew Digby Wyatt. William Dyce himself painted the reredos and chancel, considered by Beresford Hope to be 'no whit inferior to the vault of S. Jacques at Liège, or Sta. Anastasia at Verona'.

However, All Saints' was to spawn its imitators, notably the 'Rogue Goths' (*see* Chapter 7), who showed off too much for some tastes, and were so given to restless 'Go' that they were censured by their peers. 'Great' Scott was none too happy with some of these developments, for in his *Personal and Professional Recollections* (1879) he complained of

> no end to the oddities ... Ruskinism, such as would make Ruskin's very hair stand on end; Butterfieldism, gone mad with its endless stripings of red and black bricks; violent strainings ... and great successes in producing something very weak; attempts at beauty resulting in ugliness, and attempts at ugliness attended with unhoped-for success. All these have given a wild absurdity to much of the architecture of the last seven or eight years [i.e. *c.*1864–72].

There can be no question of Butterfield's impact with his great church. Contemporary opinion found nothing effeminate or luxurious in All Saints': on the contrary, it was full of virility. To *The Ecclesiologist*, All Saints' had affinities with Pre-Raphaelite paintings, and the startling use of colour was seen to parallel the exploitation of certain violent tones in the work of Millais. The overall effect, however, was austere, manly, and even Sublime. Much has been written about Butterfield's alleged hatred of beauty, his deliberate cultivation of the 'ugly', his 'holy zebra' or 'stripey bacon' style of Gothic, his use of the 'discordant', his 'ruthlessness', and his 'assaults' on the senses. Much of this, including speculations that he was uneducated, untravelled, and puritanical, is nonsense, as is the ridiculous suggestion that his work was, somehow, sadomasochistic.

All Saints' is a brilliant piece of three-dimensional design, with assured and complex massing on a difficult site; it demonstrates the practical use of materials (which have worn well) suitable for the sooty atmosphere of a Victorian city; the interior decorations were, to a large extent, permanent, and are extremely rich and colourful; and its inventive architecture was based on a rich historical set of precedents, yet it could not be confused with a mediæval church or damned as a mere copy of an *Echt*-Gothic structure. Indeed, All Saints' was an intensely modern building when it was conceived. Sensible materials, used with imagination, an ingenious plan, and a scholarly yet inventive approach to design, based on a sound understanding of precedents from many countries and periods, combine in one of the Victorian period's greatest works of architecture. Its influence was to be considerable, as Thomas James was to note in his 'On the Use of Brick in Ecclesiastical Architecture' in *The Ecclesiologist* of 1861, and G.E. Street was to recognise. The building showed that the Gothic Revival could be freed from the slavish copying of precedents. Its influence spurred designers on to new things even before it was completed: All Saints' was the Tractarian begetter of hosts of polychrome churches, and the finest memorial to the Oxford Movement, glowing, noble, and assured.

Other Churches by Butterfield

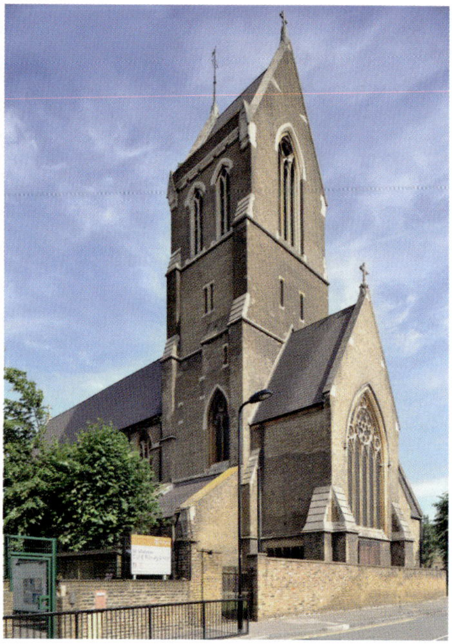

Fig. 6.4 Innovative, tall, saddleback-roofed tower over the choir in the French fashion, St Matthias's, Stoke Newington, London (1849–53), by William Butterfield (GB [2010]).

Butterfield was a prolific architect, whose designs were rarely dull. Important ecclesiastical works by him include St Matthias's, Stoke Newington, London (1849–53 – his first completed London church, the interior of which was badly damaged in the 1939–45 war – which demonstrates his control of structural massing and composition [Fig. 6.4]); All Saints', Babbacombe, Devon (1865–74 – which contains one of Butterfield's most colourful fonts); Keble College, Oxford (1868–82 – as Goodhart-Rendel said, 'one of the three or four buildings in Oxford of most architectural importance'), with a stunning chapel of 1873–6, an outstanding tour de force of strident angularity, stripey polychromy, and massive, vertical, thrusting, oversized buttresses (Fig. 6.5); St Augustine's, Queen's Gate, Kensington, London (1870–86) – a tall, strikingly polychrome building, with double bell-cote at the west end, reminiscent of the west front of the Klosterkirche, Chorin, Brandenburg (after 1273), contrasting with the ranges of stucco-faced Italianate houses on either side); and the rich assemblage of buildings at Rugby School, Warwickshire, including the chapel (1870–2 – one of Butterfield's most assured and successful compositions).

Indeed, at Keble and Rugby the polychromy is spectacular and the scale tremendous, overwhelming, Sublime. So Butterfield continued to use vivid 'structural' polychrome treatments after the 1860s, when it was starting to go out of favour with younger architects, but he often created very beautiful things, such as the exquisite font (Fig. 6.6) at the great mediæval church of St Mary, Ottery St Mary, Devon, where works of restoration took place under him and Woodyer (1847–50). Unfortunately, many of Butterfield's radiant polychrome interiors were tamed by means of plentiful applications of white paint (as was inflicted on St Augustine's, Queen's Gate, in 1927–8, by Martin Travers).

Some idea of Butterfield's importance can be gleaned from studying his works on the estates of just one high-minded aristocratic landowner, William Henry Dawnay, who succeeded his parson father as 7th Viscount Downe in 1846. An Oxford man, Downe determined to build churches, schools, vicarages, and model cottages for the workers on his estates, and commissioned Butterfield to design them. In 1853–4, in Yorkshire WR, Butterfield realised the churches, vicarages, and schools for Downe at East Cowick (Holy Trinity), Hensall (St Paul's), and Pollington (St John's), and in the NR, at Sessay, some of his earliest works for Downe were the school, lych-gate,

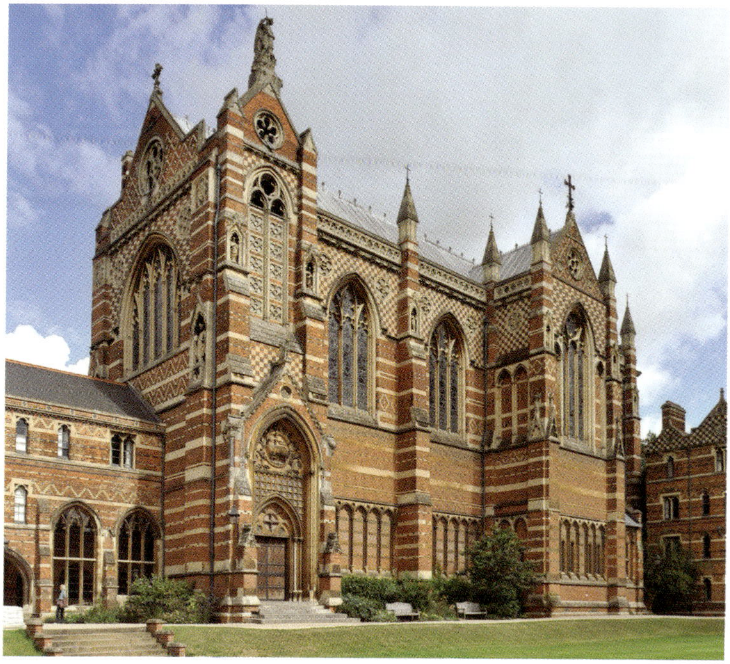

Fig. 6.5 Keble College Chapel, Oxford (1873–6), by Butterfield: a dazzling display of structural polychromy (GB [2014]).

church of St Cuthbert (1847–8), and several pleasing cottages. However, the noblest of all the churches Butterfield designed for Downe was undoubtedly St James the Great, Baldersby St James (1856–8) (Fig. 6.7), the splendid interior of which is a fine example of his structural polychrome finishes (Fig. 6.8). Downe never saw it completed, as he died in 1857, and is interred within an enclosure in the churchyard, east of the church. Butterfield's work in the village was impressive: the handsome vicarage, school, and several brick cottages (1855–9) are of historical importance for their freedom of composition, emphasis on roofs, hipped dormers, and use of sash windows, clearly influences on the work of Philip Speakman Webb, starting with the Red House, Upton, Bexleyheath, Kent (1859–60), a building for which the former vicarage at Hensall also provides design precedents. Other examples of

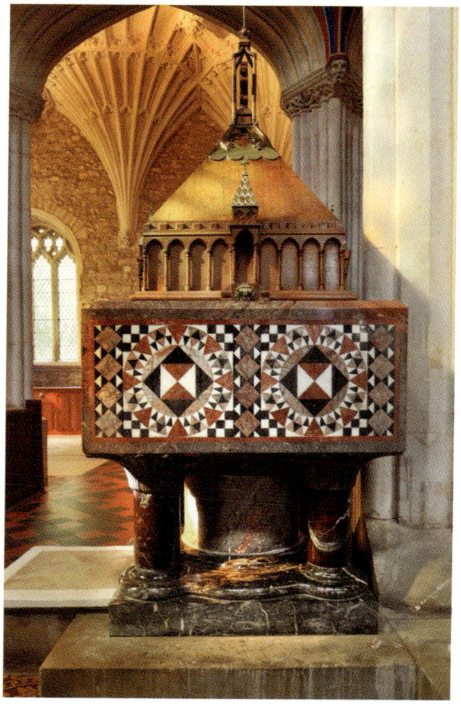

Fig. 6.6 Font by Butterfield (1850) in the restored mediæval church at Ottery St Mary, Devon, a fine example of his early polychrome inlaid work, using local marbles (GB [2014]).

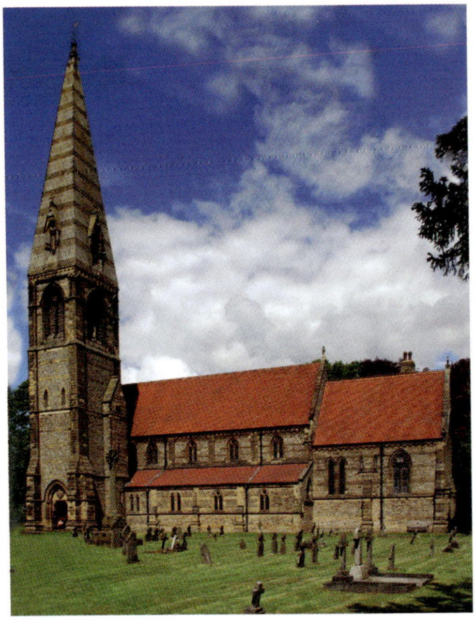

Fig. 6.7 St James's, Baldersby St James, Yorkshire (NR) (1856–8), by Butterfield, the grandest of his churches for Viscount Downe. In the style of the late 13th century, the steeple, visible for miles around, is almost detached from the church (JSC [2021]).

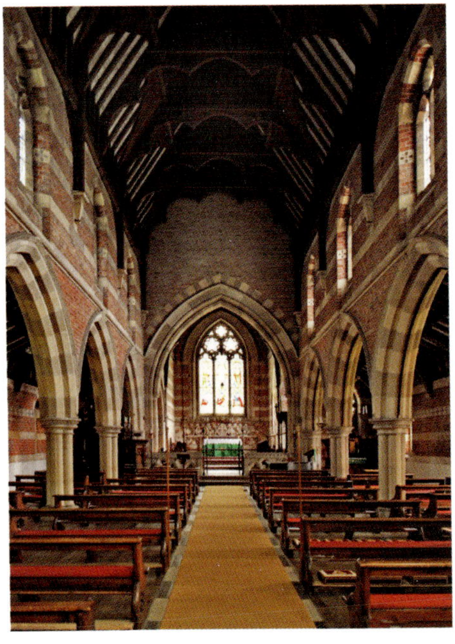

Fig. 6.8 St James's, Baldersby St James. Note the brick and stone bands, many with sunken inlaid patterns, and the busy timber roof. The chancel is panelled in alabaster, and there are low cancelli separating it from the nave (GB [2021]).

Butterfield's cottage architecture for Lord Downe were built at Butterwick, Yorkshire ER, and Ashwell, Rutland. In the latter case, the pretty cottages are similar to those in Baldersby St James, but slightly earlier. In Ashwell, too, Butterfield was responsible for the major restoration at the church (1851) (Fig. 6.9).

Eastlake declared that among the host of modern churches erected in England *c.*1850–72, none bore the stamp of originality and thought in a more eminent degree than those by Butterfield, yet later commentators completely contradicted this, sometimes with ludicrous claims. J.T. Emmett, for example, suggested that the 'speckled and spotted coloured brick patterns' of All Saints', Margaret Street, were indicative of infantilism (careful study suggests nothing of the sort); Kenneth Clark, more than half a century later, expounded on Butterfield's 'sadistic hatred' of beauty, and that there was a streak of Dickensian cruelty in the man; Summerson observed that Butterfield's alleged love of 'ugliness' amounted to 'purposeful sadism'; Pevsner, with his usual bias, saw glorious Keble College as a kind of proto-Brutalism; Reginald Turnor, quoting Christopher Hobhouse, wrote of some of Butterfield's buildings as having 'a certain evil fascination'; and even Paul Thompson, Butterfield's biographer, in 1963 seemed to adhere to the 'harsh' and 'cruel' interpretation, but shortly afterwards decided that such a view was all wrong. G.L. Hersey, however, in 1972, could still hold that in certain contexts a building such as All Saints', Margaret Street, is 'relatively sadistic, or at least brutal', and that an illustration of Butterfield's early design for the font and baptistry of All Saints', published in *The Builder* in 1853, 'really does look like a chamber for bizarre tortures – the sanctum of some ecclesiastical pervert. The

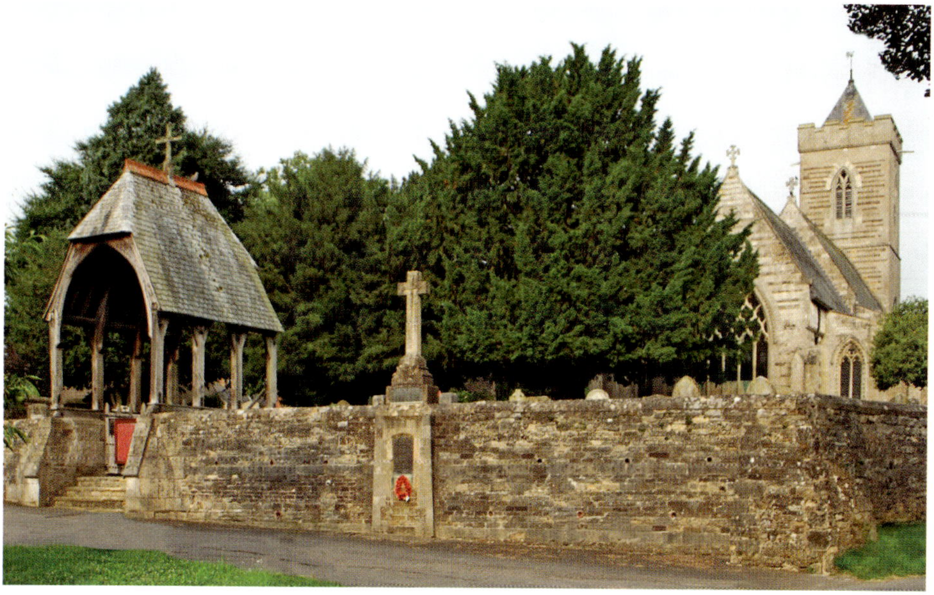

Fig. 6.9 St Mary's, Ashwell, Rutland, restored for Viscount Downe on Ecclesiological principles by Butterfield (1851), who was responsible for the east window, with reticulated tracery and ballflower decoration. Butterfield's lych-gate, with half-hipped tile roof and simple carpentry, displays a pungent originality typical of his work (JSC [2021]).

victim would be sealed into the font and the cover lowered on top of him as his cries filled the marble church'.

I find these opinions of Butterfield's work bizarre, indicative of that common English problem called Received Opinion, whereby one commentator follows what another has said, and does not exercise independent judgement. It is also called 'looking with one's ears'. To me, All Saints', Margaret Street, is a perfect setting for a scented Eucharist, with incense rising through coloured rays of sunlight, and the hard surfaces of the polychrome walls reflecting the glorious polyphony of a Byrd Mass or the heart-wrenching harmonies of a Bruckner motet.

Every stone, every brick, every tile, every element of the extraordinarily rich interior speaks of devotion, and the whole ensemble silences the garrulous, entrances the eye, brings doubt to the sceptic, and humbles the proud. It is a glorious achievement, one of the finest works of architecture anywhere in England, of any period.

The French Connection

Eugène-Emmanuel Viollet-le-Duc became a convinced Goth in the 1830s, and in 1854 the first volume of his *Dictionnaire Raisonné de l'Architecture Française du XIe au XVIe Siècle* (completed 1868) was published, from which date the Frenchman became an important arbiter of the Gothic Revival, championing the architecture of mediæval France as well as emphasising the significance of structure, purpose, dynamics, techniques, and the visible expression of means: his rationalist beliefs were enshrined in his *Entretiens sur l'Architecture* (1863–72). It was through Viollet-le-Duc's fine illustrations that a taste for French Gothic (especially early French Gothic) began to supersede previous English preferences for early Middle Pointed and the then current interest in polychrome Italian Gothic, although sometimes French and Italian themes were mingled. William Burges said of Viollet-le-Duc that 'we all crib from [him] ..., although probably not one ... in ten ever reads the text'. As Burges admitted, he, George Gilbert 'Great' Scott, Waterhouse, and many lesser men plundered the fine illustrations in the *Dictionnaire* for suitable details, and the twelfth *Entretien* may have suggested to Scott the exposed girders and ironwork of the main stair of the Midland Grand Hotel at St Pancras.

Burges called the *Dictionnaire* a 'wonderful monument of human knowledge and human industry'. However, Viollet's interpretation of Gothic was as a rational style, the construction clearly defined by buttresses supporting ribs and vaults, the whole essentially a skeletal system, with curtain walls and webs really non-structural infill. This notion of Gothic became widely accepted, especially by apologists for the much later Modern Movement (even though surviving ruined Gothic buildings might prompt different conclusions, as when the ribs of vaults had fallen away, leaving the webs still in place). Viollet had no time for Ruskin's view of mouldings as the joyous creations of happy craftsmen, but saw them as having rational functions, such as throwing the water off, preventing staining, or differentiating one part of a structure from another (e.g. a shaft from a capital or base). He saw Gothic as a purely tectonic system, one that had no connection with religion: thus his views were wholly opposite to those of Pugin and others who allied the style with 'Christian' or even 'Catholic' positions.

Nevertheless, Viollet-le-Duc's influence became perceptible as English architects 'began to introduce French details in their work', as Eastlake put it. However, Viollet's rationalism was strongly expressed, and terrified many: some were repelled by what they saw as the Frenchman's failings in sensibility, and Burges, while finding the illustrations in *Entretiens* useful, had mixed feelings about the texts, regarding some of Viollet's theories as pernicious.

Some Works by George Edmund Street

As early as 1852 G.E. Street was promoting his 'True Principles of Pointed Architecture', and arguing for development, drawing on a wider geographical area than that favoured by Pugin. In his *Brick and Marble in the Middle Ages* (1855), Street drew attention to a wide range of Continental precedents. Reaction to the strong polychrome and æsthetic of so-called 'Ruskinian Gothic' set in with the 1860s, and models for a purer, more robust, primitive, and essential Gothic began to be identified in early French buildings. Monochrome, tough, even rough, early French Gothic seemed to offer architects a new ideal: stern French exemplars, such as those of Laon Cathedral, or the massive early Gothic churches of Burgundy, seemed more vigorous, less effete, than the luxuriant Second Pointed so beloved by Ecclesiologists. French First Pointed (with its massiveness, grandeur of scale, and complete lack of frippery) was seen as more appropriate to the needs of designers of urban citadels of faith in the towns of the 1860s, for it was bold, broad, strong, stern, masculine, and uncompromisingly robust. The so-called muscular phase of the Gothic Revival had arrived.

G.E. Street was one of the most distinguished architects of the Gothic Revival: an inventive designer, his work was rarely dull, and sometimes rose to greatness. One of

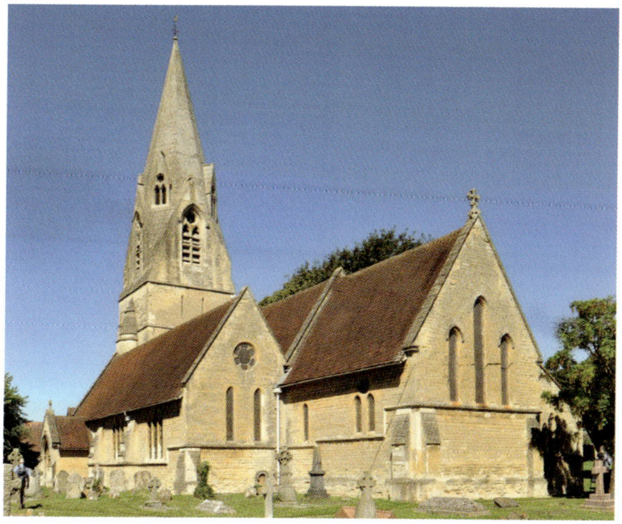

Fig. 6.10 St Mary the Virgin, Wheatley, Oxfordshire (1855–7), by G.E. Street. In the English First Pointed style, it has no clerestorey, and its nave, chancel, and aisles are separately expressed. The powerful belfry steeple (completed 1868) has an octagonal spire set on four steeply pitched gabled elements each containing openings of elementary plate-tracery. Confidently composed, it owes something to Street's first church, St Mary the Virgin, Par, Cornwall (1846–8) (GB [2016]).

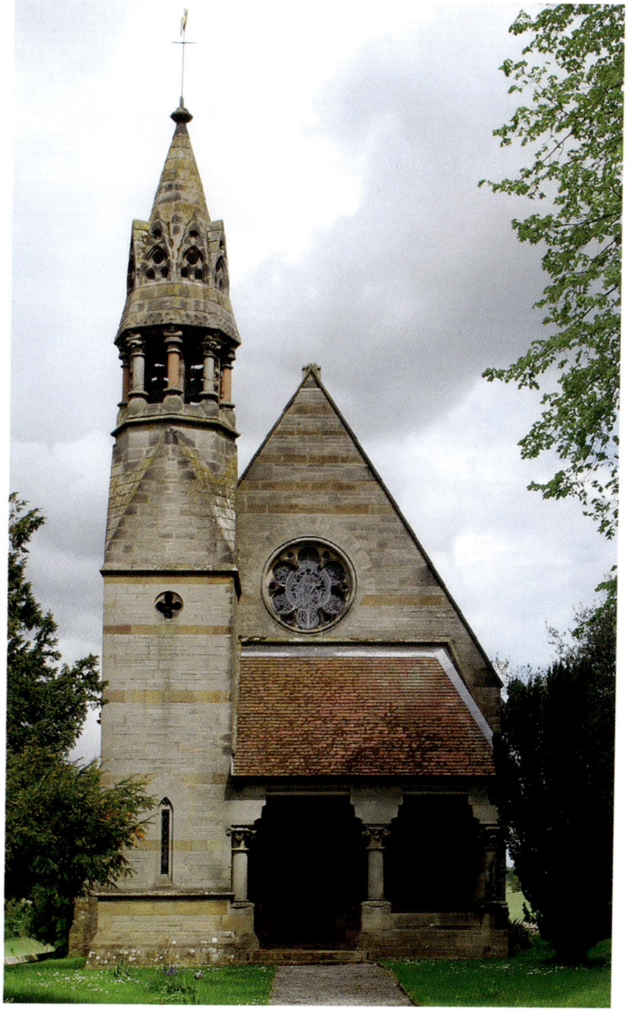

Fig. 6.11 West front of St John's, Howsham, Yorkshire (ER) (1859–60), a little Middle Pointed masterpiece by G.E. Street demonstrating his skills in making architecture of a simple building (JSC [2021]).

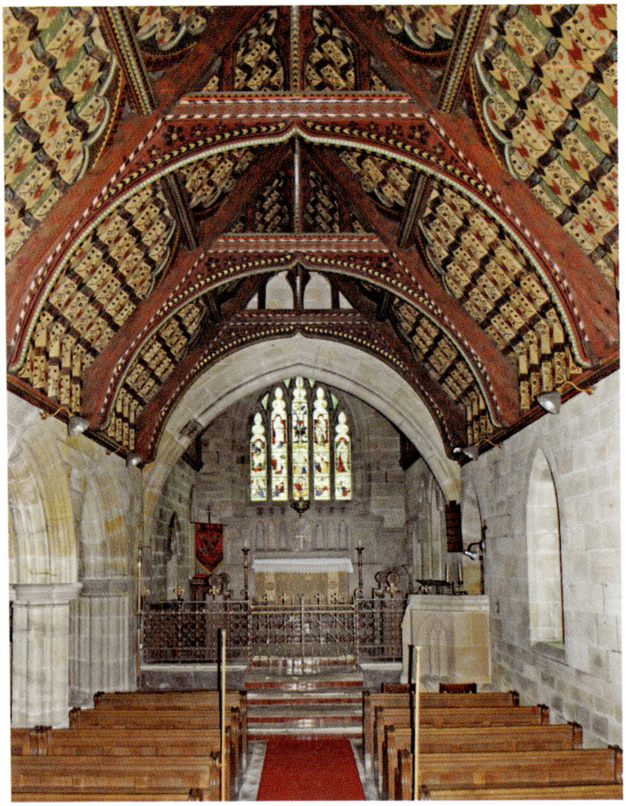

Fig. 6.12 St Peter's, Helperthorpe, Yorkshire (ER) (1871–3), by G.E. Street for Sir Tatton Sykes II, Bt, with north aisle added (1893) by Temple Moore. Note the richly coloured roof, stone pulpit, low iron screen, and chancel raised so that the altar is highly visible (JSC [2021]).

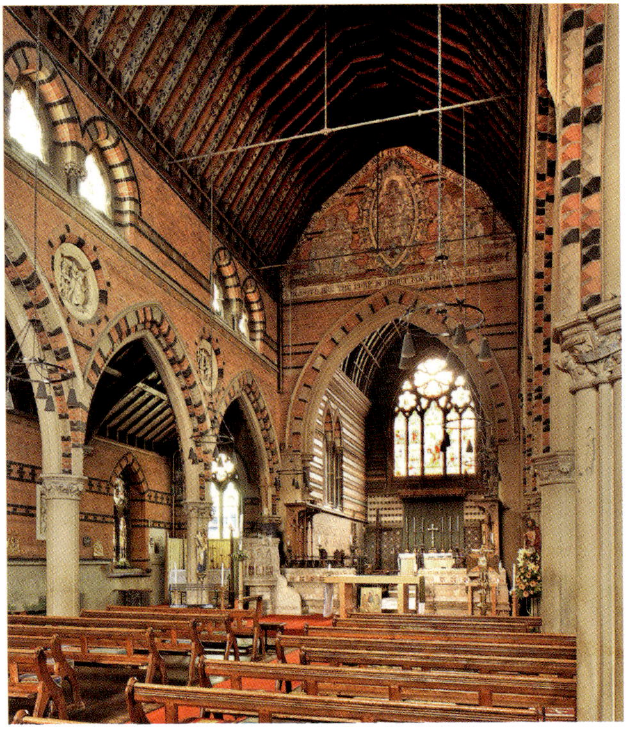

Fig. 6.13 All Saints', Boyne Hill, Maidenhead, Berkshire (1854–7), by G.E. Street. The style is Geometrical Middle Pointed, with structural polychromy of brick with stone dressings: the architectural treatment is derived from Street's studies in Italy and Germany, especially in the chancel, where walls are clad in bands of blue-black and white brick, buff and red tiles, and slabs of veined marbles and alabaster. *The Ecclesiologist* declared it was 'seldom more pleased' with any design (GB [2017]).

his happiest compositions is St Mary the Virgin, Wheatley, Oxfordshire, designed in 1855 in the English First Pointed style, with varied groups of lancets, sparing use of plate-tracery, and powerful steeple belfry, completed in 1868 (Fig. 6.10). Even finer, perhaps, is his tiny St John's, Howsham (1859–60), his first in Yorkshire ER, a little masterpiece designed for Hannah Cholmley in memory of her husband, George (d.1857). Eastlake observed that there was no better test of an architect's skill 'than when he has to design a very small village church' with sanctuary, porch, pulpit, and belfry, but Street showed how to do just that at Howsham, where he 'gave the chancel an apsidal end, decorated its windows with *escoinson* shafts, cusped the chancel-arch, reduced the pulpit to a little quadrant in plan (just the thing for a corner), planned a snug little porch with a lean-to roof for the west end, and carried up a picturesque belfry turret by its side. The effect of the whole is charming ... It is simplicity itself, but simplicity with meaning and effect' (Fig. 6.11). Street also designed several churches in Yorkshire ER for Sir Tatton Sykes II, Bt, including St Mary's, Fimber (1869–71), St Peter's, Helperthorpe (1871–3) (Fig. 6.12), St Andrew's, East Heslerton (1877), St Mary's, Thixendale (1868–70), St Mary's, Wansford (1866–8), and St Mary's, West Lutton (1872–3 – with tile-hung balustraded belfry and shingled spire, vaulted chancel, iron screen, and richly painted roof).

In Street's works of the 1850s and 1860s, a massiveness combined with deceptive simplicity can be found, and from the mid-1850s he used bold constructional polychromy, notably in All Saints', Boyne Hill, Maidenhead, Berkshire (1854–7), St James-the-Less, Westminster (1859–61), Sts Philip and James, North Oxford (1860–6), and St John the Evangelist, Torquay, Devon (1861–85).

At Boyne Hill, Street's polychrome masterpiece forms the nucleus of a group of parochial buildings of 1854–65. The interior of the church glows with rich structural colour (Fig. 6.13), and the ceiling is painted. Glass by Hardman, marble inlay and sculpture by Thomas Earp, and ironwork by James Leaver complete the exotic ensemble. Both St James-the-Less and Sts Philip and James have Continental-inspired apsidal chancels, and have a massiveness, solidity, and toughness not present in Butterfield's designs. For instance, Street's monolithic circular piers are quite unlike the clustered shafts in All Saints', Margaret Street, and he favoured the earlier, primitive plate-tracery to the more developed bar-tracery so beloved by Pugin and Scott. The Westminster church has a powerful polychrome brick interior (Fig. 6.14), but at Oxford the influence of 13th-century First Pointed Burgundian prototypes is pronounced, notably in the belfry stage of the tower, in the massive, oversized lucarnes on the broach spire, in the plate-tracery of the apsidal chancel, and in the severe lancets.

Much less massive in treatment (although the church is large), but with pronounced vertical elements, was Street's St Mary Magdalene's, Paddington, London (1867–73): the style is First Pointed, the chancel is a series of cants, and the spire rises directly from a polygonal striped belfry stage over the tower (Fig. 6.15). The building was designed for Richard Temple West (a former curate at All Saints', Margaret Street), as the first centre for High Anglicanism in what was then a poor part of the capital. The site, acquired in 1865, was a restricted wedge-shaped plot between two roads, and had a pronounced slope, which Street levelled by creating a massive arched and vaulted crypt, placing the east end within the narrow, pointed end of the site. St Mary Magdalene's interior is a robust and assured composition (Fig. 6.16), but curious as well, for the southern nave arcade has conventional clustered piers, and the northern has its arches subdivided in two on octagonal piers alternating with slender colonnettes. The tall clerestorey has intersecting tracery on the inner plane, with marble shafts. Walls are of striped brick and stone, and the roof of the nave is painted with panels of saints, etc., by Daniel Bell. More elaborately finished is the chancel, faced with alabaster, and with mosaic panels by the firm established by Antonio Salviati: the reredos has gilded figures by Thomas Earp.

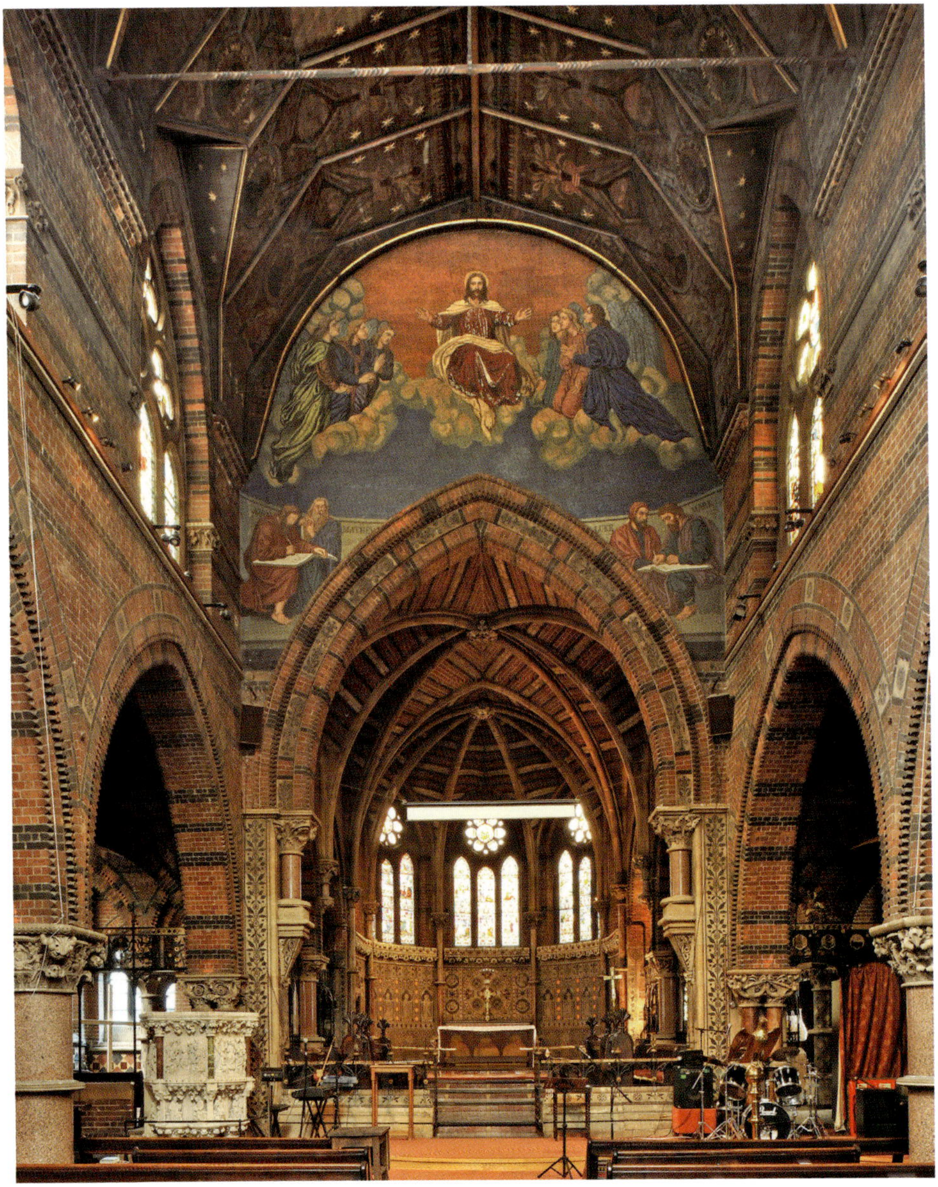

Fig. 6.14 St James-the-Less, Pimlico, Westminster (1859–61), by G.E. Street, with polychrome brickwork, mastic decoration, and Maw's red and yellow glazed tiles, apsidal vaulted chancel, and massive piers. The rasping, saw-like, harsh effects of the edges of the arcades should be noted. Over the chancel arch is a Last Judgement mosaic based on a fresco (1861) by G.F. Watts (GB [2017]).

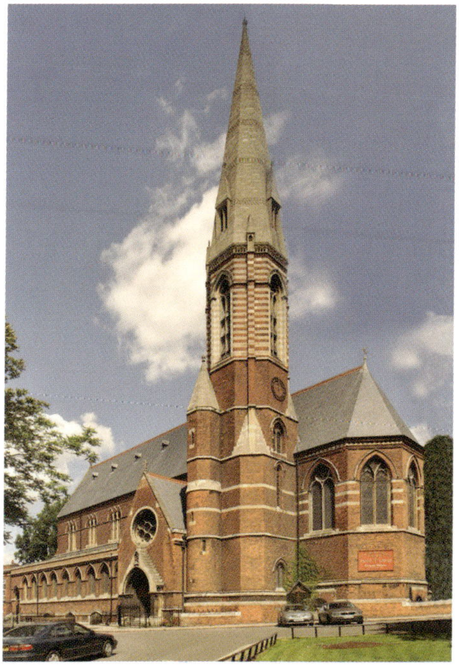

Fig. 6.15 St Mary Magdalene's, Paddington, London (1867–73), by Street. The style is First Pointed, the chancel ends in a series of cants, and the stone spire rises directly from a polygonal striped belfry stage on the tower (GB [2017]).

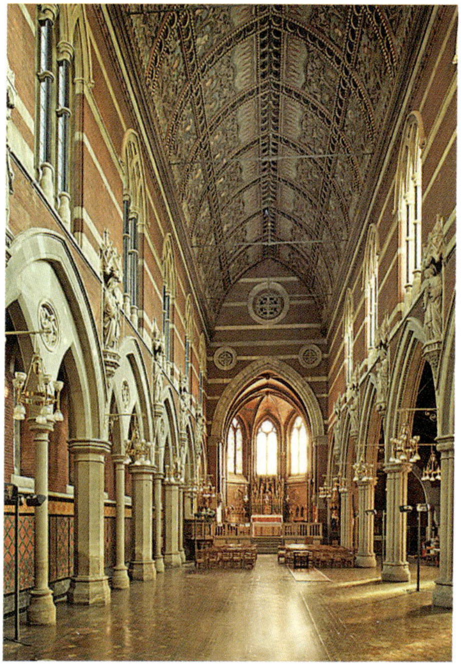

Fig. 6.16 St Mary Magdalene's, Paddington, showing the sumptuous treatment of the nave arcades and ceiling. On the left is a narrow passage aisle (GB [2017]).

In all these churches Street displayed his mastery of form, his sureness of touch in placing elements together, and his apparently effortless drawing on scholarship for his themes.

Other Mid-Victorian Churches

The 1860s were rarely dull when it came to church design, and colour was certainly well to the fore. An unexpectedly rich interior can be found in St Leonard's, part of the Beauchamp Almshouses, at Newland, Worcestershire (1862–4), by P.C. Hardwick: paired marble columns in the early French Gothic style, the beautifully decorated walls, and the splendidly opulent sedilia are particularly enjoyable (Fig. 6.17).

William White, who worked in George Gilbert 'Great' Scott's office as a young man, employed flint, brick, and stone on his small church at Smannell in Hampshire (1856), which also has tracery set flush with the outside plane of the walls, and tumbled brickwork on the porch. White's essays in large churches began with his unfinished All Saints', Notting Hill (begun 1852, consecrated 1861), but his masterpiece is St Michael and All Angels, Lyndhurst, Hampshire (1858–70). The latter is a big red- and yellow-brick First Pointed structure, with odd tracery and strange cross gables: the interior, of yellow, white, and two colours of red brick, exploits the rasping notched bricks already encountered in Street's St James-the-Less, Westminster, but White's piers have dark shafts around them, with elaborate capitals and shaft

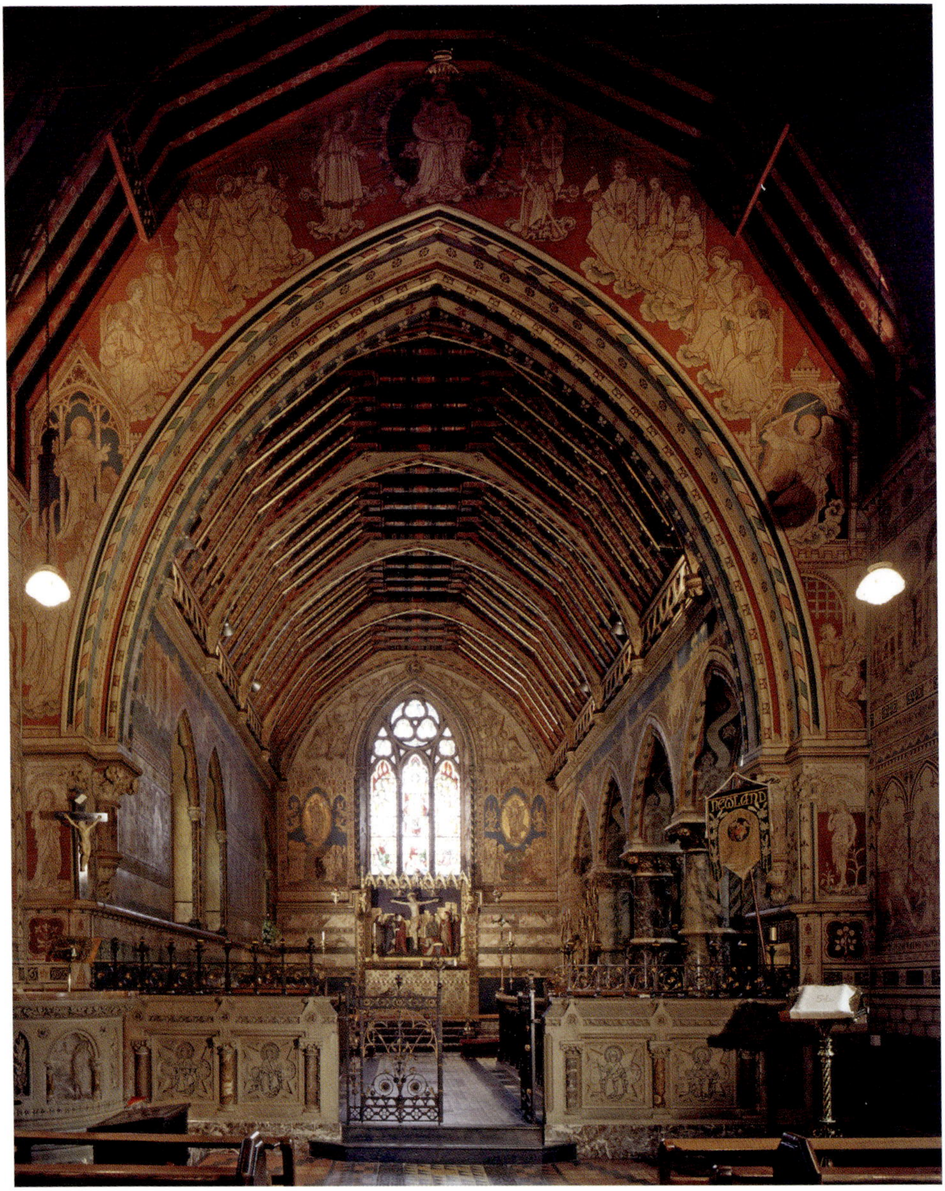

Fig. 6.17 St Leonard's, Beauchamp Almshouses, Newland, Worcestershire, by P.C. Hardwick in an early French Gothic style, consecrated 1864. The chancel is exceptionally rich, and the entire ensemble is a fine example of Victorian polychrome decoration carried out by Clayton & Bell, following a scheme devised by Dr Pusey's protégé, James Skinner, first Vicar of Newland, warden of the Beauchamp Community. Over the chancel arch is the Last Judgement, with Christ in Majesty flanked by the archangels Gabriel and Michael, with the Twelve Apostles Throned (MC B110901/RIBAC 138908 [2001]).

rings carved by George Whitfield Seale. Roof trusses are decorated with human-size angels (Fig. 6.18). St Michael's is of particular interest because of its furnishings, which constitute a monument to the Pre-Raphaelite movement.

However, the Lyndhurst church (which led *The Ecclesiologist* to regret the 'affectation of originality') lacks the insistence on robustness, muscularity, and

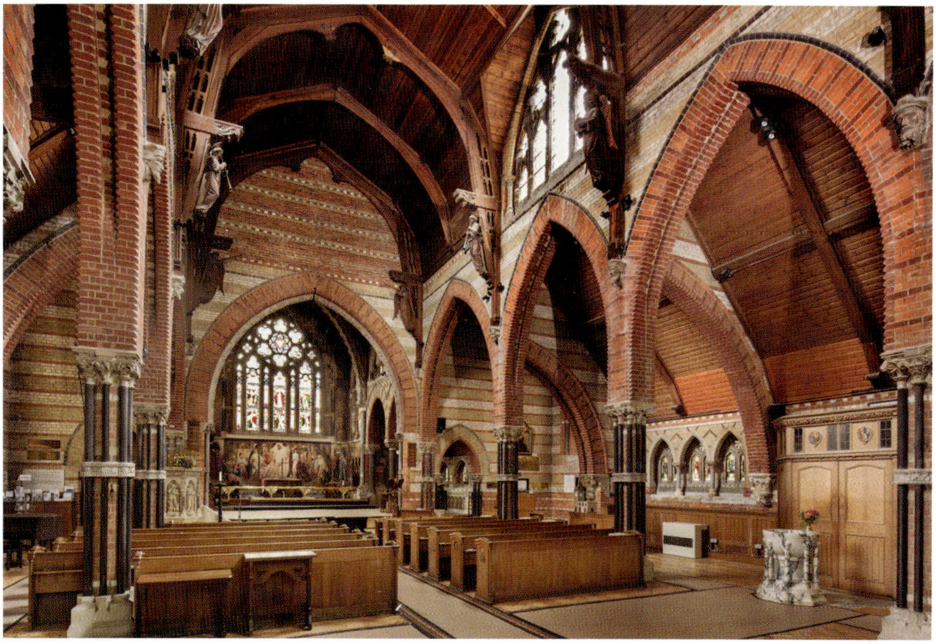

Fig. 6.18 St Michael's, Lyndhurst, Hampshire (1858–70), by William White, showing yellow, white, and two colours of red brick, and piers embellished with dark shafts of Purbeck marble with shaft rings and elaborate carved capitals supporting spiky stilted arches. The reredos beneath the complex east window was painted by Leighton (1862–4) (JOD [2017]).

primitive Gothic that were to become features of more advanced mid-Victorian work: St Michael's also cannot be upheld as an entirely successful external composition (for its elements are somewhat discordant), but its interior is of enormous interest because of its colourful individuality and richly varied furnishings. Perhaps a rather more satisfactory and robust work of White's architecture is his St Mark's, Battersea Rise, Wandsworth, London (1872–4), situated on a slope, so the east end stands on a large vaulted crypt. Curiously, the building was constructed of concrete, with a brick skin enlivened with diaper-work (Fig. 6.19).

Ecclesiologists then took the idea of the 'town church' or 'citadel of faith' pioneered in All Saints', Margaret Street, a stage further, and by the 1860s were arguing that missionary activity and a Church presence in poor parts of towns should become priorities. Beresford Hope, in his influential *The English Cathedral of the Nineteenth Century* (1861), proposed huge buildings with tall naves illuminated by clerestoreys, to stand in the urban matrix. One of the first of such 'town churches' was St Peter's, Vauxhall, London (designed 1860, built 1863–5): Eastlake felt this was a fine example of J.L. Pearson's 'originality in design', and 'one of the most successful instances of modern ecclesiastical architecture in London'. St Peter's is essentially a tall clerestoreyed brick nave continuing into an apsidal chancel, the whole with a ribbed ceiling vault, and with lean-to aisles separated from the nave by means of robust stone piers (Fig. 6.20).

Yet perhaps we have to turn to a remodelling to see lavish mid-Victorian Gothic at its most developed. This is the Albert Memorial Chapel, created in Henry III's chapel

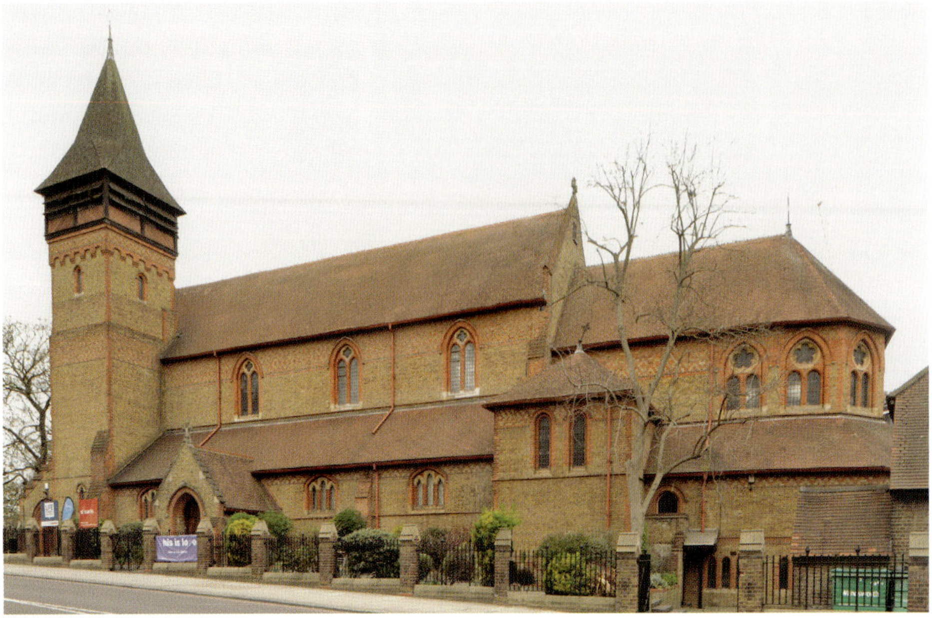

Fig. 6.19 St Mark's, Battersea Rise, Wandsworth, London (1872–4), by William White, First Pointed, with plate-tracery, and a canted east end set high over a crypt. Note the brick diaper patterns and the shingled spire over the timber belfry stage (GB [2021]).

attached to St George's Chapel, Windsor, Berkshire, where the mediæval fabric was worked over, and the interior transformed. Around the walls below the windows is a band of panels of etched marble, while on the centreline of the chapel are three monuments commemorating (from the east) Prince Albert (by Baron de Triquet[t]i); Prince Albert Victor, Duke of Clarence and Avondale (by Alfred Gilbert); and Prince Leopold, Duke of Albany (by Sir Joseph Edgar Boehm) (Fig. 6.21). In this amazingly rich interior (with vault decorated with Salviati mosaic), Continental influences from France, and especially from Germany, are very strong, and it was Continental Gothic which dominated the Gothic Revival for most of the 1860s.

George Gilbert Scott

George Gilbert 'Great' Scott's Church of the Resurrection, Dresden, Outer Longton, Stoke-on-Trent (consecrated 1853 and subsequently enlarged in 1873 and 1903), is an oddity: of red brick, its exterior aggressively diapered with Staffordshire blue bricks, and interior of yellow brick with red brick bands, it cannot be regarded as of great architectural distinction. The structural polychromy, however, is echoed in another Scott church, St Michael's, Crewe Green, Cheshire (1857–8), again of red brick, with blue-black bricks, bands of encaustic tiles, and stone dressings, stylistically looking back to the late 13th century, a building of much higher quality than the Dresden exemplar. Slightly later, and perhaps more impressive, is Scott's St Andrew's, Leicester (1860–2), a powerful exercise in elemental Continental First Pointed, built this time of red brick, blue-black bricks, and stone dressings (Fig. 6.22): it demonstrates the contemporary interest in polychrome brickwork, and shows how primitive French

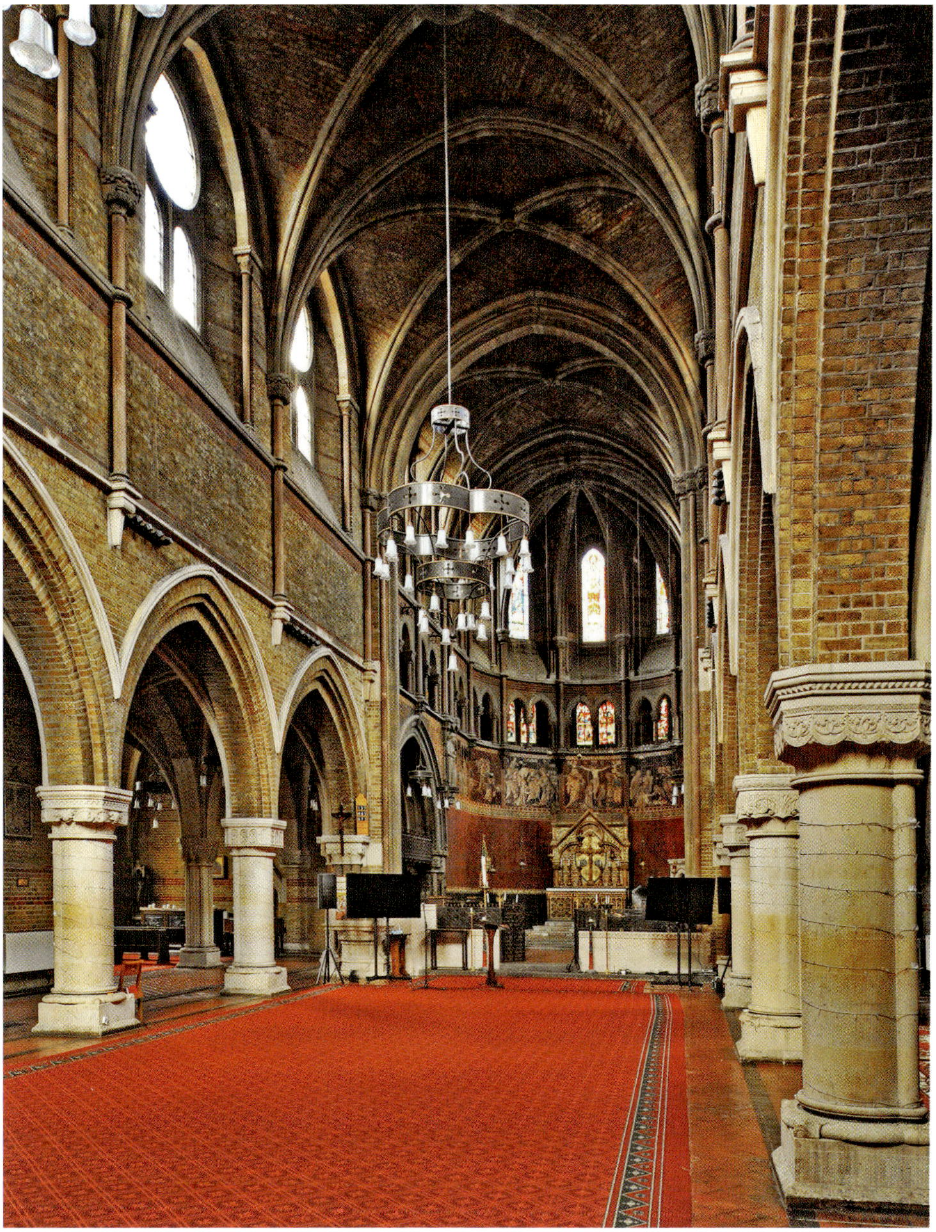

Fig. 6.20 St Peter's, Vauxhall, London (1863–5), by J.L. Pearson, showing the vaulted nave, with plate-tracery in the clerestorey, and apsidal chancel with Burgundian deep-set lancets. The style is 'muscular' early French First Pointed (GB [2021]).

influences were impinging on the Gothic Revival. Scott's St Michael's, Leafield, Oxfordshire (consecrated 1860, but not completed until 1874), is of stone, again in an early 13th-century style with lancets, quatrefoils, and a mighty octagonal crossing tower and spire, demonstrating his growing mastery of form (Fig. 6.23).

Very different is Scott's All Souls', Haley Hill, Halifax, Yorkshire WR (1855–9), built for Colonel Edward Akroyd: the tower and spire are unquestionably fine, based

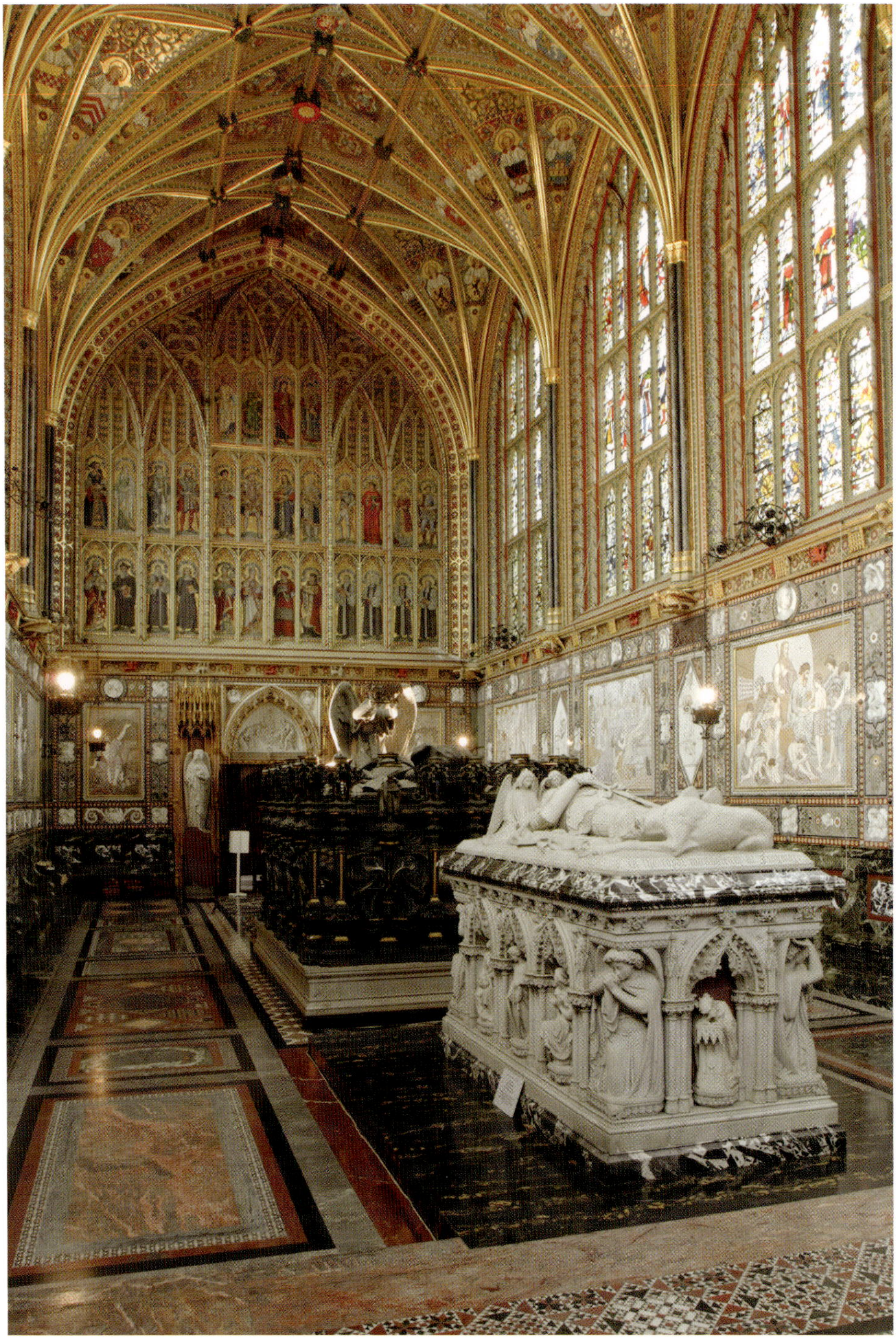

Fig. 6.21 Albert Memorial Chapel, St George's Chapel, Windsor, Berkshire, as remodelled (1862–75) by 'Great' Scott and Baron Henri-Joseph-François de Triquet(t)i, with panels around the walls (1867–c.1872) executed by Jules Destréez. On the centre line of the chapel are the art nouveau monument of Albert Victor, Duke of Clarence and Avondale, by Alfred Gilbert (1898), and cenotaph of Prince Albert (foreground) by de Triquet(t)i, with poorly observed Pointed detail (1865–73). At the feet of the Prince's effigy is his favourite dog, Eos (Royal Collections Trust/© Her Majesty Queen Elizabeth II 2021: photographer Elizabeth Vickers).

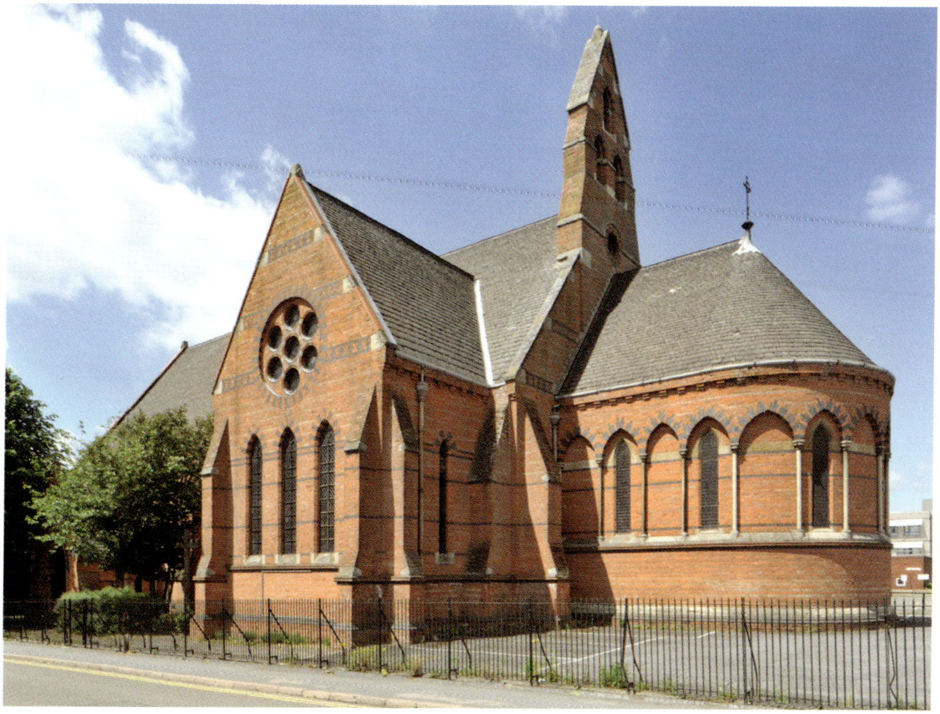

Fig. 6.22 St Andrew's, Leicester (1860–2), by 'Great' Scott, in tough, French-inspired 13th-century First Pointed, employing polychrome brickwork with stone dressings, apsidal chancel, blind arcading, lancet windows, circular plate-tracery pierced with circular openings in the transept, and a bell-cote over the chancel arch (GB [2010]).

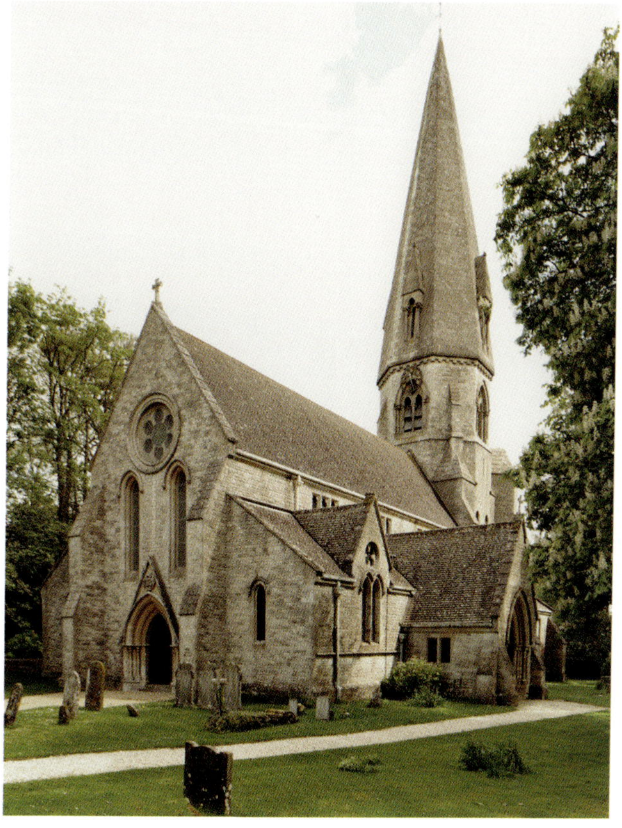

Fig. 6.23 St Michael and All Angels, Leafield, Oxfordshire, by 'Great' Scott, of 1858–60, one of his finest country churches, an assured 'muscular' composition, mostly in the First Pointed style (GB [2010]).

solidly on an understanding of historical exemplars, but the choice of contrasting Magnesian limestone and local sandstone to achieve structural polychromy, combined with excessive thinness of the masonry, proved to be problematic. The building has an impressive, finely composed interior, and sculptural decorations are lavish, with naturalistic carved foliage representing English, and especially Yorkshire, plants, mostly the work of J. Birnie Philip, who executed a great deal of stone carving for

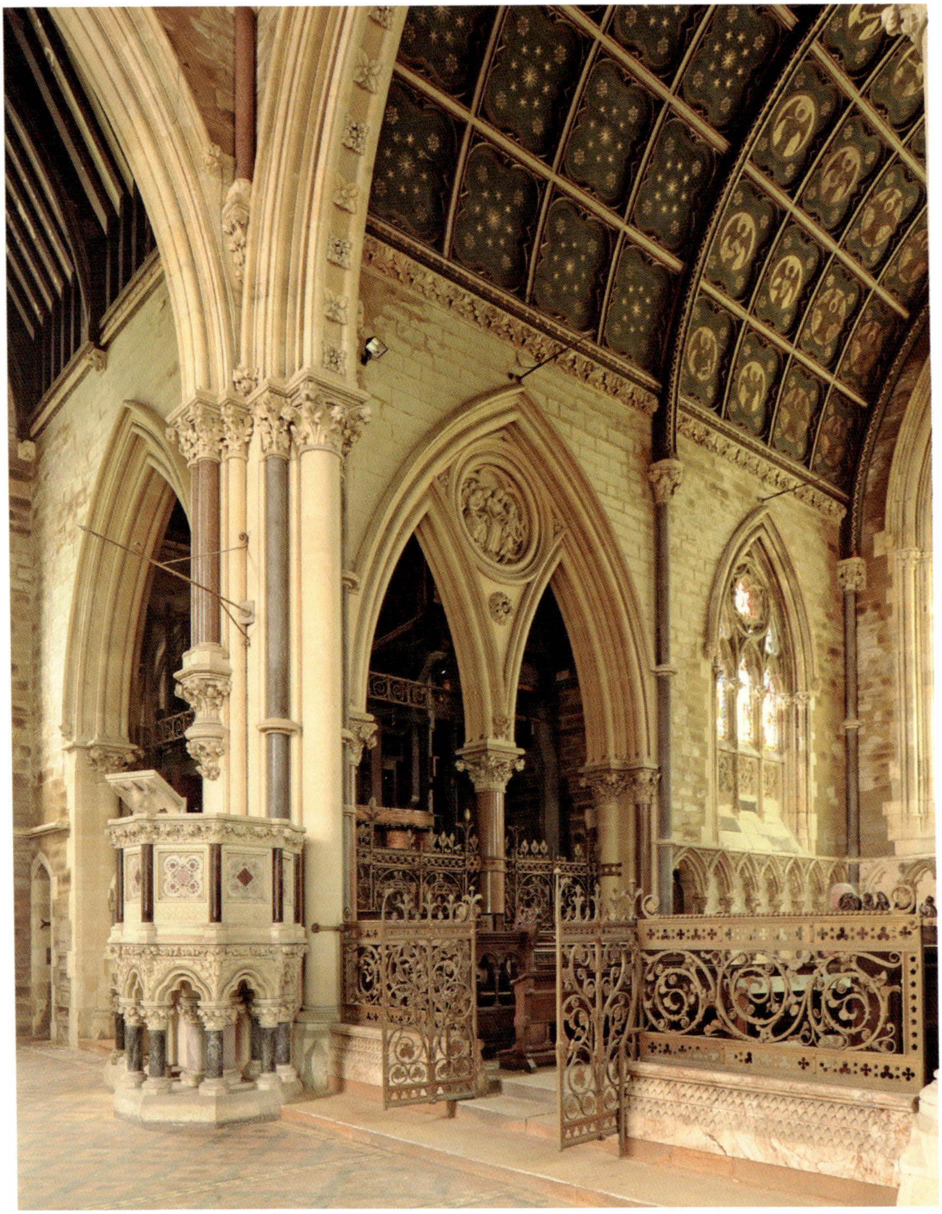

Fig. 6.24 Chancel of All Souls', Haley Hill, Boothtown (Akroyden), Halifax, Yorkshire (WR) (1855–9), by 'Great' Scott, and thought by him to be his best church. The Geometrical Middle Pointed tracery is clearly visible, and the style is a synthesis of First and Second Pointed. Nave piers and capitals are of a French early Gothic type, and resemble those in Canterbury Cathedral (GB [2010]).

Scott, notably at Lichfield Cathedral (1859–63) and at the Albert Memorial, London (1864–72). There is much figure sculpture, something *The Ecclesiologist* welcomed as 'opening a new era in church art'. Unfortunately, much of the painted decoration has been lost (the building was empty and disused for many years until it was taken over by the Churches Conservation Trust), but the choir of angels on the sanctuary ceiling, designed by Clayton & Bell, survives to give an indication of how magnificent the interior once was. Wrought-iron screens in the chancel arc by Skidmore of Coventry, tiles by Minton, and the pulpit, of Caen stone, with marble colonnettes and geometrical inlay reminiscent of Cosmati work (called after the marble-workers of Rome active in the 12th–13th centuries), is one of Scott's grandest and most lavish (Fig. 6.24). The building is contemporary with Square Congregational Church, Halifax, and may be seen as an Anglican response to an ambitious Nonconformist statement (it is a sad reflection on our times that the Anglican church was, in 2022, in the hands of a Trust, while the Congregational building had been demolished [1976–7, except for the steeple]).

Another impressive Scott church is St George's, Doncaster, Yorkshire WR, a big late-Geometrical essay with a tower in the Perpendicular style, largely replicating the form of the mediæval parish church which had been destroyed in a fire (1853). The exterior is richly decorated, and the windows display something of Scott's facility in the design of tracery (Fig. 6.25). Scott had to endure much interference, especially from the bullying anti-Ritualist Edmund Beckett Denison, one of the major donors to the fund for rebuilding the church: Scott himself noted Denison's 'unpleasant way of doing things' in his *Personal and Professional Recollections*. Scott appointed a local stonemason, George Stephen Cleverley, as clerk of works: interestingly, the young John Bentley assisted Cleverley by explaining the working drawings, setting

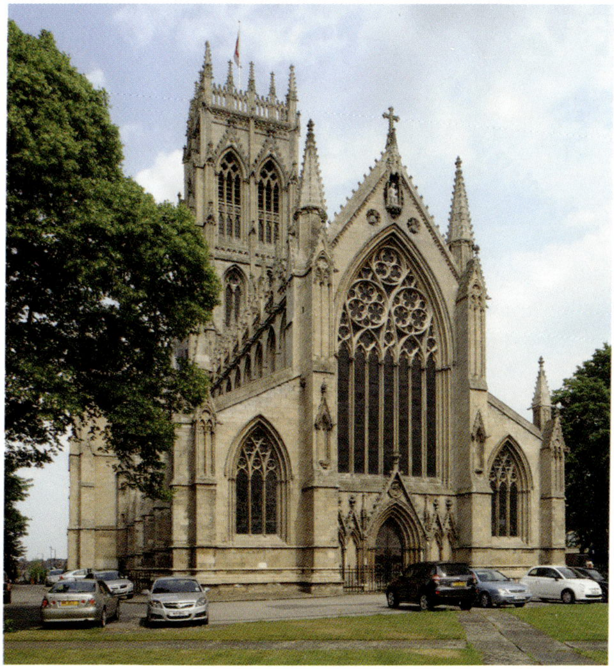

Fig. 6.25 St George's Minster, Doncaster, Yorkshire (WR), from the west, by 'Great' Scott (1854–8), it is the grandest of his many parish churches, with a majestic crossing tower. The church it replaced was all Perpendicular, which Scott re-employed in the tower, but elsewhere, fenestration displayed Geometrical Middle Pointed tracery (GB [2010]).

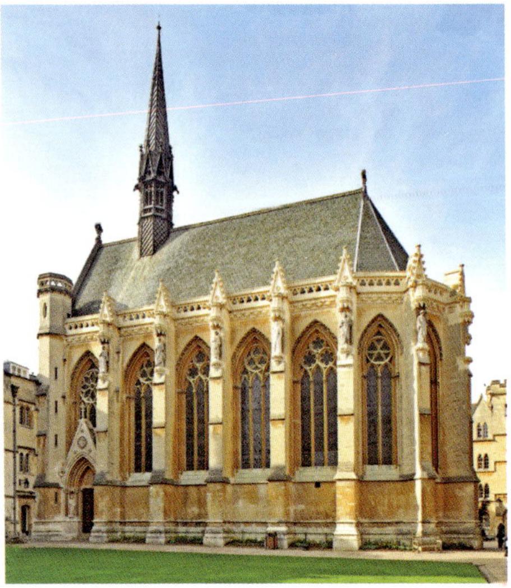

Fig. 6.26 Exeter College Chapel, Oxford (1854–60), by 'Great' Scott, loosely based on Sainte-Chapelle in Paris (1239–43), with bold buttresses, an apsidal east end, and a handsome *flèche* surmounting the western gable (GB [2011]).

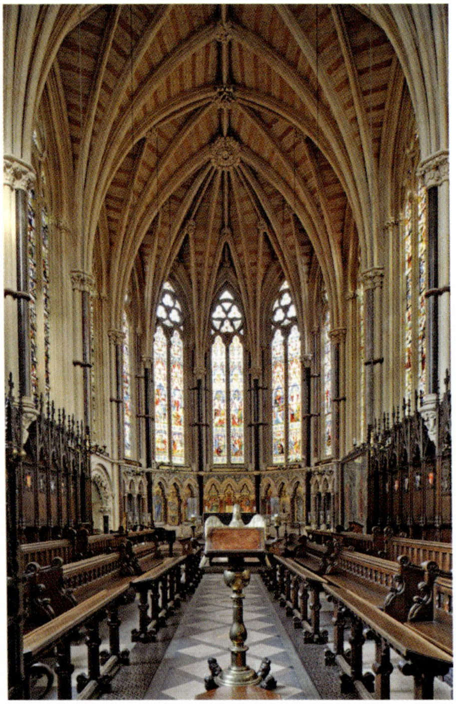

Fig. 6.27 Exeter College Chapel, Oxford, showing the vaulted ceiling, tall traceried windows, and exquisite carvings, much by J. Birnie Philip. Stalls and canopies by G.F. Bodley (GB [2011]).

out full-size details, and even making templates for the masons. Scott's lofty interior is enhanced by the naturalistic carvings and other sculpture, again by Philip, and Minton once more provided the tiled floor. Others involved in beautifying the building included Skidmore and Clayton & Bell.

Then there are two chapels Scott designed for the universities of Oxford and Cambridge. That at Exeter College, Oxford (1854–60), is large for its site (Fig. 6.26), and has somewhat oversized parts. The interior (Fig. 6.27) is very impressive, largely because of its great height: it is vaulted; the attractive iron-and-brass internal gates are by Skidmore; the arcading around the apse has Salviati mosaic decoration; and Clayton & Bell did most of the stained glass. At St John's College, Cambridge, Scott's chapel is a bit later (1863–9), with the Oxford chapel arrangement of a transept-like ante-chapel at the west end, and again a polygonal apse which is awkwardly related to the other rectangular buildings and the court. Tracery follows work of *c.*1300, and the tower over the crossing of the chapel and ante-chapel sits over a crossing marked by piers of Peterhead granite.

The Sainte-Chapelle theme, albeit with Anglicised elements, toning down the Gallic, recurs at the dramatically sited St Mary's at Itchen Stoke, Hampshire (1865–6), designed by Henry Conybeare for his brother, Charles Ranken Conybeare. It is an impressive performance by a man more noted for his engineering in Bombay, Ireland, and Wales, although he did publish work on mediæval architecture.

7

Church Architecture of the 1850s, 1860s, and Early 1870s

We want a style ... which will be pleasing ..., yet be susceptible of every gradation of beauty, till it reach the noblest and most exalted objects to which art can aspire. If we can devise such a style ... let us endeavour to develope [sic] it out of that of some former period ... and happily we find such a nucleus to work upon in the native architecture of our own country.

George Gilbert Scott (1811–78):
Remarks on Secular & Domestic Architecture, Present & Future
(London: John Murray, 1857), 8–9.

The church of St John, in Tue Brook, a suburb of Liverpool, ... recently completed from the design of Mr G.F. Bodley, ... has returned to that type of Middle Pointed art which reached its highest grace towards the middle of the fourteenth century.

Charles Locke Eastlake (1836–1906):
A History of the Gothic Revival
(London: Longmans, Green, & Co., 1872), 369.

Ruskin

'Great' Scott recognised Pugin and John Ruskin as influences on English architecture. Both, it has to be said, were bigots: Pugin was anti-Protestant; Ruskin was anti-'papist'; each equated architecture with moral worth; and both argued polemically, omitting anything inconvenient to their causes.

In *The Stones of Venice* (1851–53), Ruskin made an extraordinary attempt to dissociate Gothic architecture from 'popery', trumpeting against its ensnaring attractions: 'Romanism', he wrote, 'instead of being a promoter of the arts, has never shown itself capable of a single great conception since the separation of Protestantism from its side'.

One of the effects of such writing was to remove anti-Gothic prejudices among Evangelicals and Nonconformists alike: Ruskin's polemics painted Gothic as fit to 'frame a temple for the prayer of nations', despite the undoubted fact that all mediæval Pointed ecclesiastical architecture was pre-Reformation, and therefore, in the past, the architectural style of R.C. churches throughout Europe. Ruskin's advocacies for a Christian social order draped a mantle of romantic democracy over the Gothic Revival.

'Ruskinian Gothic' is a term connected with colour in the materials used in a building (rather than applied to surfaces), naturalistic sculpture, and Italian mediæval architecture. In his *Seven Lamps of Architecture* (1849) Ruskin celebrated Continental Gothic, contrasting it with that of mediæval England, which he opined was thin and insubstantial, even in 13th-century examples. To him, the colours and patterns of Italian Gothic were infinitely superior, and his writings helped to contribute to a climate in which rich textures, strong modelling, and violent colouring were introduced to the Victorian Gothic Revival. Colour in Italian architecture often consisted of inlaid marbles set in smooth surfaces, and helps to explain much about influences that flavoured English architecture from the 1850s, not least because of the *Rundbogenstil* movement that had developed in Germany. Ruskin advocated courses of differently coloured stones, which he claimed were analogous to geological beds, and argued against interrupting this horizontal layered effect with vertical divisions such as shafts, colonnettes, or buttresses. However, Victorian experiments involving, for example, contrasting bands of limestone and red sandstone in wall construction, to emulate different colours of marble in Italian work, brought problems.

It seems extraordinary that a visitor to Venice could virtually ignore the glories of Renaissance architecture there, but this is what Ruskin did. Even Classical elements, such as triglyphs, were declared by Ruskin to be ugly because they were not based on any natural organic forms, yet he detected just those in Venetian Gothic billet mouldings: to claim such things yet denounce triglyphs as unnatural suggests odd thought processes. How he seduced opinion with his carefully crafted words in this way defies belief: architectural theories are not reckoned by their content but by their (often baleful) influence. Ruskin's name and Venetian Gothic became inextricably linked, and he was regarded as the begetter of a type of polychrome Victorian Gothic loosely based on eclectic motifs originating in Italy: he was the populariser of a tendency that was already present in Ecclesiological circles in the 1840s, and which had been encouraged by Benjamin Webb, *The Ecclesiologist*, and G.E. Street.

The last architect argued for massiveness, powerful contours, depth of recesses, freedom in distributing openings in a façade (concentrating windows in some areas, and leaving other parts of walls blank), and the use of structural colour. He also favoured a rugged toughness, even in matters such as tracery, although the pseudo-morality and humbug about 'organic' ornament, mercifully, are absent. Street argued for the development of Gothic, and for borrowing from mediæval buildings of many European countries. What is more, he supported Pugin's concepts of the 'true Picturesque' (where elevations, forms, and silhouettes of buildings grew naturally from the plans), but purged them of symbolism, moralising, and irrational polemics. The combination of Ruskin's popular writings, advocacy of brick and polychromy by Ecclesiologists, and Street's suggestions of casting the net ever wider for sources of Gothic Revival architecture proved irresistible: the unfortunate term 'High Victorian' Gothic architecture was born, and dominated the Revival until the 1870s. What, however, one might ask, is 'Low Victorian'?

Some Definitions and Muscularity

'Definitions are difficult', Eastlake observed,

> but if, by way of classifying the works of modern Gothic architects, it were possible to arrange them ... in three general divisions or schools, such a classification might ... take the following form ...

> First. The Traditional or Correct School, which aims ... at a literal reproduction of art in the Middle Ages: admitting no compromise, abhorrent of eclecticism, selecting one style for absolute imitation, excluding ... nothing for which there is authentic precedent ...
>
> Second. The Adaptational or Artistic School, which holds Mediæval art in high respect, but considers ... it may be modified to suit ... the present age ...
>
> Third. The Independent or Eclectic School, ... regardless of authority, of local peculiarities, of dates and proprieties of design, so long as it satisfies individual taste ... not hesitating to unite in one building the distinctive characteristics of English and foreign Gothic ... inclined to startling proportions ...
>
> Between these three groups ... there are ... men who are pledged to no fixed principles of taste, and who have passed from one extreme to the other as the ... fleeting fashions of the day have guided them.

Eastlake saw in some work of the 1850s and 1860s a 'muscular' type of architecture: models tended to be more archaic, such as early Burgundian Gothic of the 13th century, as previously mentioned; and vivid polychromy fell from grace. Among the most successful 'muscular' 'town-churches' were those by James Brooks, erected of brick in the East End and other parts of London: these include St Chad's, Shoreditch, Hackney (begun 1867) (Fig. 7.1), which has plate-traceried windows puncturing plain unbuttressed walls. Brooks employed wide, high naves; tiny, almost vestigial aisles; lofty clerestoreys; wide, short lancets of the Burgundian type; plate-tracery; apsidal east ends (but not invariably); and French Gothic of the 13th century.

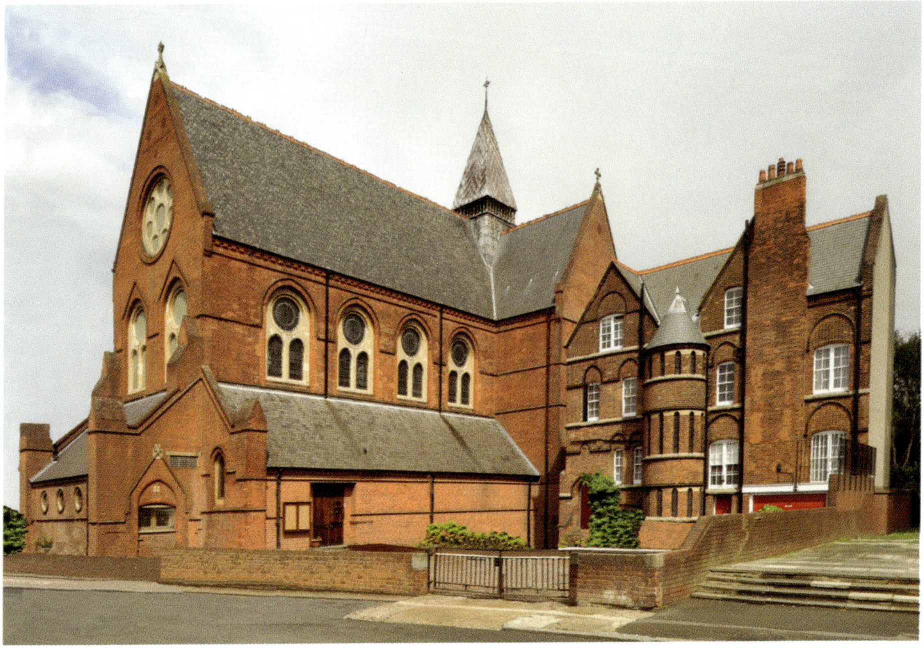

Fig. 7.1 St Chad's, Shoreditch, London (1867–9), by James Brooks. Built under the ægis of the Shoreditch and Haggerston Church Extension Fund, it and the adjoining clergy house were in an early French Gothic style, of brick, with plate-tracery (GB [2021]).

'Go', 'Roguery', and Reactions

'Great' Scott commended the task of 'rendering' iron construction beautiful to 'the special care of the architects' engaged in the Gothic Revival. It was unfortunate that iron began to be favoured by Goths of the Evangelical persuasion and who were addicted to 'Go', implying work that was restless, animated, and embarrassingly loud. 'Go' suggested empty fashion, discord, clashing colours, excessive liveliness, coarseness, furious vigour, exaggeration, vulgarity, and generally something overdone.

One of the problems was that Ruskin's *Stones of Venice* was strong fare, to be consumed with caution. Under his mesmerising spell, indeed, an architecture was beginning to appear in English streets derived from exemplars featuring coloured marbles that basked in much sunnier climes. Too many elements, such as notched arrises, coloured layers of bricks and tiles, and petrified foliage, could be seen to have drawn their inspiration from Ruskin's prolix writings. E.W. Godwin saw dangers in the sudden, almost universal outbreak of Anglo-Venetian Gothic, stating it was as far removed from the Gothic of Venice as a bleached mutilated skeleton was from the glowing living body.

The trouble with 'Ruskinian Gothic' was that during the 1860s it became over-decorated and over-coloured. John Pollard Seddon began the reaction with a scathing attack prompted by the Music Hall erected on the site of the Exeter Exchange in The Strand, London, opened on 15 October 1864, and designed by E. Bassett Keeling. It was said of Keeling that he knew how to provide places of architectural entertainment for Sundays without either 'profanity' or 'popery', a reference to his 'Rogue' churches, but the Music Hall received a barrage of vitriolic abuse. Seddon mocked 'Acrobatic Gothic', calling it the 'hair-stand-on-end' style' with 'knobs, bosses, and balls, notches and chamferings with villainous spiky iron-work'.

Condemnation would have damaged Keeling's career less had the venture been a commercial success. John Hollingshead observed that it was a 'failure' from the first, and the architecture 'had something to do with it. A decorator's studio, overloaded with samples picked up from all nations was the only thing the place suggested'. Apart from damage to Keeling's reputation, a more immediate problem was his financial involvement and subsequent bankruptcy.

Keeling was not alone, of course, for there were others identified as 'rogue-elephants' whose ferocious architecture did not meet with Ecclesiological approval. Goodhart-Rendel bracketed Keeling, Joseph Peacock, and Robert Lewis Roumieu as a 'trio of architectural rakes' each doing his best to 'debauch' the Gothic Revival. He noted that around 1860, the Gothic Revival was vulnerable, for those were the days 'of the longest whiskers, the most spacious crinolines, and the biggest stripes and checks. Fashions in architecture were similarly exaggerated, and strong influences had to be exerted by the leaders of the profession to ensure that if young men went as far as Mr. Street did they should at any rate go no further'. The style pandering to the same mood in Paris, the style of Davioud (a pupil of Viollet-le-Duc), was nicknamed the *Style Rageur*: *raguer* is French for to chafe, gall, or irritate, so applied in France to a phase of architecture characterised by perversity, discordance, and aggressive originality.

The effusions of Ruskin, Butterfield's work at All Saints', Margaret Street, and after, and Street's investigations into Italian polychromy 'had thrown into the Gothic pot much strong seasoning ... The dominant Gothic party insisted that architecture must above all be "vigorous" and in contemporary office slang the highest praise for a design was to say that it had plenty of "go"'. Ecclesiological circles, however, 'bristled with principles rigidly upheld, and if led by duty to design what was sensational abhorred sensationalism as such. When Butterfield hit what he regarded as a frivolous and self-indulgent age full between the eyes he did it of high purpose', but it was generally perceived that was not the case with the Strand Music Hall.

It is strange that such a perceptive critic as Goodhart-Rendel could not 'get to the bottom of the deep disapproval' of the Music Hall, nor could he find 'the reason for its early demolition'. The reason it closed and was demolished was because it failed financially and the company went into liquidation. It seemed to Goodhart-Rendel that the hall's interior had 'a raffish look that might account for its contemporary disapprobation were it not that the same look appears in his churches and there aroused no comment'.

That last remark is untrue, for St Mark's, Notting Hill (1862–3 – demolished 1970s), was denounced as an 'atrocious specimen' of 'coxcombry', and there were other criticisms that cannot have done Keeling any good, especially when church-building committees were accused in the *Building News* of 'irresponsibility' in the choice of architect, but that was after the Music Hall debacle. The sort of eclectic soup dished up by Keeling and other 'Rogues' had as its ingredients components of Anglo-Venetian and early French Gothic, and was fast becoming a popular style, what J. Mordaunt Crook aptly called the 'demotic Gothic of the 1860s': but the Strand Music Hall, being a place of vulgar, popular entertainment, was some distance from the high idealism of mainstream Gothic Revival. It took something to attract the wrath of the entire architectural establishment, but that is what happened.

Some 'Rogue' churches gloried in repetitive notchings and chamferings; had roof structures expressed in an outlandish, restless way; and appeared to want to jar the beholder with saw-toothed arrises on every side, threaten with scissor-shaped trusses, and shout loudly with barbaric, harsh, polychromy. Antics of carpentry recur in the roofs of E.B. Lamb's churches: his St Margaret's, Leiston, Suffolk (1853), has a wildly busy mass of carpentry leaping out from low walls; and St Mary Magdalene's, Addiscombe, Croydon, Surrey (1868–70), has an interior comparable only to some of Lamb's other work, e.g. Christ Church, West Hartlepool (1850–4), and St Martin's, Gospel Oak, Camden (Fig. 7.2). A critic in *The Ecclesiologist* described such oppressive roof structures as 'a chaos of carpentry', and expressed the hope that they would not prove injurious to the health of those who sat beneath them. Lamb designed for Low Church worship, emphasising visibility and preaching: his churches are exemplars of how far removed some Victorian ecclesiastical architects could be from mere imitation of the mediæval past.

Like Lamb, Keeling exploited carpentry in his roofs and gallery fronts, but he also employed an unmatched degree of spiky, rasping sharpness, and his polychromy was extremely violent. While he claimed his churches were in a style of 'Continental Gothic, freely treated', some critics denounced them. His two most extraordinary London churches were St Mark's, Notting Hill, and St George's, Campden Hill (1864–5 – altered and damaged almost beyond recognition [Figs 7.3 and 7.4]). St Mark's had arcades on spindly cast-iron piers and spiky arches of red, black, and white brick voussoirs, the arrises of which were notched, like those of the scissor trusses

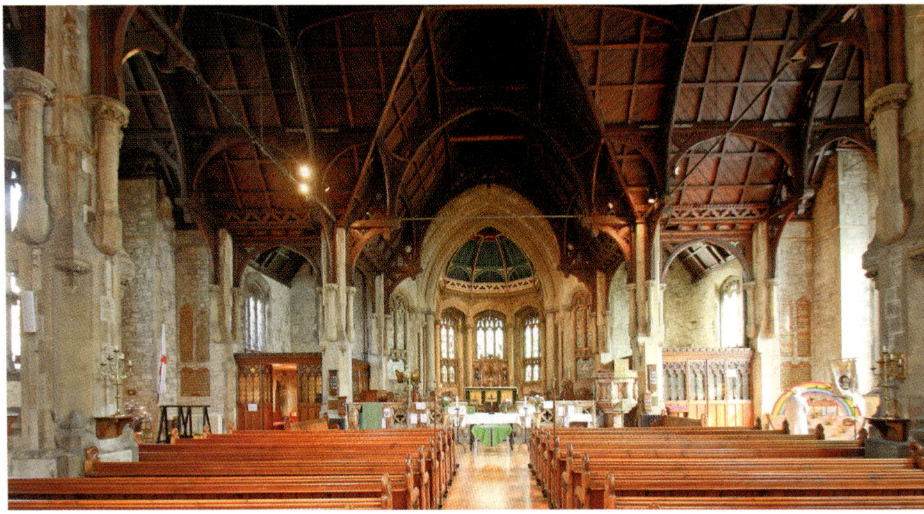

Fig. 7.2 St Martin's, Gospel Oak, London (1864–5), by E.B. Lamb, designed to suit a Low Church emphasis on visibility and preaching, with a menacing, over-busy roof construction, typical of Lamb's work (JS [2011]).

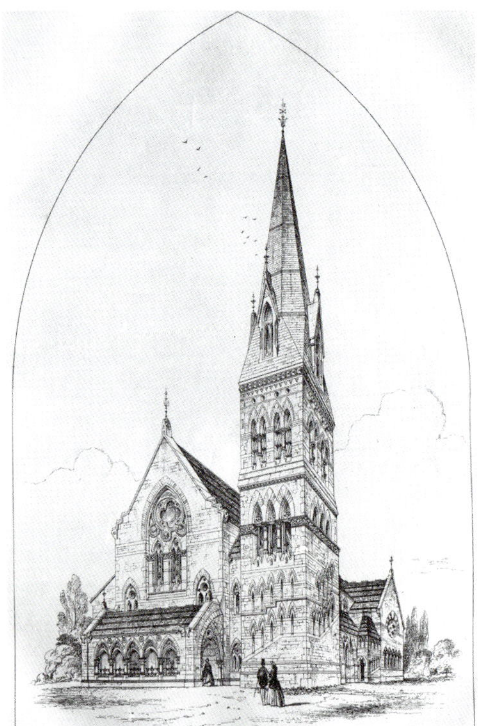

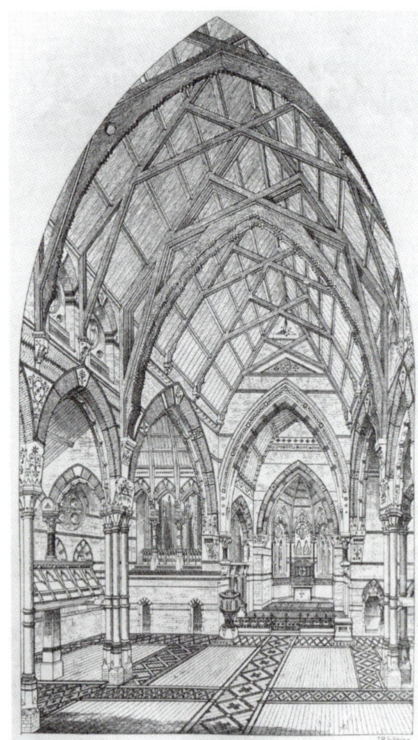

Fig. 7.3 Left: St George's, Campden Hill, Kensington, London (1864–5), by E. Bassett Keeling. It no longer sports its spire (from *The Building News* **xi** [22 July 1864] 363, coll. JSC).

Fig. 7.4 Right: St George's, Campden Hill (1864–5), by E. Bassett Keeling, showing the slender cast-iron piers, gallery, polychrome notched brickwork, and frantic roof structure. The galleries were later removed, weakening the structure's integrity, so the piers had to be encased in concrete. The apse has been demolished (from *The Building News* **xi** [30 September 1864] 729, coll. JSC).

carrying the roof; and St George's had violent, harsh polychromy, scissor trusses, and much notching, with arcades carried on cast-iron clustered shafts. Galleries were provided, not approved of by Ecclesiologists, who sought severity, unmoulded planes, and a more primitive, early Gothic style based on Continental precedent. Zulu war shields rather than Burgundian Gothic were suggested by Keeling's sharply pointed arches that, even for the 1860s, were beginning to be too full of 'Go'.

Eastlake doubtless had Keeling in mind in referring to 'those younger architects who for a while mistook licence for freedom in design and conceived that the conditions of Gothic art were not thoroughly fulfilled unless ... every edge in masonry or woodwork' was 'notched or chamfered'. From the 1860s, clustered piers (especially thin, stovepipe, cast-iron piers) were gradually eschewed, while polychrome surfaces became quieter, and violent jaggedness was superseded by something more austere, archaic, and tough as the Revival moved towards the 1870s. By the 1860s Keeling's galleried interiors were very old fashioned, while his external treatment using Bath, Red Mansfield, and Kentish Rag (unsuitable for the London climate) soon showed signs of distress.

No approval came to Chester Cheston for one of the wildest pieces of 'Rogue' Gothic ever conceived. The enormous church of St Mark, Dalston, London, was designed in 1862, and work began in 1864, but consecration did not occur until 1870. Inside (a vast auditorium), piers are slender, of cast iron, and carry high pointed arches of polychrome notched brick. The style is vaguely First Pointed Continental Gothic (with a strong dose of stripey Zulu colouring): there are lots of lancets and a large western wheel window. The entire ensemble has to be seen to be believed (Fig. 7.5).

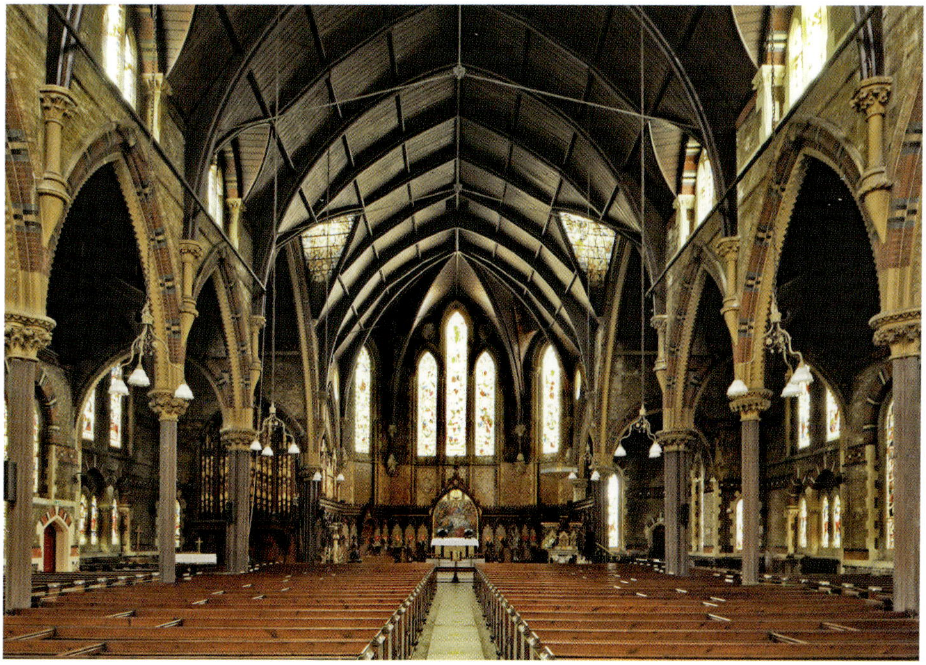

Fig. 7.5 St Mark's, Dalston, London (1862–70), by Chester Cheston, in a wildly 'Rogue' Gothic style, showing the thin cast-iron piers, notched striped arches, and restless, polychrome effects. Coloured glass in the ceilings on the nave sides of the transept arches was possibly suggested by Keeling's contemporary Strand Music Hall (GB [2021]).

To men of the up-and-coming generation of architects, the 'Rogues' were guilty of 'architectural rants', their 'Go' suggesting 'rage', being 'in a restless state', 'in constant motion', and being 'slightly drunk' (Keeling actually died of liver cirrhosis, aged 49). J.T. Micklethwaite contributed several articles to an ephemeral journal called *The Sacristry* in 1870, but they were republished in his important book, *Modern Parish Churches* (1874): he denounced 'Go', over-pedantic antiquarianism, and vulgar commercialism as the enemies of good architecture. However, even more important, Micklethwaite turned against his own master, Scott, and, with others of his generation, repudiated as an aberration almost the whole mid-Victorian Gothic architectural output. Advocating a return to rational principles of ecclesiastical design, the study of liturgical requirements to determine the plan and volume of a church, the need to evolve a type of architectural solution for the future, the abandonment of ecclesiological antiquarianism (and dreamy mediævalism), and, most significantly, a return to principles of design established by Pugin and R.C. Carpenter, he pointed the way forward to the evolution of late Victorian church architecture.

William Burges

Nevertheless, despite Micklethwaite's strictures, there were some talented men who still drew heavily on Continental prototypes yet created architecture of great beauty and integrity, avoiding 'Rogue' excess. Two of the most gifted were William Burges (himself highly critical of 'Rogues') and John Loughborough Pearson.

Burges, a former partner of Clutton, was one of the most successful synthesisers of early First and Middle Pointed styles, notably in his two spectacular churches of St Mary, Studley Royal (1870–8) (Figs 7.6 and 7.7), and Christ the Consoler, Newby Hall, Skelton-on-Ure (1870–6) (Figs 7.8 and 7.9), both Yorkshire WR. Burges got these jobs largely through George Frederick Robinson, 1st Marquess of Ripon, an immensely rich romantic mediævalist and Christian Socialist, who, when he inherited Fountains Abbey in Yorkshire, longed to restore it as a 'working-man's university' (how wonderful that would have been, especially if Billy Burges had been in overall control as architect!), and actually built a private chapel at his house at Studley Royal dedicated to 'Our Lady of Fountains' so that She should have 'something of Her own again'. Burges's name was suggested to Ripon through John Patrick Crichton-Stuart, 3rd Marquess of Bute, who had 'perverted' (as termed by those who disapproved) to the Roman Church while

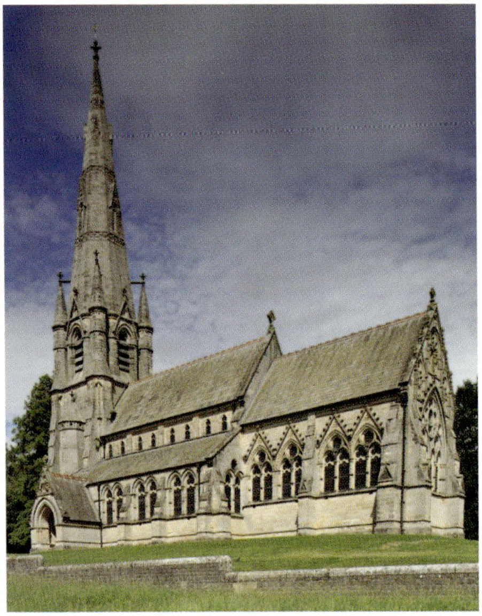

Fig. 7.6 St Mary's, Studley Royal, Yorkshire (WR) (1870–8), by William Burges. The 'muscular' treatment of First and Early Second Pointed (of the Geometrical type) was heavily influenced by Continental exemplars (GB [2021]).

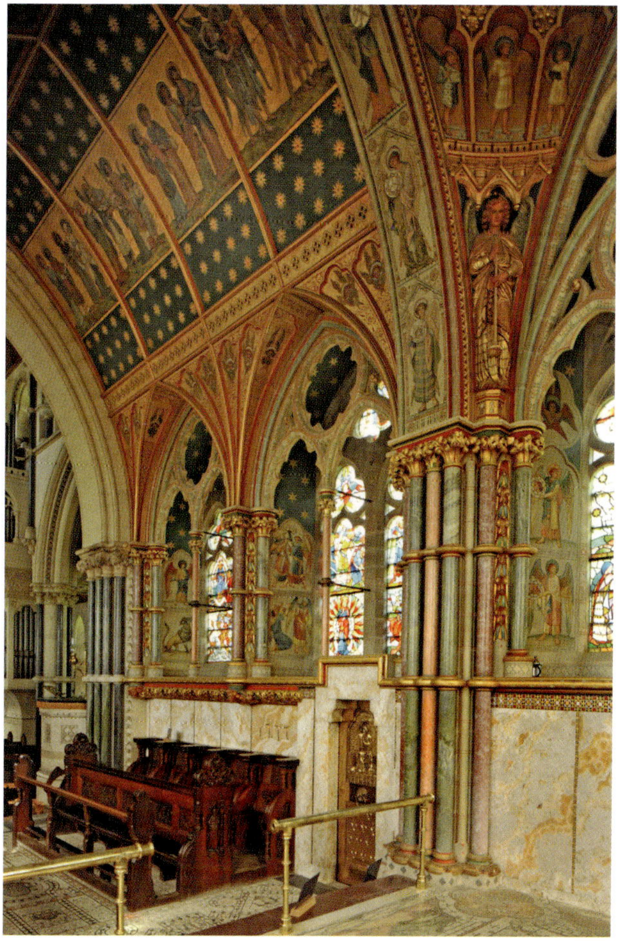

Fig. 7.7 Chancel north wall, St Mary's, Studley Royal, from the domed sanctuary. Burges's inventive genius is displayed in the luscious colouring. Wall dados are lined with alabaster, there is double tracery to the windows, and the walls are decorated with carved and painted ornament. Sculpture was by Thomas Nicholls, stained glass was made by Saunders & Co., and the designers of the details were Frederick Weekes and Horatio Walter Lonsdale, all under Burges's direction. Apostles, prophets, and martyrs in procession enliven the chancel ceiling (GB [2021]).

still up at Oxford, and for whom the architect had carried out spectacular works at Cardiff Castle from 1866.

These two stupendous Yorkshire churches (among the very finest exemplars of the Victorian Gothic Revival, which show that it was, in fact, far, far more than a 'revival') were triggered by the capture (1870) by Greek brigands of Ripon's neighbour and brother-in-law, Frederick Grantham Vyner (who had been up at Oxford with Bute). A huge ransom was demanded for his release, and troops were sent to the rescue, but in the ensuing mayhem Vyner was killed. His mother, Lady Mary Vyner, and his sister, Henrietta Anne Theodosia (née Vyner), Marchioness of Ripon, employed the ransom money to erect two churches as his memorial on their estates, and Burges was commissioned. St Mary's (consecrated 1878) has a light-filled, colourful interior, a Paradise Lost in the nave and Regained in the chancel and sanctuary, a theme emphasised by the colouring in the materials used. The interior of Christ the Consoler (consecrated 1876) does exactly that: it consoles, suffused in dappled light reflected from many coloured stones, reds, greens, blacks, whites, the effects enhanced by low vaults carried on compressed shafts. Every detail is lovingly designed with reference to historical precedent, yet is completely original and personal, from door hinges to

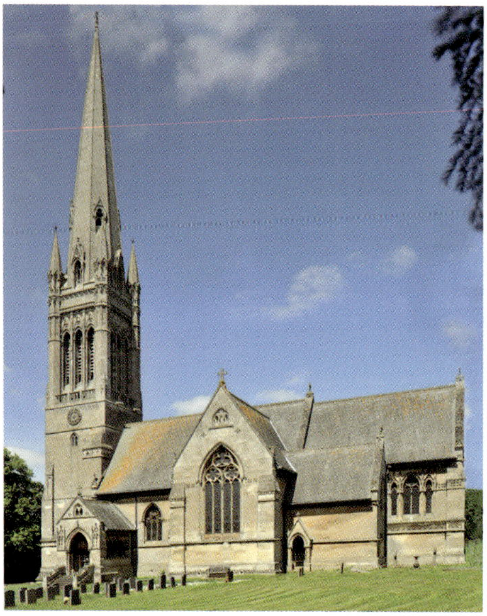

Fig. 7.10 St Mary's, South Dalton, Yorkshire (ER) (1858–61), by J.L. Pearson for Lord Hotham, an essay in 13th-century Gothic, sometimes called 'the cathedral of the Wolds'. The splendid steeple seems to owe debts to those of St Wulfram's, Grantham, Lincolnshire, and also perhaps to Salisbury Cathedral (GB [2021]).

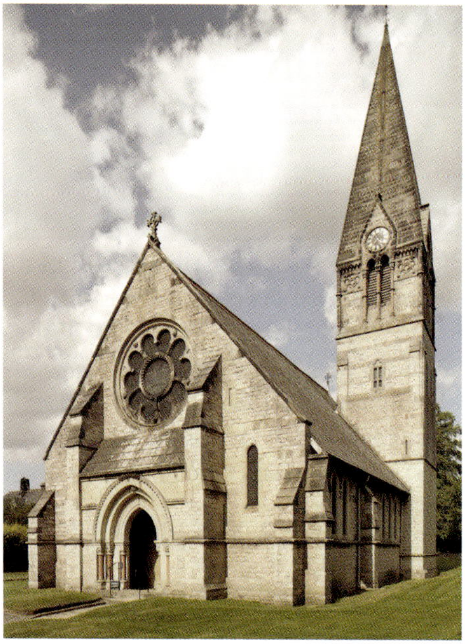

Fig. 7.11 Christ Church, Appleton-le-Moors, Yorkshire (NR) (1862–5), by J.L. Pearson, from the south-west. Eastlake (1872) called it 'scholar-like and noble', and identified it as 'modelled on the earliest and severest type of French Gothic' (GB [2011]).

Leonard's in nearby Scorborough, also by Pearson, as a 'thank offering for many blessings' (*see* front cover).

Pearson's Christ Church, Appleton-le-Moors, Yorkshire NR (1862–5), was the immediate successor to St Peter's, Vauxhall (*see* Fig. 6.20), although it is not vaulted, but its plan is essentially Romanesque, with an apsidal chancel, and architecture modelled on the severest French Gothic, in complete contrast with South Dalton: Eastlake noted that the difference between them 'in point of style is extraordinary'. At Christ Church, the west front is pierced by a large wheel window in the gable under which is a narrow narthex wedged between two buttresses: the square tower with pyramidal spire is deftly handled (Fig. 7.11). Pearson's inspiration was Continental, especially the vigorously carved 'severe and primitive' nave arcade capitals (Fig. 7.12), and the whole building, a little masterpiece, is far more impressive in its way than the much larger St Mary's.

Christ Church was commissioned by Mary (née Hyett), widow of Captain Joseph Shepherd, who made a fortune in shipping. One outstanding feature is the tiny mortuary chapel, with groin-vaulted ceiling, north of the chancel, intended for Shepherd's entombment, but in the event both Shepherds were interred at Lastingham, Ryedale, NR. The exquisite chapel at Appleton is enriched with mural decorations of figure subjects suggested by Psalm cvii, verses 23–30 ('They that go down to the sea in ships ... he bringeth them unto their desired haven').

Pearson was also responsible for St Mary's, Freeland, Oxfordshire (1869–71), with nave, unbuttressed apsidal chancel, and north-eastern tower with saddle-back roof placed against one side of the chancel near its junction with the nave. Nave windows have plate-tracery, and

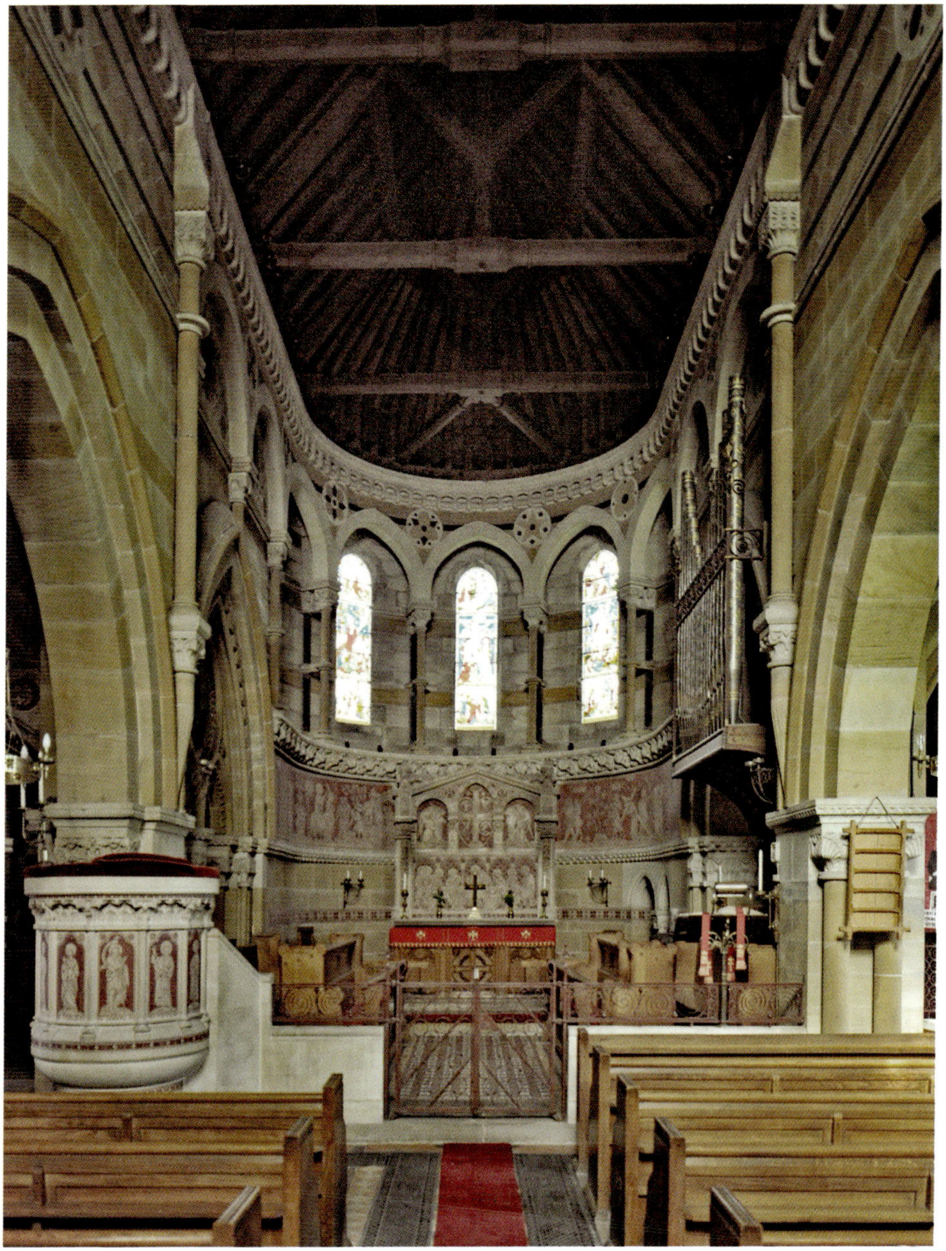

Fig. 7.12 Christ Church, Appleton-le-Moors (1862–5), by J.L. Pearson. The style is predominantly early French First Pointed, deftly handled in this marvellous interior (GB [2021])

the apse is pierced with lancets. Pearson's use of apses was always masterly, and St Mary's is a superb example of his skill in handling architecture based on French early 13th-century precedents. The interior demonstrates the Ecclesiologists' theories concerning the 'beauty of holiness', with its aisleless nave and decorations by Clayton & Bell: the chancel has a rib vault of pinkish-grey stone carried on red wall shafts, and 13th-century-style paintings enlivening the walls (Fig. 7.13).

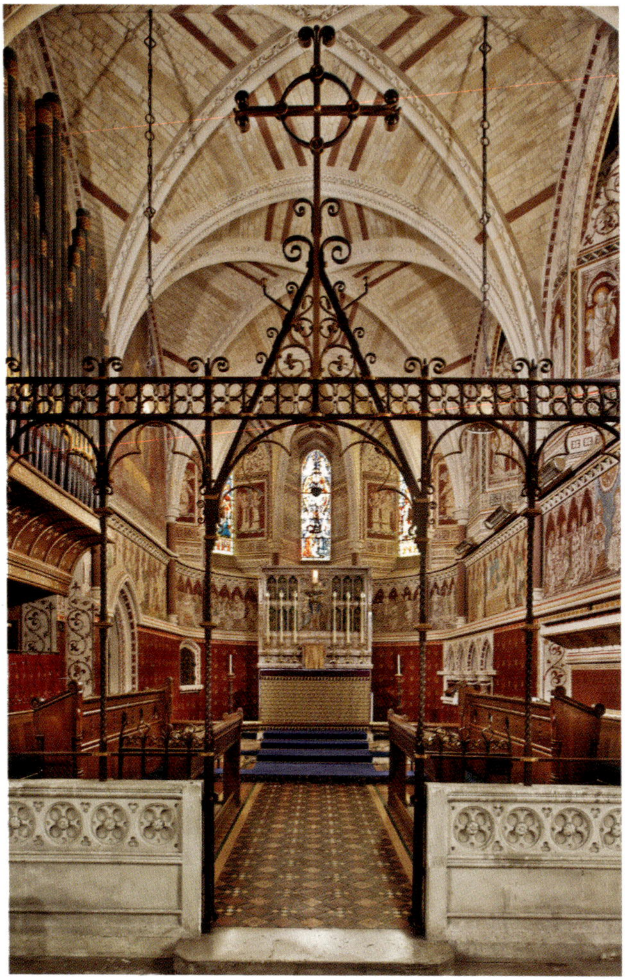

Fig. 7.13 St Mary's, Freeland, Oxfordshire (1869–70), by J.L. Pearson, showing the sumptuous, vaulted chancel, with wall paintings by Clayton & Bell, completed 1890. Note the wrought-iron screen and cancelli defining the chancel, floor covered with Minton tiles, and deep-red dado with fleur-de-lys and rosette decorations (JOD [2016]).

Extensive works were carried out (1856–7) under Pearson's direction at two much-decayed and much-altered Norman churches in Yorkshire ER for Sir Tatton Sykes I, 4th Baronet: one was St Mary's, Kirkburn, and the other St Michael's, Garton-on-the-Wolds. He rebuilt the chancel of the latter in Romanesque style incorporating some original features: *The Ecclesiologist* predictably doubted whether enough remained to justify a Romanesque reconstruction in preference to the 'choice of Middle Pointed'. However, Street was brought in by the 5th Baronet in 1872, and under him the amazing scheme of interior decoration was realised, with wall paintings by Clayton & Bell (1873–6), who also made the stained glass (Fig. 7.14). The paintings were restored (1986–91) by Donald Smith and Wolfgang Gärtner (Fig. 7.15).

St Augustine's, Kilburn, Westminster, London (1870–7 – erected to Pearson's designs under the ægis of an Anglo-Irish, Anglo-Catholic clergyman, R.C. Kirkpatrick, for a largely middle-class congregation), was also inspired by early French Gothic, this time of Normandy, where models for parts of the exterior (the steeple and the turrets) were from the 13th-century Abbaye-aux-Hommes (St-Étienne), Caen, but the interior, with its very deep internal wall-piers (invisible from the outside) and

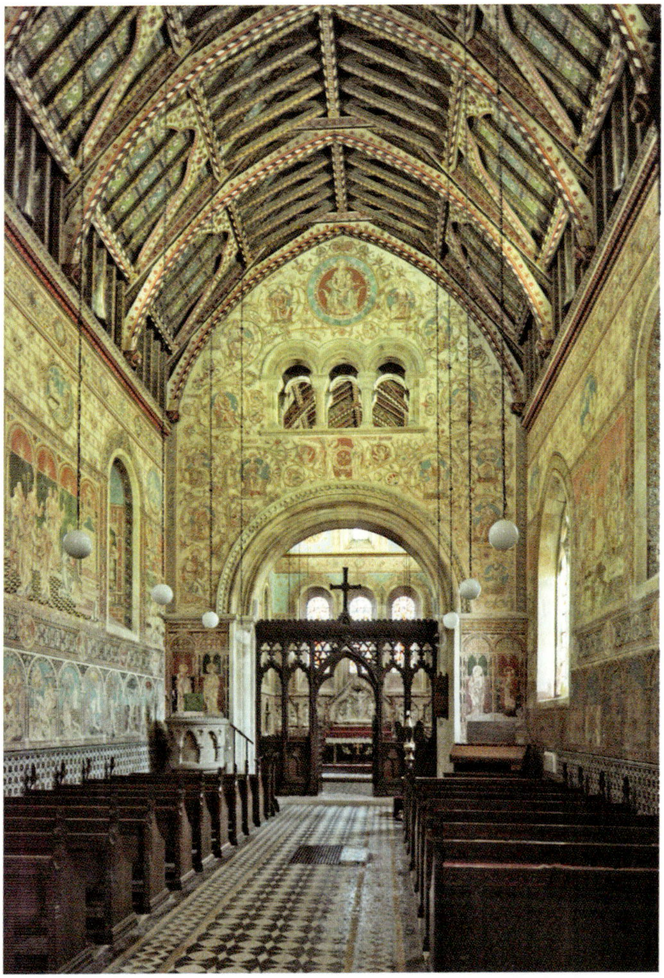

Fig. 7.14 St Michael's, Garton-on-the-Wolds, Yorkshire (ER): chancel-arch with a triple opening above, all by Pearson, and the remarkable scheme of decoration by Clayton & Bell, initiated by Street from 1873, using the spirit-fresco method devised by Thomas Gambier Parry. The oak screen is by Street (1875), made by Rattee & Kett. Paintings around the chancel arch show the Tree of Jesse with the Virgin and Child at the apex: below (left and right) are the Four Doctors of the Western Church (GB [2021]).

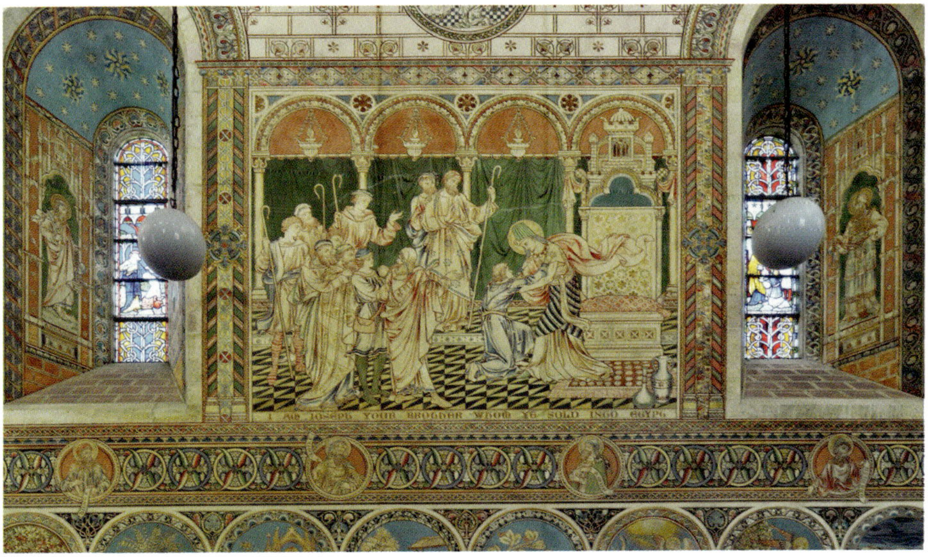

Fig. 7.15 Detail of wall paintings on the nave north wall, St Michael's, Garton-on-the-Wolds, showing Joseph identifying himself to his brothers. In the roundels below are (left to right) the Old Testament minor prophets Hosea, Joel, Amos, and Obadiah, while the window reveals show Abraham (left) and Aaron (right) (GB [2021]).

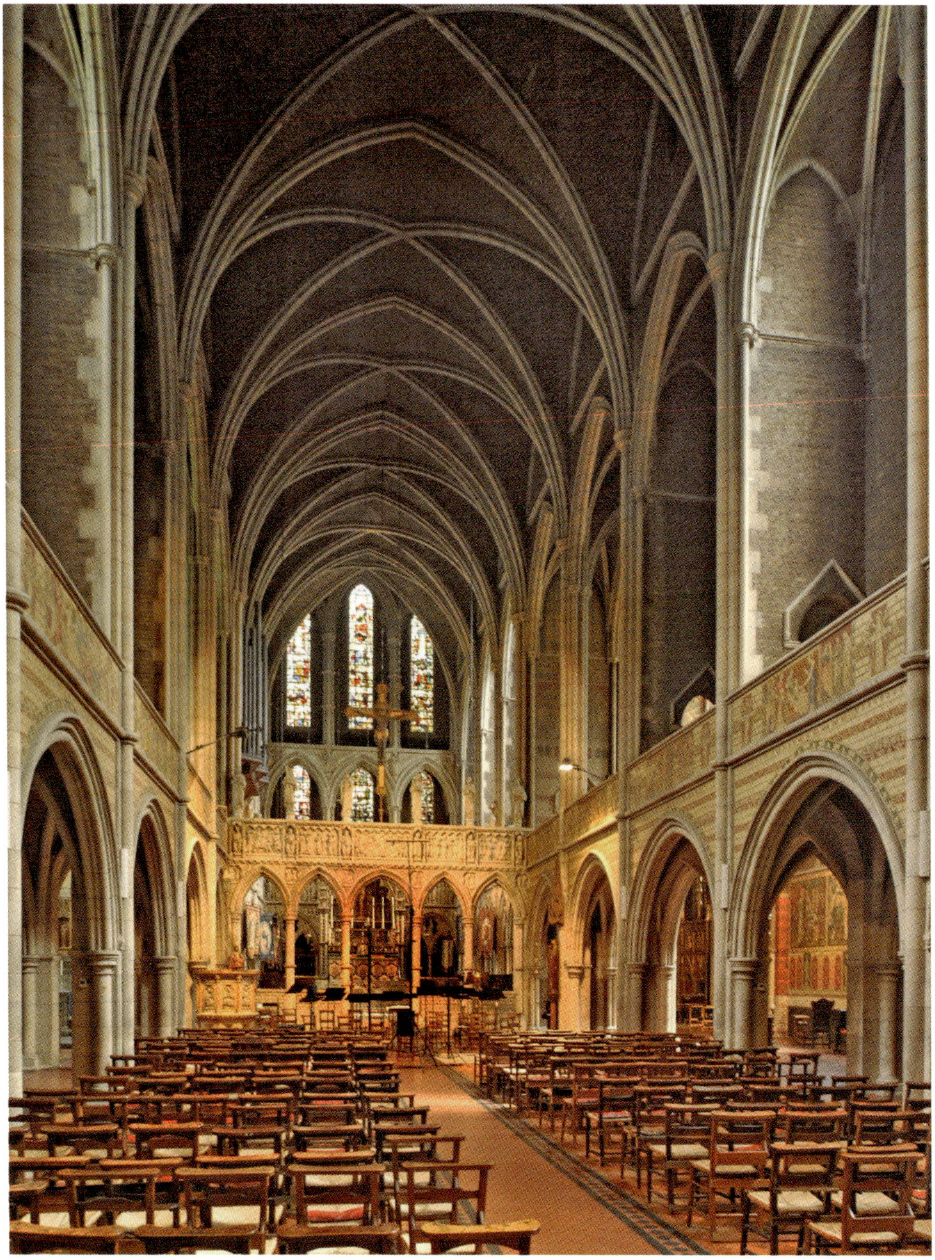

Fig. 7.16 Pearson's St Augustine's, Kilburn, City of Westminster, London (1870–7), a brilliant synthesis of Gothic features derived from several European buildings, especially from Normandy (GB [2019]).

narrow passage aisles (a scheme wholly unlike English mediæval exemplars) was derived from two important French prototypes – Albi Cathedral (1282–1390) and the Church of the Cordeliers, Toulouse (mid-14th century). Frederick Moore Simpson, in an important paper on 'Architectural Developments During Victoria's Reign' published in *The Architectural Review* (1897), observed that the Church of the Cordeliers plan (one not unlike that of King's College Chapel, Cambridge) was one 'eminently fitted for English church worship'. He noted that it made an enormous impact on the planning of churches in the last three decades of Victoria's reign.

Nearly all Pearson's windows are tall lancets, although there are sometimes a few examples of elementary plate-tracery and he often employed elaborate rose or wheel windows. Many of his churches gain *gravitas* from having stone or brick vaults, and St Augustine's is no exception. Brick, too, is the material used inside and out, with stone dressings and First Pointed details. The chancel is defined by a screen, but otherwise the interior forms an unbroken space, ten bays long, entirely covered by vaulting. Arcades support a gallery extending round the church and crossing the transepts, and the architectural effect is mysterious, grand, and Sublime (Fig. 7.16).

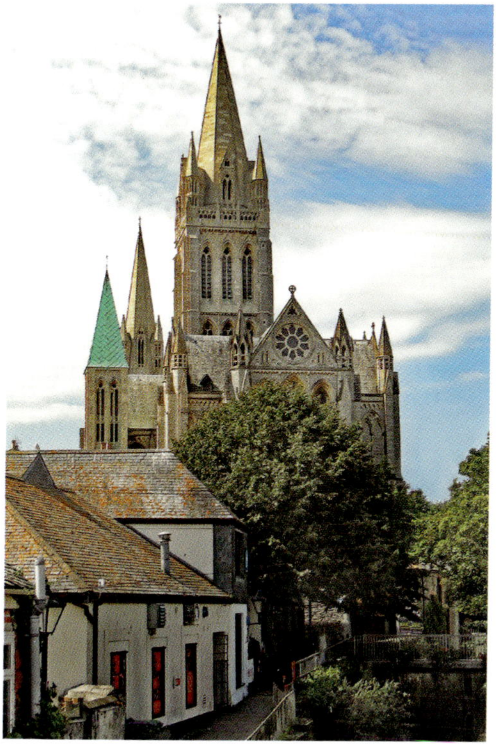

Fig. 7.17 Truro Cathedral, Cornwall (1880–1910), by J.L. Pearson. The central and western steeples resemble that at St Augustine's, Kilburn, so their source is St-Étienne, or Abbaye-aux-Hommes, Caen. Otherwise the building is entirely First Pointed Early English, strongly influenced by Lincoln Cathedral (DNS [2011]).

French Gothic was quoted again by Pearson at Truro Cathedral, Cornwall (1879–1910), a scholarly building in which French (especially Caen) and English First Pointed are convincingly synthesised. In composition there are echoes of Lincoln Cathedral (also suggested by the three steeples and two sets of transepts). The Lincoln connection was no whim, for when the See of Truro was revived (1876), the bishop appointed was E.W. Benson, chancellor at Lincoln from 1872, and Pearson himself was involved in restoration work there from 1875. At Truro the central and western towers and spires (Fig. 7.17) have similarities to the steeple at Kilburn, so their source is St-Étienne, Caen, with a dash of Coutances Cathedral, but the rest of the ensemble is mostly Early English (e.g. Whitby Abbey), though with many French quotations (e.g. Caen and Bayeux), not least the sexpartite vault over the nave. The circular baptistry is one of the richest, most successful, and scholarly elements of the whole design.

Again 13th century in style, combining both French and English elements, is Pearson's Sts Agnes and Pancras, Sefton Park, Liverpool (1882–5), built at the expense of Howard Douglas Horsfall, a wealthy stockbroker. South of the chancel is a Lady chapel with screen (1903) and reredos (1904) by G.F. Bodley, and it is to the work of Bodley and his contemporaries that we now turn.

The Liturgical Background

Eastlake singled out Blomfield, Brooks, Burges, Champneys, E.W. Godwin, G.G. 'Middle' Scott, and Seddon as rising stars in the contemporary Gothic Revival firmament. It would be difficult, he wrote, to 'attempt so much as a general definition of the several qualities of excellence for which these artists' designs are remarkable ... however, it may be said that they have become known to fame, if not exactly as contemporaries, yet at short intervals within the last ten years' (i.e. the 1860s to 1872).

As experiments with Continental Gothic and 'structural polychromy' began to pall, taste moved away from the massiveness, rhetoric, and Sublime over-emphasis of 'muscular Gothic', and a new delicacy began to become apparent in work of several gifted, scholarly Goths. A return to Pugin and Carpenter was seen by several pupils of 'Great' Scott as a means of purifying the Revival and making a fresh start.

Early in the 20th century, buildings such as Butterfield's Keble College, Oxford, and works of Street and others, were ridiculed as 'Victorian monstrosities'. Undergraduates and young dons believed that Keble was by Ruskin, and that it was the ugliest building in the world, having been told it was so. This was partly because late Victorian commentators had turned away from mid-Victorian taste (some polychrome interiors were painted out in the early years of the 20th century and afterwards), and it was not until H.S. Goodhart-Rendel and others (including W.R. Lethaby) began to defend architects active in the 1850s and 1860s that reputations started to be rehabilitated. Yet there were many who saw late Victorian Gothic Revival as a fulfilment of early promise, and the logical artistic pinnacle of the work of Pugin, Carpenter, and other early Goths. Kenneth Clark, in the epilogue to his *The Gothic Revival*, had no doubts: 'nearly all' the best work of the Gothic Revival 'was done after the death of Gilbert Scott', he noted, but 'nearly' is important here, for Burges's masterpieces were created during Scott's lifetime, as were others by Bodley.

Most late Goths, steeped in religion, religious buildings, and liturgical requirements, were real scholars, many of them Anglo-Catholics. In the early 21st century few commentators or critics have religious faith, and are ignorant of the requirements of ritual. Yet at the end of the 19th and beginning of the 20th century *The Architectural Review* (founded 1896) was not only edited (1896–1901) by an Anglo-Catholic Churchman (Henry Wilson), but had several committed Churchmen on the editorial board. Significantly, Wilson saw art, architecture, and religion as closely allied, and admired Roman Catholicism for its visible integration with daily life and art in Western European towns and cities. It became recognised that R.C. Carpenter had introduced Pugin's architectural style and ideals into the Anglican Church with his church of St Mary Magdalene, Munster Square, London (*see* Fig. 5.5), a building that owed much to the old Austin Friars church in London (destroyed).

It became clear that churches with chopped-up interiors were unsuitable for 'Modern Gothic', the protagonists of which (Bodley, Garner, T.G. Jackson, Micklethwaite, 'Middle' Scott, and Sedding) were all Churchmen, and, with the exception of Sedding (a pupil of Street), had all been pupils of 'Great' Scott (and all reacted against the architecture of their masters). Bodley was the eldest of these, and already established; the others were very much the up-and-coming men. It is probably significant that the liturgies at St Alban's, Holborn, and All Saints', Margaret

Street, were, in 1870, considerably influenced by Roman Catholicism, while the English strand was evident at St Mary Magdalene's, Munster Square.

Roman tendencies were therefore associated with Butterfield's architecture, and the English with Carpenter's: to Micklethwaite and others the Carpenter/Pugin model was the more desirable to emulate, merging it with large, open volumes, accommodating the 'people at large', emphasising equality of everybody before the Eucharist, and recognising that church buildings should bring Christianity to all, especially the urban poor.

The Revival of English Late Gothic Styles

Bodley's career spanned virtually the entire Victorian period. Much of his early designs share characteristics with mid-Victorian work, and in the late 1850s he was as 'muscular' a Goth as any. For example, contrasting accents can be found in his powerful All Saints', Selsley (King's Stanley), Gloucestershire (1858–62), in the early French Gothic style, with a mighty saddleback-roofed tower and much plate-tracery (Fig. 7.18).

In 1858, the year John Purchas's *Directorium* was published, Bodley was commissioned by Charles Beanlands, who had been Wagner's curate at St Paul's, Brighton (by R.C. Carpenter, as previously noted), to design St Michael and All Angels, Brighton (1858–61) – later gloriously extended from 1865 to designs by Burges and John Starling Chapple. Although St Michael's is 'muscular', the stained-glass windows contain a considerable proportion of white glass, and the colouring was influenced by late mediæval English and Flemish glass, pointing to a new direction for English Gothic Revival away from French and Italian Gothic exemplars. This stained glass was by Morris, Marshall, Faulkner, & Co., the first significant ecclesiastical commission for this firm, founded in 1861, which was also involved in Bodley's mature work at St Martin-on-the-Hill, Scarborough, Yorkshire NR (1861–3). Of St Martin's, *The Ecclesiologist* said that the style was 'severe Early Pointed, the tower ... in particular showing evident marks of extremely early French style', but inside the building Bodley limited his use of structural polychromy and applied his first large-scale design of painted decoration, harking back to Pugin and mediæval examples, although it was largely confined to the chancel, and was completed in 1864. St Martin's is particularly interesting for its lovely

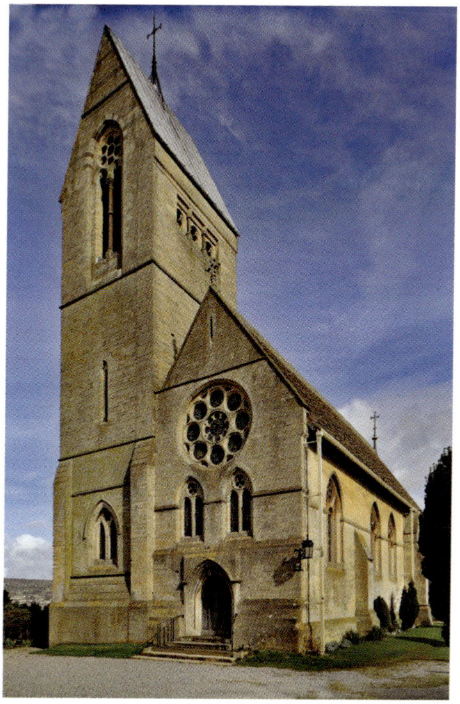

Fig. 7.18 All Saints', Selsley, King's Stanley, Gloucestershire (1858–62), an early masterpiece by G.F. Bodley in a French-inspired early First Pointed style, showing the west front, saddleback tower, and some plate-tracery. West door inserted 1887–8 (GB [2014]).

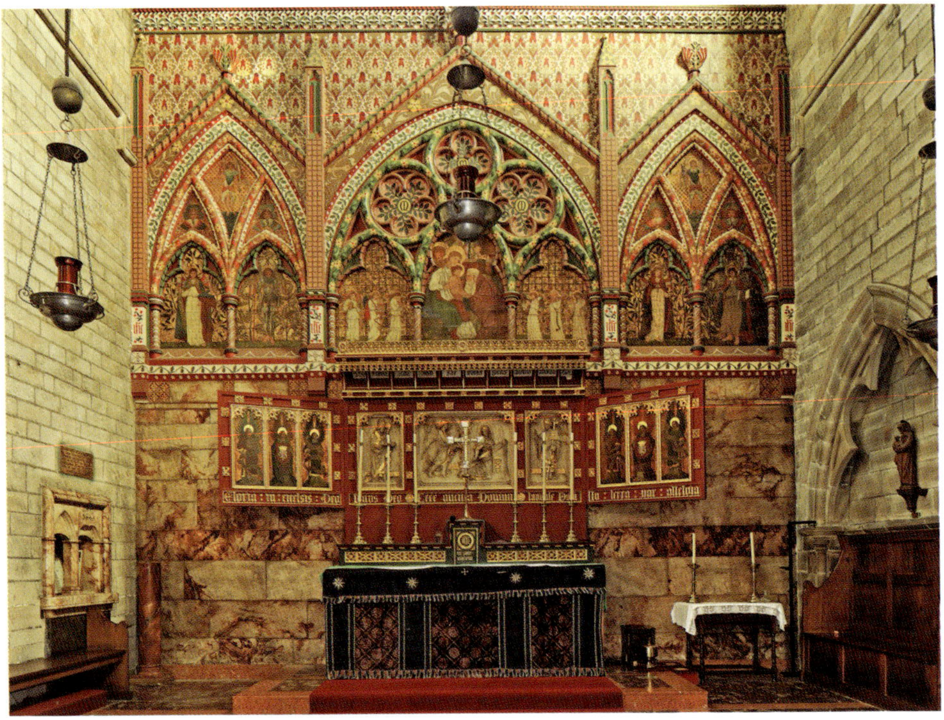

Fig. 7.19 East end of St Martin-on-the-Hill, Scarborough, Yorkshire (NR) (1861–3), by Bodley. The central element is derived from the 13th-century blind-tracery of the lavatorium at Kirkham Priory, an Augustinian foundation in the ER, north-east of York. In the centre is an Adoration of the Magi designed by Burne-Jones, and painted decorations are by George Campfield, William Morris's chief glass painter. The allusion to the destroyed priory may suggest the revival of religious traditions so violently disrupted by the Dissolution and the Reformation. Bodley's reredos, installed 1890, reflects the architect's later, more delicate manner (GB [2013]).

Pre-Raphaelite interior to which Dante Gabriel Rossetti, Ford Madox Brown, William Morris, and others contributed. Bodley designed the rood screen and reredos (Fig. 7.19).

Now these connections are interesting with respect to Bodley's change of direction. Clearly the influence of Morris and his firm was significant, but so was that of Purchas, who became curate at St Paul's, Brighton (1861), when St Michael and All Angels was consecrated, and he and Bodley were acquainted. It is clear that the plan of the sanctuary of St Michael's was modelled on Purchas's work: indeed, Bodley's later designs for sanctuaries, with their large reredoses and high gradines, owed virtually everything to Purchas's *Directorium Anglicanum*, the second edition (1866) of which, edited by Frederick George Lee, contained illustrations by Edmund Sedding, brother of John Dando Sedding. Both had worked in Street's office and were deeply sympathetic to Anglican Ritualism. They worshipped in St Mary's, Crown Street, Soho, where John Charles Chambers had been appointed (1856) perpetual curate, and Richard Frederick Littledale (an associate of J.M. Neale, one of the founders of the Cambridge Camden Society) joined him there (1861). As Anthony Symondson has pointed out, St Mary's was a 'river of ritualistic activity into which many tributaries flowed': the Seddings lodged with Chambers while they worked in Street's office;

Littledale introduced Edmund to Purchas; and Purchas introduced young Sedding to Lee. Thus Lee's version of Purchas's *Directorium* acquired Sedding's illustrations, pronounced 'full of Catholic feeling' and 'correct taste' in 'Christian art', but which owed perhaps more to 19th-century Continental R.C. design in Northern Europe than to pre-Reformation English models.

So Roman Catholic liturgical practices and design became important to certain strands of Victorian Anglicanism. J.D. Sedding's ecclesiastical leanings were ritualistic Anglo-Catholic, and he, in turn, influenced most of his pupils to follow suit. Symondson has made clear that Edmund Sedding's association with the *Directorium* connected Neale through Littledale with the 'progressive architectural movements' of the late 19th century, and Neale was a patron of both Street and Bodley.

All Saints', Cambridge, and Bodley's Later Work

With All Saints', Jesus Lane, Cambridge (1862–71), Bodley decisively broke with mid-Victorian Continental Gothic: All Saints' is unquestionably English- and Pugin-inspired work in the style of the late 13th and early 14th centuries, and makes a return to the 'homely and sweet' native styles, as *The Ecclesiologist* put it, so was recognised at the time as an important precedent. Several commentators claimed Bodley's change of style at All Saints' was forced on him by conservative dons at the University of Cambridge. However, *The Ecclesiologist* saw things differently: it noted, 'with some satisfaction', that Mr Bodley 'had ... restricted himself to pure English forms. The time for a reaction from exclusively French or Italian types' had arrived. A cursory trawl through the architectural and ecclesiological press of the time shows that opinion was already moving away from mid-Victorian 'muscularity' towards English exemplars: 'conservative dons' had nothing to do with this.

It was with St John the Baptist, Tue Brook, Liverpool (1868–71), however, that Bodley's acceptance of 14th-century English exemplars became complete, and the resultant masterpiece makes this glowingly apparent (Fig. 7.20). Eastlake noted that here Bodley had revived the leading elements of the style 'carefully and ably', and had introduced very beautiful colour 'which pervades the whole building from its primary construction to the last touch of embellishment'. Indeed, not 'all the scientific treatises on polychromy could have supplied a better scheme', wrote Eastlake, who felt that in 'this truly remarkable work the genuine grace of Mediæval art seems at length to have been reached'. The church was erected at the sole cost of Eliza Ann Reade (née Thornton), wife of the Revd John Chorley Reade (the incumbent, remaining there for nine years), and Eastlake felt that 'for correctness of design, refined workmanship, and artistic decoration' the building could 'take foremost rank among examples of the Revival'. In so many ways St John's displays Bodley's scholarship and sense of rightness in ecclesiastical art, for he designed and supervised virtually everything. The chancel arch acquired a mural by C.E. Kempe, and there is some decent glass by Morris & Co. Altogether, the interior is a wonderful, lovely ensemble, and in the 1990s still looked marvellous (having been beautifully restored in the 1970s by Stephen Dykes Bower). St John's is one of the half-dozen or so first-rate Anglican church interiors in which colour and architecture blend into a satisfying whole.

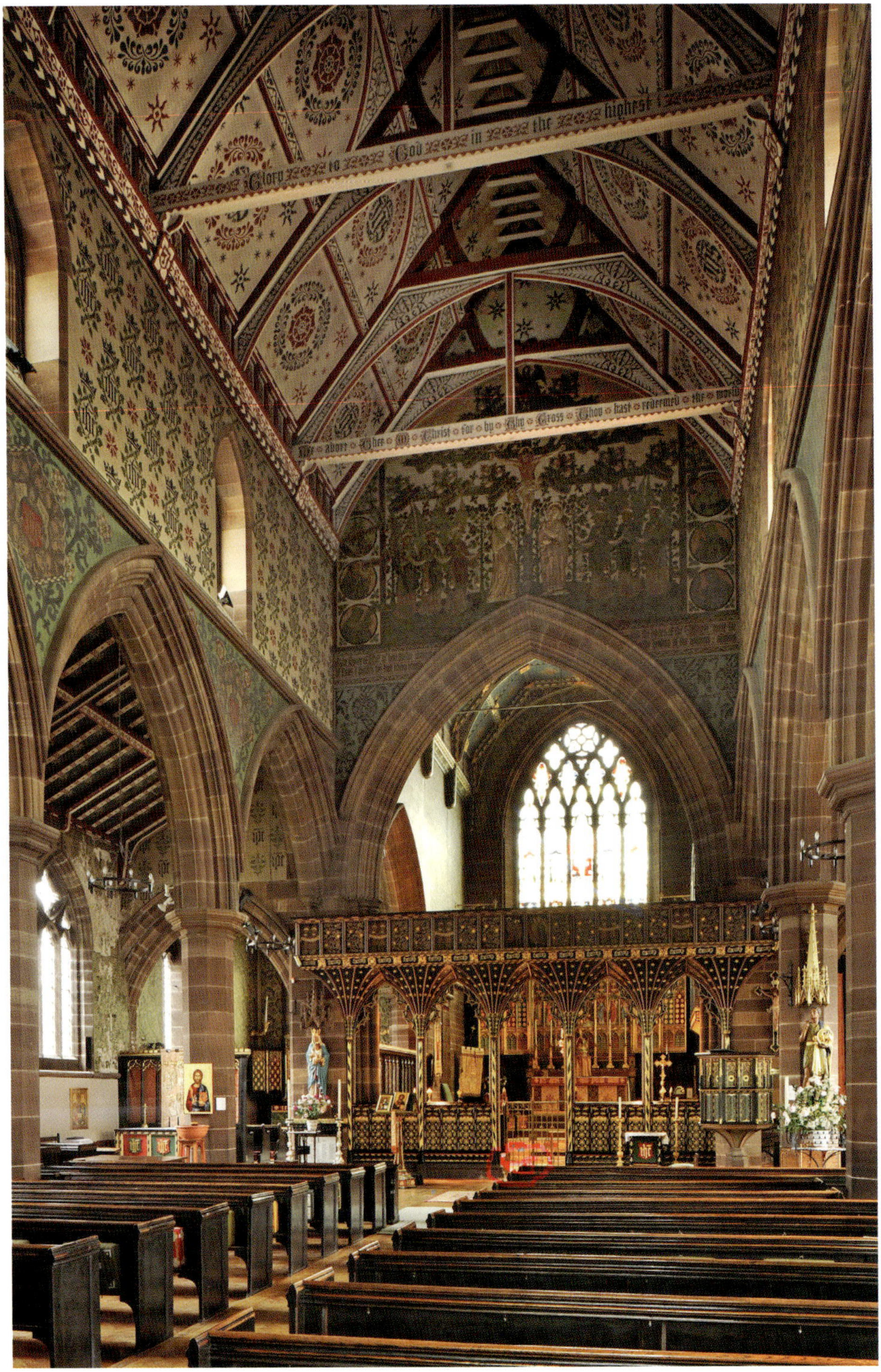

Fig. 7.20 St John the Baptist, Tue Brook, Liverpool (1867–71), by Bodley, showing S.E. Dykes Bower's brilliant partial restorations and simplifications (1968–71) of the original colour scheme by C.E. Kempe, F.R. Leach, and W.M. Shaw. The fine high chancel screen was the first designed by Bodley (GB [2013]).

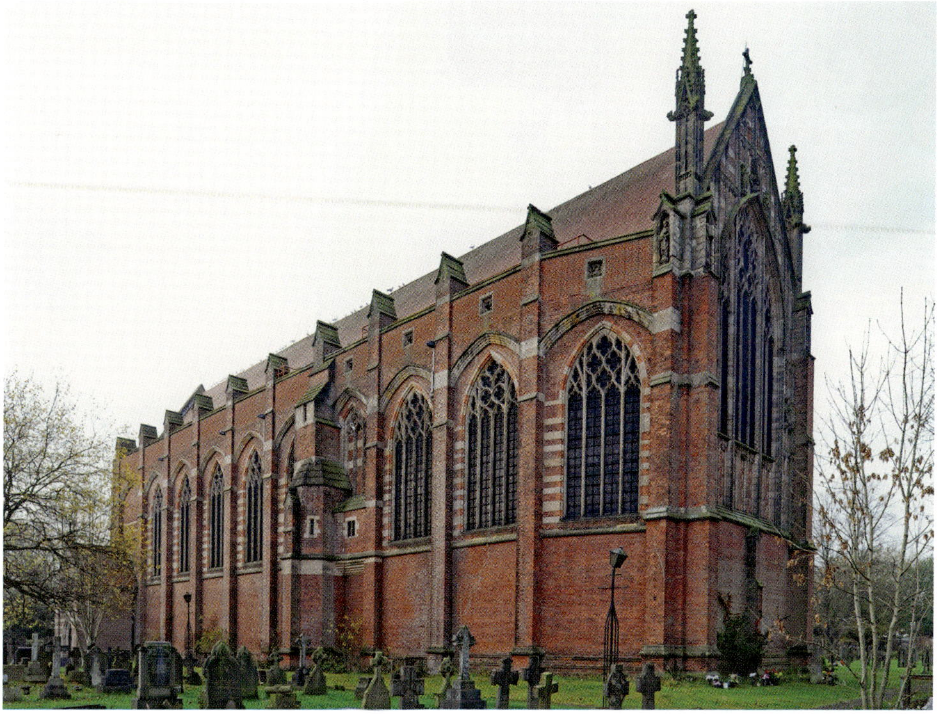

Fig. 7.21 St Augustine's, Pendlebury, Greater Manchester (1870–4), by Bodley & Garner, the whole of brick, with stone dressings, with the east window set high above the reredos inside. Windows have late Second Pointed flowing tracery: buttresses appear shallow because they are mostly within the building (GB [2013]).

In 1869 Bodley went into partnership with Thomas Garner, who had 'pronounced English sympathies' in architectural terms. The first of a series of outstanding churches designed by them was St Augustine's, Pendlebury, Lancashire (1871–4): the architects reverted to delicate tracery of the 14th-century type, and there were other aspects that deserve note, as they proved profoundly influential (Fig. 7.21). Inside are massive wall-piers pierced to create narrow passage aisles giving the congregation access to seats in the nave. Apart from Albi (which is the exemplar usually quoted), the Church of the Cordeliers, Toulouse, is sometimes mentioned, but it is more likely that Bodley & Garner took as their starting point the well-known Dominican church, Gent, Belgium, a plan and perspective of which had been published in *The Building News* (30 July 1869), and which reappeared in *Church Design for Congregations: Its Development and Possibilities* (1870) by James Cubitt, a publication that has not had the attention it deserves. The arrangement of a monumental undivided interior (without a chancel arch); the wide, spacious nave, and narrow passage aisles; daring mixture of tough, early French Gothic and delicate English 14th- and 15th-century detail; and uncluttered, unified volume, covered with a coloured timber wagon vault, was a taste of things to come (Fig. 7.22). The east window is vast, and has flowing Curvilinear tracery of the 14th-century type, but with certain features reminiscent of 15th-century work. In addition, the rood screen and reredos look to a late Gothic and Flemish ancestry. Bodley & Garner went a lot further than Pearson did at Kilburn in Anglicising the Albi (or, more obviously, Gent) type and ensuring visibility: it marks

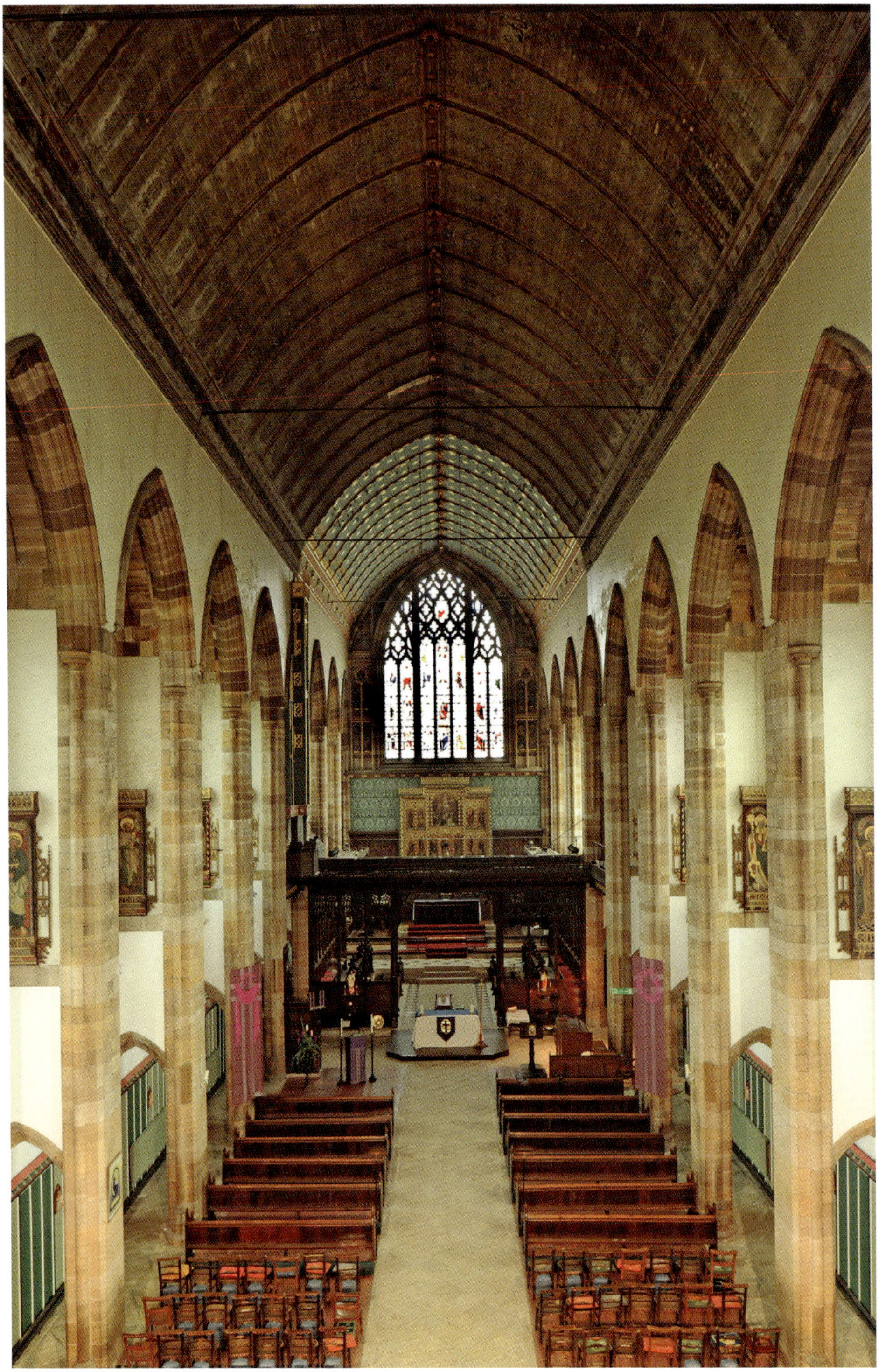

Fig. 7.22 St Augustine's, Pendlebury, showing the wall-piers (pierced by arches to form aisle passages, and carrying transverse vaults to stiffen the walls). The rich chancel decorations are typical of Bodley's return to late mediæval styles (GB [2013]).

the beginnings of the 'modern' Victorian church. Like many of the finest ecclesiastical buildings of the Gothic Revival, St Augustine's was built at the expense of a wealthy individual, in this case the banker, Edward Stanley Heywood.

Bodley & Garner's Holy Angels', Hoar Cross, Staffordshire (1872–1900), where scholarship, refinement, and sumptuous detail were combined in the one estate church for a small congregation, was commissioned as a memorial to Hugo Francis Meynell Ingram, of Hoar Cross and Temple Newsam, who died in a hunting accident. It was paid for by his widow, the Honourable Emily Charlotte (née Wood), daughter of the 1st Viscount Halifax. Holy Angels' was consecrated in 1876, but later lengthened by a bay, acquired a Lady chapel and another chapel north of the 'chantry chapel', and a narthex was added in 1906 to designs by Cecil Greenwood Hare, who took over Bodley's practice after the latter died. The date of commencement of the building of Holy Angels' is interesting, for it was shortly after work started on Christ the Consoler at Skelton-on-Ure, yet the styles of the two churches could hardly be more different.

Pendlebury and Hoar Cross are examples of different approaches to church design: the former, large, tough, and austere, is essentially one big space with powerful wall-piers carrying the nave arcade, has no transepts, and the chancel is not emphasised architecturally either inside or out; the latter is ultra-refined and luxuriant in its welter of beautiful decorations, and consists of a nave (without clerestorey), lean-to aisles, transepts (with tall crenellated panelled tower in the Perpendicular style over the crossing), chancel taller than the nave, and the chapels mentioned above (Fig. 7.23). Apart from the tower, the style is mostly Second Pointed, with side windows mostly

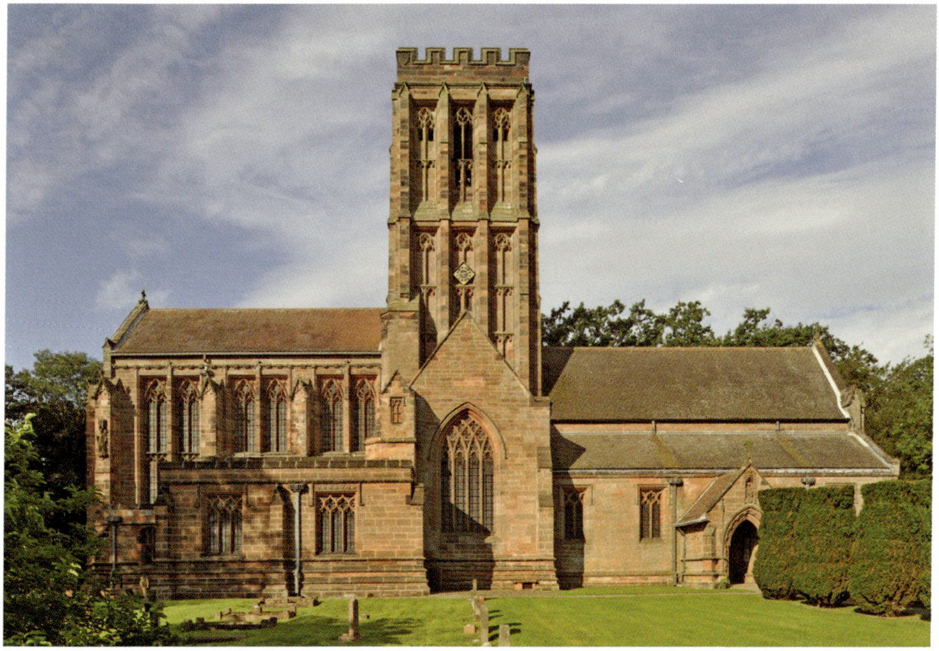

Fig. 7.23 Holy Angels', Hoar Cross, Staffordshire (1872–6), by Bodley & Garner, showing the tower derived from the late 15th-century St Mary's, Ilminster, Somerset, the design of which was influenced by Wells Cathedral's crossing tower. The style is entirely Second Pointed, although the tower is just beginning to turn to Perpendicular (GB [2013]).

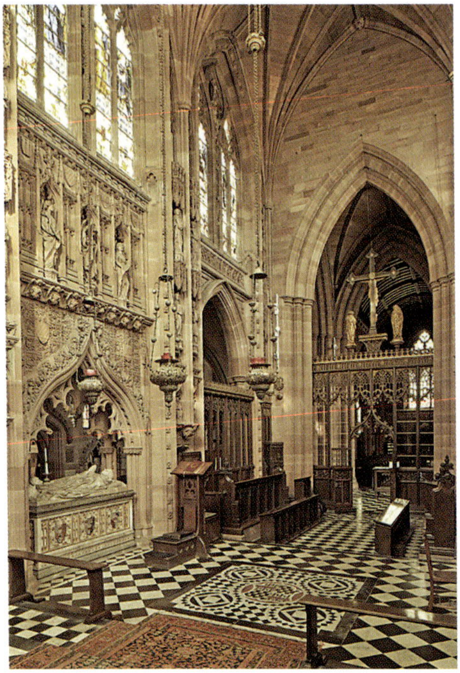

Fig. 7.24 Holy Angels', Hoar Cross: chancel looking west towards the rood screen, with, on the left, the canopied tomb of Hugo Meynell Ingram, inspired by the mid-14th-century Percy tomb in Beverley Minster, Yorkshire (ER) (GB [2013]).

square headed with hood moulds, and larger windows with intricate tracery. Like Pugin's churches, Holy Angels' is compartmented inside. Pendlebury emphasised structure, but Hoar Cross showed how delicate late English Decorated and Perpendicular could be (Fig. 7.24).

Holy Angels', then, was really partly a mausoleum, erected both as a tomb and a memorial by a woman whose religious views had been profoundly influenced by her brother, Charles Lindley Wood, who had become an Anglo-Catholic while up at Oxford. In 1868 Wood agreed to Pusey's request that he should become president of the English Church Union, the organisation founded in 1860 to maintain the Catholic heritage of the Church of England and to defend those who were under attack for their religious principles. Wood played no small part in bringing to an end the persecution of Ritualist clergy, and he was an important ecumenist, active in attempting a rapprochement with Rome. He probably influenced his sister's choice of architects for Holy Angels'.

Another beautiful (and stunningly well-sited) Bodley & Garner church (though apparently designed by Bodley alone) is St Mary the Virgin, Clumber Park, Nottinghamshire (1886–9), commissioned by Henry Pelham Archibald Douglas Pelham-Clinton, 7th Duke of Newcastle-under-Lyme (a great-nephew of Beresford Hope), when he was just 21 (Figs 7.25 and 7.26). St Mary's consists of an aisleless nave, a chancel with a chapel to the south and sacristies to the north, short transepts, and a central tower with octagonal spire. It is vaulted, and was Bodley's own favourite design, yet he did not manage to complete the furnishings, as a quarrel with the duke led to his dismissal. The rood screen, stalls, and other enrichments were by the Revd Ernest Geldart; the stained glass was by Bodley's former pupil Kempe; and the statue of the Virgin was by another pupil, John Ninian Comper.

Newcastle's intensely Ritualistic piety (in stark contrast with his family's history of profligacy) seems to have prompted Clumber Chapel as a statement of his sense of Christian responsibility. Nevertheless, there clung about scented Ritualism, and indeed revived Gothic, a suspicious taint: the lavish chapel at Clumber, not least its dedication to the Blessed Virgin Mary (devotion to whose cult offended Protestant sensibilities), had unwholesome associations for some. A nostalgic pæderasty was not always that far removed from a romantic longing for a revived Catholic Ritualism in the minds of many. It may be of interest to point out that Oscar Wilde's 'Dorian

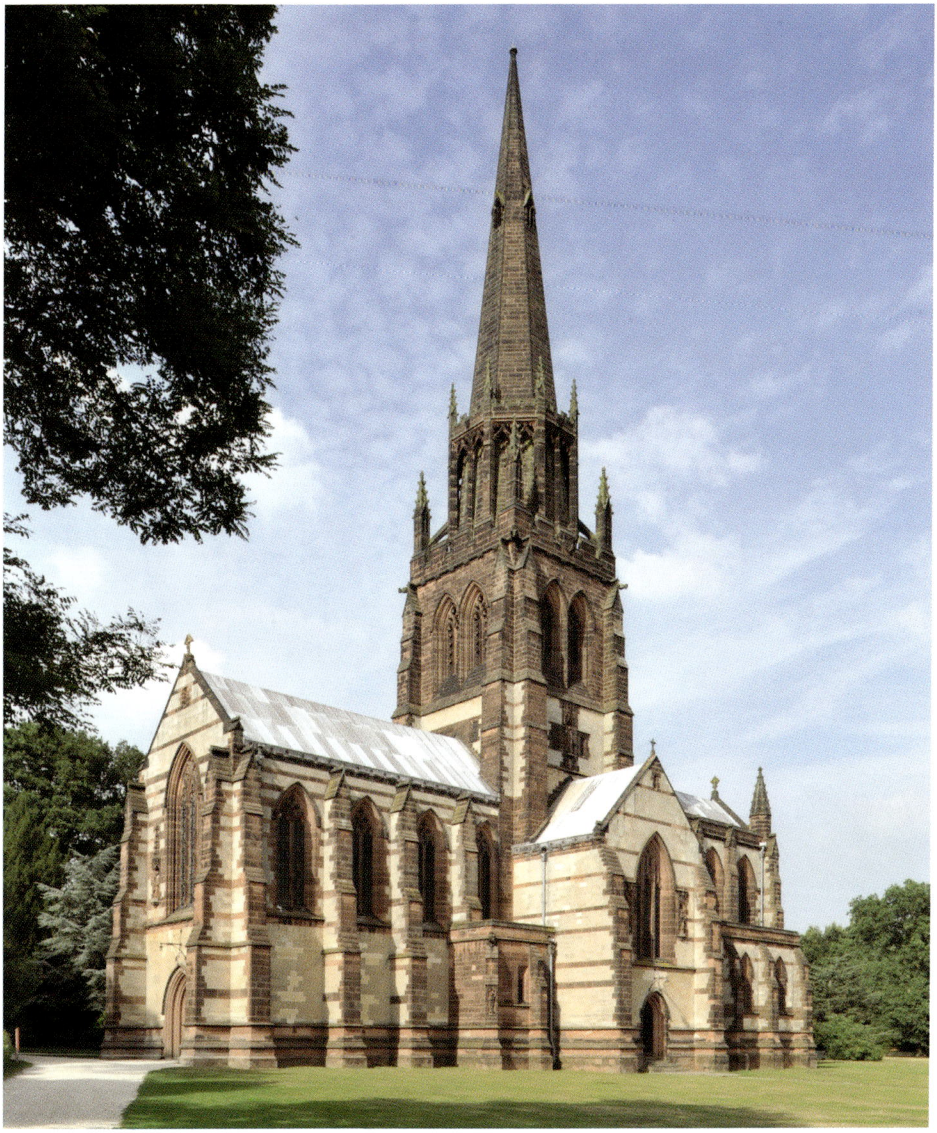

Fig. 7.25 St Mary the Virgin, Clumber Park, Nottinghamshire (1886–9), nominally by Bodley & Garner (but actually by Bodley alone), showing the structural polychromy. The spire is modelled on that of the uncommonly fine mediæval St Patrick's, Patrington, Yorkshire (ER), and the chancel is almost the same length as the unaisled nave, which has blind arcading along its walls, and a wall passage above (GB [2013]).

Gray' owned a large house in Nottinghamshire and took great delight in everything 'connected with the service of the Church', not least his magnificent collection of vestments with orphreys starred with medallions of saints and martyrs, notably St Sebastian (of course). There is no evidence that Newcastle indulged in depravities practised by 'Dorian Gray', the publication of which (July 1890), created more than a frisson of fear in some quarters, appearing to justify the suspicion that Æstheticism, Ritualism, Anglo-Catholicism, and everything associated with those, including Gothic, posed some kind of moral danger, threatening the very fabric of society.

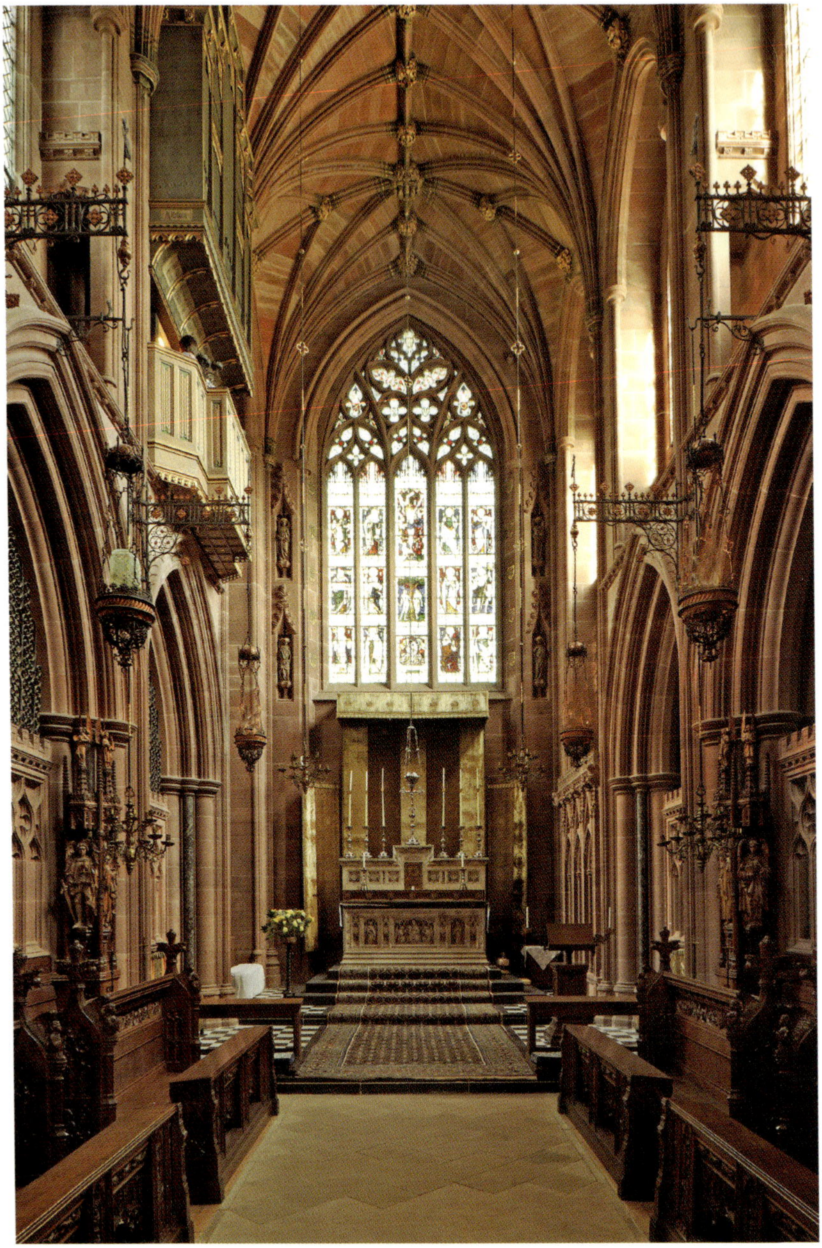

Fig. 7.26 St Mary's, Clumber Park: chancel showing the great east window with late Decorated tracery. A wall passage runs above the arcading on the right (GB [2013]).

Today, Clumber church stands, separated from the lake by a stretch of greensward, and backed by fine mature trees: one has to try to imagine it as intended, as a church in the park of a great house (demolished in the 1930s). It remains as a poignant memorial to the 7th Duke and his Anglo-Catholicism.

8

The Late Victorian Anglican Church in Several Manifestations

Where the Chancel can be of considerable length, then there is no doubt that a high Rood Screen is the greatest possible ornament to the interior, but ... requires very considerable depth behind it to give it its true value. It is curious, however, the prejudice one frequently meets against a Screen.

TEMPLE LUSHINGTON MOORE (1856–1920):
Architectural Association Journal, **xxii** (1907), 36.

Bodley fills an important position in the history of English ecclesiastical architecture. If Pugin, Scott, and Street were the pioneers whose work went hand in hand with the Oxford movement in its early days, Bodley is their counterpart in the last quarter of the nineteenth century.

PAUL WATERHOUSE (1861–1924):
Entry on Bodley in *The Dictionary of National Biography Supplement* (January 1901–December 1911) (Oxford: Oxford University Press, 1920), 189.

Introduction

At Bodley & Garner's St Augustine's, Pendlebury, the dominant architectural theme is structure, and the interior is one great space. Another church, the design of which goes even further as a celebration of one huge Sublime volume, is St Bartholomew's, Brighton (1872–4), by Edmund Evan Scott for the Anglo-Catholic Arthur Wagner. When the latter's father, H.M. Wagner, became Vicar of Brighton and West Blatchington in 1824 there were only the mediæval parish church of St Nicholas and a couple of proprietary chapels to minister to Anglicans: when A.D. Wagner died in 1902 there were 17 churches, 5 of which, lavishly fitted out for High Anglican worship, were paid for out of his own pocket. Of those five, shamefully, two (All Saints' and St Anne's) have been demolished.

Arthur Wagner imbibed his Ecclesiology at Cambridge in the 1840s: from the start of his career he was a convinced Ritualist. Fabulously rich through inherited wealth (the Wagners, originally from Germany, settled in London in 1717, and became hatters to both royalty and the British Army), his life was devoted to building churches for the care of all, especially the poor, in Brighton. He became vicar when a parish was assigned to Carpenter's St Paul's, in 1873. Wagner not only beautified St Paul's, but financed the erection of other Brighton churches, including the Annunciation (begun 1864 to designs by William Dancy, with later work from 1881 by E.E. Scott, F.T. Cawthorn, and Martin Travers), the enormous St Bartholomew's, and the

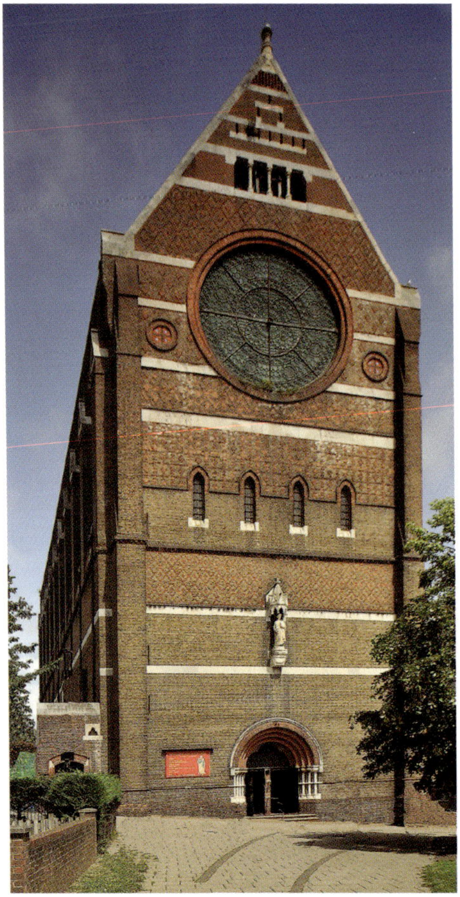

Fig. 8.1 St Bartholomew's, Brighton, East Sussex (1872–4), by E.E. Scott. The huge front has a canopied statue set on the wall high over the west door, and above are four small lancets and an enormous circular window. The side elevation is articulated at high level by buttresses (the external expression of the wall-piers), between which are lancets (GB [2021]).

magnificent St Martin's (1874–5 – the first major work by Somers Clarke, with later fittings unsurpassed for their date). He also paid for the Church of St Mary the Virgin, Buxted, East Sussex (1885–6 – by Scott & Cawthorn), financed several schools, and even houses for poorer parishioners, and in 1855 founded an Anglican Sisterhood, the Community of the Blessed Virgin Mary, which established a house at Buxted (St Margaret's Cottage [1878]) for the reclamation of prostitutes.

Although Wagner commissioned some of the best architects of the day, for St Bartholomew's he went to a local man, E.E. Scott, whose great church, of plain brick, outshone Wagner's other creations (Fig. 8.1). Its nave is higher than Westminster Abbey's: almost devoid of ornament, its architecture is tougher and bolder than anything by Brooks or Street. Articulation of the nave walls is by massive wall-piers forming three-sided recesses, and so is derived from Albi, Toulouse, and Gent. The east end was embellished in the Arts and Crafts manner by Henry Wilson (Fig. 8.2).

Father Wagner's churches were visible expressions of his Ritualism (known locally as 'The London, Brighton, & South Coast Religion'), and were often defaced with graffiti. As he moved (with many of his contemporaries) towards a more pronounced Anglo-Catholicism, he came under the scrutiny of the guardians of Evangelical Protestantism: his curates were denounced as 'papists', and he was beaten up by thugs.

It is impossible to understand the complexities of Victorian ecclesiastical architecture without reference to the concerns of the time, and this is as true of the later part of the Victorian Age as it was of the beginning. For example, Wagner's Sisterhood of the Community of the Blessed Virgin Mary was a response to the huge numbers of brothels that existed at the time in Brighton and Hove, some of which had children working in them. Thus some explanation is necessary to put the physical fabric in context, not least because many (perhaps even most) people will be unfamiliar with the subject today.

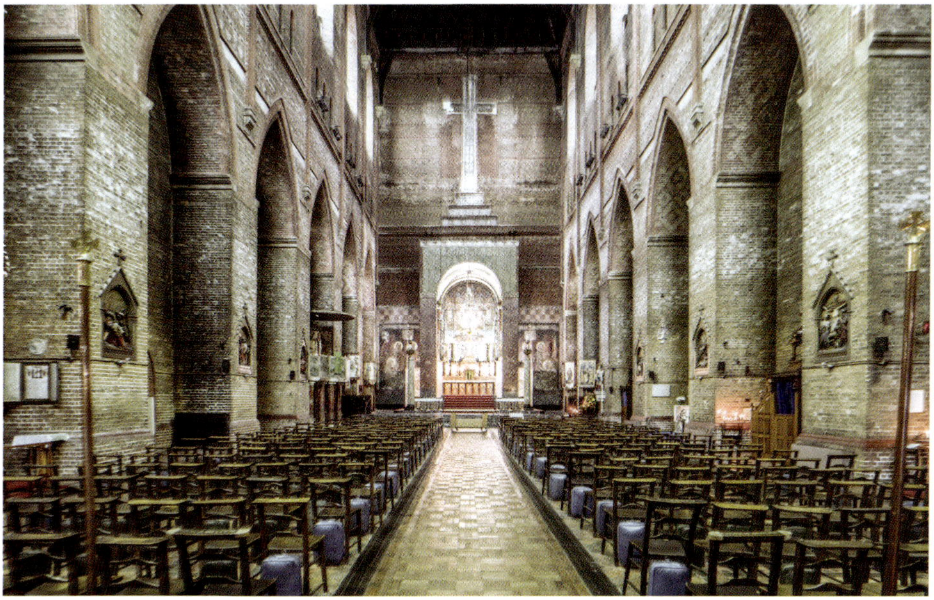

Fig. 8.2 St Bartholomew's, Brighton, showing the internal wall-piers forming arched recesses, suggestive of nave arcades. Above is a vestigial triforium of three slit lancets to each bay, and above that are the tall clerestorey windows. The east end, fitted out by Henry Wilson, terminates the vista in a composition of Sublime power (JS [2018]).

Anglo-Catholicism and Controversy

Anglo-Catholicism is Catholicism of the Anglican type which, according to the traditions and scholarship of the English Church, had always maintained a certain amount of independence. Tractarians held that the English Church, even as Reformed, was the national 'branch of the Church Catholic' in its historical sense, emphasised by the deference paid by the Church of England to tradition. Revived architectural style, rituals, and liturgies formed an essential part of this.

Historical continuity lay behind much of the revival of both Anglicanism and Gothic: early in Victoria's reign efforts were expended on the recovery of the meaning and nature of the Sacraments, because those were no longer widely understood (even, it seems, by clergymen, especially of Evangelical persuasion). During the 1840s and 1850s, apart from the well-publicised secessions to the R.C. Church, the main controversies in the Church of England were connected with Baptism and the Eucharist. As far as architecture was concerned, both Sacraments were important, bringing about architectural responses, but of the two the Eucharist was by far the more significant.

In the 1850s, George Anthony Denison (at Oxford when the Tractarians began their activities), Archdeacon of Taunton, defined his doctrinal position on the Eucharist in three sermons in Wells Cathedral (1853–4). He affirmed the Real (though non-material) Presence of Christ in the sacred Elements, and the consequent adorability of the Sacrament (though not of the sensible species). This doctrine defines the actual and objective presence of the Body and Blood of Christ in the Eucharistic Sacrament. Thus Denison upheld the Sacrament as a true symbol (i.e. a representation of something that it is), thereby receiving Inward Grace, while the Protestant/Calvinistic/

Evangelical persuasions denied the reality, claiming that the Body and Blood were present only in an allegorical sense (i.e. representing what it is not in itself).

The Low Church Evangelical Alliance (an association of individual Christians of different denominations established [1846] to oppose Ritualism and promote a scripture-based Christianity) instituted a prosecution, and in 1856 Denison's views were declared contrary to the Articles of Religion by John Bird Sumner, Archbishop of Canterbury. Previously, in relation to the Gorham case, Sumner (chosen, significantly, by a Whig premier [Lord John Russell] as primate) had concurred with the judgement of the Privy Council that a clergyman of the Church of England 'need not believe in baptismal regeneration'. Bishop Phillpotts of Exeter therefore accused the archbishop of heresy, and the Anglican Church lost several clergy to Rome. Denison was sentenced to deprivation, but appealed to the Court of Arches, resulting in a reversal on a technical point in 1857, and an appeal against this decision was dismissed (1858) by the Privy Council's Judicial Committee without any determination of the substantive question, all of which (as in the Gorham case) merely served general confusion. The Anglican Church's position vis-à-vis the State was seen by High Churchmen as anomalous, and led to audible stampedes of clerical boots to Rome and Dissent.

High Church, Tractarian, or Ritualist parties within the Anglican Church had always attracted displeasure in certain quarters. Some practices introduced by High Church clergy again came before the Privy Council's Judicial Committee in the case of *Westerton v. Liddell* (1857), when 'Ritualistic' services came under attack from those who disapproved of what were regarded as 'crypto-popery' leading to 'perfumed Rome'. However, the result of this case (which included a declaration that liturgical candles were 'contrary to law' except, absurdly, for the purpose of 'giving necessary light') was not regarded as entirely discouraging to Ritualists, and over the next two decades there was an increase in ritual usage, such as vestments, altar lights, and incense.

In 1860 the English Church Union (of which, as noted above, Charles Lindley Wood [from 1885 2nd Viscount Halifax] became president in 1868) was formed to uphold High Church principles and to assist clergy who attracted Evangelical disfavour. However, the latter responded by forming (1865) the Church Association to prosecute Ritualists and prevent their practices. Matters came to such a pass that a Royal Commission was appointed (1867), which recommended that parishioners hostile to Ritualism should be assisted to stop it: between 1867 and 1871 the Privy Council's Judicial Committee was openly hostile to Ritualism.

Ritualists' position in London had not been helped when Tait was enthroned as Archbishop of Canterbury (1869): it will be recalled that he had contested claims made in Newman's *Tract xc* (also torn to shreds by Wiseman). Tait had been appointed Bishop of London in 1856, and in 1859 he withdrew the licence of Alfred Poole, Curate of St Barnabas's, Pimlico, objecting to his practice of hearing Confession. Poole appealed to the then Archbishop of Canterbury, who upheld Tait's sentence. In 1859 Tait also had to contend with the uproar occasioned by Ritualistic innovations at St George-in-the-East, Wapping, by Charles Fuge Lowder (who had served as a curate [1851–6] under Liddell), on whose head fell the wrath of a blaspheming mob of 'anti-papist' rioters, and, later, of the Church Association. Lowder, however, nothing daunted, secured the site of St Peter's, London Docks, in 1860, and a new church, designed by Frederick Hyde Pownall in the French First Pointed style, with

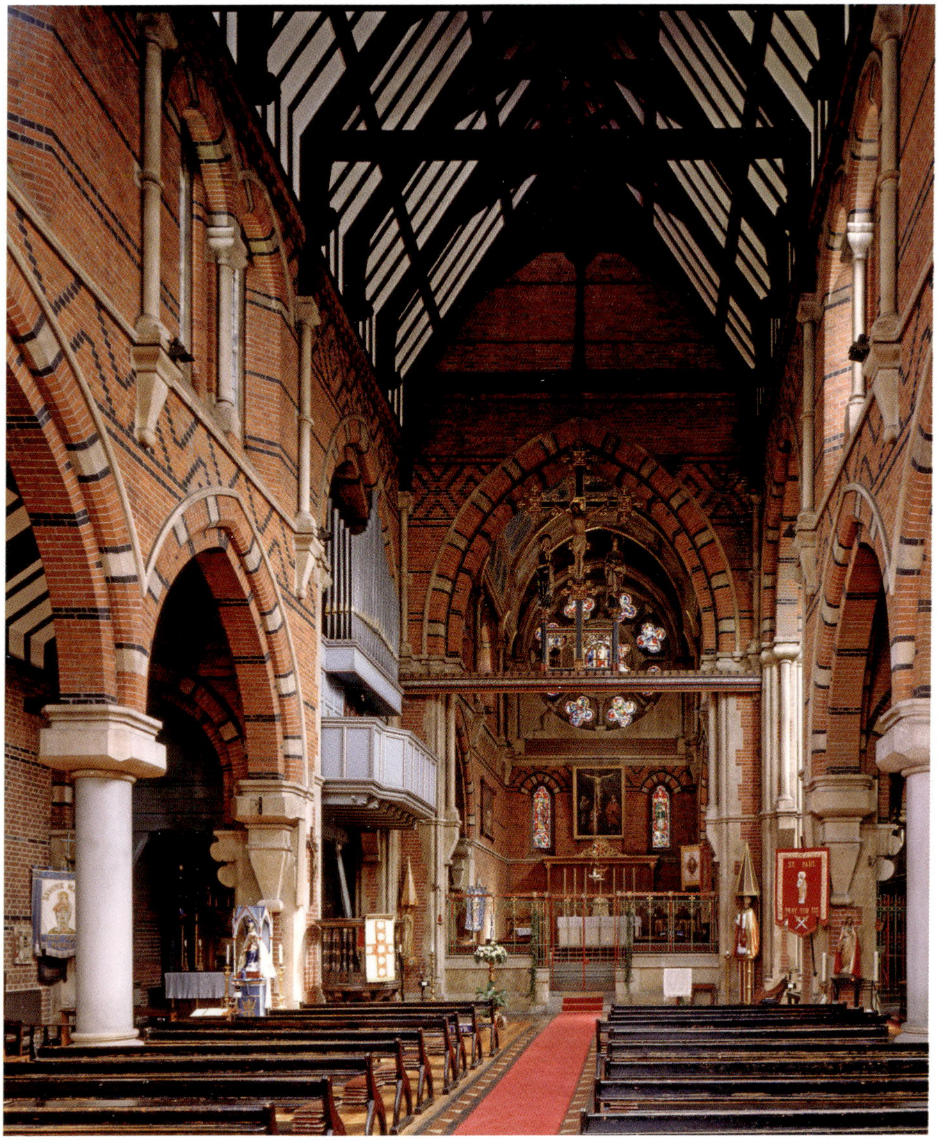

Fig. 8.3 St Peter's, London Docks, by F.H. Pownall (1865–6), showing the bold structural polychromy. Pier capitals were never carved. The modest iron screen does not obstruct the view of the altar: the rood beam, planned in 1880 in memory of Father Lowder, was completed after the 1914–18 war (MC B220405/RIBAC 138912 [2005]).

a handsome polychrome interior of patterned brick, was duly consecrated (1866) (Fig. 8.3): Lowder's Confraternity of the Blessed Sacrament ministered to the poor and sick during the 1860s cholera epidemics, rendering his position secure, and he became known as 'Father Lowder'. Having won the love and respect of his parishioners, he was protected by them from the Church Association which tried to disrupt proceedings at St Peter's: as his biographer observed, 'their emissaries were glad to get away without broken heads'. St Peter's is a moving monument to Anglo-Catholicism and its mission to the deprived of East London.

John Purchas, distinguished ecclesiologist and liturgiologist, when Perpetual Curate (from 1866) of St James's Chapel, Brighton, was also prosecuted (1869) for his Ritualistic practices, including the so-called 'Six Points' (facing east during the celebration of the Eucharist; using the mixed chalice; employing unleavened bread; placing 'lights' on the altar; wearing linen vestments; and burning incense), and charged with infringing the laws of the Established Church. Judgement was given against him in the Arches Court of Canterbury, but even that was not enough for his opponents: after an appeal was made (1870), the Privy Council's Judicial Committee (predictably) ruled against Purchas on practically all the issues raised, something High Churchmen pronounced as 'tyranny'. But Purchas, who had made over all his property to his wife, neither paid the costs awarded against him nor discontinued his practices. Official and public hostility was perceived by High Churchmen to be persecution, and, as a result, Ritualism became widespread, for there is nothing like persecution to intensify religious devotions: many clergymen believed that Ritualistic practices were incumbent upon them (yet those practices were condemned as illegal by mechanisms set up outside the Church and by some shades of opinion within it), and that approved rubrics of the Church were sloppily disregarded by most Evangelicals.

Tait's times as Bishop of London and Archbishop of Canterbury, therefore, were not easy, and marred by violent controversy, for, just as he commenced his tenure of the Throne of St Augustine, disestablishment of the Anglican Church in Ireland became a reality, and it will be recalled that it was earlier political interference with the Church of Ireland which had prompted Keble's outrage and the birth of the Oxford Movement. The Public Worship Regulation Act (1874) attempted to end several years of dispute, but even that was insufficient, for, in 1878–81, five Anglican priests were imprisoned for disobeying the orders of secular courts, and led to greater conflict. Such heavy-handed tactics and the ludicrousness of the prison sentences proved counterproductive, so Ritualistic usages within the Church became widespread: even Edward King, Bishop of Lincoln from 1885, had proceedings instituted against him (1889), and was cited before the Archbishop of Canterbury (by then Edward White Benson [primate from 1883]), to answer charges of sundry offences committed during the administration of Holy Communion. These included facing the 'Holy Table' while celebrating, causing the 'Agnus Dei' to be sung after consecration, and making the sign of the cross in the air. The archbishop heard the case, and in the end pronounced (1890) no admonition or condemnation, although the sign of the cross and mixing in the chalice during the service were proscribed. The Church Association, outraged, appealed to the Privy Council's Judicial Committee, but in 1892 the appeal was dismissed and the archbishop's judgement upheld. The 'Lincoln Judgement' aided the progress of Ritualistic and Doctrinal movements, which became known as Anglo-Catholicism. Furthermore, the publication (1889, with ten further editions within a year) of the influential *Lux Mundi* (Light of the World), a collection of 12 essays by liberal Anglo-Catholic theologians, edited by Charles Gore (Bishop of Oxford from 1911), strengthened the movement through a creative interaction between patristic theology, Anglo-Catholicism, and Broad Church liberalism. *Lux Mundi* celebrated the Logos (the Word of God Incarnate, the active principle living in and determining the world) in evolution, art, science, faiths, and socialism. Yet matters were by no means plain sailing. Anglo-Catholicism attracted further strong and violent opposition, notably from the Protestant Truth Society, founded in 1890 by John Kensit, a militant agitator: he organised a band of itinerant preachers called 'Wicliffites' who raided Ritualistic churches throughout the country, interrupted services, and even attempted to secure the election to Parliament of those opposed to Ritualism.

Bigots were gleeful, and High Churchmen were appalled, by events in the 1890s. Pope Leo XIII began to speak of 'separated brethren', and in his letter *Ad Anglos* (1895) revealed his concern for the conversion of England and the likelihood of a reunified Catholic Church, but on Rome's terms. Prompted by certain French and Belgian clergy, who proposed that Anglican Orders should be recognised as valid by the R.C. Church, the Pope appointed a commission to examine the subject, but that commission (loaded with conservative Italian clerics) reported adversely, and in the bull *Apostolicæ Curæ* (13 September 1896), Leo pronounced that ordinations performed by the Anglican Rite were absolutely null and utterly void, thus dismissing the validity of Apostolic Succession from the Anglican priesthood ordained by 16th-century bishops. The hurt experienced by men such as Halifax, who had worked for most of their lives to promote reunion, was very great.

The bull provoked further anti-Roman Catholic controversy, and encouraged attacks on Anglo-Catholicism and on Ritualism generally. It also led to Garner's conversion to Roman Catholicism, which seems a reason why his partnership with Bodley ended (1898), and Garner was by no means alone, for many other Anglicans, clergy and lay, seceded. In 1899 the archbishops of Canterbury and York condemned the use of incense and lights in processions, and in 1900 Reservation of the Blessed Sacrament was also denounced, but not effectively enforced. So lax did matters become that a Royal Commission on ecclesiastical discipline was appointed (1904), which reported (1906) that many practices were 'clearly inconsistent with and subversive of the teaching of the Church of England'. Nevertheless, Anglo-Catholicism survived, while also patronising artistic endeavours to enhance worship within the Church.

Thus Ritualism advanced, especially as a means of expressing the Eucharistic doctrine as a grave and dignified ceremony. What had started as the Oxford Movement in the 1830s and 1840s evolved into a vigorous Anglo-Catholicism, and from around the end of the 1860s Anglican ecclesiastical architecture was greatly stimulated by Catholic principles similar to those that had fired Pugin. So powerful was the Anglo-Catholic response to persecution that very soon craftsmanship was encouraged in the production of ornaments, furnishings, artefacts, and everything required for ceremonial. The close involvement of leading architects with the theological and liturgical issues of the time strongly affected design: all were Anglo-Catholics; all believed that the 20th-century Anglican Church would be Anglo-Catholic; and all were men of great talent and learning.

Apostolicæ Curæ was a very serious blow, however, and its aftershocks cannot be underestimated, though the archbishops of Canterbury and York published a robust reply (1897). One church dating from the early years of these ferocious Ritualist controversies was St Agnes's, Kennington, London (1874–91 – destroyed), where the architecture and furnishings provided a perfect setting for Anglo-Catholic worship. It was designed by George Gilbert 'Middle' Scott, who for a time shared a drawing office with Bodley and Garner in Church Row, Hampstead, and Scott introduced

J.D. Sedding to them. Many points made in later years in papers given by Bodley, Scott, and Sedding are identical, and these probably derived from discussions held at Church Row.

Scott's designs for St Agnes's were published (1875), and aroused storms of disapproval, for they were influenced by the late 14th- and early 15th-century Perpendicular that had been anathematised from the time of Pugin. Gradually, however, the sensitive refinement of Scott's work gained admirers. Furniture included parclose screens enclosing the chapels; the carved, painted, and gilded triptych, or *Flügelaltar* (designed by Scott and Temple Moore, based on the 15th-century German exemplar at Oberwesel), set well before the east window, leaving a passage behind it; and the rood screen and loft constructed to be used liturgically.

Like Pearson's St Augustine's, Kilburn (*see* Fig. 7.16), St Agnes's had come into being as a result of attempts to suppress Ritualism in the parish, and was founded by a mediævalist in order to establish an Anglo-Catholic place of worship. The church soon became famous for pre-Reformation English ceremonials based on the Sarum Use: plainsong, well-designed embroidered vestments, processions with banners, and singing from the rood loft gladdened Anglo-Catholics and outraged Evangelicals. Kennington curates were also mediævalists, and in due course carried their ideals to other parishes: in short, St Agnes's was a catalyst in very many ways for the evolution of ecclesiastical and liturgical design for decades to come. Nevertheless, its architecture, the beauty of its rituals, and its mediævalism were extremely suspect in certain quarters: such suspicions were exacerbated when its architect became a Roman Catholic (1880).

The Arts and Crafts Influence

A return to intricacy and finely crafted work (that took its inspiration from English late-Gothic art) coincided with the rise of the Arts and Crafts Movement, an English social and æsthetic phenomenon that grew from a dissatisfaction with the quality of design in mechanically manufactured artefacts, especially after the 1851 Great Exhibition. It had its origins in an admiration for traditional art and craftsmanship, and in a romantic longing to recapture the ethos of mediæval craft guilds: these notions can be traced to the theories of Jean-Jacques Rousseau (who sensibly advocated the teaching of manual skills to everybody), the writings of Pugin, and the polemics of Ruskin. The key figure of the movement was William Morris, who founded the firm of Morris, Marshall, & Faulkner in 1861, producing wallpapers, the ornamental parts of stained-glass windows, printed patterns, furniture, and much else. The movement influenced young architects and designers, crusaded to make towns beautiful, sought to reform society so that ugliness would be abolished, and argued for the preservation and protection of old buildings, doing the minimum to conserve buildings without altering their character. However, the Arts and Crafts Movement, which grew out of the Gothic Revival, also influenced that Revival, notably in its last phase as may be seen to advantage in two Anglican churches in London when questions about planning, liturgical requirements, visibility, and so on were very much in the air.

The first is St Cuthbert's, Philbeach Gardens, Earl's Court, London (1884–7), by Hugh Roumieu Gough, a lofty, brick structure with lean-to aisles, the whole

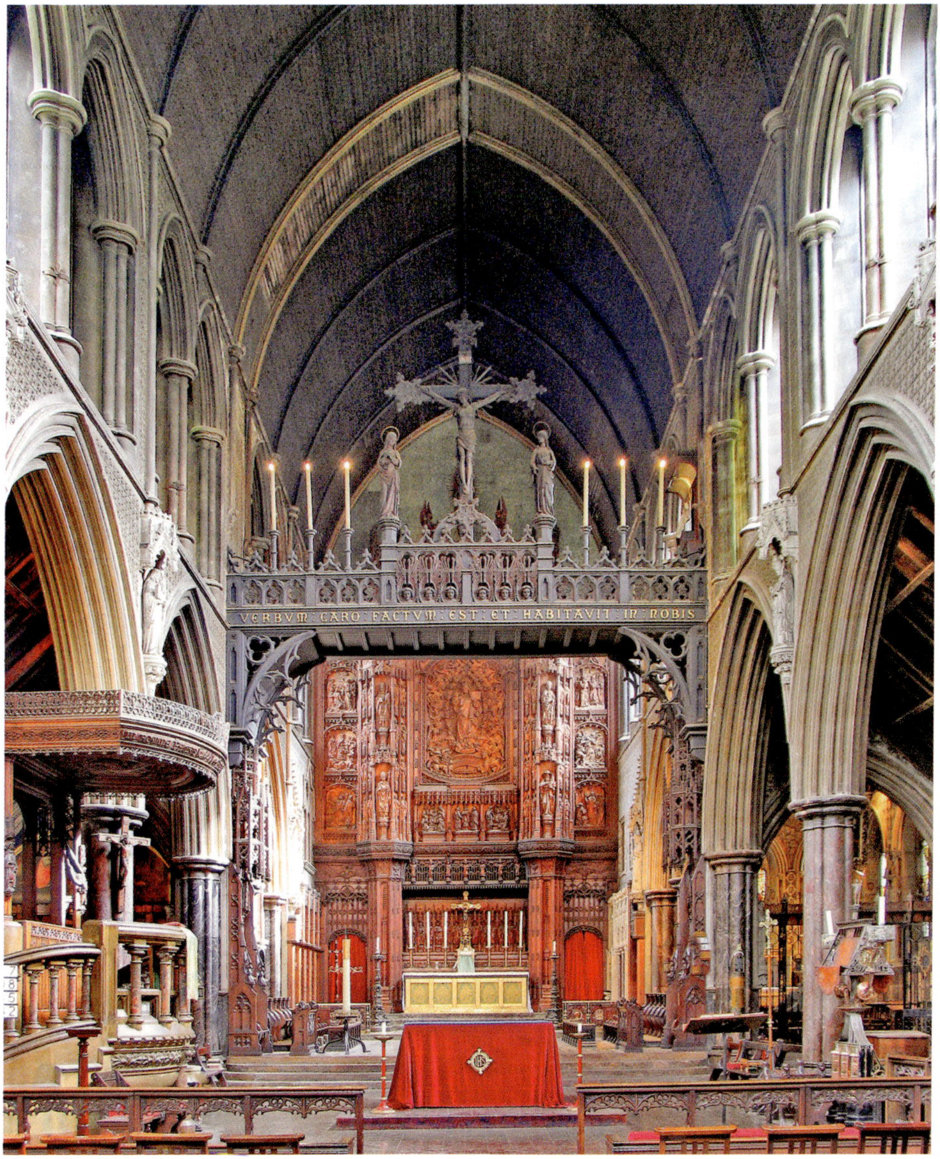

Fig. 8.4 St Cuthbert's, Philbeach Gardens, Kensington, London (built 1884–7), by H. Roumieu Gough, showing the nave arcades owing much to First Pointed Cistercian types. Piers are of polished Torquay marble. Beautification of the church (1887–1914) converted a bare interior into a monument of Anglo-Catholicism. Gough designed the rood loft (1893), but the reredos or retablo (1899–1914), in a Spanish mediæval style, was by the Revd Ernest Geldart. Decorations of surfaces were carried out by specially created guilds of newly trained craftsmen working in the Arts and Crafts spirit (JS [2006]).

modelled on Transitional and Cistercian mediæval types (the immediate model was Tintern Abbey), with a French-influenced *flèche* on the roof, the dominant architectural language being First Pointed. Gough's barn-like interior was lavishly beautified (1887–1914), so that it became a monument to Anglo-Catholic taste as well as to the Arts and Crafts Movement (Fig. 8.4). Among those involved in this sumptuous work were W. Bainbridge Reynolds, the Revd Ernest Geldart, J. Harold Gibbons, and Gilbert Boulton. The Revd Henry Westall, vicar from 1883, made St Cuthbert's the most flourishing High Church foundation in Kensington, with the result that on Good Friday, 1898, it was raided by Kensit and his cronies, who disrupted the Adoration of the Cross (a mediæval practice revived at St Cuthbert's). Kensit was duly depicted on one of the misericords in the chancel complete with the ears of an ass. The beautification of St Cuthbert's was carried out by craftsmen (many of them amateurs 'united in piety and generosity') who were organised into guilds, working under professionals.

Thus at St Cuthbert's certain tendencies, imported from Belgium (Brugge in particular) by W.H.J. Weale (founder of the Guild of St Gregory and St Luke, and another convert to Roman Catholicism, who had been closely involved in the Guild of Sts Thomas and Luke in Flanders), were developed. This Flemish connection has been often overlooked, yet Weale was active in Brugge from the mid-1860s, and the Dominican church in Gent was illustrated by Cubitt as early as 1869, that is, just before St Augustine's, Kilburn, and St Augustine's, Pendlebury, were built.

The second London church where Arts and Crafts influences can be studied with benefit is The Holy Trinity, Sloane Street, Chelsea (1888–90), designed by John Dando Sedding, who had studied with Street, and who was intimately connected with the Arts and Crafts Movement. Sedding was a passionate Anglo-Catholic, and perceived religious art and architecture as being at the core of European culture: he saw art, and especially ecclesiastical art, as essential to the civilising and redemption of the urban masses. Devoted to the Incarnation, from which the Sacraments flowed, Sedding argued that the altar must be the centre of Christian worship, for there God, operating through and in matter, made the Incarnation real and living in the Eucharistic Sacrament, something with which Evangelicals would have insuperable difficulties. Sedding saw Christ in art and architecture: if He were not, then art and architecture would be meaningless. The reference to Psalm cxxvi in the *Vulgate* (*Nisi Dominus ædificaverit domum, in vanum laboraverunt qui ædificant eam* – unless the Lord has built this house, its builders have laboured in vain – given as Psalm cxxvii in *The Book of Common Prayer*) is clear: it was something many involved in the creation of Victorian churches obviously held in sincere belief.

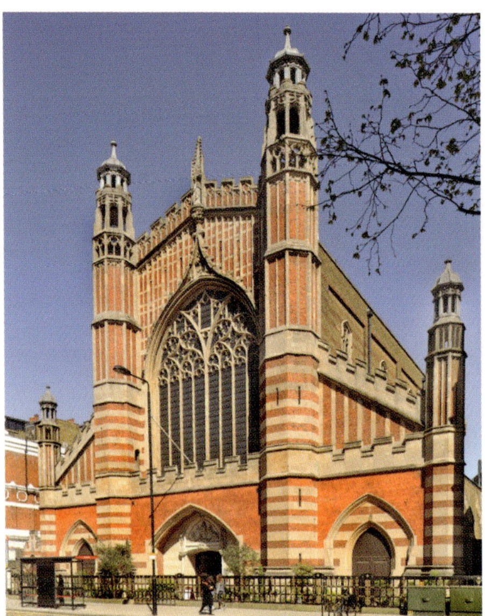

Fig. 8.5 The Holy Trinity, Sloane Street, Chelsea, London (1888–90). The style has returned to that of late Perpendicular of the St George's Chapel, Windsor, Berkshire, type, although window tracery was in a sumptuous Second Pointed Curvilinear style (GB [2021]).

With The Holy Trinity (Fig. 8.5), Sedding achieved his ambition to create a church fully decorated and furnished by contemporary artists. His starting point was the Perpendicular style as it was around 1500. Taking up certain

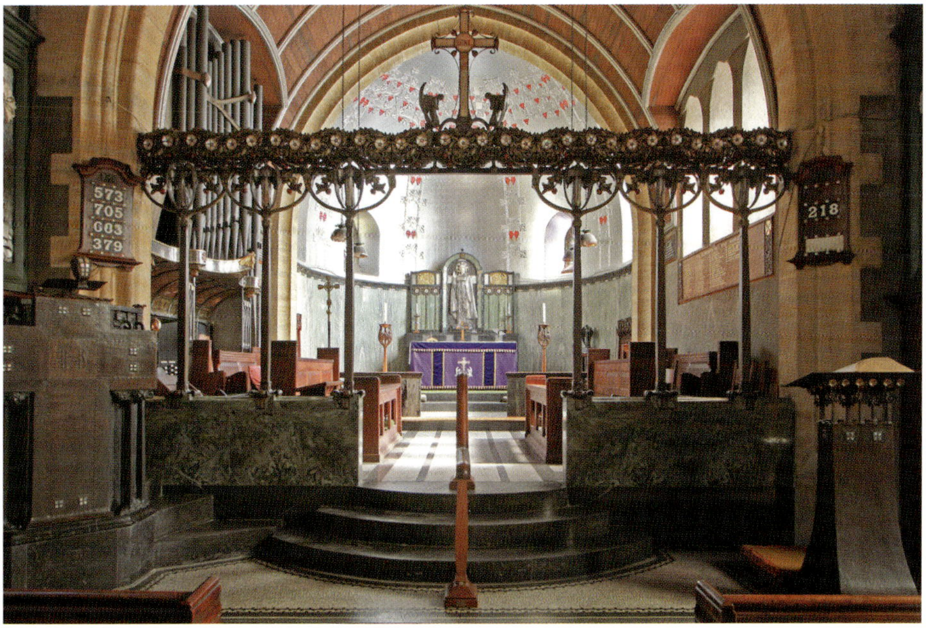

Fig. 8.6 St Mary the Virgin, Great Warley, Essex (1902–4), by C.H. Townsend, with exquisite art nouveau fittings, including the screen, by W. Reynolds-Stephens (JS [2011]).

'threads of the Gothic tradition' (as he put it), he wove 'them into the weft of modern' needs and theories, and in the furnishings and fittings Gothic, Renaissance, and Arts and Crafts themes were mixed with spicings of Byzantine and art nouveau elements adding to an already rich brew. The church was largely funded by George Henry, 5th Earl Cadogan: it is a repository of fine examples of design from the 1890s to the 1914–18 war, including work by Morris & Co., Burne-Jones, William Reynolds-Stephens, and many others. Reynolds-Stephens later designed the beautiful art nouveau fittings (including the screen and font) in the tiny St Mary the Virgin, Great Warley, Essex (consecrated 1904), designed by C.H. Townsend (Fig. 8.6).

Our Holy Redeemer, Exmouth Market, Clerkenwell, London (1887–95), was also by Sedding: an Italianate Renaissance Revival building, it has a starkly simple pedimented west front, with some

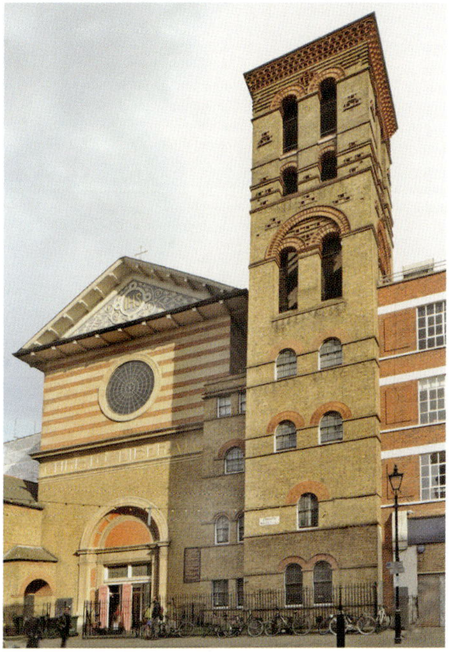

Fig. 8.7 Italianate Early Renaissance Revival west front of Our Holy Redeemer, Exmouth Market, Finsbury, London (1887–8), with a vast Tuscan pediment crowning it. The campanile (1892–5), by Henry Wilson, mixes Early Christian and Italian Romanesque styles, and would not look out of place in Rome or Ravenna (GB [2021]).

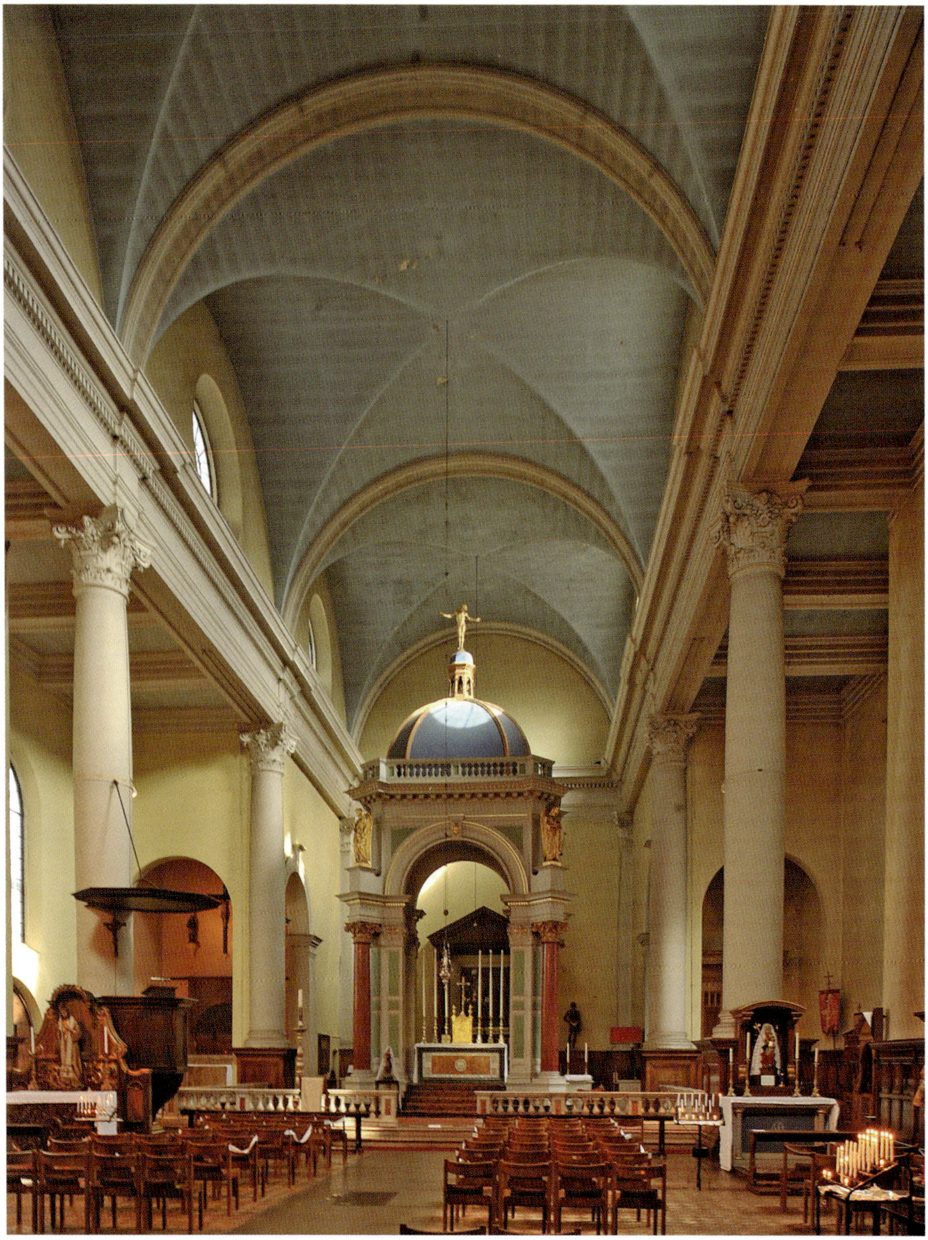

Fig. 8.8 Our Holy Redeemer, Exmouth Market, showing the four-bay vaulted space, with continuous entablature supported on Corinthian columns with capitals carved by F.W. Pomeroy. Note the massive ciborium sheltering the high altar: based on the exemplar in Santo Spirito, Florence (c.1600–1), it reflects R.C.-influenced liturgies used in the church (GB [2021]).

allusions to Inigo Jones's St Paul's, Covent Garden (1631–2) (Fig. 8.7). Intended to serve a poor district, a Renaissance style was selected as the means by which the congregation would be exposed to the Eucharistic Sacrament. To this end the sanctuary was raised, the altar protected by a handsome ciborium enhancing the Italianate effect, and there was no intervening screen. This arrangement adopted the scheme of a cross within a square which Wren had used in several City churches, so even the basic geometry harks back to Renaissance and Carolean models, and the Classical allusions also connect the building with R.C. exemplars. From its beginnings Our Holy Redeemer eschewed mediævalising Ecclesiology (Fig. 8.8).

Another church by Sedding and after his death in 1891 his successor, Henry Wilson, may be highlighted here: St Peter's, Ealing (1889–93), which demonstrates how late Gothic forms could still be drawn upon and used with virtuosity and originality. The west front is an extraordinary invention (Fig. 8.9), a variation, perhaps, on the massive west window of Sts Peter and Paul's Priory Church, Leominster, Herefordshire.

One of the most delightful, yet not well-known, churches with which Sedding was involved is St Martin's, Brabyns Brow, Marple, Cheshire, erected 1869–70 at the expense of Anne Hudson to designs by Edmund Sedding (d.1868) and completed by his brother. The main interest, however, lies in the contributions made by Henry Wilson in designing the Lady chapel (1895–6) and north aisle (*c.*1909), but it is the exquisite Lady chapel which deserves close examination (Fig. 8.10). It was paid for by Mrs Hudson's daughter, Maria Anne, and is a fine example of the Arts and Crafts influence on late Victorian ecclesiastical work, to which Christopher Whitworth Whall contributed.

St Agatha's, an astonishing late Victorian church, was erected (1893–5) as part of a mission from Winchester College to what was a slum district outside the dockyards at Landport, Portsmouth. Its inspiration, and part of its funding, came from an Anglo-Irish Anglo-Catholic priest, Father Robert Dolling, its first incumbent, and its architect was J.H. Ball, a pupil of Waterhouse.

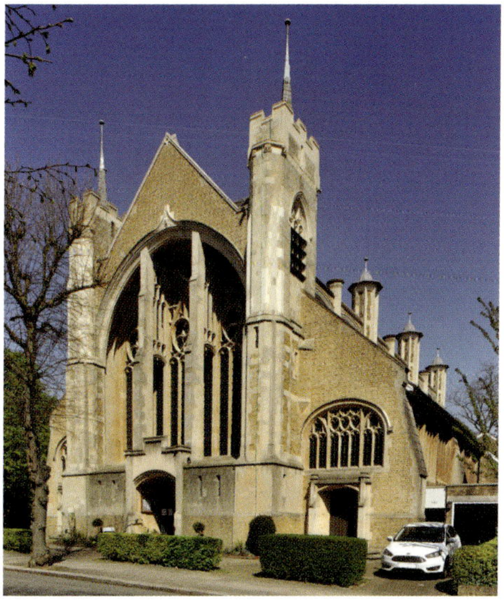

Fig. 8.9 St Peter's, Mount Park Road, Ealing, London, designed (1889) by J.D. Sedding, posthumously realised 1892–3 by his partner, Henry Wilson. The west front, like Holy Trinity, Sloane Street, has turrets on either side, but in this case, they flank a deeply recessed window partly concealed behind flying buttresses in the form of free-standing mullions connected to the window by openwork tracery (GB [2018]).

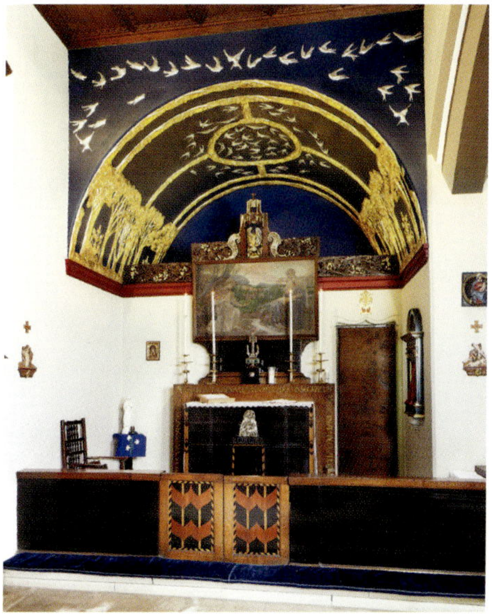

Fig. 8.10 Lady chapel, St Martin's, Marple, Cheshire (1895–6), by Henry Wilson and Christopher Whall. The beautiful apse is decorated with gilded gesso trees and flights of swallows, and the altar and Communion rail are decorated with delicate inlays. Whall painted the Annunciation (1896), set in a carved and gilded frame (AH [2011]).

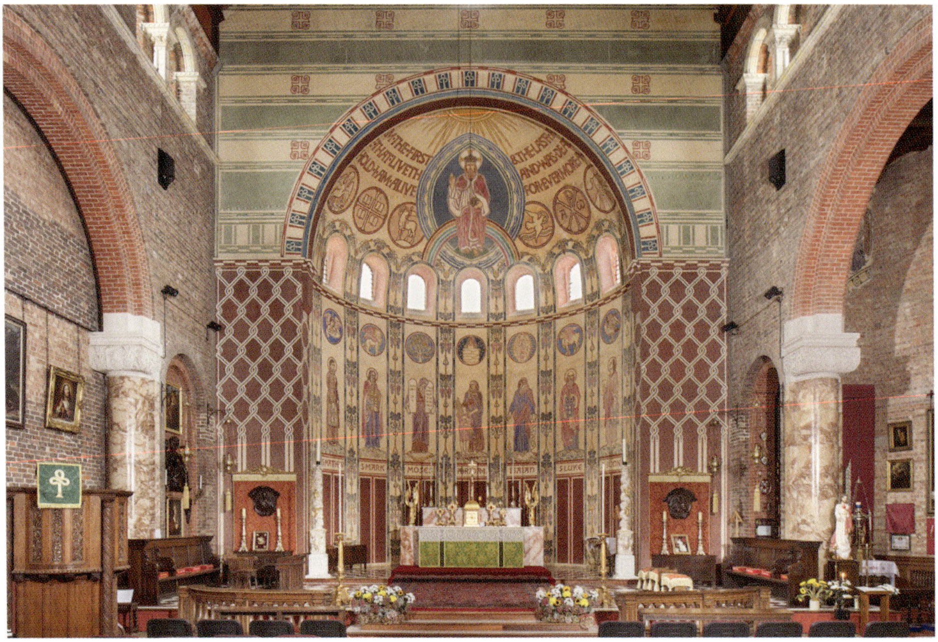

Fig. 8.11 Chancel, St Agatha's, Landport, Portsea Island, Portsmouth, Hampshire (1893–9), in the Early Christian basilican style designed by J.H. Ball, decorated from 1901 in sgraffito by Heywood Sumner. Christ, seated on the arc of a rainbow, is depicted in the hemi-dome, set in a vesica with many-lined border, the radiant sun represented overhead. There are texts on either side of the vesica, below which are six medallions with Christian symbols. The apse is pierced at high level with seven semicircular-headed windows, below which are more medallions with symbols, and below those are figures of the Evangelists and major prophets. The entire composition is unified by means of borders embellished with vine stems and leaves (JOD [2017]).

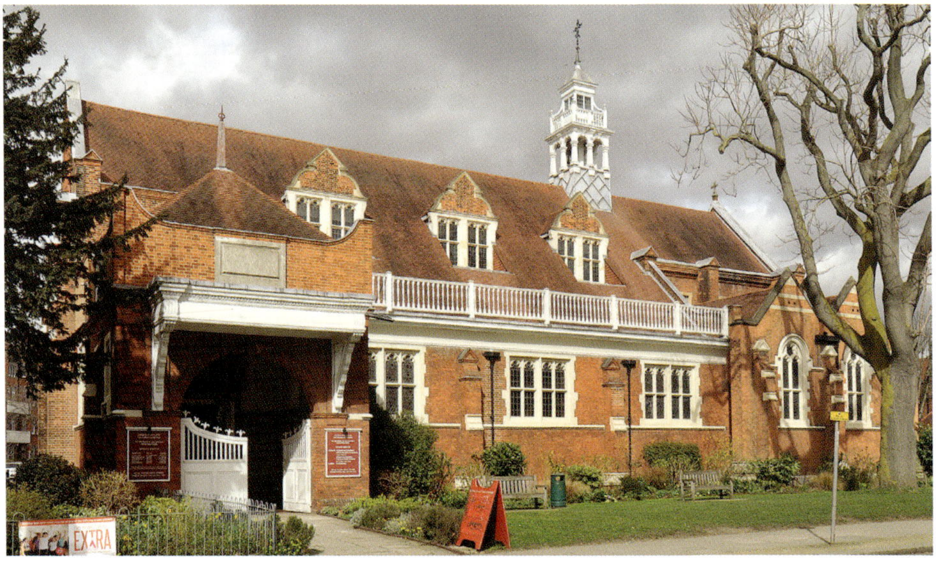

Fig. 8.12 St Michael and All Angels, Bedford Park, Chiswick, London (1879–82), by R.N. Shaw. It combines aspects of Perpendicular Gothic with features derived from 17th- and 18th-century English domestic architecture (GB [2018]).

The Anglo-Catholic rituals, and Dolling's intention to have a third altar in his new church to be used for requiem Masses, aroused the opposition of Randall Davidson, Bishop of Winchester, so Dolling resigned his living. The episode was said to have formed Davidson's determination not to be the primate who drove the High Church party out of the Church of England (he was enthroned at Canterbury [1903]). St Agatha's was based on an Early Christian Italian basilica, and is now known as the 'Cathedral of the Car-Parks', as the tight urban fabric in which it originally nestled was destroyed by bombing and modernist town planning, so that the building presents much of its external fabric to public view, which was never originally intended. Made redundant (1955), St Agatha's lost its Lady chapel through the widening of Charlotte Street (1964), and was threatened with demolition (1973). Hampshire County Council acquired it, but, amazingly, it became a church again, adopted by the Personal Ordinariate of Our Lady of Walsingham, established by Pope Benedict XVI to allow Anglicans to enter into full communion with the R.C. Church, while retaining much Anglican tradition (one might regret that this could not have been done more than a century earlier, when much hurt could have been avoided). Unfortunately, before it was rescued, many of St Agatha's furnishings were dispersed (some were ignorantly destroyed, although a few survived and have recently been returned). However, one of the glories of the church is its semi-domed apse, with its beautiful sgraffito decorations by Heywood Sumner (Fig. 8.11).

The Arts and Crafts Movement is also associated with the Domestic Revival, or Old English style, involving Picturesque compositions using elements from vernacular architecture. Certain aspects of these were occasionally employed in ecclesiastical architecture: R. Norman Shaw used a free eclectic mix (including a Perpendicular lower part with certain upper features derived from the 17th and 18th centuries) at St Michael and All Angels, Bedford Park, London (1879–82) (Figs 8.12 and 8.13), but at Hopwas, Staffordshire, John Douglas used brick and timber-framed gables and upper-works at his St Chad's (1881), which at first glance looks like a piece of domestic architecture (Fig. 8.14). Both Shaw's and Douglas's churches reflect their architects' interest in incorporating vernacular architectural elements. Another, perhaps more remarkable and very personal, Shaw church should be mentioned here: that of All Saints', Compton, Leek, Staffordshire (1885–7). Although Shaw gave nods to Gothic, historical allusions are almost non-existent, and the architecture has distanced itself from them in its very free variants and assured inventions (Fig. 8.15).

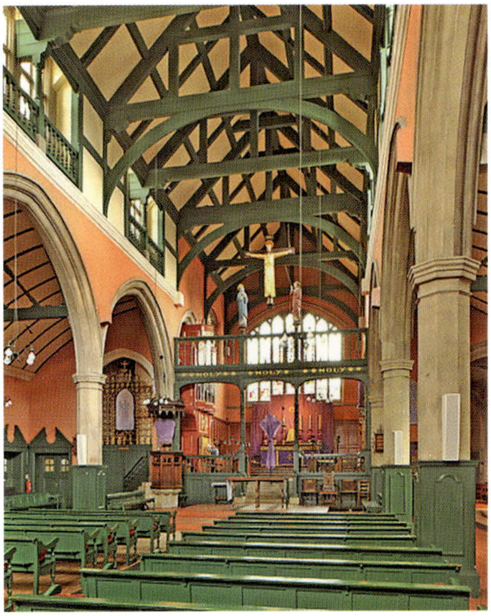

Fig. 8.13 St Michael and All Angels, Bedford Park. The pulpit is in a 17th-century style, and the whole ensemble is a marriage of late Gothic Revival with Arts and Crafts detail (GB [2018]).

Just before Shaw's Bedford Park church, Philip Speakman Webb – who

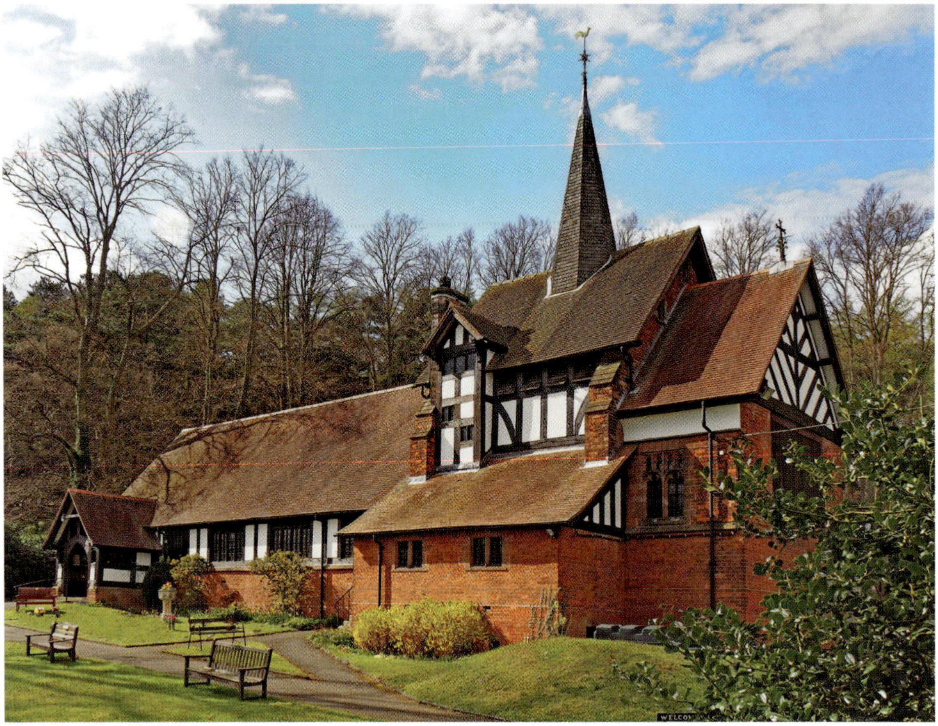

Fig. 8.14 St Chad's, Hopwas, near Lichfield, Staffordshire (1881), by John Douglas, showing the markedly domestic appearance to which the brick- and timber-framed construction contributes (CJP [2021]).

Fig. 8.15 All Saints', Leek, Staffordshire (1885–7), by R.N. Shaw. The chancel seems very tall, thanks to the fall of the terrain and the placing of the windows high in the wall, and the low tower, small clerestorey, and massive, assured treatment of the buttresses show how adaptable Gothic could be: this is no mere copyism (GB [1988]).

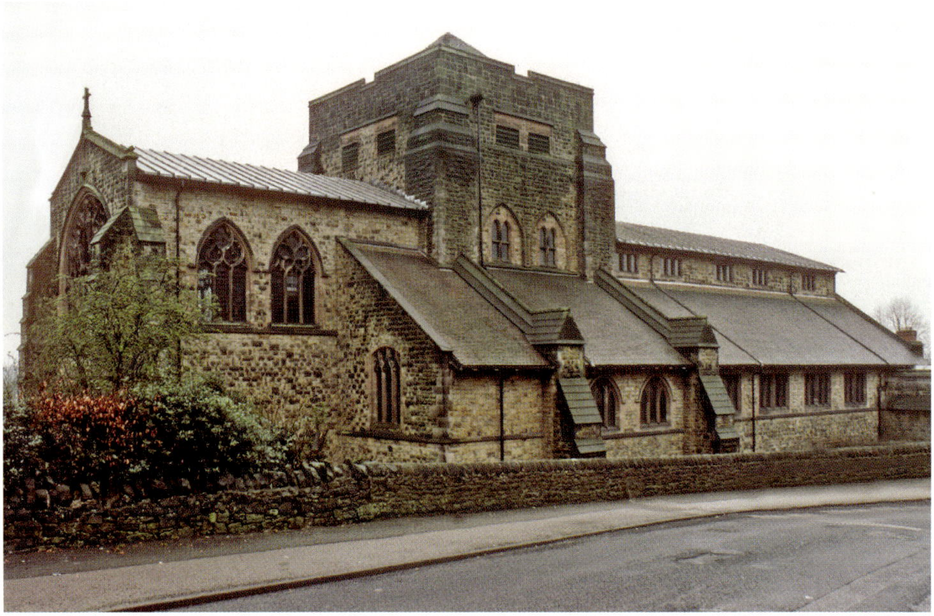

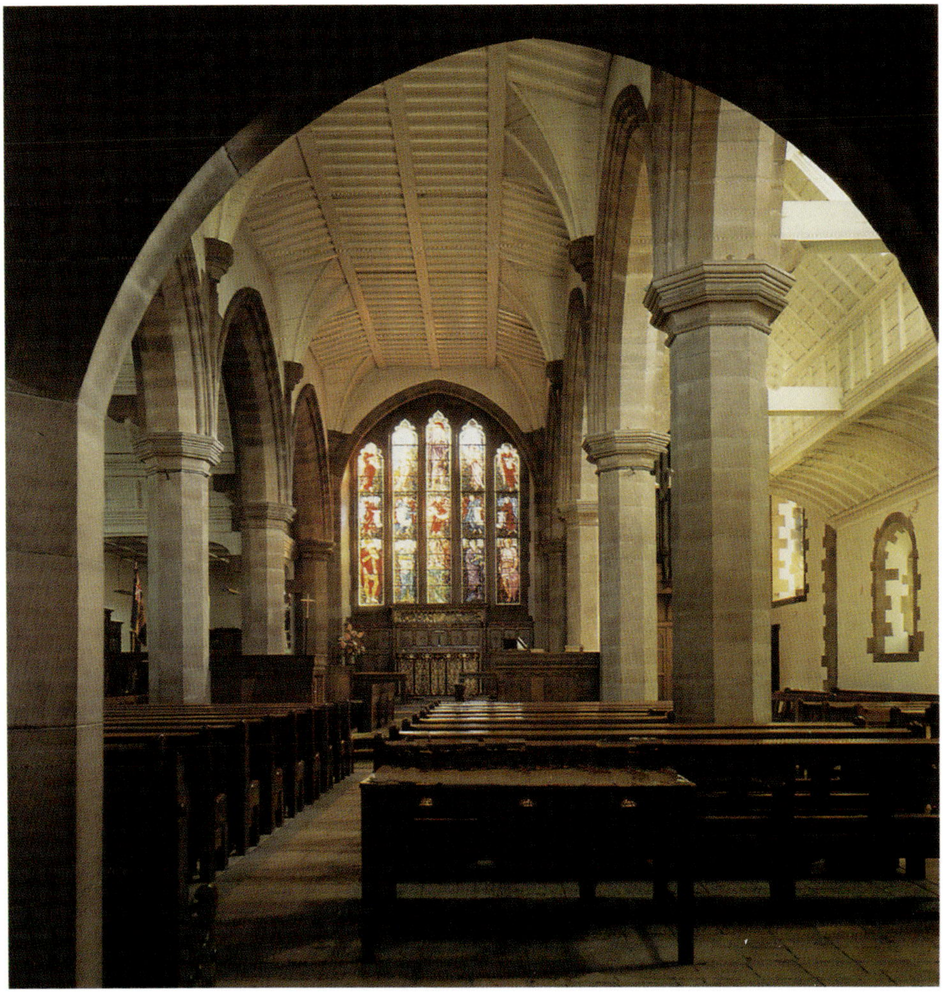

Fig. 8.16 St Martin's, Brampton, Cumbria (1874–8), by Philip Webb. The north aisle has a ceiling treated as transverse tunnel vaults, while the south aisle has a timber lean-to roof with tie-beams and dormers, and the nave ceiling is flat except for the fan-like coving. The five-light east window, like the rest of the glass, was designed by William Morris and Edward Burne-Jones, made 1878–80 (MC/RIBAC L270989 [1989]).

had worked for Street and who had joined Morris, Marshall, Faulkner & Co. in 1861 (and so had imbibed both the Gothic Revival and an Arts and Crafts outlook) – built his only church, St Martin's, Brampton, Cumbria (1874–8), for the Howard family, Earls of Carlisle. Webb mixed styles, and stained-glass windows were by Morris and Burne-Jones, displaying occasional proto-art nouveau forms (Fig. 8.16).

Edward Schroeder Prior designed St Andrew's, Talbot Road, Roker, Sunderland (1906–7), supervised during its construction by A. Randall Wells, who had acted as clerk of works at Lethaby's All Saints', Brockhampton-by-Ross, Herefordshire (1901–2), one of the most perfect syntheses of Gothic and Arts and Crafts elements. All Saints' was funded by Alice Foster as a memorial to her parents: it incorporates unreinforced concrete vaults and thatched roofs, and the architectural language was remarkably fresh and new, redolent with references, but avoiding direct quotations. Even the tracery,

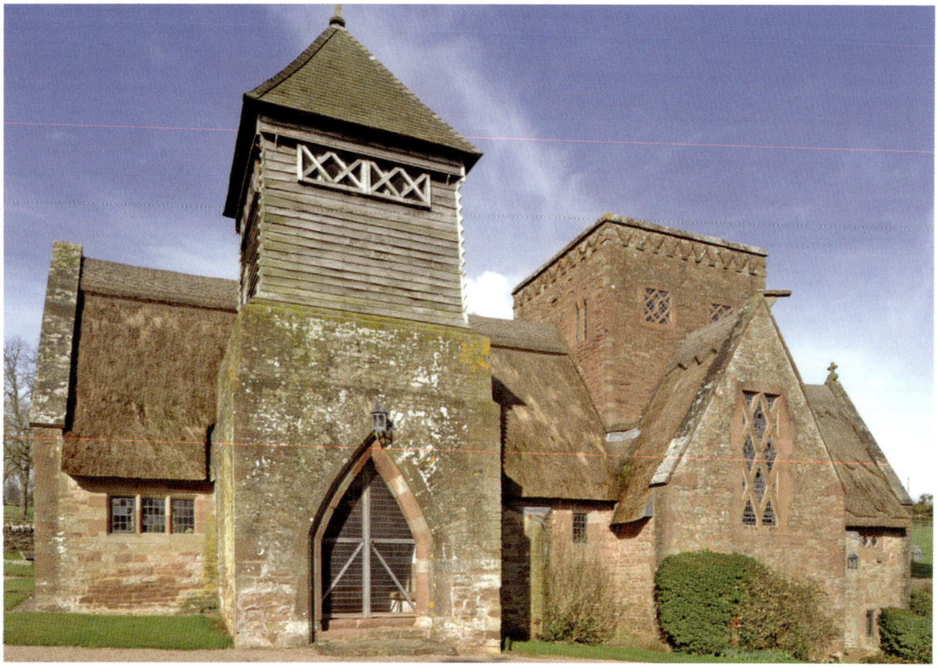

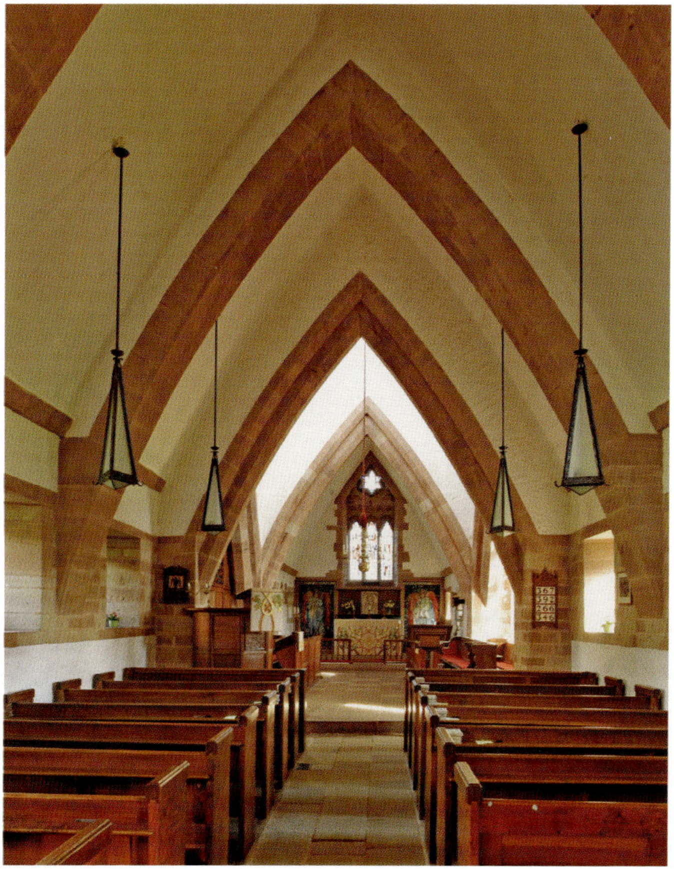

Fig. 8.17 All Saints', Brockhampton-by-Ross, Herefordshire (1901–2), by W.R. Lethaby, with A. Randall Wells as clerk of works. The tower over the southern porch has its upper stage clad in oak boarding, a feature of several Herefordshire belfries, e.g. at Yarpole. The crossing tower terminates with a zigzag frieze, and tracery owes little to historical precedents (GB [2018]).

Fig. 8.18 All Saints', Brockhampton-by-Ross, with its tunnel-vaulted interior and tough transverse pointed arches. Vaults are of concrete, lime washed (GB [2018]).

though Gothic in spirit, owed little to archæology. No student of the Arts and Crafts Movement, of Victorian churches, and of the influence of the Vernacular Revival on design should miss this charming building (Figs 8.17 and 8.18).

Further Remarks on Anglican Liturgiology

In 1879, the distinguished physician, and liturgical scholar, John Wickham Legg, who published a phenomenal amount of work on medical matters, notably on hæmophilia (he was physician to Prince Leopold, Duke of Albany, who suffered from that disease), founded the St Paul's Ecclesiological Society in order to further studies in liturgiology and allied subjects. Legg was also the founder (1890) of the Henry Bradshaw Society (named after the Cambridge librarian and scholar), which printed rare liturgical texts: Legg himself edited the *Westminster Missal* (1891–7), and the *Sarum Missal* (1916). However, Legg also provided a vast amount of scholarly evidence to show that from 1660 to 1833 traditional Anglican Church doctrines and practices prevailed far more commonly than the Oxford Movement acknowledged, and attempted to redress the skewed view of Georgian Anglicanism held by Tractarians. Critical of a growing tendency among Anglo-Catholics to introduce current liturgical practices from France or Belgium, without proper historical inquiry, he was also suspicious (as well he might be) of liberal theology and change for the sake of change. Indeed in 1909 and 1911 he published rather ferocious pamphlets opposing any revisions of the Prayer Book, claiming that the generation then running things lacked both the knowledge and the taste to do so with any success. What Legg would have said about recent developments must remain a subject for bemused speculation.

Legg's writings generally were recognised as having no parallels, and even R.C. commentators (e.g. Henry Thurston, in the Introduction to the 1937 edition of *The Mass* by Adrian Fortescue) acknowledged that liturgical studies and research into the origins of the Mass owed much to Anglican scholarship. Legg concluded that, like Pugin, modern liturgiologists should take their inspiration from the Middle Ages, and remember the Prayer Book directed that chancels should remain 'as in times past'. He declared that mediæval liberty of practice was preferable to the attempts of the R.C. 'Congregation of Rites to establish all over the world the iron uniformity which is the aspiration in most things of the nineteenth century', something R.C. architects themselves found restricting. He also opined, with accuracy, that all that was 'Roman' was 'not ancient', and, remembering the High Churchmen of old, that not every pre-Tractarian clergyman was a Puritan.

Legg found Bodley's work unsatisfactory for basing his altars too closely on Purchas's publications and on contemporary Continental models that were erroneously imagined to be derived from mediæval precedents. Indeed, he regarded Bodley's designs as having taken much from those evolved during the Counter Reformation, dressed up in German *Spätgotik* garb (Legg had studied in Germany, and knew that country well). The problem with buildings like St Augustine's, Pendlebury, for Legg, and those who thought like him, was that it was rather like a large room 'with an altar at one end', and not sufficiently rooted in English liturgical history. Perhaps more to Legg's taste were the Puginian/Carpenterian themes derived from St Mary Magdalene's, Munster Square: these were also influences on J.T. Micklethwaite

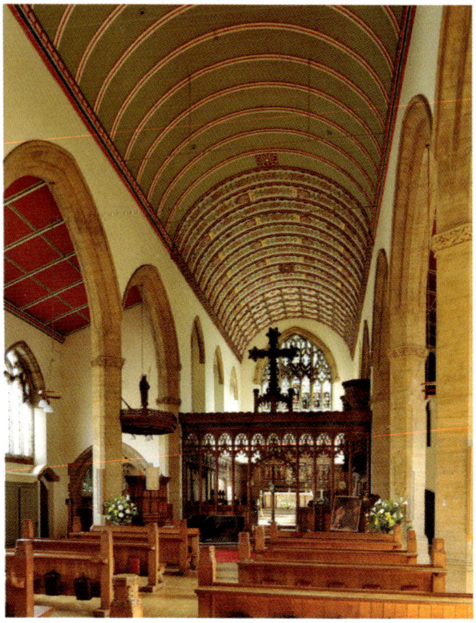

Fig. 8.19 St Paul's, Wimbledon Park, London (1888–96), by J.T. Micklethwaite and G. Somers Clarke. Furnished and glazed by Kempe, this interior comes close to realising the ideal of an authentic mediævalising architectural setting for soundly based Anglican liturgy (GB [2021]).

when he designed St Paul's, Augustus Road, Wimbledon Park, London (1888–96), in partnership (1876–92) with George Somers Clarke. There, the tall and handsome nave arcades support a wagon roof (there is no clerestorey), and stylistically the building is a satisfying mixture of Second Pointed and Perpendicular. Kempe provided the handsome Perpendicular rood screen (Fig. 8.19).

So the wheel had moved full circle, and the Gothic Revival had returned to the period beloved by Pugin – English Second Pointed – but carried out with far greater bravura than in the 1840s. English churches were being built and fitted out with wonderfully crafted artefacts, the like of which had not been seen since

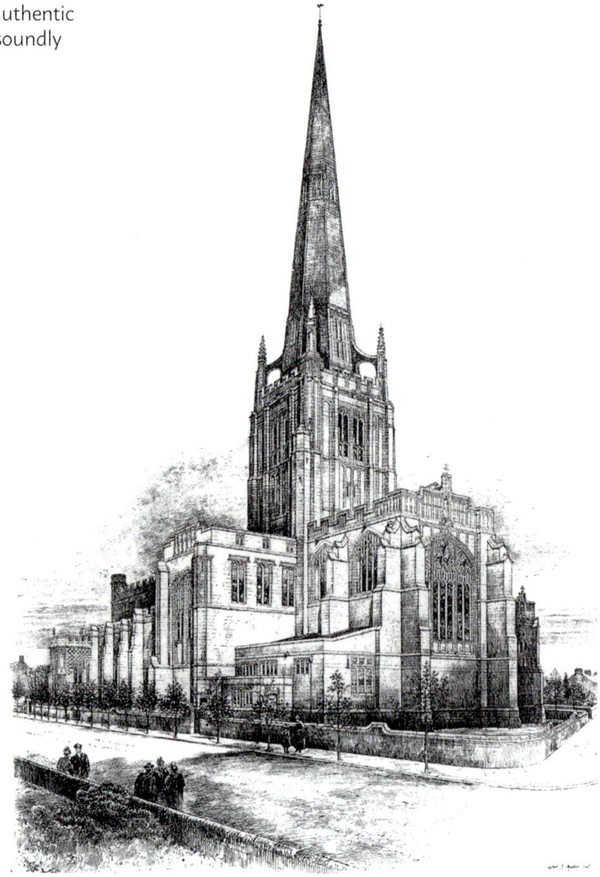

Fig. 8.20 St George's, Stockport, Cheshire (1892–7), a refined, coherent Perpendicular essay, from the south-east, largely the work of H.J. Austin of Paley, Austin, & Paley, and drawn by him. The spire, with its thin flying buttresses, is derived from that of St James's, Louth, Lincolnshire (1501–15). This sensitive interpretation of Perpendicular was characteristic of the Gothic Revival during the last years of Queen Victoria's reign (*Academy Architecture* **xi** [1897] 39, coll. GB).

the 1520s, and it was to the late mediæval period that architects increasingly turned for inspiration. Bodley's late style was followed by numerous architects, including E.G. Paley and his partner H.J. Austin, whose noble church of St George, Stockport, Cheshire (1892–7), mostly Austin's work, is a late and ripe example: the style was Perpendicular, and powerful, assured, spectacular Perpendicular at that (Fig. 8.20). It was not cheap, and was financed by Major George Fearn, a local brewer, whose munificence helped to create the grandest church for miles around. The panelled effects of external wall surfaces were an innovation, used with verve and imagination. St George's always had its admirers: it made it into Hermann Muthesius's splendid book on English church architecture, published in Berlin (1901). Indeed, even Pevsner recognised that Austin 'raised the work of the practice to the level of the best in the country' (a statement with which I would agree), and grouped St George's with Bodley's St Mary's, Eccleston, Cheshire (1894–1900), as among the most majestic of the representations of Victorian 'historicism' (a view from which I would dissent, as the Eccleston church, in many ways, is a disappointment).

St Mary's owed its existence to Hugh Lupus Grosvenor, 1st Duke of Westminster, whose monument (designed by Bodley, with effigy carved by Léon-Joseph Chavalliaud) occupies a position between the chancel and the south chapel. The church is largely Second Pointed, although the furnishings (by Watts & Co.) show a blend of the 'refined

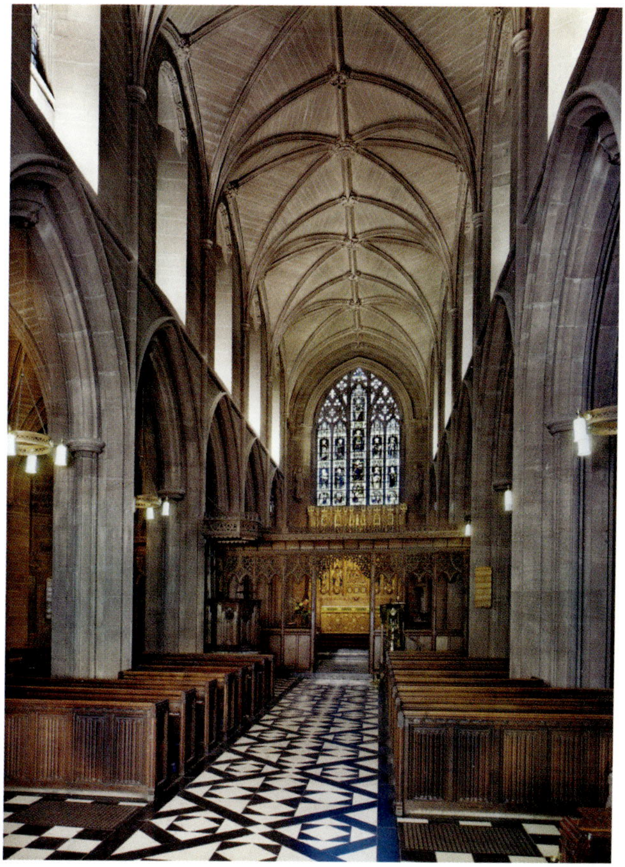

Fig. 8.21 St Mary's, Eccleston, Cheshire, by Bodley. Entirely of ashlar, rib-vaulted throughout, there is no structural change marking the chancel (a feature of many late mediæval English churches, especially in East Anglia, where chancels were simply screened off, although there was usually a greater richness in the treatment of the timber ceilings: no such increase of richness is visible here). Ornament is confined to the roof bosses and furnishings, including the fine reredos (by Farmer & Brindley) and screen (where some colour and gilding might have relieved the slightly chilly effect of the entire ensemble) (AH [2011]).

and inventive ornament' based on 14th- and 15th-century exemplars for which Bodley is celebrated. The rather dull exterior, all in finely cut red sandstone ashlar, shows it consists of a nave with aisles, a porch, and a west tower, but there is no architectural expression of a chancel visible from outside. The interior (Fig. 8.21), a large space entirely enclosed in sandstone, despite its octopartite ribbed vaulting, groupings of mouldings and shafts on the arcade piers, and screens defining the chancel, though good examples of Bodley's work, is rather dry, and there is an argument that some scholarly applications of colour and gilding would greatly improve the ensemble.

Some Other Churches

In the last decade of Victoria's reign various architects developed free Gothic styles, often drawing on Perpendicular themes. Numerous churches were built at that time, for the Church of England, despite its trials and tribulations, was very much alive, and attracted more and more worshippers, something not unconnected with the beauty and dignity of the liturgy. Many liturgical issues discussed above led to a type of church in which the Eucharist played a far more important role than was the case when Queen Victoria ascended the throne.

One of 'Middle' Scott's most gifted pupils, Temple Lushington Moore, produced memorable compositions based loosely on mediæval precedents (such as St Columba's and St Cuthbert's, both in Middlesbrough, Yorkshire NR) at the beginning of the 20th century. St Columba's (1898–1902) has a western tower canted on one side to fit a very tight site hemmed in by streets in a poor working-class area, and indeed the whole plan imaginatively fills the awkward site, which accounts for its odd shape, rather like a squashed, distorted octagon (Fig. 8.22).

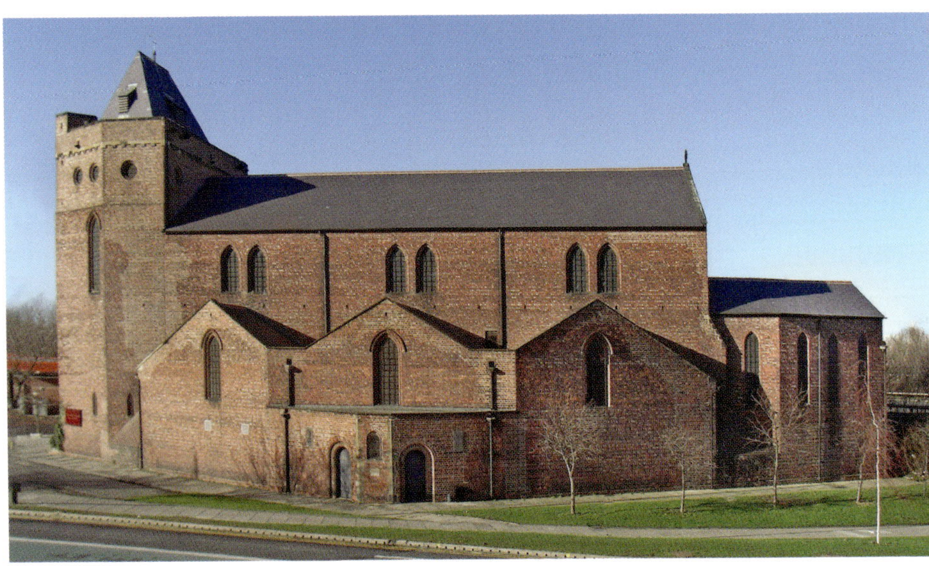

Fig. 8.22 St Columba's, Middlesbrough, Yorkshire (NR) (1898–1902), by Temple Moore, a severe, fortress-like brick building owing much to Moore's admiration for the huge brick Gothic churches of northern Germany. Designed to fit tightly within a dense housing development (now demolished), it is now somewhat naked and marooned (GB [2008]).

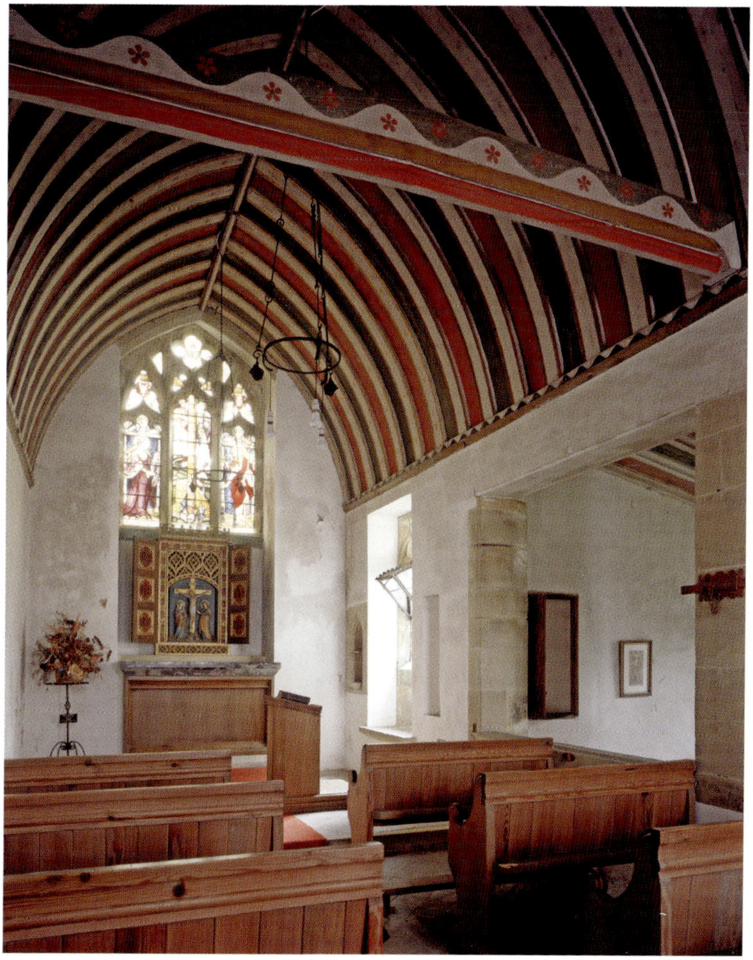

Fig. 8.23 St Mary Magdalene, East Moors, Yorkshire (NR) (1881–2), showing the east window and the opening to the south aisle/baptistry, designed by 'Middle' Scott and completed by Temple Moore, who was responsible for many of the delightful details [MC A280901/RIBAC 138904 [2001]).

Moore had worked on St Agnes's, Kennington, with 'Middle' Scott, and imbibed many of Scott's liturgical-architectural concerns. Among his finest works is the completion of Scott's tiny St Mary Magdalene's, East Moors, Yorkshire NR (1881–2): this delightful building consists of a nave and chancel covered by a pretty, painted wagon roof, the division between them suggested by a painted beam spanning from wall to wall, and a south aisle of two bays, again with a painted roof, this time lean-to (Fig. 8.23). Every detail is charming, including the beautifully designed waterspouts.

Other churches by Moore include St Mark's, Mansfield, Nottinghamshire (1894–7 – with no structural division between nave and chancel, no clerestorey, and instead of aisles, passages through the massive piers) (Fig. 8.24); St Botolph's, Carlton-in-Cleveland, Yorkshire NR (1895–97 – with low, square-headed aisle and clerestorey windows, and Moore's favourite device of elongated piers merging into the arches of the nave arcades without capitals); and St Mary's, Sledmere, Yorkshire

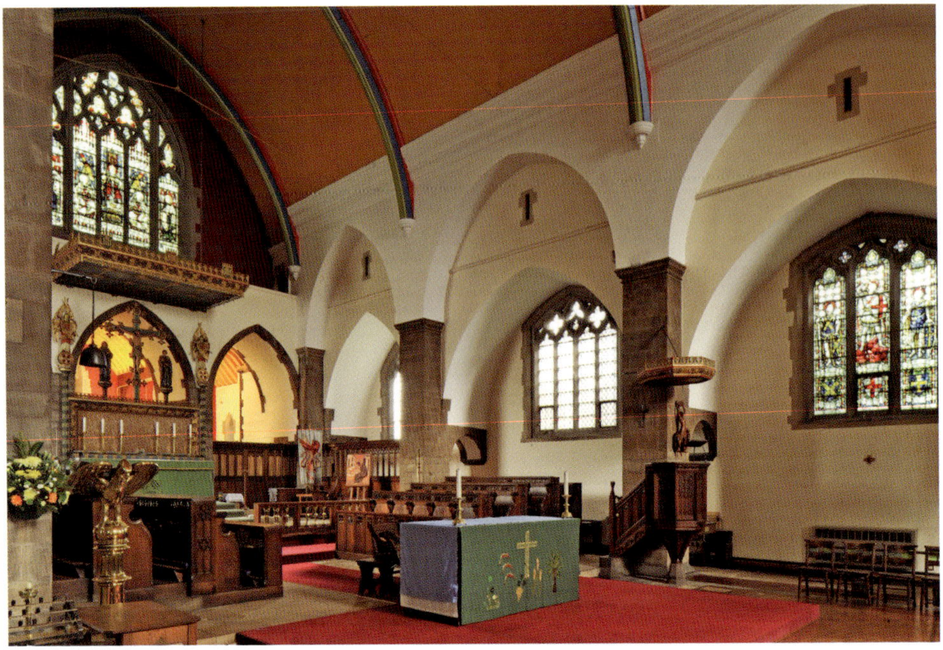

Fig. 8.24 St Mark's, Mansfield, Nottinghamshire (1894–7), showing the superarches, secondary arches, tiny apertures, and passage aisles, an austere, simplified scheme. Beyond the high altar, on the left, is the Lady chapel. This arrangement gave excellent visibility to the high altar from the nave, uninterrupted by piers, columns, or other obstructions. Moore's sumptuous turn-of-the-century high altar (with riddel posts, vignette frame to the reredos, elegant brattishing, and Watts fabrics for hangings), most regrettably, has been spoiled (GB [2012]).

ER (1893–8 – reckoned by Pevsner, with predictable bias, to be 'large, quite perfect, and patently dull', but by Goodhart-Rendel [with more perspicacity] to be 'perhaps one of the loveliest churches in England'). The last was for Sir Tatton Sykes II, Bt. Moore also designed some exquisite church furnishings. One of his happiest creations is the lovely rood screen (1892–3 – later coloured by Bodley) in St Swithin's, Littleham, near Bideford, Devon (Fig. 8.25). Moore was a much greater architect than Pevsner-inspired commentators have admitted, and his work was refreshingly free from stylistic or theoretical inhibitions.

William Douglas Caröe, who studied with Pearson in the early 1880s, produced a fine free-Gothic design for St David's, Exeter (1897–1900): it has a wide tunnel-vaulted nave, with each bay expressed by transverse arches, and the tall, narrow aisles are passages through the internal buttresses from which spring vaults (Fig. 8.26). Caröe's St Barnabas, Walthamstow (1902–3), forms a happy group with its church hall and vicarage: Alastair Service rightly referred to the 'endless felicities' of Caröe's design.

Towards the end of the 19th century, Bodley's pupil, J.N. Comper, experimented further with English Perpendicular, and came closest to fulfilling the ideas of liturgiologists such as Legg. In Comper's hands the Gothic Revival became delicate and jewel-like: among his small-scale works may be mentioned the exquisite St Sepulchre's Chapel, created as a memorial to Dr West, in the crypt of St Mary Magdalene's, Paddington (1895). The contrast with Street's powerful fabric of the 1860s and 1870s could not be more marked (Fig. 8.27).

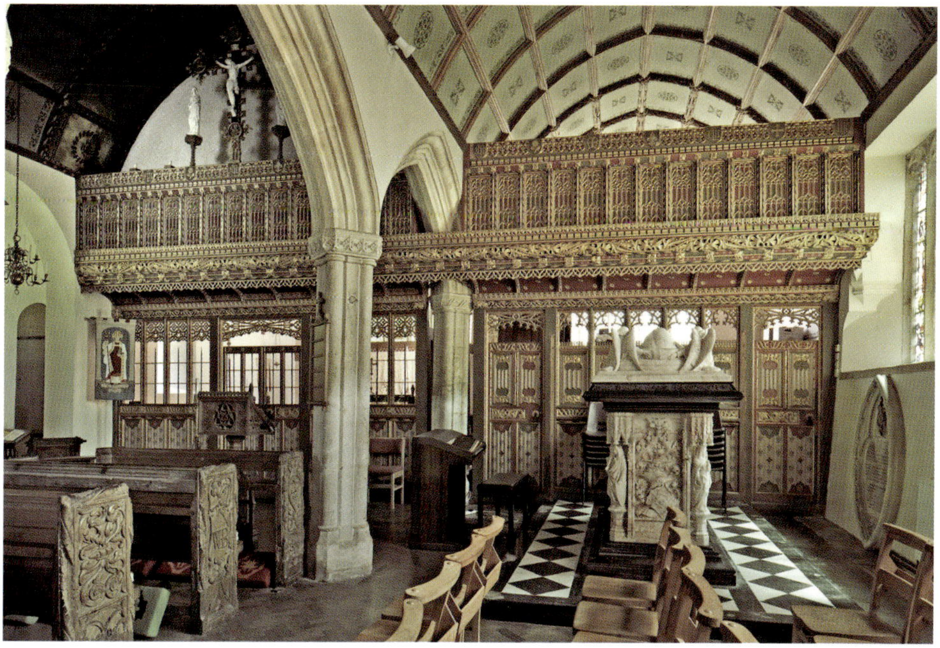

Fig. 8.25 Prodigious screens in St Swithin's, Littleham, near Bideford, Devon (1892–3), by Temple Moore, coloured by Bodley, based on mediæval exemplars in the Welsh Borders, notably that in St Issui's, Partrishow, near Crickhowell, Breconshire, Powys (*c.*1500). In the foreground, right, in the south aisle, the tomb-chest with effigy commemorating Lt-General Henry Hope Crealock was also designed by Moore and made (1894) by Farmer & Brindley (GB [2017]).

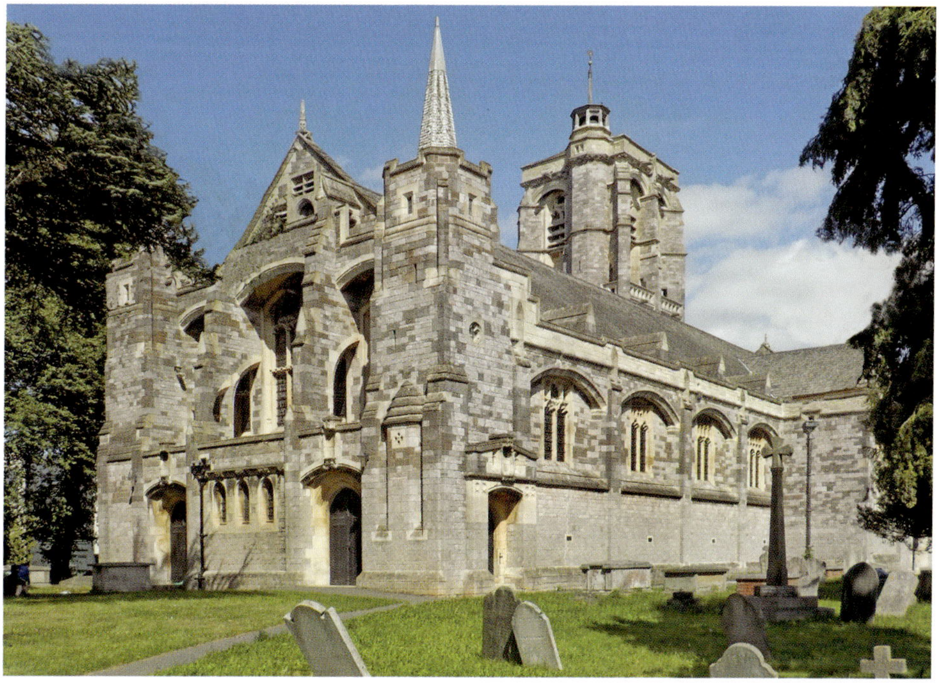

Fig. 8.26 St David's, St David's Hill, Exeter, Devon (1897–1900), by Caröe, from the south-west, a highly original interpretation of Gothic (GB [2021]).

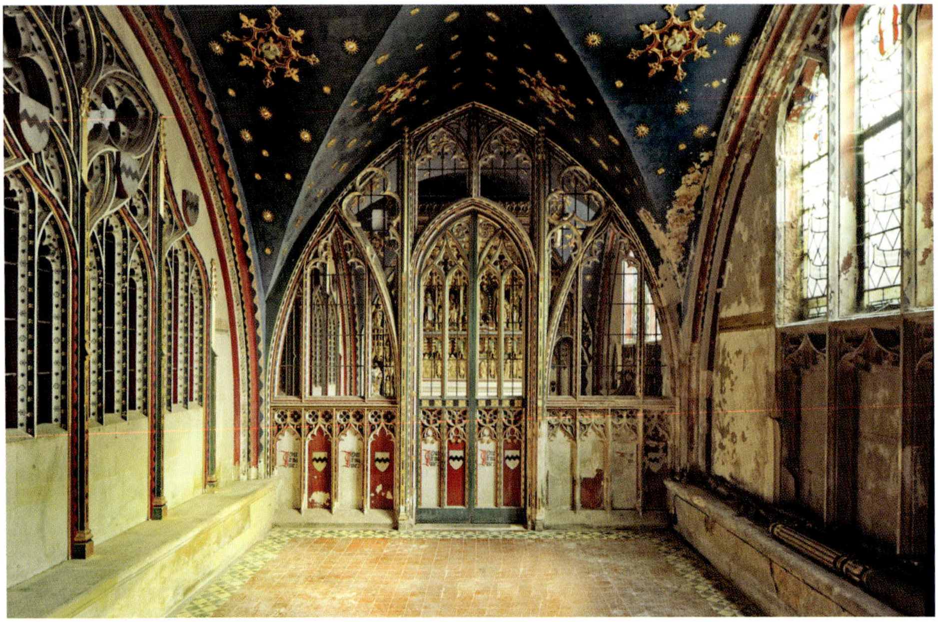

Fig. 8.27 St Sepulchre's Chapel, crypt of St Mary Magdalene's, Paddington, London, by J.N. Comper, his first important work, an exquisite reinterpretation of Perpendicular detailing, boldly coloured (mostly completed 1895). It is in complete stylistic contrast with the earlier architecture of the church (*see* Figs 6.15 and 6.16). The spectacular altar, with carved, gilded, painted reredos has a projecting panelled canopy above, a motif Comper was to use often, and can just be seen through the glorious screen. The sumptuous decorations, including a star-spangled vault and walls inscribed with quotations from the Sarum Missal, were revived by Sebastian Comper in 1967, and there were subsequent restorations (GB [2021]).

Comper's architecture, however, was not 'pure' Perpendicular, for he drew on late mediæval precedents from Northern Europe, and especially from manuscript sources and the ecclesiastical art and artefacts of Flanders. As noted above, it is curious that many commentators on the Gothic Revival have tended to gloss over the Flemish connection: Belgium was easy to reach in the 19th century, its towns are close together, and its size means that very many buildings can be visited in a short time. Comper's *Practical Considerations on the Gothic or English Altar and Certain Dependent Ornaments* (1893) impressed Micklethwaite, Legg, and others, and had a lasting effect. Other important models for Comper were the great churches of East Anglia, in which chancels and naves occupied the same volume, only demarcated by screens and (sometimes) by a celure. He sought solutions to the problem of designing chancels and churches that would be historically and æsthetically valid, that would respect the ideals of the Oxford Movement, and be acceptable within the constraints of Anglican rubrics relating to order and ornament.

In 1858 William White had designed the delightful little Church of St Petroc Minor (aka St Petrock) at Little Petherick, Cornwall, for the Tractarian rector, Sir Hugh Molesworth, Bt. The Molesworths were patrons, and in 1887 John Athelstan Laurie Riley (later Seigneur de la Trinité, Jersey) married the Hon. Andalusia Louisa Charlotte Georgina Molesworth, becoming patron in 1898. Riley, a devout Anglo-Catholic, favouring the Sarum Use, was closely involved as a layman with the Church of England, and it was he who involved Comper in work at the church, starting with the exquisite rood screen and loft, completed 1908 (*see* back cover). After Andalusia's death in 1912, Comper designed the Riley chantry chapel to the south of the chancel: it contains a fine monument, and Riley's heart was interred in the chapel after his death in 1945.

St Cyprian's, Clarence Gate, London (1901–3), was Comper's first complete church (though it was designed when [1888–1908] he was in partnership with William Bucknall), and the building was inspired by the stately mediæval St Mary's, Attleborough, Norfolk. Although strictly speaking it is not Victorian, it represents the culmination of late Victorian tendencies in Anglican church design. Like Attleborough, it has a prodigious screen running across the nave and aisles, and the white-painted walls set off Comper's lavish gilded and coloured furnishings (many of which were gradually added over the next two decades) (Fig. 8.28). Comper himself described St Cyprian's as following the 'fully developed type of the English parish church' in which the high altar is made 'public to the whole body of worshippers' without violating 'the earlier tradition ... which veiled the altar from view'.

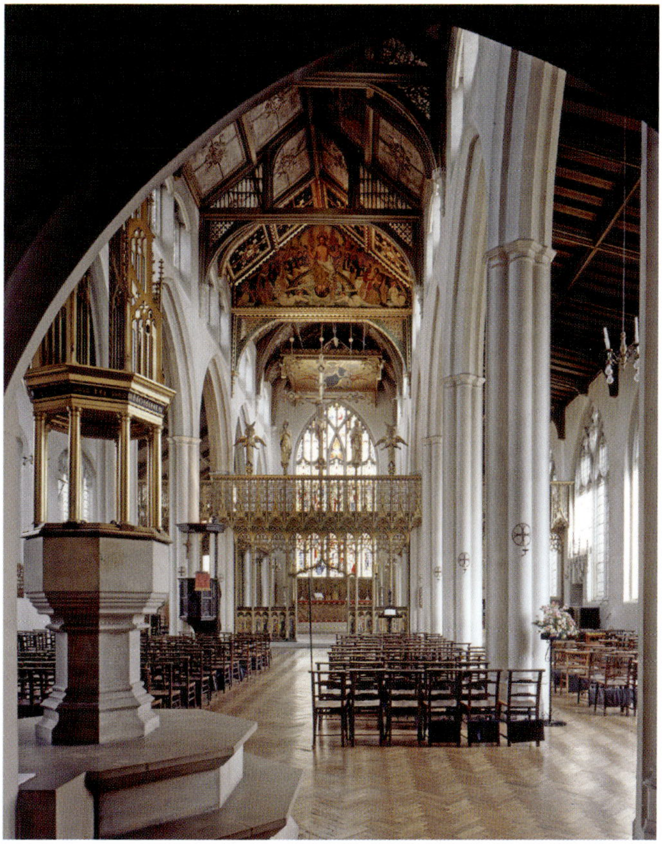

Fig. 8.28 St Cyprian's, Clarence Gate, London (1901–3), by Comper, showing the 'last development of a purely English Parish Church', in which Perpendicular precedents are clear. All fittings were designed by Comper, including the rood screen (completed 1924), the font and font cover (1930–2 – which drew on Classical as well as Gothic themes), and the celure over the high altar (1948) (MC A210901/RIBAC 138905 [2001]).

As Comper pointed out, this was the 'ideal of the English parish church before and after the introduction of the Book of Common Prayer', and it was 'for the realisation of this ideal that the new church of St Cyprian' had been prepared. Its design neither sought nor avoided originality, and its aim was not to reproduce any period of the past, but only to fulfil the needs of the time, 'and to do so in the last manner of English architecture which for us in England is the most beautiful manner of all'. In his *Further Thoughts on the English Altar: or Practical Considerations on the Planning of a Modern Church* (1933), Comper described St Cyprian's as a 'lantern', with the altar as 'the flame within it'.

In Comper's later St Mary's, Wellingborough, Northamptonshire (1904–31), the palette was more varied, pulling together threads from late Perpendicular fan vaulting (with pendants for the nave ceiling), Renaissance details (for the screen and font surround), and other allusions. As Anthony Symondson sagely observed, in St Mary's 'Anglo-Catholic aspiration, the fruit of liturgiology, the incarnational principles of theology, the indebtedness of Christian tradition to history, and the primacy of beauty in the service of God' can all be found, where the 'accretive legacy' of European church architecture may be studied with benefit. Of this church, Comper said that only 'to its contemporaries does [it] owe nothing'.

Of all his generation, perhaps only Comper retained a strong intellectual and practical connection with the liturgical problems of church building. His greatest strengths were in synthesis, and in the design of detail (his restoration of the rood screen in Sts Peter and Paul, Eye, Suffolk, is felicitous). However, terrible damage was done to Comper's reputation by Pevsner, who dismissed his work as irrelevant because it did not fit his Gropius-worshipping vision of the future, and, besides, Comper, like Voysey and Baillie Scott, loathed modernism and everything it stood for, not least its Godlessness.

In 1899 appeared the *Parson's Handbook* by Percy Dearmer, which went into many subsequent editions. Dearmer became Vicar of St Mary's, Primrose Hill Road, London, in 1901, where he put many principles enshrined in his book into practice. St Mary's (begun 1871), by Michael Prendergast Manning, was in a tough, no-nonsense style of Middle Pointed, of red brick with stone dressings, but Dearmer whitewashed the interior and set up an 'English' altar. For many years high altars had been set raised and approached by steps, with candlesticks placed on shelves: Dearmer, drawing on Legg and Comper, insisted there was no authority for this arrangement, and that English mediæval altars were set low, had very little on them apart from a couple of candlesticks, and had ends screened by curtains. Dearmer reinforced the view that much that passed as authentic mediæval ceremonial was based on R.C. Counter Reformation practice (some of it often of quite recent date), and that true English ceremonial was simple, dignified, and beautiful.

Dearmer's book was enormously influential. Far too many churches were whitened (including many where structural and other polychrome decorations were ruined or obscured), and during the 1920s and 1930s 'English' altars with riddel posts and curtains became almost de rigueur. Although his *Parson's Handbook*, in the words of the *Dictionary of National Biography*, 'was an attempt to recall the Church to the native English tradition in matters of liturgy and ceremonial', and Dearmer 'saw that art is ... an essential and integral expression of the worship offered to God in religion', he has been criticised for watering down the Anglo-Catholicism of men like Legg and Comper, and trivialising their principles.

Epilogue

One of the last and grandest works of the Gothic Revival is the Cathedral Church of Christ in Liverpool in Honour of His Resurrection, designed by Moore's former pupil, Giles Gilbert Scott, who became Garner's assistant. An architectural competition was held (1885) in attempts to find a suitable design, but another, of 1902, was won (1903) by Scott, whose youth and Roman Catholicism were perceived as problematic, so Bodley was called in to add Anglican respectability and keep an eye on the younger man. Although this great building was designed and erected after the Victorian period had ended (it was begun on site in 1904), it is included here because it is the climax of one of the most creative periods in English architectural history, and because it is essentially a 19th-century building.

Arthur Stanley George Butler, in his entry in the *Dictionary of National Biography* (1971) on Scott, wrote that when looking 'at the whole exterior [of Liverpool Cathedral] sixty years later one is struck by the dependence on mass rather than intricacy, and on well-proportioned stone surfaces, deftly pierced by windows betraying no more than a Gothic ancestry'. When Scott died, he had been connected with the building for 58 years, compared with Sir Christopher Wren's 34-year association with London's St Paul's Cathedral. Pevsner sourly opined that 'Scott, though younger than Wren, was more tired towards the end, and the style of his building has worn worse than Wren's'. This is a serious misjudgement, for Liverpool Anglican Cathedral contains one of the most impressive interior spaces ever conceived: there the mature, late Gothic Revival triumphantly evolved into the Sublime. Scott and Bodley's collaboration is most obvious in the Lady chapel (1906–10), with a stone-vaulted ceiling, the precedents for which were clearly Continental. The very beautiful *Flügelaltar* adds to the overwhelmingly German flavour (Fig. 8.29).

The story of Gothic did not end with Comper, Temple Moore, or Scott. It continued with the work of S.E. Dykes Bower, who was influenced (among others) by F.C. Eden, a pupil of Bodley. Dykes Bower, in the 1960s and 1970s, showed how Gothic could be used to extend the early 16th-century parish church of St James in Bury St Edmunds, Suffolk, where he carried out enlargements, visibly confirming its recent status as a cathedral. This was achieved when hardly anything comparable was being done, and at a time when architectural and critical opinion gave 'no encouragement to stylistic appropriateness' or good manners in design, but only to what was, in Dykes Bower's words, 'spuriously represented' as 'modern' or 'contemporary'. At Bury St Edmunds Dykes Bower demonstrated his belief that 'more permanent satisfaction and interest would derive' from architecture demonstrating 'that new work should look, not different, but natural and harmonious; that gave opportunity for the exercise of skills and craftsmanship not extinct but only neglected and under-used'.

'Building for our own time' is a dismal over-used phrase, and nearly always a clarion call demanding the tenth-rate and the ugly. Dykes Bower often talked of 'beauty' in architecture, a word never used by modernists: a brave man, he accomplished much in a climate in which indifference, hostility, and wilful misunderstanding of everything

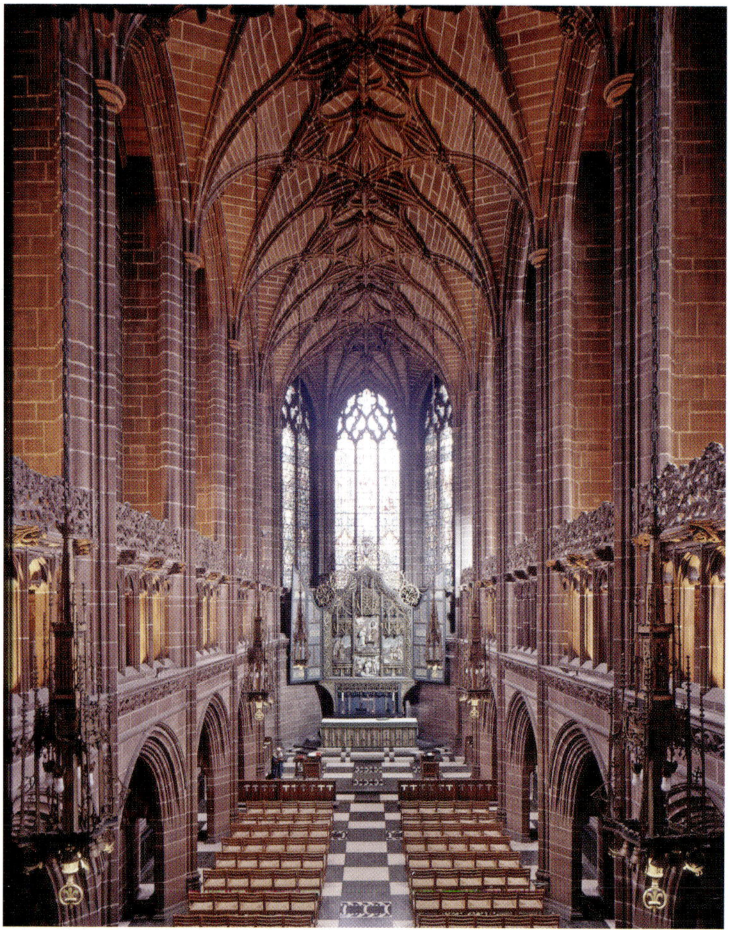

Fig. 8.29 Lady chapel (1906–10) of the Cathedral Church of Christ in Liverpool in Honour of His Resurrection, by Giles Gilbert Scott, with *Flügelaltar* by Scott and Bodley, made by Rattee & Kett. The style owes much to German precedent (MC F180901/RIBAC 138906 [2001]).

he stood for made his task very much more difficult than it need have been. The bullying commissars of cultural totalitarianism did not help one of the great exponents of the late Gothic Revival.

At the beginning of the 21st century the Gothic Design Practice, headed by Dykes Bower's former assistant, Warwick Pethers, with Hugh Mathew, realised a noble Gothic design for the upper stages of the crossing tower at Bury St Edmunds, crowning Dykes Bower's work. Based on precedents at Long Melford, Suffolk (1897–1903 – by Bodley), Cattistock, Dorset (1876 – by 'Middle' Scott), and the 'Bell Harry' tower at Canterbury Cathedral, Kent (1494–1501 – by Wastell), Pethers' work is a triumph of scholarly architecture (Mathew was responsible for the coloured vault under the crossing tower), but hostile elements succeeded in severing (2006) Pethers' involvement, a sorry tale, and one reminiscent of earlier vile treatment meted out to Dykes Bower, notably by offensively doctrinaire modernists in Cambridge.

It is a fitting, if somewhat disagreeable note on which to end this chapter.

9

Non-Anglican Buildings for Religious Observance

The Protestant House of Prayer reveals a very different temperament and … world from the church of mediæval Catholicism. Not even the most sympathetic lover of Gothic can deny that … mediæval churches were singularly ill-adapted to preaching and congregational worship, with their echoing vaults and long-drawn aisles.

ANDREW ALASTAIR LANDALE DRUMMOND (1902–66):
The Church Architecture of Protestantism. An Historical and Constructive Study
(Edinburgh: T. & T. Clark, 1934), 19.

All Protestantism, even the most cold and passive, is a sort of dissent.

EDMUND BURKE (1729–97):
Speech on Conciliation with America (22 March 1775) in
The Works of The Right Honourable Edmund Burke **iii** (London: Thomas M'Lean, 1823), 53.

Introduction

In the last quarter of the 19th century the round-arched, Romanesque, Early Christian, or Byzantine styles (collectively known by the German name *Rundbogenstil*) were exploited as the range of historical precedents available to designers widened once more. The 'moral' arguments in favour of Gothic were starting to wear thin, and, in any case, the Gothic Revival had been the style of the High Church, Anglo-Catholic, Tractarian traditions in the Anglican Church (although there were signs of deviations, as the impact of masterpieces such as Westminster Cathedral started to be felt), so it was natural that Nonconformists, Evangelicals, and Roman Catholics would endeavour to cast their stylistic nets over wider seas than mere Gothic ponds. Nevertheless, it is surprising how many groups (even Nonconformists) sought to ape the Anglicans, probably because Pugin had done his work well, and partly because of the social position enjoyed by the Established Church.

Architectural style seems to have associations with caste and class: Gothic, from around 1840 until the end of the century, was certainly respectable, and in any case, Ruskin had successfully identified the Renaissance and Baroque styles with 'popery', while setting up a highly selective palette of Gothic as suited to his notions of romantic democracy and dissociated from Ritualistic and papistical practices. As has been indicated above, Ruskin effectively removed prejudices against the Gothic styles among Evangelical Anglicans and Nonconformists by connecting them with the good and moral life, and by arguing that as Gothic had been abandoned by 'glittering', 'perfumed', idolatrous Romanists, it was free from taint: his limited range of approved Gothic could safely be embraced by non-'papists' who were unlikely to catch the Roman contagion. However, as we have seen, Anglo-Catholics were not averse to some of the architectural tendencies apparent in some R.C. churches, so there was a great deal of cross-fertilisation and overlapping in matters of ecclesiastical church building, arrangement, and furnishing.

Sometimes, Gothic of a deliberately foreign type was used for specific reasons. One of the oddest of oddities of the late Victorian period is the R.C. church and mausoleum of the ex-Emperor Napoléon III, the ex-Empress Eugénie, and Napoléon-Eugène-Louis-Jean-Joseph, Prince Impérial, at Farnborough, Hampshire (1887–8), designed by Hippolyte-Alexandre-Gabriel-Walter Destailleur in the French *Flamboyant* style of late Gothic, with an incongruous dome on top (Fig. 9.1): it is in the grounds of St Michael's Abbey, which has a centrepiece capped by a tall *flèche* also designed by Destailleur, and Romanesque and First Pointed elements derived from the buildings of the former Benedictine Abbey at Solesmes (Sarthe) in France. Here was an example of French Gothic being used for a purpose, to connect the Bonaparte dynasty with France by means of a stylistic allusion, and to show that a part of France was enshrined in Hampshire.

With regard to the Byzantine style, Bentley's great cathedral at Westminster has already been described (although it

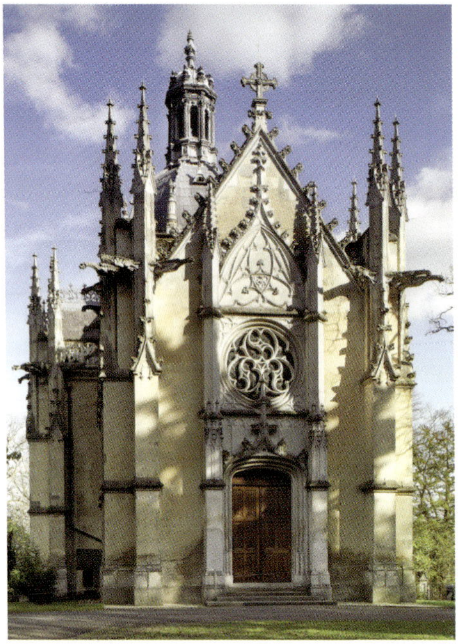

Fig. 9.1 Mausoleum of Emperor Napoléon III, Empress Eugénie, and the Prince Impérial of France at Farnborough, Hampshire (1887–8), by H.-A.-G.-W. Destailleur. It is in the French *Flamboyant* style of late Gothic, and has an incongruous dome on top (AH [2010]).

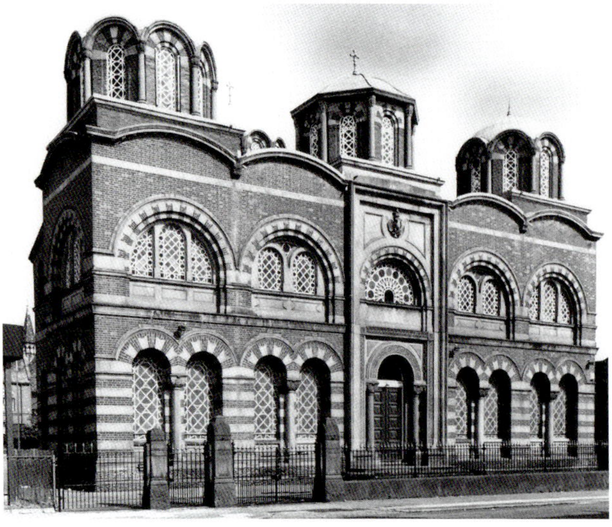

Fig. 9.2 Greek Orthodox Church of St Nicholas, Toxteth, Liverpool (1865–70), by Henry Sumners, in a Byzantine Revival style, with big cupolas (JSC [1994]).

is much more than Byzantine, as was made clear), but several years earlier, Liverpool acquired its large Greek Orthodox church of St Nicholas, Toxteth (1865–70), the design of which was closely modelled on the former church of St Theodore, Constantinople (*c.* 1100). That Byzantine church had been illustrated in James Fergusson's *Illustrated Handbook of Architecture* (1855), and a competition was held to provide designs for the Toxteth building, which was won by W.H. & J.M. Hay in 1864. However, St Nicholas's, with its high Byzantine cupolas, of brick with stone dressings, was erected under the supervision of Henry Sumners, then in partnership with William Culshaw, and was opened in 1870 (Fig. 9.2): thereafter authorship was disputed. Later, John Oldrid Scott exploited the Byzantine style with his impressive St Sophia's Greek Orthodox Cathedral of Western Europe, Moscow Road, Bayswater, London (1877), clearly alluding to traditional Greek Orthodox buildings based on ancient Byzantine prototypes of the Eastern Roman Empire.

Not far from this cathedral is the spectacularly showy New West End Synagogue, St Petersburgh Place, London (1877–9), by George Ashdown Audsley and Nathan Solomon Joseph (Figs 9.3 and 9.4), the design of which is closely based on that of the synagogue at Prince's Road, Toxteth, Liverpool (1874–82), designed by G.A. Audsley and his brother, W.J. Audsley. Both buildings mix Gothic, Byzantine, and Moresque themes: at Toxteth, for example, the materials are common bricks, with red-brick and terracotta dressings, while the portal is stylistically Gothic, in the early 13th-century manner, but set within a Moresque lobed arch, and the wheel window is entirely North European Gothic. Inside, the Ark of the Torah scrolls is formed to resemble a Byzantine church, with five cupolas. Thus, as far as synagogues were concerned, they tended to be designed in ways that avoided a resemblance to buildings of Christian denominations, except for the use of selected morsels here and there within some overall exotic confection. Indeed, Byzantinesque styles, craftily mingled with Moresque elements, seem to have been favoured for synagogues, though there are one or two Egyptianising examples, Egypto-Classical essays, and other eclectic buildings for Jewish observances. Clearly, architects looked back to the ancient synagogues of mediæval Spain (hence the Moresque themes), in some instances, but also drew on Byzantine, Egyptian (there is a good example of an Egyptian Revival former synagogue in

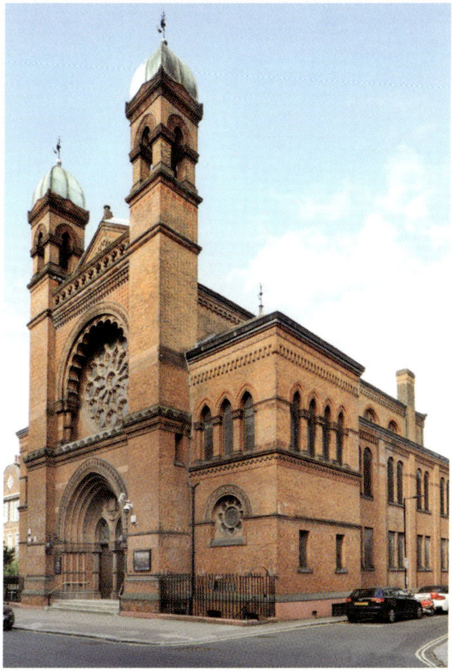

Fig. 9.3 New West End Synagogue, St Petersburgh Place, Bayswater, London (1877-9), by Audsley & Joseph, resembling the Synagogue at Prince's Road, Toxteth, Liverpool (1871-4), by G.A. & W.J. Audsley. It has Romanesque and Gothic elements, but the arch, behind which is the North European Gothic wheel window, has Moresque lobed features. Here, however, unlike the Toxteth exemplar, the flanking turrets have survived (GB [2021]).

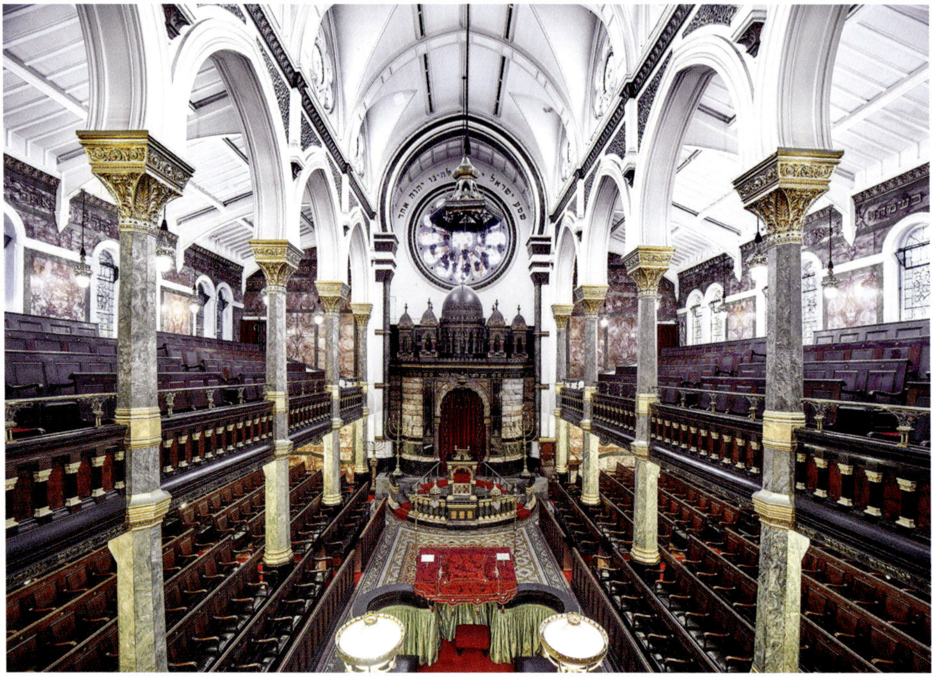

Fig. 9.4 New West End Synagogue, St Petersburgh Place: the sumptuous interior with tall arcades on octagonal piers with Moorish capitals. The internal arrangement is very similar to that of the Toxteth synagogue (DA [2020]).

King Street, Canterbury, Kent [1847–8], designed by Hezekiah Marshall), and Classical elements in others. Interiors were often very rich, with the foci on the Ark of the Torah scrolls and on the reading platforms. Sometimes the style of synagogue architecture could be described as Oriental Gothic, or even as Orientalising Byzantine-Gothic. Thus synagogues did not always escape entirely from the Gothic Revival, and the resulting buildings are often curious stylistic mixtures, while Classical and round-arched elements were also employed, often promiscuously mixed with other styles in inventive and imaginative ways. One of the very finest of Victorian synagogues, designed by the distinguished firm of Jewish architects, Henry David Davis & Barrow Emmanuel, was erected (1867–70) as the West London Synagogue in Upper Berkeley Street, St Marylebone, Westminster. With its huge arched front and Germanic *Rundbogenstil* architecture, it looks as though it had travelled from Berlin and settled in London. As with the other synagogues mentioned here, it has a marvellously ornate interior.

One of the most extraordinary of exotic late Victorian places of worship is the delightful Shah Jahan Mosque, Oriental Road, Woking, Surrey (1889), designed by William Isaac Chambers for Dr Gottlieb Wilhelm Leitner, a distinguished orientalist, traveller, and linguist, of Austro-Hungarian Jewish descent, who founded a centre for Oriental Studies in Woking (Fig. 9.5). This was the first purpose-built mosque in Britain, although in 1891 a large Georgian house at 8 Brougham Terrace, West Derby Road, Liverpool, had been purchased by a convert (1887) to Islam, a Liverpudlian solicitor called William Henry Quilliam (who became known as Sheikh Abdullah Quilliam), for use as a Muslim Institute, which included a mosque, a library, schools,

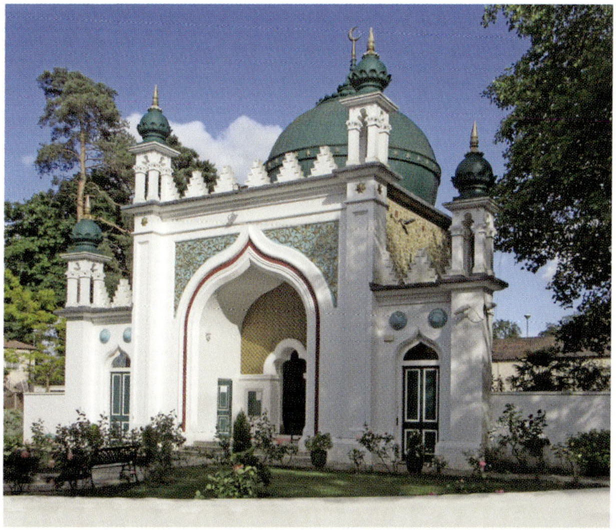

Fig. 9.5 Shah Jahan Mosque, Woking, Surrey (1889), by W.I. Chambers, the first purpose-built mosque in Britain. It has an onion dome crowning the composition, and a pretty frontispiece that could be mistaken for a distant cousin of Brighton Pavilion. Crenellations are of the almena type, characteristic of Moorish architecture (e.g. the Antigua Mezquita, Córdoba, Spain) (Hassocks5489/Wikimedia Commons/GB [2015]).

a lecture hall, a printing press, and a home for illegitimate children. Quilliam later was closely involved in the running of the Woking mosque. The Sultan Shah Jahan was Begum of Bhopal, and she contributed handsomely to the costs of erecting Chambers's lighthearted little building, which is precisely orientated towards Mecca.

Picturesque Orientalism, however, went down like a lead balloon with the editor of *The Building News*, who was unduly sniffy about the structure, wishing it had been erected in Jericho or in some other place 'never to have troubled us'. Here again was a deliberate use of an architectural style to signify that the building was not a church, not a chapel, not a synagogue, but a mosque, very Indian in style, rather than Arabic (despite the crenellations), but it is also interesting because it is a late 19th-century throwback to a style of Regency exotica to be found in places such as Sezincote or Brighton, and therefore not likely to be taken seriously by architecture critics indoctrinated with the effusions of Pugin and Ruskin.

The Buildings

The main Nonconformist groups have been outlined previously, and the essentials of Nonconformist church architecture sketched. Nonconformist churches (or chapels) were built in great numbers in the Victorian period: however, they have not attracted the attention they deserve (until recently) for many reasons, not least because they were seldom by the 'big names' among Victorian architects, and because, like many Evangelical Anglican churches, they often lacked architectural distinction: thus they did not enjoy the imprimatur of that arbiter of taste, *The Ecclesiologist*, in matters of church architecture.

At the start of the Victorian period, Nonconformist chapels tended to be simple preaching-boxes. The plan was usually a rectangular room with seats facing a pulpit opposite the entrance doors, galleries (and therefore with fenestration of two tiers of windows for illumination around the building to light the volumes above and below the gallery), some sort of vestibule arrangement and stairs to the galleries, and usually a Classically-inspired entrance front to the whole ensemble, so architectural enrichment or show was reserved for the entrance or street frontage. Many such buildings were delightful, in their own terms, unpretentious, serene, and not infrequently distinguished as architecture, in a quiet, unobtrusive way.

Early enthusiasm for Gothic was not shared by Nonconformists, who abhorred a style so intimately connected with pre-Reformation England (until Ruskin identified Classical styles as more immediately Romanist, and proscribed all varieties of Gothic of which he arbitrarily disapproved). Yet, as discussed earlier, Nonconformists had been discriminated against until the reforms of the 1820s, and shared aspects of that discrimination with Roman Catholics. Gothic and Nonconformity are uneasy bedfellows, and it has to be recognised that Georgian chapels are usually more harmonious compositions than their often hamfisted Victorian Gothic successors. Our idea of Victorian churches embraces the strident polychromy of Butterfield, the muscularity of Street and Brooks, the scholarly delicacies of Bodley, and the nobility of Pearson, while the rasping, rattling barbarities of Keeling and Cheston can intrigue. Yet Nonconformist architecture is perhaps nearer the spirit of 'Roguery', and that is probably partly why much of it has sometimes failed to be taken seriously.

Yet as Gothic churches became numerous and the Pointed styles attained fashionable status, antipathy towards Gothic for Nonconformist buildings began to wane. Charles Barry Sr designed Upper Brook Street Unitarian Chapel in Manchester (said to be the first Gothic Nonconformist chapel in England) in the First Pointed style, erected 1837–9, and the same style was used in the Dukinfield Unitarian Chapel, Cheshire (1840–5), by Richard Tattersall (Fig. 9.6), although the great west window is Geometrical Gothic. Dukinfield marked the beginning of a series of distinguished Unitarian chapels, including the impressive Hyde Chapel, Gee Cross, Hyde, Cheshire (1846–8), not far from Dukinfield, which to all intents and purposes looks like an Anglican parish church from the outside: the chapel eschews the central pulpit of Dukinfield, has a chancel complete with Communion table (although the font is also in the chancel), and is in the Second Pointed style (even with a broach spire), and clearly was influenced by the views of Ecclesiologists and buildings for the Anglican Church. The architects were Henry Bowman and Joseph Stretch Crowther (he had been a pupil of Tattersall 1838–42) of Manchester, who were very up to date and progressive in their architectural ideas, and who entered into partnership in 1846. Their building is of considerable architectural importance because it is one of the first Nonconformist places of worship to be so entirely a copy of an Anglican church. The same architects were responsible for the Mill Hill Unitarian Chapel, City Square, Leeds (also 1846–8), in which the Middle Pointed style is mixed with Perpendicular windows (Fig. 9.7) in an extraordinarily impressive design much influenced by St Peter's parish church, Leeds (1837–41). Indeed, the building does not really look like a Nonconformist church at all: it even has a reredos with mosaics by Salviati (*c.*1884).

All of which brings us to an interesting point: Nonconformists, in spite of their history, often found themselves opposing or rivalling Anglicans in daily life: socially and economically they increased their influence, and played an enormous part in Victorian political life (notably in local, municipal government). Such a rising profile required architectural expressions, so the modest late Georgian or Classical pedimented chapel (although built in numbers well into Victoria's reign) was often

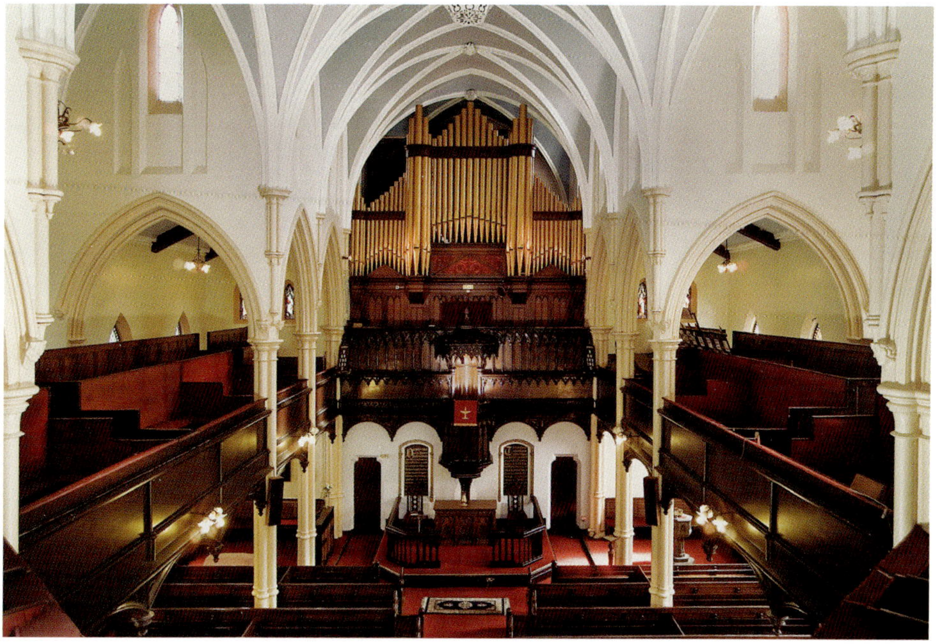

Fig. 9.6 Unitarian Church, Dukinfield, Cheshire (1840–5), by R. Tattersall in the style of *c.*1300, an early use of Second Pointed adapted to what was essentially a preaching-box, cruciform on plan, with aisles and transepts, and lofty interior with arcades on very thin quatrefoil piers (with cast-iron cores). There are three galleries, and at the east end an arrangement of organ, high central pulpit with sounding-board, Communion table, and boards with Lord's Prayer and First Commandment (the latter stressing the One-ness of God): this is quite unlike the chancel of a Roman Catholic or Anglican church (© Beccy Lane Positive Image Photography [2007]).

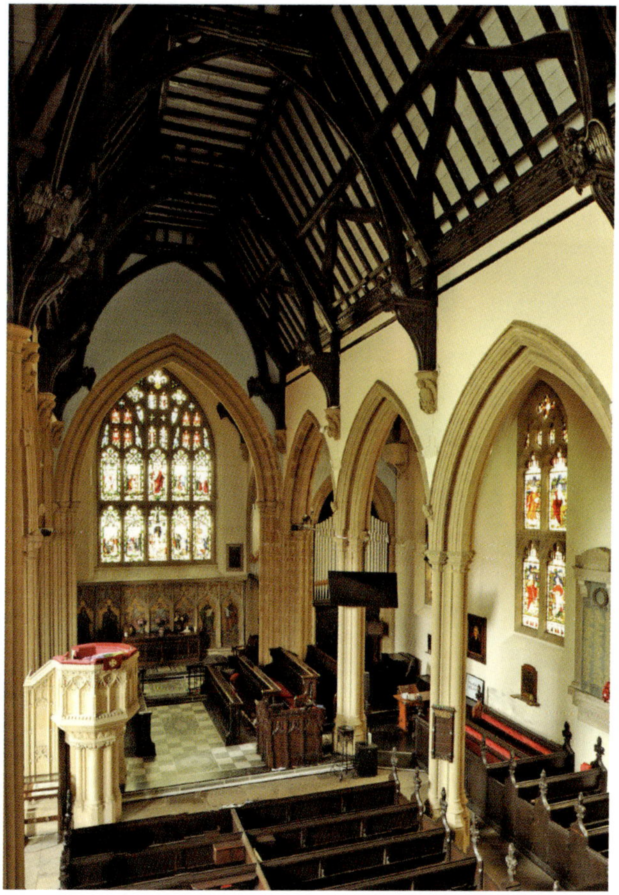

Fig. 9.7 Mill Hill Unitarian Church, Park Row, City Square, Leeds, Yorkshire (WR) (1848), by Bowman & Crowther, much influenced by Anglican church design, mixing Second Pointed and Perpendicular elements (GB [2021]).

replaced by a much grander edifice that aped the fashionable Gothic of the Anglicans from the 1850s. A good example was the impressive Square Congregational Church, Halifax, Yorkshire WR (1855–7), by Joseph James: it was a fine essay in the Second Pointed style, and was partially funded by Sir Francis Crossley, the carpet manufacturer and philanthropist. Doubtless, competition with the steeple of James's building would partly explain the slightly taller spire of Akroyd's Anglican All Souls', Haley Hill, Halifax (1856–9). However, James's Gothic church was demolished 1976–7 following a disastrous fire of 1971, leaving only the ambitious tower and spire (the latter feebly derived from Pugin's St Giles's, Cheadle) standing, yet, ironically, the Classical Georgian chapel (1771–2), which it replaced, still survived. It should be noted that not only was a style being aped, but that the term 'church' was substituted for 'chapel': architectural ambitions and a rising social profile went together.

From the 1850s, indeed, Nonconformists sometimes succeeded in adapting Gothic to their own needs, but, more often, the use of the style, and an attempt to achieve a Gothic solution to what was essentially the creation of a preaching-box, produced less than satisfactory results, for the large, static congregations of Nonconformist services and the central position of the pulpit were at odds with a type of mediæval church architecture that evolved because of pre-Reformation liturgy and practice. Later, from the 1870s, Nonconformity began to develop more experimental architecture which reflected the centralised type of plan suited to preaching: Waterhouse's Congregational chapels at Lyndhurst Road, Hampstead, and at Duke Street, Mayfair (both in London and both of the 1880s), are good examples of this new freedom.

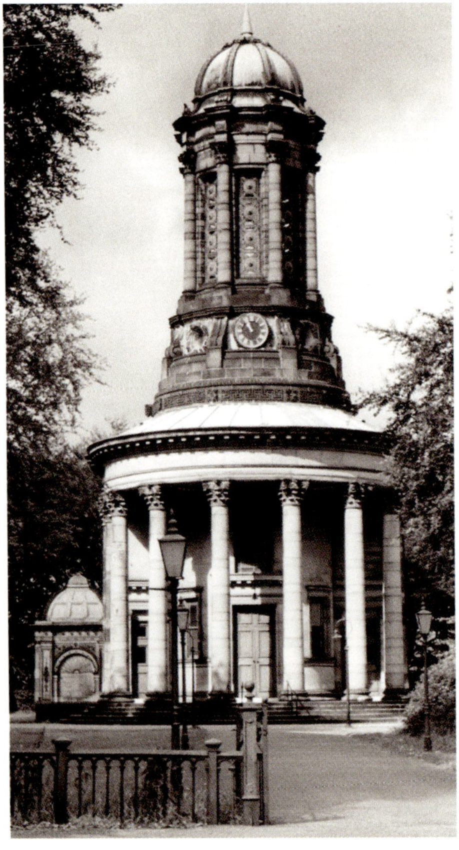

Fig. 9.8 Classical Congregational Church at Saltaire, Yorkshire (WR) (1858–9), by Lockwood & Mawson. Attached to the church on the left is the mausoleum of Sir Titus Salt, Bt, founder of Saltaire (JSC [1971]).

Henry Francis Lockwood, then in partnership with Thomas Allom, designed the extraordinary Great Thornton Street Wesleyan Methodist Chapel, Hull, Yorkshire ER (1841–3), which was firmly Classical, with a fine octastyle Corinthian portico and Doric wings on either side, but it, alas, has been demolished. Lockwood, with his partners Richard and William Mawson, were architects for the distinguished Classical Congregational Church at Saltaire, Yorkshire WR, built (1858–9) for Sir Titus Salt, the industrialist and philanthropist, prominent Congregationalist, sometime Mayor of Bradford, and local MP: it has an impressive semicircular

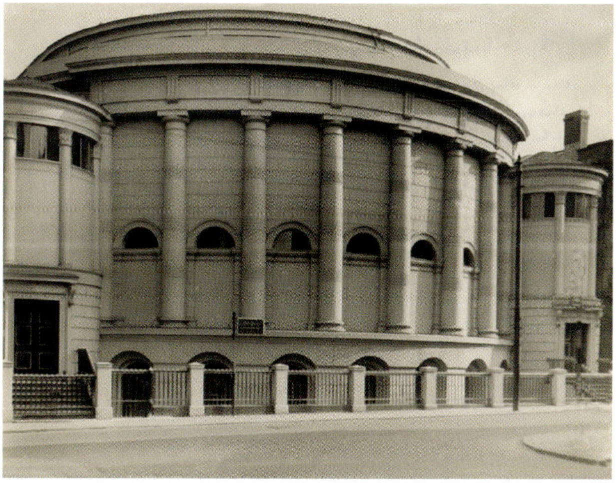

Fig. 9.9 Former Baptist Chapel, Belvoir Street, Leicester (1845), known as the 'Pork Pie', by J.A. Hansom. The curved front, featuring an engaged Giant Tuscan Order, expresses the auditorium's shape within. It is flanked by semicicular elements (loosely based on the Choragic monument of Lysicrates, Athens [334 BC]) containing the entrances and stairs to the gallery: column capitals on those elements are of the Corinthian palm type derived from the Tower of the Winds, Athens (c.50 BC) (ROL&R: F. Lumbers coll. Acc. No. 126 [1962]).

Corinthian portico above which is a circular belfry with engaged Corinthian columns, and attached to the north side is Salt's mausoleum (Fig. 9.8).

Classical too was the Particular Baptist Chapel, Belvoir Street, Leicester (1845), designed by J.A. Hansom – the R.C. architect of St Walburge's, Preston, mostly remembered today as the inventor of the Patent Safety Cab that bore his name and as the founder (1842) of *The Builder*. It was part of an education centre in 2021 (Fig. 9.9).

John Tarring seems to have worked solely for the Congregationalists, producing uninspired designs that looked rather like Commissioners' churches. Indeed, from the middle of the century, various denominations seem to have employed architects of their own persuasion (a curious exception was the choice of the R.C. Hansom by the Baptists of Leicester), but this did not always result in architecture of distinction. The batterings many buildings received in the pages of *The Ecclesiologist* and *The Builder* tended to make congregations in search of designers turn to specialist and more distinguished professionals. Furthermore, some denominations tried to evolve some sort of party line in matters of design, and the Wesleyan architect-clergyman Frederick James Jobson brought out his important book, *Chapel and School Architecture* (1850), in which he insisted chapels were not theatres, concert halls, or warehouses, and should not look like these building types. Like the Commissioners, Jobson favoured Gothic, not only because it suggested the 'House of God', but because it was reasonably economical: however, he insisted upon good sightlines and clear acoustics, and that the processional way down the centre of the nave (essential in Anglican churches) should never be used, because it was necessary to seat the congregation. Thus a Nonconformist arrangement of pews was nearly always a large section of seats in the middle of the space with access passages on either side.

As indicated above, Joseph James was one of the better architects producing designs for the Nonconformists in the middle of the century. Mention has been made of his fine Second Pointed Congregational church in Halifax, but only two years earlier he had produced a similar and equally scholarly Middle Pointed church for Barnsley, Yorkshire WR. Other competent Gothic essays, with swashbuckling spires, include the Unitarian Church, Todmorden, Yorkshire WR (1869), a Second

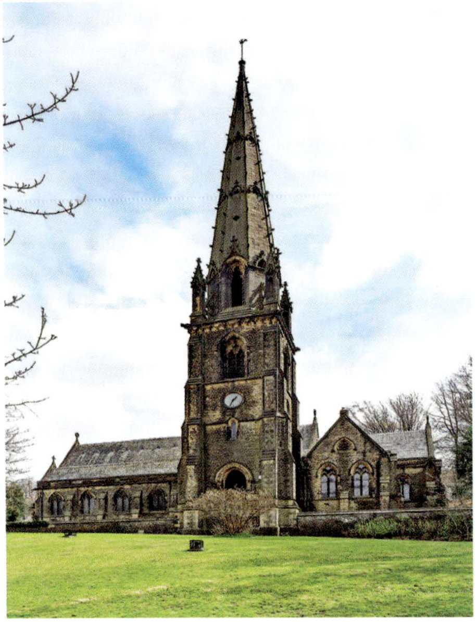

Fig. 9.10 Unitarian Church, Todmorden, Yorkshire (WR) (1865–9), by John Gibson, one of the most splendid Nonconformist places of worship in the North of England, all in the Second Pointed style (PP [2021]).

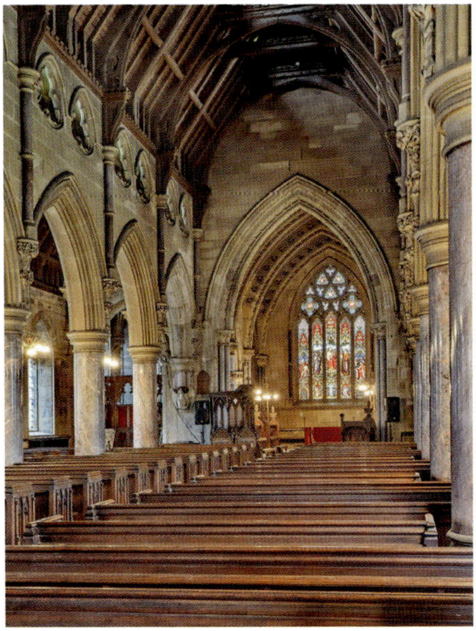

Fig. 9.11 Todmorden Unitarian Church: piers are marble cylinders, and the entire ensemble is very grand, much influenced by Anglican ecclesiastical design (PP [2021]).

Pointed ensemble by John Gibson, which would easily pass for an Anglican parish church (Fig. 9.10). Set high among trees above the town, the church was a memorial to John Fielden, cotton manufacturer and philanthropist, by his sons, Samuel, John, and Joshua: it has a fine interior, much influenced by the Tractarian revival of Gothic (Fig. 9.11).

Thomas Worthington designed excellent Unitarian churches: two examples of his work are Brookfield Church, Gorton, Manchester (1869–71), a Middle Pointed essay of high quality, with a superb Tractarian-inspired interior (though adapted for Unitarian worship); and Monton Church, Monton Green, Eccles, Lancashire (1875), another scholarly building that looks like an Anglican establishment. Thomas and his son, later Sir Percy Scott Worthington, were responsible for the Ullet Road Unitarian Church, Sefton Park, Liverpool (1896–1902), one of the most ambitious Unitarian churches in England, with Second Pointed features, but with much Arts and Crafts detail in the cloister, library, vestry, and hall. The entire ensemble is built of hard, red brick, with red sandstone dressings. Stained glass was by Morris & Co., the beaten-copper doors were by Richard Rathbone, and the frescoes in the library and vestry were by Gerald Moira. Light fittings were designed in the art nouveau style.

From around 1865, however, there was a gradual retreat from Gothic by Nonconformists in general, although architects such as Worthington continued to handle the style with considerable elan, and to adapt it for Nonconformist use. For the Unitarians, however, many churches were erected that looked indistinguishable (at least on the outside) from respectable Ecclesiologist-inspired Anglican parish churches. As has been indicated above, not all Nonconformists turned to Gothic with ease, because the form of a mediæval church was unsuitable for their purposes. Especially interesting is the use of the *Rundbogenstil*, an early example of which is the Central Baptist Chapel, Bloomsbury Street, London (1845–8), by John Gibson: it has a broad front of white brick with thin stripes, two towers, and a large wheel window. Some Nonconformists also began to develop an interest in plan-forms freed from Gothic restrictions, and more centralised plans with arms containing galleries began to appear, harking back to earlier arrangements of the 18th century. In 1870 Cubitt's *Church Design for Congregations* appeared, which discussed such matters. Cubitt was also to publish *Wren's Work and its Lessons* (1884) and the *Popular Handbook of Nonconformist Church Building* (1892): he himself designed the Union Chapel, Islington (1876), with its octagonal interior and arms, and the former Welsh Presbyterian Church, Charing Cross Road, London (1888).

Many Nonconformist churches began to require other structures attached to them: these consisted of meeting rooms, living accommodation for caretakers, church halls, and Sunday schools. The latter provided important educational facilities in the decades before the Established Church began to involve itself in expanding educational efforts at the beginning of the Victorian period. After the passing of important enactments concerning education, the Sunday schools assumed a new significance for the teaching of religion, so buildings to house schools were erected attached to places of worship. Tight urban sites required ingenious planning solutions, and so some remarkable multifunctional Nonconformist architectural compositions can be found. Among these, the Congregational Chapel, Upper Street, Islington, London, of 1888, by Alfred Augustus Bonella and Henry John Paull – a handsome building obviously influenced by the work of R. Norman Shaw – may be mentioned (Fig. 9.12).

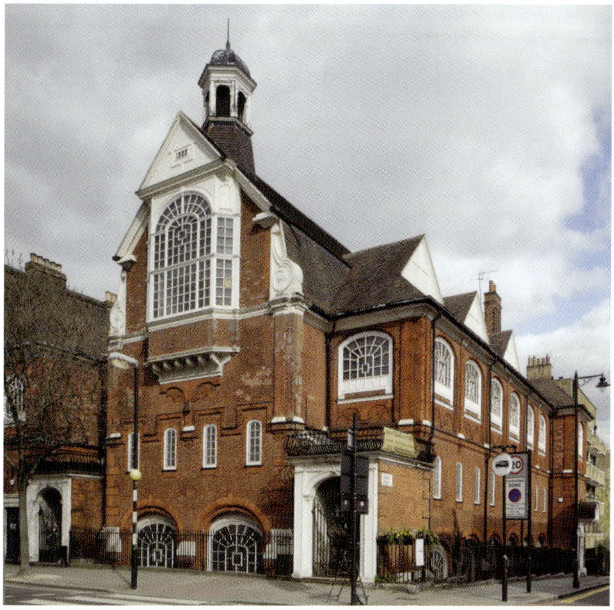

Fig. 9.12 Congregational Church, Islington, London (1888), by A.A. Bonella and H.J. Paull, showing how the Domestic Revival by Norman Shaw and others was being absorbed at that time (AH [2021]).

The *Rundbogenstil* returned with a vengeance in this later phase of Nonconformist church building, notably at the King's Weigh House Congregational Church, Duke Street, Mayfair, London (1889–91), by Alfred Waterhouse: this is a hard essay built of brick and much biscuit-coloured terracotta. Waterhouse was also responsible for the Congregational Church, Lyndhurst Road, Hampstead, London (1883–4), which is essentially an irregular hexagon with attachments, while the Mayfair building is an elliptical arrangement set on a rectangular base. Brick and terracotta also feature in Hampstead, but this time the colour is darker, with purple brick and majolica dressings. Another terracotta *Rundbogenstil* example is the Talbot Tabernacle in Northern Kensington (1887) by William Gilbee Habershon and J.F. Fawckner.

But of all Nonconformist late Victorian churches, one of the most delightful, architecturally, is Christ Church, Port Sunlight, Cheshire, designed from 1900 by William and Segar Owen, built 1902–4. It was the personal gift of William Lever, who intended it to be independent, but became Congregationalist. Beautifully constructed of red sandstone, it is in that very flattened, panel-like Gothic style in which Paley, Austin, & Paley so often worked, richly detailed, with very dense tracery. It is a successful, charming building, and at its west end is the lovely open narthex-like vaulted canopy protecting the bronze effigies (by Sir William Goscombe John) of Lord and Lady Leverhulme. T. Raffles Davison wrote of Christ Church that 'its solidly built red stone walls and stone slated roof, and its finely appointed interior with a wealth of enriched oak timber work, commands one's attention whether as architect or layman. It speaks of strength and endurance and a sincere love and study of our traditional English Gothic'.

Quite so: and one can only regret that humane environments, such as that created at Port Sunlight, with all its finely crafted, beautifully detailed buildings, ceased to be valued by modernists, who rejected everything that went before, and imposed an inhumane dystopia almost everywhere now apparent.

Afterword

As the century neared its end there was a renewal of the idea of the City Mission, or evangelising the urban masses. Many Nonconformist chapels, or churches, or complexes of buildings were erected in an overblown and showy manner that recalled the distortions of architectural detail in contemporary theatres and music halls. Materials such as terracotta and faïence were used in abundance, and the designs of such buildings seem to have been conceived to look as 'un-churchy' as possible, with the intention of attracting, rather than repelling, possible converts.

A spectacular example of a showy Wesleyan establishment in London was erected to designs by Jonas James Bradshaw and John Bradshaw Gass, both Lancastrians, both Nonconformists, and related to each other: the building was the Leysian Mission (now Imperial Hall), City Road, Finsbury, London, designed right at the end of Queen Victoria's reign, and completed in 1906. Its front was extremely richly treated, with plenty of luscious scrolled Arts and Crafts ornamentation, some Gothic canopies and brackets, all in terracotta, the composition capped with a short domed tower.

It would be superfluous to comment further, and mention of that extraordinary building is a suitable termination to this brief survey.

10

Epilogue

We have not originated a new style, but are called upon to re-awaken one which has for centuries lain dormant; and it is absurd to argue that, because those who originated it did not scruple, during its progress, at destroying specimens of the earlier varieties, to make way for what they thought better, we are equally free to destroy their works to make way for our own.

GEORGE GILBERT SCOTT (1811–78):
A Plea for the Faithful Restoration of our Ancient Churches
(London: John Henry Parker, 1850), 25–6, 33.

Church Restoration

No study of Victorian churches can afford to omit a mention of the importance of church restoration, for such work is likely to have taken as much of the energies of the architects and builders of the period as did new structures. Some of the biggest architectural names involved in designing new churches were also those associated with ancient ecclesiastical fabric, and foremost among them was that of 'Great' Scott.

At the beginning of the Victorian era, many churches were in a poor state of repair, and to our eyes often would have looked distressingly bare, unkempt, and plain. Fittings and furnishings were very frequently of dates much later than the end of the Middle Ages: they included tall panelled Georgian 'box pews', 'three-decker' pulpits, Jacobean or Caroline Communion rails, and a plethora of funerary monuments, not all of which were without historical or æsthetic merit by any means, and indeed over-zealous Victorian clear-outs unquestionably led to losses that should not have occurred. Not unusually, mediæval features, such as piscinæ, sedilia, and altars, were hidden behind plaster, buried, or had been destroyed. Mediæval stained-glass windows were rare, and skills in restoring or recreating them had to be learned from scratch. Those Victorian architects, reared on Ecclesiology, and cognisant with mediæval architecture, felt duty-bound not only to preserve mediæval churches, but to restore them, with all their furnishings and fittings. Box pews, Commandment boards, pulpits, and much else were ruthlessly swept out, and new work in the Gothic style put in. Some architects sought a feeling of completeness, of homogeneity, in their restoration work, so a church and its fittings, begun, say, in the Norman period, and added to over the next 700 years, might be reborn in the Second Pointed style, so much genuine Romanesque, Pointed, Perpendicular, Elizabethan, Jacobean, Caroline, Carolean, Restoration, and Georgian work was obliterated in the process.

At the splendid mediæval Cathedral of Sts Chad and Mary, Lichfield, Staffordshire, much of what we see today is by 'Great' and J.O. Scott, of 1857 onwards, including mouldings, capitals, statues, and window tracery. Thus Lichfield Cathedral is largely a Victorian building, and it is really none the worse for that, as it is a very satisfying whole, and has much of great beauty outside and within it. Yet it had been very badly damaged during the 17th-century Civil War, and in 1646 the central spire collapsed, doing extensive damage, so nearly all the clerestorey windows of the choir date from the 1660s. By 1760 the building was almost devoid of ornament, and some drastic works were carried out (1788–95) under Wyatt 'The Destroyer', including the virtual reconstruction of the central spire. Yet more rebuilding took place in the late 18th and early 19th centuries under Joseph Potter, including substantial repairs to the south-west tower and spire (1794), restoration of the vaulting of the north transept (1795–7), and much renewal of the west front (1820–2). Potter was followed by a four-year sequence of works under Sydney Smirke (1842–6), and then the Scotts took over from 1857, continuing until 1901: they had a lot to unpick and put right.

The results are undoubtedly impressive, and the building hangs together very well, but to take the west front alone, the great window is entirely Scott's work, as is the gable over it, and all the statues date from 1876–84, replacing cement and stucco figures of 1820–2. A study of various pre-1857 illustrations, including plate-glass negatives, suggests that only the tracery and window openings of the apse preserve anything of the mediæval fabric. That in no way denigrates Scott's scholarly and very satisfactory work: much of the original building had decayed beyond repair, been badly damaged by iconoclasts, and extremely destructively treated by soldiery during the Civil War. Further 17th- and 18th-century attempts at 'restoration' had in fact obliterated a great deal, so the interventions of the Scotts really created a scholarly piece of architecture, based on what remained of a badly mauled mediæval building, and what emerged was largely a very fine Victorian cathedral church. Particularly felicitous is the truly beautiful crossing screen: the craftsmanship is outstanding (Fig. 10.1).

Scott also carried out thorough works of restoration at Salisbury (exterior 1863–7, tower and spire 1866–8, west front 1866–70, Lady chapel interior 1869–71, choir interior 1871–6, nave interior 1876–8), where one of his main tasks was to correct and undo the efforts of Wyatt (who demolished the mediæval pulpitum, among other things). However, Scott's reredos and superb iron screen were scrapped in 1959 (some panels from the screen were made part of the Communion rail in St Mary's Church, Alderbury, Wiltshire – a building by the 'Rogue', S.S. Teulon). *The Friends of Salisbury Cathedral Thirty-First Annual Report* (May 1961, 27–8) smugly rejoiced at the removal of 'the distracting fussiness of the choir screen, the reredos, the encaustic tiles'.

The lovely screen (1862) designed by Scott and made by Skidmore for Hereford Cathedral was exhibited at the International Exhibition of that year in South Kensington, and was a Victorian monument of the highest quality: it was not born of mere imitation, but was a work of confident, assured design in its robust employment of Gothic motifs, a spectacular example of the exuberant richness possible using metal. This did not prevent the cathedral authorities disposing of their 'Victorian monstrosity' in 1967, which can now be admired in the Victoria & Albert Museum: such vandalism is all too common. Had it not been for the Victorians, and especially men like Scott, our cathedrals and parish churches would either look pretty grim, or

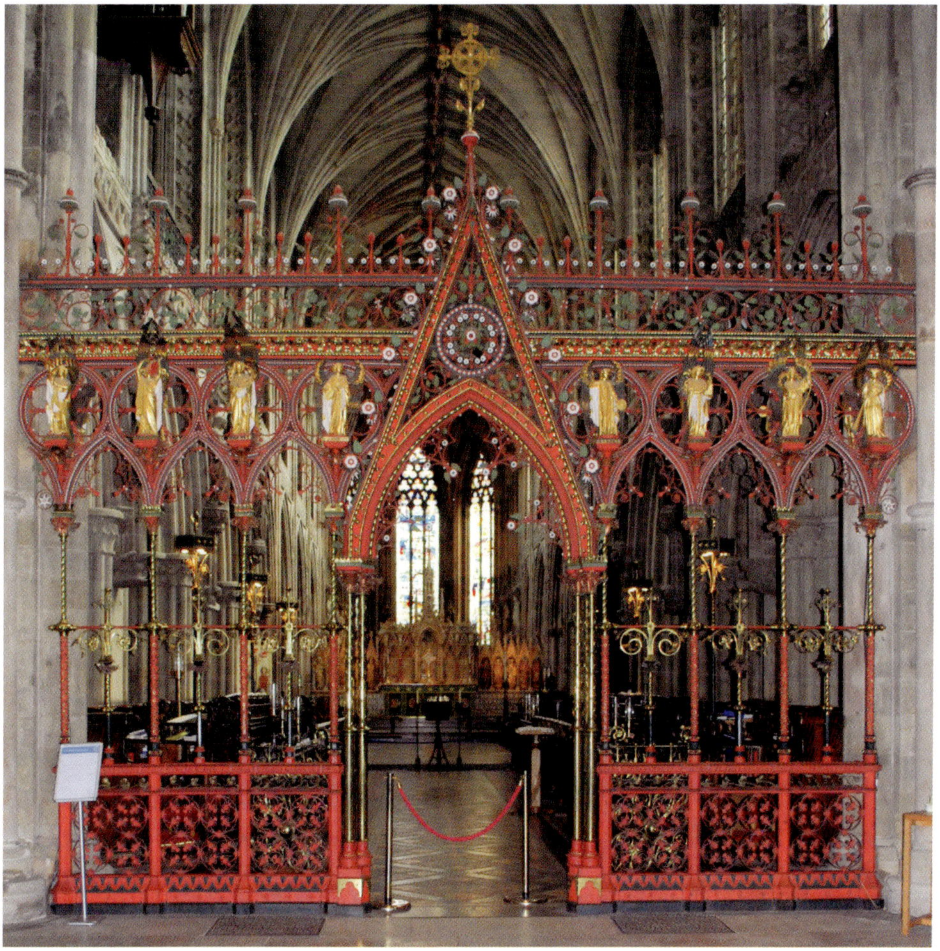

Fig. 10.1 'Great' Scott's beautiful crossing screen (1859–63), of iron, brass, and copper, made by Francis Skidmore, with figure work by John Birnie Philip, in Lichfield Cathedral, Staffordshire (JSC [2016]).

would, in some cases, have collapsed. The chapterhouse at Westminster Abbey was a mess until Scott virtually recreated it (1864–5), and the celebrated octagon over the crossing at Ely Cathedral, Cambridgeshire, was renewed in its entirety under Scott's direction. 'Great' Scott also carried out major works at Worcester Cathedral, where several screens made by Skidmore can still be seen, including that at the crossing.

For Victorian church fittings see the catalogue (1971) of the exhibition entitled *Victorian Church Art* held at The Victoria & Albert Museum (1971–2): the range of designs was breath-taking, and no unbiased sensibility could fail to respond to the beauty of these marvellously crafted artefacts.

'Great' Scott restored a huge number of cathedrals and other mediæval buildings (some 300): in 1855 alone he received commissions for such works at the cathedrals of Hereford, Lichfield, and Peterborough. Although he set out sound principles for restoration, he was not always able to abide by them when pressurised by clergy and committees, but nevertheless his work in the field of restoration was based on scholarship and knowledge, and not all architects of his generation were so endowed.

Restoration has often aroused passions, and there is no doubt that many 'restorations' of mediæval fabric were pretty drastic, and obliterated much genuinely old work in favour of mechanical and unsatisfactory new detail. Scott wrote sensitively about the problems of restoration in his *Plea for the Faithful Restoration of our Ancient Churches*, yet he could be among the worst offenders: his mid-19th-century work at St Mary de Castro, Leicester, is one of the least impressive of all his efforts in the field, while William Butterfield (not a name one would immediately associate with restoration, as his architecture is so uncompromisingly hard and unmediæval) could be sensitive and unobtrusive, as in the marvellous restoration work at the great church of St Mary, Ottery St Mary, Devon, under the ægis of the Coleridge family (there is a beautiful polychrome font by Butterfield of 1850 in the church [*see* Fig. 6.6]), although he, too, could be over-zealous, as in the church of St Mary, Ashwell, Rutland (where, as previously described, he carried out a full Ecclesiological 'restoration' for William Henry, 7th Viscount Downe in 1851). At Ashwell, it has to be said, the character of the church is now more Victorian than mediæval, and Butterfield 'restored' the building within an inch of its life (*see* Fig. 6.9).

Ruskin, in *The Seven Lamps*, had denounced radical, conjectural, and drastic 'restoration', and said that such work could never be restoration at all. When Scott proposed his draconian, over-zealous overhaul of Tewkesbury Abbey, Gloucestershire, opinion was strongly opposed. It was in response to so-called restorations that William Morris was to found (1877) 'Anti-Scrape' or SPAB (the Society for the Protection of Ancient Buildings), for real mediæval buildings seldom had an appearance of completeness, as they were added to over a long period, and acquired many examples of different styles in the process. Architects had a regrettable tendency to assess what was the dominant style of a building, and then to make the whole ensemble a Victorian version of that style: if no style were clearly dominant, then an arbitrary decision would be made, and one style would be imposed, willy-nilly. Largely through the growing influence of the Arts and Crafts Movement, untidiness, elements from different periods and in different styles all jumbled together, and diversity, began to be appreciated, and a gentler approach to older buildings began to be adopted, which we would now term 'conservation', involving the retention of as much old fabric as possible.

In a brief study such as this there is insufficient space to discuss the designers of furnishings and fittings, but no haunter of churches can fail to be impressed by much of the Victorian work. In the field of stained glass alone there are many fine examples in which sensitive design, scholarship, and excellent colouring go together: the best work was by Morris & Co., Kempe, Clayton & Bell, Burlison & Grylls, and other contemporaries. In metalwork, Francis Skidmore of Coventry provided some lovely objects, including superb screens designed by Scott, as fine examples of mid-Victorian work as can be found anywhere. In virtually every aspect of furnishing and fittings, Victorian design and workmanship can arouse our admiration, although it has to be said that much fails to rise to the occasion, and poor-quality work is truly awful. At their best, Scott, Street, Pearson, and Butterfield could be very good, while Bodley and Garner rarely put a foot wrong, and Burges could, and can, astonish us with his inventiveness. History has not been kind to the 'Rogue Goths': it is impossible to see a Bassett Keeling interior in all its rasping, thumping, polychrome glory now, since the church of St Paul, Anerley Road, Norwood, was demolished in the 1970s; Teulon's work has often been badly treated; but Lamb's frantic carpentry (*see* Fig. 7.2) can still be enjoyed, if that is the correct word.

The most skilled Victorian architects could produce buildings that, by any standards, are wonderful creations, great works of architecture, and repositories for superbly designed and crafted fittings and furnishings. Pearson's St Augustine's, Kilburn (*see* Fig. 7.15), and Truro Cathedral (*see* Fig. 7.17) are unquestionably great buildings, and Pugin's 'perfect Cheadle' could move the hardest of hearts (*see* frontispiece and Figs 4.5 and 4.6). St Cuthbert's, Philbeach Gardens, Earl's Court, London, is a treasure house of marvellous things, and ought to be better known (*see* Fig. 8.4).

Closing Remarks

And yet, any serious student of Victorian churches, no matter how enthusiastic, must suffer from increasing bouts of melancholy. There can be no doubting the quality of what must be one of the loveliest churches in England, Bodley's Holy Angels' at Hoar Cross, as perfect and of a piece as no mediæval church ever is, having been chopped around, altered, added to, subtracted from, vandalised, and abused, but it is really a mausoleum, adrift in the countryside, remote from the experience of most, and infinitely sad (*see* Figs 7.23 and 7.24). There are also those great urban minsters, once served by devoted young Anglo-Catholic clergymen, working themselves to the bone to bring decent behaviour, standards, education, and the Sacraments to the great masses of poverty-stricken poor that we know existed in Victorian England, even working in the horrific conditions of cholera epidemics at great risk to themselves, and having to fight lack of hygiene, ignorance, prejudice, and hostility with every fibre of their being: the buildings are now marooned, either in urban dystopias, or in places where the demographic shifts have been colossal, involving increasing numbers following other faiths. There has also been a remarkable rise in certain Christian sects, groupings, and wings which have no interest in traditional liturgies or in buildings and ecclesiastical furnishings for their forms of worship. Most tellingly, indifference towards religion in general among a very large part of the population has led to the abandonment of a great many churches. There is even evidence of a growing hostility to both the buildings that represented Christianity and to Christianity's servants.

Arnold's 'melancholy, long, withdrawing roar' has for ages been so distant it cannot be heard any more, and the 'naked shingles of the world', unwashed by any sea for generations, are now so covered with detritus they cannot even be seen. But there is discernible a far-off sound that ominously heralds a violent storm, a massive change, when a new tide will sweep in, a tidal wave of massive power and destructive force, and it will not then be in any way connected with Arnold's 'Sea of Faith' as he understood it. Derelict, abandoned, wrecked churches, and equivocating, virtue-signalling, unimpressive clergy will be unable to withstand it. This book, therefore, is something in the nature of a memorial, even an elegy, for something that was often of great beauty, imbued with a powerful spirituality that today seems to have been dissipated.

The riches of Victorian ecclesiastical architecture were created in less than 70 years: 'Gothic' styles had to be learned; craftsmen had to adapt to the demands made by Ecclesiology-inspired designers; and materials (such as encaustic tiles) were specially produced for church work. Victorian churches are among England's greatest buildings, and contain some of England's best design, craftsmanship, and originality of detail.

Such a legacy is of the greatest importance to our country's heritage: it may, in the end, only be remembered by a few as something that was wonderful, yet was lost through widespread indifference to the terminal decline of all that once was held to be of value, the finest architecture that England ever produced.

Select Glossary

It is the fate of those who toil at the lowest employments of life ... to be exposed to censure, without hope of praise; to be disgraced by miscarriage, or punished by neglect ... Among these unhappy mortals is the writer of dictionaries ... Every other author may aspire to praise; the lexicographer can only hope to escape reproach.

SAMUEL JOHNSON (1709–84):
A Dictionary of the English Language
(London: J.&P. Knaptor, *et al.*, 1755), Preface.

Developement [sic] ... cannot be expected from that most numerous class of architects, who veil their own ignorance of existing styles by an affected contempt for those who look to what has been as in any degree a stepping-stone to what shall be. These persons aim at avoiding servility through the medium of ignorance, and run down as mere copyists those who have taken the pains to attain a knowledge of the only styles which we can, as Christians or as Englishmen, call our own.

GEORGE GILBERT SCOTT (1811–78):
A Plea for the Faithful Restoration of our Ancient Churches
(London: John Henry Parker, 1850), 112–113.

This Glossary is intended for the guidance of readers, and has no pretensions to comprehensiveness. Some assumptions have to be made regarding familiarity with common architectural terms, e.g. 'buttress', etc., so they are not included here for reasons of space. Those mystified by purely architectural terms, therefore, are referred to *The Oxford Dictionary of Architecture* by James Stevens Curl and Susan Wilson (Oxford: Oxford University Press, 2015, 2016, available in print and online), a volume which should satisfy the most voracious appetites for such terminologies, as well as providing potted biographies of many dead architects.

Entries here deal mostly with ecclesiastical or ecclesiological matters. Some are reproduced or derived from work by me previously published and © Oxford University Press, to which body I am indebted. Others are drawn from many sources listed in the Select Bibliography. As most English churches are connected in one way or another with Western Christendom, the majority of terms given here relate to the Western Catholic, not the Eastern Orthodox, traditions. Italicised terms in the definitions have their own entries.

Absolution. Remission or forgiveness of sins declared by ecclesiastical authority.

Advent. The Coming of the Saviour, i.e. the season preceding the *Nativity* of Christ, now including the four preceding Sundays before Christmas.

Agnus Dei. *Lamb* with a *halo*, supporting a banner or the Cross, or both: an emblem of Christ.

aisle. Part of a church on either side of the *nave*, *choir*, and *chancel*, separated from those elements by *arcades* or colonnades carrying the *clerestorey*. Aisles are lower than naves, except in *hall churches*.

allegory. Description of a subject under the guise of some other subject of aptly suggestive resemblance. It therefore represents something which it is not in itself. *See* **attribute**, **symbol**.

altar. Elevated table consecrated for celebration of the *Eucharist*, usually of stone (though after the *Reformation* replaced with wooden *Communion* or Holy *tables*) found at the east end of a church and in *side chapels*. The *high altar* is situated on the principal east–west axis at the east end of the *chancel*. The sides (*horns*) of altars are termed *Epistle* (south) and *Gospel* (north). An altar frontal is the detachable finish or cover for the front of an altar, facing the nave, aka *antependium*, altar front, or altar facing. An altar rail defines the *sacrarium* from the rest of the chancel. An altar screen or altar wall behind an altar separates the sacrarium from the *ambulatory* or *chapels* to the east, and is often of richly carved work. An altar slab or altar stone is the slab (*mensa*) forming the top of an altar, often carved with five crosses indicating the *Five Wounds of Christ*, and, in *Roman Catholic* churches, having a *relic* inlaid in the centre. An altar tomb is a monumental tomb-chest or high tomb resembling an altar (but never used as such), sometimes supporting recumbent effigies or memorial brasses on top, and always has solid sides. It is sometimes embellished with statuettes called *weepers* in niches around its sides. Altar tombs are sometimes protected by ornate canopies.

ambo (*pl.* **ambones**). Raised *lectern* or *pulpit* in the *nave*, set before the steps of the *chancel*, used for the readings of the Epistle and the Gospel.

ambulatory. *Aisle* linking the *chancel aisles* behind the *high altar*: it can be canted, semicircular, or straight on plan, with *chapels* to the east and the *sanctuary* to the west.

Anabaptist. Member of a German Protestant sect (1521) that held infant *Baptism* was invalid, and that Baptism should be of adults only.

Anglican. Of the Reformed *Church of England* and other churches in communion therewith (e.g. the Church of Ireland). The Anglican Church claims to be part of the One, Holy, Catholic and Apostolic Church. It professes the faith uniquely revealed in the Holy Scriptures and set forth in the Catholic Creeds, but repudiates certain tenets of the *Roman Catholic Church* as corruptions, and claims independence of the Roman papacy. The *Established Church* in England, it acknowledges the sovereign as Supreme Governor, with the Archbishop of Canterbury as its senior Churchman (*primate*). Anglicanism falls into three main groups: *High Church* (which gives a high place to the authority and claims of the episcopate and the priesthood, to the saving *Grace* of the Holy *Sacraments*, and to those points of doctrine, discipline, and ritual by which Anglicanism is distinguished from *Protestant Nonconformity* [*see* **Dissenters**] and Continental *Calvinism* – in its most ritualistic *Catholic* observances it is sometimes known as *Anglo-Catholic*, *Ritualist*, or even *Bells and Smells*); *Broad Church* or Middle-of-the-Road – which avoids incense, many ritualistic trappings, images, *Stations of the Cross*, etc.; and *Low Church* – which has a more Protestant character, shies away from anything suggesting Catholicism (even the Cross, and certainly vestments, images, and candles). *See* **Evangelical**.

Anglo-Catholicism. Catholicism of *Anglican* type, according to English views: it is the doctrine or perception of the Anglican Church as part of the *Catholic* (i.e. universal) *Church*, and emphasises *Ritualism* and the continuity of *High Church* principles with the pre-*Reformation*, pre-*Tridentine* Church in England – though in fact it absorbed much post-Tridentine and even 19th-century aspects of *Roman Catholicism*. *See* **Catholic**; **Ritualism**; **Tridentine**.

Annunciation. Intimation of the *Incarnation* by the Angel Gabriel to the Blessed Virgin Mary.

antependium. *See* **altar**.

apse (*pl.* **apses**). Recess, generally semicircular or part-polygonal on plan, often half-domed or vaulted, projecting from an external wall, the interior forming a large, deep volume. It often terminates the *nave* of a *basilica*, and contains the *high altar*. Apsidal *chapels* are found at the east ends of *transepts* and *chancel aisles*.

arcade. Series of arches on the same plane supported by *piers*, *colonnettes*, or columns, either free-standing, or attached to a wall (blind arcade). A nave arcade divides a *nave* from an *aisle*.

archbishop. Chief *bishop*, the highest dignitary of an episcopal Church, superintending the bishops of his *province*. A *metropolitan*.

Arminianism. Doctrine, named after Jacobus Arminius, embraced by several *Protestant* sects, notably the followers of John Wesley, which opposed George Whitefield's *Calvinistic* view of absolute predestination and irresistible *Grace*. *See* **Methodism**; **Wesleyanism**; **Whitefieldian**.

art nouveau. Style of architecture/decorative arts that flourished (*c.*1880s–1914), featuring asymmetrical compositions; attenuated blooms, foliage, roots, and stems with sinuous flowing lines, as though floating in water; female figures (dream-maiden or *femme-fleur*) with long, wavy strands of hair; stylised rose-bowls; intertwining plant-forms; and indeterminate whiplash curved tendrils. It evolved from some late *Gothic Revival* motifs.

Arts and Crafts. Work done under the ægis of the Arts and Crafts Exhibition Society, founded 1888, in essence attempting to re-establish craftsmanship threatened by mass production. The most important personality associated with it was William Morris, who sought to revive mediæval standards and methods of making beautiful artefacts while holding truth to materials, constructional methods, and function to be the essence of good design, drawing on traditional and *vernacular* precedents. In architecture it was associated with the *Old English Domestic Revival*, and informed the design of certain church furnishings, so flavoured some exemplars of the late *Gothic Revival* in the period 1884–1918, usually, but not always, designed by members of the Art Workers' Guild.

Ascension. Ascent of Jesus Christ to Heaven on the fortieth day after His Resurrection.

Assumption. Reception of the Blessed Virgin Mary into Heaven.

attribute. Object recognised as appropriate to, and symbolic of, any office or person, i.e. suggesting a characteristic quality. Most saints have attributes, often associated with their martyrdom (e.g. St Bartholemew and the knife with which he was flayed, and St Lawrence and the gridiron on which he was roasted).

Augsburg Confession. *Protestant* statement of belief drawn up mainly by Melanchthon (the græcised name of Philip Schwartzerd, Professor of Greek at the University of Wittenberg), based on Luther's articles, and presented to the Holy Roman Emperor Charles V at the Diet of Augsburg in 1530. It specifically condemned Roman Catholic 'abuses': withholding the Cup during Communion; compulsory celibacy among the clergy; considering that the Mass was a sacrifice; compulsory Confession, festivals, and fasts; monastic vows; and secular authority exercised by bishops. It also clarified the main doctrines held by Lutherans: the Creeds of the Catholic Church; support for the doctrines of St Augustine against those of the Pelagians (who denied Original Sin) and Donatists (who held that their own party was the only true Church and that *Baptisms* and Ordinations carried out by others were invalid); affirmation of justification by faith and the exclusive mediatorship of Christ; opposition to *Anabaptism* on the meaning and administration of the *Sacraments*; and the organisation of the Church, the ministry, and Christian rites.

aumbry. Recess in a church wall in which sacred vessels are kept, usually near an altar. Also, in Anglican churches, used for the *Reservation of the Blessed Sacrament*.

aureole. *Halo* or *Glory* surrounding the figure of Christ, the Virgin, or a Saint. If almond shaped, it is formed of two interlocking segmental arcs, the whole figure called a *mandala* or *vesica piscis*. A circular halo surrounding a head only is called a *nimbus*.

Backsteingotik. Simplified mediæval *Gothic* architecture constructed of brick, of the type found in northern Germany.

baldacchino. Permanent canopy, especially over an altar, usually carried on columns. It does not have a domed top or a cupola at its apex, unlike a *ciborium*.

balustrum. *Altar rail* or *chancel screen*.

Baptism. Immersion of a person in water or application of water by pouring or sprinkling as a religious rite, symbolising moral and spiritual purification, and signifying initiation into the Christian Church. It is a *Sacrament* carried out in churches at a *font*.

Baptist. Member of a *Protestant* religious body that holds *Baptism* should be administered by total immersion only to believers.

baptistry. Building or part of a church containing the *font* used for the *Sacrament* of *Baptism*.

Baroque. Florid form of 17th- and 18th-century Classical architecture, characterised by exuberance, movement, convex and concave flowing curves in plan, elevation, and section, and cunningly contrived and complex spatial inter-relationships.

basilica (*pl.* **basilicas**). Building-type with a clerestoreyed *nave*, two or more lower lean-to *aisles* on each side of the nave, and an *apse* at the end of the nave, often used in church plans.

bell-cote *or* **bell-gable**. Gablet, usually set over the west wall of a church or over the east wall of the *nave*, immediately above the *chancel arch*, containing a bell or bells suspended within arched openings. If set over the chancel arch, a bell-cote is called a *sancte-cote*, as it carries the sanctus bell.

Bells and Smells. *See* **Anglican**.

bench-end. Terminal timber facing of a church pew, frequently decorated.

Benedictine. Monastic Order based on the Rule of St Benedict, regularised in the ninth century. The exemplary plan for the monastery of St Gall, Switzerland (*c.*820), is similar to the layout of many subsequent establishments.

bishop. In the Eastern, Western, Anglican, and other Churches, a clergyman consecrated for the spiritual government and direction of a *diocese*, ranking beneath an *archbishop* and above the *priests* or *presbyters*.

Byzantine. Architectural style that developed in the Eastern Roman Empire from the 4th century, and continued where the *Orthodox Church* was dominant long after the fall of Constantinople in 1453.

Calvinism. Doctrines of the Protestant reformer John Calvin. It was largely opposed by *Arminianism*.

campanile (*pl.* **campanili**). Italian bell-tower, usually free-standing: any bell-tower in an *Italianate* or *Early Christian* style.

cancellus (*pl.* **cancelli**). **1.** Latticed *screen*, especially one (cancello) dividing the *sacrarium* or *presbyterium* (hence *chancel*). **2.** In the plural, balustrades or railings defining the *choir*, usually attached to *ambones* (*see* **ambo**).

Candlemas. Feast of the Purification of the Blessed Virgin Mary (2 February), celebrated with a great display of candles.

canopy. **1.** Ornamental hood surmounting an *altar*, *font*, *niche*, *pulpit* (where it is called a *tester*), *stall*, statue, *tabernacle*, throne, tomb, etc., supported on brackets, *colonnettes*, etc., or suspended. **2.** Canopy of honour, ceele, *ceilure*, *celure*, *cellure*, or seele is a richly coloured and gilded panelled ceiling over an *altar*, *chancel*, *chantry chapel*, *mortuary chapel*, etc. **3.** A *town canopy* is a structure resembling an arcaded gabled opening, often with elaborate pinnacles, finials, etc., set over a niche or protecting a statue. It was common in funerary architecture, set horizontal (i.e. 90° from the usual vertical position as a protection from the weather), on tomb-chests over the heads of effigies, and was depicted in two dimensions on *incised slabs* and funerary 'brasses'. **4.** A canopy over an altar is usually called a *baldacchino* or *ciborium*.

cardinal. **1.** One of the ecclesiastical princes constituting the Pope's Council, or Sacred College, and to whom the right of electing the Pope has been restricted since 1173. **2.** A Virtue: the Theological Virtues are Faith, Hope, and Charity; and the Natural Virtues are Justice, Prudence, Temperance, and Fortitude. Cardinal Sins are Pride, Greed, Lust, Envy, Gluttony, Wrath, and Sloth, countered by Humility, Charity, Chastity, Gratitude, Temperance, Patience, and Diligence. **3.** Point of the compass (i.e. north, south, east, west).

Carolean. Of the period of King Charles II.

Caroline. Of the period of King Charles I.

cathedra. **1.** Chair or seat of a *bishop* in his church. **2.** Episcopal *see*.

cathedral. Church containing the *cathedra*, therefore the principal church of a *diocese* or *see*.

Catherine-wheel. Circular *Gothic wheel window*, the radiating *colonnettes* suggesting spokes. *See* **marigold**; **rose**; **wheel window**.

Catholic. **1.** General, or universal, so the whole body of believers, as distinguished from an individual congregation or sect. **2.** *Ritualist* or *Sacramentarian* aspects of worship.

Catholic Apostolic Church. Church (aka *Holy Catholic Apostolic*) founded in England *c.*1835 by disciples (*Irvingites*) of Annan-born Edward Irving: a strange mixture of *Presbyterianism*, *Ritualism*, and arcane beliefs, it emphasised prophecy, modern miracles, and an imminent Second Coming. It is now virtually extinct.

Catholic Church. The whole, universal, Christian Church. It was claimed that the *Church of England*, even as Reformed, was the national branch of the Catholic Church. Thus the unreformed Western Church was termed the *Roman Catholic Church*.

celure, ceilure, cellure. **1.** Part of the roof of a church, panelled, decorated, and coloured, immediately above the *altar* or *rood*, aka *canopy of honour*, *ceele*, or *seele*. **2.** Richly decorated ceiling over an *altar*, *chancel*, *chantry chapel*, *mortuary chapel*, etc.

chancel. Liturgical eastern part of a church, used by those officiating in the services, and often defined by a *cancellus* (from which the term is derived) or *screen*. It contains the *sanctuary* and the *altar*, and often embraces the *choir*, especially in larger churches where the chancel is part of the main body of the building east of the *crossing*.

chancel aisle. *Aisle* parallel to a *chancel*. *See* **ambulatory**.

chancel arch. Arch at the liturgical east of the *nave*, often carrying a gabled wall above, separating the nave from the *chancel*. It is often splendidly decorated, and beneath it may be found a screen (with or without a *rood*). Above the roof (usually higher or lower than that of the nave), the gable was sometimes crowned with a *bell-* or *sancte-cote*.

chancel screen. *Screen* separating the *chancel* from the body of the church. A large stone chancel screen is a *pulpitum*. Many English chancel screens survive: they have galleries (*lofts*) which are approached by narrow stairs (many of which have also survived the screens themselves) in the masonry of the church, and often supported *roods*, so can also be referred to as *rood screens*.

chantry chapel. Chapel or separate part of a church established for the daily or frequent saying of Masses on behalf of the soul of the founder or founders of the chantry or endowment. Chantry chapels were usually enclosed by screens (with or without a *canopy*), and were frequently erected over the burial-place of the founder, so incorporated an *altar*, *reredos*, *tomb-chest*, and *effigy*.

chapel. **1**. Building for Christian worship, not a *parish church* or *cathedral*, often without certain privileges normally attached to a parish church. **2**. Room or building for prayer and worship in or attached to a castle, college, etc. **3**. *Oratory* in a burial aisle, mausoleum, *mortuary chapel*, or elsewhere, with an *altar* where Masses might be offered for the dead (i.e. a *chantry chapel*), often containing funerary monuments. **4**. Screened compartment in a large church, usually in *aisles*, to the east of *transepts*, or to the east of the high altar, with its own altar, separately dedicated, and often of great magnificence. **5**. Place of worship subordinate to the parish church, erected for the convenience of parishioners (chapel of ease), when the parish was very large and distances great, or where populations increased. **6**. Place of Christian worship other than buildings of the *Established Church* in England, so usually applied to *Nonconformist* establishments.

chapter-house. Building for assemblies, business, meeting, maintenance of discipline, etc., associated with cathedral, collegiate, and monastic churches, often situated on the east side of the cloisters, but sometimes on the north side of the church with access through a vestibule or trisantia. In larger establishments (e.g. Lincoln Cathedral) chapter-houses were polygonal on plan, with stalls around the perimeter.

cherubim. Angel of the Nine Orders of Angels with attributes of the knowledge and contemplation of Divine things.

chevet. Apsidal or canted liturgical east end of a large church, with an *ambulatory* off which *chapels* radiate.

choir *or* **quire**. **1**. Part of a large church appropriated for the singers, with *stalls*, situated to the liturgical east of the *nave*, and partially or fully screened. **2**. In a cruciform church that part east of the *crossing*, including *choir*, *presbytery*, and *sanctuary* around the *high altar*, wholly or partially screened.

choir aisle. *Aisle* parallel to and adjoining the *nave* of a *choir*. *See* **ambulatory**.

choir loft. Upper part of *choir screen* or *pulpitum*, or a balcony in the *choir*.

choir rail. Rail, low balustrade, or *cancelli* separating the *choir* from the *nave*.

choir screen. Partition, railing, screen, or wall of any sort (pierced or solid) separating the *choir* from the *choir aisles*, *ambulatory*, *retrochoir*, and sometimes the *nave*, although *chancel screen*, *jubé*, *rood screen*, or *pulpitum* were formerly preferred to describe the last case.

choir stall. Raised seat, one of a series of fixed *stalls* in a *choir*, backing on to a *choir screen* (where there are *choir aisles*) and on to a *pulpitum* where that exists. Seats were usually hinged, with brackets (*mercy-seats*, *misericords*) underneath, to aid surreptitious partial sitting during the long mediæval offices. In *cathedrals*, choir stalls have richly embellished canopies of open-work, enhanced by pinnacles and much ornament.

choir wall. As *choir screen*, but of masonry between *choir* and *choir aisles*.

Chrismon. Sacred monogram, an arrangement composed of the first three Greek letters (Chi [X], Rho [P], and Iota [I] of ΧΡΙΣΤΟΣ, Christ's name, also called a Christogram, which suggests the Cross as well as *Pax* (peace). Other symbols associated with Christ are Alpha (A) and Omega (Ω), the Beginning and the End; INRI (*Iesus Nazarenus Rex Iudæorum* [Jesus of Nazareth King of the Jews], or *In Nobis Regnat Iesus* [Jesus Reigns in Us], or *Igne Natura Renovatur Integra* [Nature is Regenerated by Fire – referring to the Spirit and to Redemption]); IHS (variously explained as the first two and last Greek capital letters of ΙΗΣΟΥΣ, Christ's first name [IHC, the Iota, Eta, and Sigma (given as Σ, C, or the Latin S)], an abbreviation of *Iesus Hominum Salvator* [Jesus the Saviour of Man], *In Hoc Signo* [In This Sign (Thou shalt Conquer)], and *In Hac Salus* [in this (Cross) is Salvation]); and the fish, which is a symbol of Christ, Christianity, St Peter, and *Baptism*, as fishes cannot live without water. The first two letters of the Greek for 'fish' (ιχθύς) also give the initial I and X (for Ιησούς Χρίστος = Jesus Christ), a symbol of Faith and *Baptism*.

church. Edifice for public Christian worship, distinguished from a chapel or *oratory*, which in some respects are not truly public in the wider sense. The simplest type of church plan consists of an area for the congregation known as the *nave*, and a smaller part (usually divided from the nave by an arch) known as the *chancel*, for use by the officiating clergy and containing the *altar*. The basilican form has a clerestoreyed nave, lean-to *aisles*, apsidal east end, and some kind of porch or narthex. Centralised church plans derive from *Byzantine* domed spaces, and from circular or polygonal mausolea associated with important tombs and *martyria*. Large, elaborate churches have several chapels, two or more *transepts*, towers, other structures such as cloisters, porches, a *baptistry*, and a *chapter-house*.

Churchman. Clergyman, ecclesiastic, or member of the Established Anglican Church, frequently with High Church leanings.

ciborium (*pl.* **ciboria**). Fixed domed canopy over an altar, supported on four columns. *Compare* **baldacchino**.

Cistercian. Strict monastic Order founded at Cîteaux (1098) as an offshoot of the *Benedictine* rule. Cistercian architecture was severely simple. *Chancels* had straight, rather than apsidal, east ends, and *chapels* off transepts were also squared off.

Classicism. Principles of Greek and Roman art and architecture. Classical architecture is derived from precedents drawn from antiquity that were respected as having authoritative excellence.

clerestorey. Upper parts of walls carried on *arcades* or colonnades in the *nave*, *choir*, or *transepts* of a church, rising above the lean-to roofs of the *aisles*, and pierced with windows.

clustered pier. Compound *pier* with separate *colonnettes* or *shafts* attached to it and each other by means of bands of a shaft. In English *First Pointed* work, shafts were often of dark Purbeck polished marble, contrasting with the lighter stone behind. The Victorians also used detached shafts, often of polished granites.

collegiate church. Church endowed for a body corporate, or chapter, of dean and canons, attached to it.

colonnette. Small column, baluster, or slender circular *shaft*.

Commissioners' churches. Following the Napoleonic Wars, it was feared that England might suffer from upheavals similar to those that had beset France, so, faced with irreligion, an increasing population (much of it restive), and Nonconformity, the authorities decided to build *Anglican* churches, numbers of which (also known as Waterloo churches) were erected under the ægis of the Commissioners for Building New Churches appointed under An Act for Promoting the Building of Additional Churches in Populous Parishes (58 Geo. III, c.45), 1818.

Commonwealth. The Republican government established between the execution of King Charles I (1649) and the Restoration of the *Carolean* monarchy (1660).

Communion. **1**. Participation in the *Sacrament* of the Lord's Supper. **2**. The Sacrament itself. *See* **Eucharist**.

Communion rail. Rail in front of an *altar* at which communicants kneel to receive the Elements.

Communion table. Wooden table in *Protestant* churches, replacing the stone *altar*, introduced as a deliberate denial of the doctrine of Eucharistic sacrifice.

confessional. Booth, box, or cubicle in which confessions are heard.

Confirmation. Rite administered to baptised persons in various Christian Churches to convey Special Grace, confirming or strengthening recipients in their faith: in the *Roman Catholic* and *Orthodox* Churches reckoned to be one of the *Seven Sacraments*. In the Anglican Church it is administered solely by bishops.

Conformity. Compliance with the form of religion legally established, i.e. with the rites, discipline, and doctrines of the *Anglican Established Church*. Anybody who did not conform as defined above was a *Nonconformist or* a *Dissenter*.

Congregationalism. Form of *Protestant* Church government in which each congregation is independent in the management of its own affairs, yet acknowledges itself to be part of the Universal Church.

Consubstantiation. Doctrine of the Real Substantial Presence of the Body and Blood of Christ co-existing together with the bread and wine of the *Eucharist*. *See* **Transubstantiation**.

corona (*pl.* **coronæ**). Circlet or loop suspended over an *altar*, often carrying candles, called a corona lucis.

Cosmati work. Inlaid geometrical polychrome patterns of stone, glass, mosaic, and gilding set in marble. Cosmati patterns were revived in the 19th century.

credence. Table or shelf on the south side of the *sanctuary* of a church near the altar, sometimes associated with the *piscina* (*see* **fenestella**), where the Elements to be offered for Consecration were placed before the oblation.

cross. Two straight members set at 90° to each other, one vertical and the other horizontal.

It is the principal symbol of Christianity. The commonest types are the Latin with the three topmost arms of equal length and the bottom arm longer; the Greek, with the arms of equal length; and the clover-leaf or *bottonée* cross, with three clover-like leaves at the end of each identical arm.

crossing. Part of a *cruciform* church where the *transepts* cross the east-west *nave*, often with a tower over it.

Crucifixion. Crucifixion groups were set up on *rood beams*, and usually featured Christ on the Cross with Sts Mary and John. Sometimes the timber base was carved with skulls, bones, etc., and called a *Golgotha*.

cruciform. Cross-shaped: e.g. a church with *transepts*.

crypt. Vaulted chamber, sometimes of considerable size, beneath a church, wholly or partly underground, usually under *chancels* and *chancel aisles*, often divided into *nave*, *aisles*, and *chapel*.

curate. **1**. One entrusted with the care of souls, i.e. any ecclesiastic who has the spiritual charge of a body of laymen. **2**. Clergyman who has the spiritual charge of a parish or parochial district (i.e. the parson of a parish). **3**. Clergyman engaged for a stipend to perform ministerial duties in a parish as a deputy or assistant of the parish priest or incumbent.

curtain wall. Part of a straight wall between two advancing structures, e.g. buttresses or piers. In a church it is usually pierced with large windows illuminating the *aisles*.

Curvilinear. *See* **Gothic**.

cusp. Point formed by the intersection of two curved lines or members, e.g. the projecting point between small arcs or *foils* in *Gothic* tracery.

dagger. Light shaped like an *ogee*-ended elongated lozenge resembling a dagger in *Second Pointed* or *Decorated Gothic tracery*.

deacon. In episcopal Churches, a member of the third Order of the Ministry, ranking below *bishops* and *priests*, and having the functions of assisting the priest at the celebration of the *Eucharist*, visiting the sick, etc.

Decorated. *See* **Gothic**.

diaper work. *See* **Gothic**.

Diet. An assembly or council of the Holy Roman Empire of the German Nation. Martin Luther appeared before the Diet of Worms (1521) to defend his doctrines in the presence of Emperor Charles V. The Diet of Speier (1529) reversed innovation, and 6 princes and 14 cities read a solemn protest: this prompted their being labelled *Protestants*. *See* **Augsburg Confession**.

diocese. Sphere of jurisdiction, or the district under the pastoral care, of a *bishop*.

Dissenters. Those who refused to conform to the requirements of the *Established Church* (*see* **Anglican**). In early use Dissenters included *Roman Catholics*, but from *c*.1660 the term came to mean *Protestant Nonconformists* who remained separated from the *Anglican* Church, and included Presbyterians, Baptists, Quakers, Independents, Unitarians, Congregationalists, and, later, Methodists.

dog-tooth. *See* **Gothic**.

Domestic Revival. *See* **Old English**; **vernacular architecture**.

Doom. Pictorial representation of the Last Judgement. In a church it often took the form of a mural painting over the *chancel arch*, with Christ in the middle, Hell and the damned on His left (the south or right when viewed from the *nave*), and the Blessed on His right (north). It was also the subject of stained-glass windows and carvings on the tympana of doorways.

dorsal, dossal, dossel. **1**. *Reredos*. **2**. Cloth suspended at the rear of an altar. **3**. Ornamental hanging suspended at the backs of *sedilia* or elsewhere. **4**. Stall with a back to it.

dove. Symbol of the Holy Spirit. With an olive branch it represents peace.

eagle. Symbol of St John the Evangelist, and therefore an important motif in the design of *lecterns*, St John being considered the supreme witness to the divinity of Christ.

Early Christian. Style of church architecture that evolved in the Roman Empire from the 4th to the 6th centuries AD, usually of brick, and often on the *basilica* plan, with windows and doors treated with semicircular-headed openings. Early Christian basilicas incorporated colonnaded or arcaded *clerestoreyed naves*, and usually had apsidal east ends. The style was revived in the 19th century as part of the *Rundbogenstil*.

Early English. *See* **Gothic**.

Easter. Festival of the Christian Church commemorating the Resurrection of Christ, corresponding to the Jewish Passover. It is observed on the first Sunday after the paschal full moon.

Easter sepulchre. Recess under an arch or canopy associated with a tomb-chest, situated on the north side of a *chancel*, in which Christ was 'buried'. At the end of the Good Friday liturgy, the priest put off his Mass-vestments, and, barefooted, clad in his surplice, carried a *pyx* containing the Third Host (consecrated the day before) and the Cross (which had been kissed by the people during the liturgy) to where the sepulchre was made ready. Both pyx and Cross were wrapped in linen and placed in the sepulchre, which was duly censed, covered with a richly embroidered pall, and had numerous candles glowing before it. In the early hours of Easter Sunday all candles in the church were lighted, the clergy processed to the sepulchre (which was censed), the Host was removed to the pyx above the high altar, and the Cross was raised from the sepulchre and carried around the church before being placed on the altar at the north side of the church, where it was venerated. The empty sepulchre remained an object of devotion for days thereafter.

ecclesiology. The study of churches, church history, traditions, decorations, and furnishings. *The Ecclesiological Society*, members of which were known as Ecclesiologists and who adhered to the philosophy of Ecclesiology, was a powerful force in promoting and developing the English *Gothic Revival*, and its journal *The Ecclesiologist* (1841–68), was influential, not least in the making (and breaking) of architectural reputations.

Edwardian. Of the time of King Edward VII, often characterised by an opulent *Baroque* revival, but also the period when some of the very finest English Arts and Crafts late *Gothic* work was created.

Edwardine. Of the period of King Edward VI.

effigy. Sculptured representation of a figure, normally shown clothed or in armour, lying on its back on a tomb-chest.

encaustic. **1**. Painting with wax colours and fixing them during firing so that the colours are burnt in. **2**. Type of tile decorated with patterns formed with different colours of clay inlaid in the tile made of another colour, then fired, and usually glazed. Encaustic tiles with yellowish patterns on a dark red ground were commonly used in *Gothic Revival* churches.

English altar. Type of late mediæval altar arrangement with *riddels*, *riddel posts*, and, sometimes, a *tester*.

Epistle. Letter from an Apostle, forming part of the Canon of Scripture in the New Testament of the Holy Bible, extracts from which are read from the south side of the *altar*.

Epistle side. *See* **altar**.

Erastianism. Control of the Church by the State. It is named after Thomas Erastus, who did not, in fact, advocate the full subordination of Church jurisdiction to the State. However, from the British parliamentary enactments of the 1820s and 1830s, Churchmen perceived 'Erastianism' to be gaining the upper hand in English Church affairs.

Established Church. The Church as by law established as the public or State-recognised form of religion. *See* **Anglican**.

Eucharist. **1**. The *Sacrament* of the Lord's Supper or Communion. **2**. The consecrated Elements (the bread and wine), especially the bread. **3**. The box or closed vessel (*pyx*) containing the consecrated bread.

Evangelical. Protestant who maintains that the essence of the Gospel consists in the doctrine of Salvation by faith in the Atoning Death of Christ and denies that either Good Works or the *Sacraments* have any saving efficacy. Evangelicals within the *Anglican Church* were associated with the *Low Church* party. In more recent times some Evangelicals have been influenced by American Revivalism and Biblical Fundamentalism.

Evangelists. Sts Matthew, Mark, Luke, and John, often represented by winged creatures: man (Matthew), lion (Mark), ox (Luke), or eagle (John).

excubitorium. Elevated gallery or loft in a church from which watch could be kept over a shrine (*watching loft*) or a place from which monks could be summoned to services.

Extreme Unction. One of the seven *Sacraments*, the anointing of a person nearing death by a priest with oil blessed for the purpose by a bishop. The rite consists of the separate anointing of the five senses and the feet, and the repetition at each anointing praying for forgiveness, thus healing the soul against the difficulties faced in mortal illness.

family pew. Arrangement of seats in a church contained within a high panelled screen around them, also called a box pew, usually rented by one family.

Fathers of the Church. Large group of orthodox and personally holy writers known as the Early Fathers, in art usually represented as Sts Ambrose, Athanasius, Augustine, Basil, Gregory the Great, Gregory Nazianzen, Jerome, and John Chrysostom.

fenestella. **1**. Opening in an altar or shrine affording a view of the *relics* within. **2**. Niche in the south wall of a *chancel* containing the *piscina* and (sometimes) the *credence table*. **3**. Opening for a bell in a *bell-cote* over a gable.

fereter. **1**. Permanent or portable shrine for *relics*. **2**. Bier, catafalque, *tomb-chest* or other construction of a similar funerary type.

feretory. Enclosure defined in some way (e.g. by means of a screen) in a church or chapel, containing a *fereter*.

First Pointed. *See* **Gothic**.

fish. *See* **Chrismon**.

fish bladder. Form found in *Second Pointed Curvilinear tracery* looking like a tadpole, with a round or pointed head and a curving pointed tail, also called a *mouchette*.

Five Wounds of Christ. The wounds to the Saviour's hands, feet, and side, caused during the *Crucifixion*, and represented on the *mensa*, or altar slab by five incised crosses, one at each corner and one in the middle.

Flamboyant. *See* **Gothic**; **tracery**.

foil. In *Gothic tracery* any circular lobe tangent to the inner side of a larger arc or arch, meeting other lobes in points termed *cusps* projecting inwards. Prefixes describe how many foils occur: *trefoil* = 3; *quatrefoil* = 4; *cinquefoil* = 5; *sexfoil* = 6; *multifoil* = many foils, etc.

font. Basin for the blessed water used during the *Sacrament* of *Baptism*. It is commonly formed from a large block of stone, hollowed out and carved with Christian symbols, supported on a short *pier* or cluster of *colonnettes* set on a stepped plinth or platform. It may have an elaborate coloured *font cover*.

Free Gothic. **1**. Revival of *Gothic* forms and motifs, freely used in an eclectic mix. **2**. Late 19th-century style, in which Arts and Crafts and other references/styles were mingled, creating a non-archæological, scholarly, yet highly individual style.

fresco. Mural painting, carried out while the plaster is still wet and fresh (buon fresco).

frontal. *See* **altar**.

gallery. Galleries or scaffolds were erected in post-*Reformation* churches above aisles and at the west end to accommodate more people. They were detested by Ecclesiologists.

Georgian. Architecture of the period of the first four Kings of the House of Hanover (1714–1830).

Go. Pejorative Victorian term used to describe work by *Rogue* Goths that was restless, too animated or 'acrobatic', and embarrassing. It implied empty fashion, hamfistedness, clumsiness, discord, clashing colours, excessive liveliness, coarseness, loudness, decadence, furious vigour, recklessness, exaggeration, vulgarity, and generally something overdone.

Golgotha. *See* **Crucifixion**.

Gospel. The body of religious doctrine taught by Christ and His Apostles, i.e. the Christian revelation, religion, or dispensation, the record of Christ's life and teaching contained in the books written by the Four *Evangelists* (Matthew, Mark, Luke, and John) in the New Testament, extracts from which are read in services from the north side of the *altar*.

Gospel side. *See* **altar**.

Gothic. Architectural style, properly termed *Pointed*, that developed in Europe from the latter part of the 12th until the 16th century, and in certain locations (e.g. Oxford) even continued into the 17th century. As its more appropriate name suggests, it is the architecture of the pointed arch, pointed rib vaults, *piers* with clusters of *shafts*, deep buttresses (some of the flying type), window *tracery*, pinnacles, spires, battlements, and a soaring verticality. Gothic is arcuated (as opposed to trabeated), giving a dynamic impression of thrust and counter-thrust, and is a remarkably coherent style in which forces are expressed and resisted, and non-structural *curtain walls* were pierced by huge areas of glazed window.

First Pointed (known in England as *Early English* Gothic or the *Lancet* style) evolved and prevailed from the late 12th to the late 13th century. Windows were first of all tall and thin, with pointed tops, of the *lancet* type, set singly or in groups in walls. *Trefoils* and *cinquefoils* (*see* **foil**) occurred over smaller openings, and important doorways (e.g. at the west of a church) were often divided into two by a central shaft (*trumeau*), with a *quatrefoil* or *vesica piscis* carved above, associated with sculpture in the *tympanum*. West doorways were usually elaborated with numerous *Orders* and enrichments. Mouldings consisted largely of convex and concave rolls, producing strong effects of light and shade, and were deeply cut. Early English ornaments, found on horizontal mouldings, were the nail-head (consisting of a repetitive row of small pyramidal forms usually found on the abaci of bell-capitals) and the larger, spikier dog-tooth resembling a pyramid with V-shaped notches pointing towards the apex, forming one of a closely spaced series within a cavetto moulding. Foliate stylised ornament was deeply carved and vigorous, often with the leaves arranged in threes. *Piers* had clusters of *shafts* (usually of black or dark-grey *Purbeck marble*) around them, held in position by bands of freestone, and contrasting with the lighter stone of the pier proper. Ribbed vaulting was commonly employed. *Tracery* seems to have begun as flat masonry slabs pierced with lights (known as *plate-tracery*), but towards the end of the 13th century bar-tracery was used, consisting of moulded mullions, etc. These bars could intersect at window-heads, forming Y-tracery, but also formed symmetrical patterns involving circles and *foils*: this type of arrangement is termed *Geometrical* tracery, for obvious reasons, and reached perfection in the early *Middle Pointed* period of the late 13th century, which followed the earliest phase of *First Pointed*. Capitals were of the foliate stiff-leaf type, or simple bell-capitals. Buttresses were prominent, deep, and narrow, to take the thrust of the stone-vaulted ceilings, and marked the divisions of the length of the church into bays: they terminated in gables or stepped arrangements (pinnacles only came into general use towards the end of the First Pointed style, and were often treated as bundle-piers). The use of the pointed arch enabled rib vaults to be constructed over rectangular spaces without incurring the problems caused when the less flexible geometry of semicircular *Romanesque* arches had been employed: the pointed arch was rather like a 'hinge', freeing up the geometry of construction and junctions. Roofs, like Romanesque structures, were steeply pitched, sometimes dramatically so. First Pointed merges with *Middle Pointed*, and there were overlaps with *Second Pointed*.

Second Pointed (known as *Decorated Gothic* in Britain), as the term suggests, has more elaborate enrichment, with decoration (especially *diaper work*, decorative patterns on plain, flat, unbroken surfaces consisting of repeated simple figures [e.g. squares, lozenges, polygons] closely connected with each other, sometimes with embellishments in the form of stylised flowers) covering surfaces. Its chief characteristic, however, is the complexity of *tracery* and vaulting. At the end of the *First Pointed* period, as noted above, *plate-tracery* evolved, then *bar-tracery* arranged in geometrical patterns. So *Geometrical* bar-tracery is usually seen as characteristic of the *Middle* or early Second Pointed styles. Nail-head and dog-tooth ornament were superseded by fleuron, four-leafed flower, and *ball-flower* enrichment, while crockets on pinnacles and canopies, and other ornament, multiplied. Floral and foliate decorations tended to be treated more naturalistically. The late phase of Second Pointed saw the development of *Curvilinear* or Flowing tracery made possible by use of the *ogee* (or S-shaped) curve: this, in turn, gave rise to the appearance of *fish bladders*, *daggers*, or *mouchettes* in tracery, and the invention of complex *reticulated*, or net-like, patterns in windows that became very large. Ogees led to the creation of flame-like shapes in the lights of upper parts of traceried windows: these shapes suggested the term *Flamboyant* to describe later elaborate Pointed architecture on the European Continent. Ogee curves contributed to a sense of remarkable richness and flowing, elegant lines. Vaulting became more elaborate, with intermediate and lierne ribs forming star-shaped patterns. Roofs remained steeply pitched. By Second Pointed is meant the style of mediæval architecture as developed from the late 13th until the second half of the 14th century.

Third Pointed or *Perpendicular Gothic*, which started in the first half of the 14th century (*c.*1330), continued into the 16th century, even surviving in places like Oxford into the 17th century, so it was the longest-lived style of Pointed architecture in England, lasting for about three centuries, and was the first style of Gothic to be revived. Unlike *First* and *Second Pointed*, it has no true Continental counterpart, and should really be regarded as the national architectural style of England. It is arguably the greatest contribution England ever made to architecture, although the *Gothic Revival* and aspects of the *Domestic Revival* and *Arts and Crafts Movement* were also important and original English cultural inventions. It rejected the flowing *ogee* forms (though ogees survived for a time), replacing them with panel-like motifs, which, towards the later phase of the style, acquired very flat, depressed arches. So Perpendicular is the last of the styles of Gothic which flourished in England in the mediæval period, and its developed characteristics gave it the alternative (and more accurate, preferable) title of the *Rectilinear* style. It is recognisable because of its delicate patterns of vertical and horizontal bars, especially in *tracery* and blind-tracery over wall surfaces. Transoms were often ornamented with miniature battlements, and mullions do not branch out, but rise straight to the undersides of window openings and are also sometimes carried down over wall surfaces, thus continuing the rigid panel effects. Arches over openings and spaces became very depressed (of the four-centred type). Vaulting became more complex, unifying the entire space: at first, vaults were of the lierne type, and then evolved into the fan pattern, which carried the panel-like motifs on over ceilings as well as walls. There is no parallel to fan-vaulting on the European Continent: it is a powerfully individual English invention. A further important feature of Perpendicular design was the introduction of rectangular frames around apertures: this created spandrels (often elaborately ornamented) between the rectangular frames and the four-centred arches, enhancing the disciplined, unifying, panel-like treatment of interiors. The rectangular frames over openings became hood-moulds outside terminating in label-stops carved as shields or hearts. On occasion windows filled entire walls between buttresses, and the rhythms of window tracery were repeated as blind-tracery over internal wall surfaces: some Perpendicular interiors were so covered with repeated panel motifs (even over the fan-vaulted ceilings), that an architecture of tightly controlled, logical, modular unity was created, as never before. A characteristic of Perpendicular *clerestoreys* is that they contained very large windows, and so were airy, light, and vast: as naves were heightened to accommodate huge ranges of Perpendicular windows, roofs had to be flattened, and disappeared behind parapets decorated with battlements. The use of repeated panels over surfaces, in window tracery, and in fan vaults; the adoption of rectangular hood-moulds; the flattening of roofs; the adoption of crenellated parapets to conceal those roofs; and the elaboration of lierne and, later, fan vaulting gave the Perpendicular style its chief motifs. During the Perpendicular period, *chancels* were not distinctly compartmented, but were part of the main volume of the church (this influenced architects of late Victorian churches): they were demarcated by means of sumptuous timber screens, often gloriously coloured, over which was a *rood loft* and *rood*. Such screens were commonly ornamented with grapevine, trail, vignette, vine-scroll, or vinette running enrichment, often coloured, and crested with brattishing. Chancel ceilings were frequently given more elaborate treatment than those of naves and aisles: additional colour was the means usually employed. Some of the most exquisite Perpendicular work may be found in *chantry chapels* and tombs (e.g. in Tewkesbury Abbey and Winchester Cathedral).

Gothic Revival. Movement that began in England to revive Gothic forms with a full understanding of their original character. Although there is probably an overlap between 17th-century *Gothic Survival* (in the sense that it was an unconscious continuation of the late *Perpendicular* style) and Gothic *Revival*, it is clear that 17th-century buildings such as the church of Holy Trinity, Staunton Harold, Leicestershire (1653–6), and the cathedral church of St Columb, Londonderry (1628–33), were erected in Gothic because Holy Trinity's founder wished to make a stand against the Republican-Puritan regime of Cromwell, and the builders of St Columb's (the City of London) desired to distance themselves from the Palladian style favoured by the Stuart Court. They are therefore Gothic Revival.

In the early 19th century many Gothic churches were built that were often unconvincing in terms of archæology and scholarship, and did not resemble mediæval buildings. Simple *Georgian Commissioners' Gothic* churches with rudimentary *First Pointed* or *Perpendicular* windows often purported to be Gothic. What became the scholarly Gothic Revival in which real mediæval exemplars provided the precedents for design really began with the works of Rickman in the second decade of the 19th century, with the publications of Bloxam in the third and fourth decades, and with the polemics of A.W.N. Pugin in the fourth and fifth decades. *Ecclesiology* and the religious debates of the 1830s and 1840s also helped to promote the Revival, as did the popular success of the Palace of Westminster (from 1836) by Barry and Pugin.

A growing body of scholarship began to inform the 19th-century Gothic Revival, and the ambitious programme of church building was increasingly served by architects thoroughly immersed in the style. The building industry had to adapt too, craftsmen trained, and the lost language of the Pointed styles learned anew. In England the Revival began with Perpendicular; turned to *Second Pointed* (English first, then Continental), largely due to the arguments of Pugin and the Ecclesiologists, who perceived 14th-century Gothic as fully developed with advantages over the 'undeveloped' *Lancet* style of *First Pointed* and the supposedly 'decadent' Perpendicular; then embraced Continental Gothic (especially that of Italy, in which possibilities of *structural polychromy* had attracted commentators including Street and Ruskin). The mid-Victorian Gothic Revival of the 1850s and early 1860s was thus often coloured, incorporating polished granites, marbles, many-coloured brick-and-tile-work, becoming more free in expression and less archæologically derivative in the process. Gothic Revivalists then sought a more robust and 'primitive' Gothic, and so turned to the powerful First Pointed Burgundian precedents of the 13th century: this produced the so-called 'muscular Gothic' of Brooks, Pearson, G.E. Street, and others.

Some practitioners, such as Sir George Gilbert 'Great' Scott, settled for *Middle Pointed* as the ideal: it was more sophisticated than the Lancet style and less fussy than *Curvilinear* Second Pointed. Lastly, however, architects such as Bodley turned to late Second Pointed and Perpendicular sources, producing exquisitely delicate work such as the church of the Holy Angels, Hoar Cross, Staffordshire (1872–1900). A feature of English late Gothic Revival was its eclecticism and its close connection with the Arts and Crafts Movement, as in Sedding's Holy

Trinity, Sloane Street, London (1888–90).

Grace. **1**. Free favour of God manifest in the Salvation of sinners and the bestowing of Blessings. **2**. Divine influence which operates to regenerate and sanctify, to inspire virtue, and to impart strength to endure trials and resist temptation.

gradin, gradine. **1**. One of a series of low steps or seats raised one above the other. **2**. Raised shelf set above an altar and at its back, usually as long as the *mensa* (*see* **altar**), a third or a quarter as deep, and having the front (often painted) closed in. The narrow strip of pictures is called the *predella*. **3**. Platform, *foot-pace*, or predella on which an altar stands, projecting about a metre and a half in front of the altar and about a third of a metre on either side, approached by at least two generously sized steps. Some Victorian writers seem to use the term to describe the whole raised area of a *chancel* in which an altar stands.

guild. Craft fraternity particularly involved in protecting the interests of members. Guilds erected and maintained *guild* or *chantry chapels* for the care of the souls of departed brethren and sisters.

hagioscope. *Squint*, loricula, or aperture, cut obliquely in a wall (usually of a *chancel*), affording a visual connection between the *high altar* and *aisles* or *side chapels*.

hall church. Church with *nave*, *aisles*, and no *clerestorey*, the interior of which is of approximately uniform height throughout. It is a characteristic German type (*Hallenkirche*).

halo. Disc of radiance or *nimbus* around a head. *Compare* **aureole**.

hatchment. Achievement of Arms represented on a square panel hung diagonally in a church after the funeral of a gentleman.

helm roof. Spire on a square tower, each side of which is crowned with a gable.

Henrician. Of the period of King Henry VIII (*r.* 1509–47), sometimes also applied to that of Henry VII (*r.* 1485–1509).

heraldic. Decoration derived from heraldic motifs and/or colours, found on ceilings, screens, floor tiles, etc.

high altar. *See* **altar**.

High Church. Party or principles of the *High Churchmen* who hold views that give a high place to the claims of the episcopate and the priesthood; to the saving *Grace* of the *Sacraments*; and to those points of doctrine, discipline, and ritual by which the *Anglican Church* is distinguished from *Calvinistic Protestant* and *Nonconformist* Churches. The High Church party is associated with the *Oxford Movement*, *Tractarianism*, *Ritualism*, and *Anglo-Catholicism*.

High Victorian Gothic. Unsatisfactory term for the style of the somewhat harsh *polychrome* structures of the *Gothic Revival* in the 1850s and 1860s. Its gritty 'muscularity' owed much to Continental Gothic, but use of the term poses a question as to what might constitute Low Victorian Gothic.

Historicism. Architecture strongly influenced by the past, especially Revivalist architecture. It was facilitated by many lavish and scholarly publications, notably those including measured drawings. The term is used pejoratively by some, who also employ *pastiche* as a term of abuse, but Historicism draws on precedents, and requires care and learning, so has been rejected by modernists.

holy loft. *Rood loft*, *beam*, or *screen*.

horn. Side of an **altar**.

iconostasis. In Greek and Russian *Orthodox* churches, a screen between the *sanctuary* and the body of the church, with three doorways, often hung with icons, hence its name.

IHS. *See* **Chrismon**.

Incarnation. God becoming Man in the person of Christ, i.e. the investiture or embodiment in flesh. It is represented in art either as the *Annunciation* or the *Nativity*.

incised slab. Slab of stone with a design cut into its surface, often enhanced with black or coloured filling, commonly a funerary monument with representations of effigies, emblems, etc., and with inscriptions. A variation is a more comprehensive series of indents filled with brass or latten sheets cut to fit and themselves incised and inlaid.

INRI. *See* **Chrismon**.

intersticium. Where transepts cross the *nave* of a church, the space between the nave proper and the *chancel*.

iris. Symbol of the Virgin Mary and of Chastity, representing Reconciliation between Man and God.

Irvingite. *See* **Catholic Apostolic Church**.

Italianate. Style of architecture related to the *Rundbogenstil* drawing on Italian precedents, including *Early Christian campanili*.

Jacobean. Architecture and decoration of the period of King James I (*r.* 1603–25).

Jacobethan. Revivalist architecture of the late 19th and early 20th centuries in which *Elizabethan* and *Jacobean* elements were freely mixed.

Jesse. Genealogical tree depicting Christ's ancestry, usually in the form of a tree or vine springing from the recumbent body of Jesse, with figures denoting his descendants standing on the ends of the branches, the Virgin and Child forming the fruit at the top.

Kentish rag. Very hard, compact grey-white limestone used in polygonal rubble rough or close-pitched walling, often in *Gothic Revival* churches in London. Its irregular forms create a network of mortar joints.

Lady chapel. Chapel in a larger church, expressly for veneration of the Virgin Mary, often situated east of the *chancel* or *choir*, but in smaller churches usually to the east of one or other chancel aisle.

Lamb. Symbol of Christ as Sacrifice. If with a flag or banner, it represents the Risen Christ, and is associated with St John the Baptist; if depicted on a hill with four rivulets, it signifies the Church and Gospels.

lancet. Tall, narrow window opening with a pointed arched head, either a single insert in a wall or one of several lights of similar shape in a larger window. *Lancet style* is an archaic term for *First Pointed* (*see* **Gothic**) before the development of *tracery*.

lantern. Upper stage of a church tower, usually octagonal, treated in a very light and graceful way, and pierced with *tracery*.

Last Judgement. *See* **Doom**.

Last Supper. The subject is usually depicted on the *reredos* behind *altars*, either carved, set in mosaics, or painted.

Latin Cross. Cross with three topmost arms of equal length (though sometimes the head is shorter than the arms), and a much longer lower arm, the basic plan-form of Western *cruciform* churches.

lean-to. Structure with a roof pitching away from a taller building or wall against which it is erected, such as an *aisle* of a church, leaving the *clerestorey* rising above.

lectern. **1**. High, sloping reading desk, especially in a church, placed on the *Epistle side*, usually consisting of a column or pedestal carrying a globe on which perches an eagle with outstretched wings (a symbol of St John the Evangelist). **2**. An *ambo*.

ledger. Large flat stone slab used as the top of a structure (e.g. an altar-tomb), or covering a brick-lined grave, sometimes incised or inlaid with brasses.

Lent. Period of 40 weekdays from Ash Wednesday to the eve of Easter, observed as a time of fasting and penitence, in commemoration of Our Lord's fasting in the Wilderness.

lich-gate. *See* **lych-gate**.

lily. The fleur-de-lys, an *attribute* of the Blessed Virgin Mary.

lion. Emblem of St Mark. It is associated with the *Resurrection*.

liturgy. Form of public worship in the Christian Church, conducted in accordance with a prescribed form, especially the service of the Holy *Eucharist*. Thus liturgiology is the study of liturgies.

loft. Elevated *platform*, *staging*, or *gallery*, within a larger room or hall, such as an *excubitorium*, a rood loft, or organ loft in a church.

Lombard style. Style of architecture, essentially an amalgam of *Early Christian* and *Romanesque*, that flourished in Northern Italy in and around Como. It was revived in the 19th century as part of the *Rundbogenstil*.

Low Church. Party of the *Church of England* holding opinions that give a low place to the claims of the episcopate and priesthood; to the inherent *Grace* of the *Sacraments*; and to matters of ecclesiastical organisation. *See* **Evangelical**.

lucarne. Window or gabled aperture on the sloping sides of a *Gothic* spire.

lych-gate. Gateway with a wide-spreading pitched roof sited at the main entrance of a burial ground, a resting place for a coffin while mourners wait for the officiant at a funeral.

Magi. Three Kings or Wise Men: Balthasar (black, with myrrh), Caspar (yellow, with frankincense), and Melchior (white, with gold).

mandala. Also mandorla, mandoral. Almond-shaped figure composed of two vertical arcs each passing through the other's centre, enclosing a panel, called *aureole* or *vesica piscis*, often found on *tympana* of *Gothic* doorways. It frequently contains the figure of Christ in Majesty.

marigold. Mediæval circular window subdivided by radiating bars or *tracery*, sometimes resembling a marigold and sometimes a *rose* (if more complicated in geometry).

martyrium (*pl.* **martyria**). **1**. Building, usually circular or polygonal, built over the tomb of a Christian martyr, so essentially a mausoleum. Hundreds of Christian churches owe their existence to *martyria*. **2**. Place in a church where *relics* are deposited.

Mass. The *Eucharistic* service, especially as doctrinally viewed and administered by the Roman Catholic Church, but also used to describe the liturgy of *Anglo-Catholics*.

Mass-bell. Sanctus-bell, hung in a *sancte-cote*, so called because it was rung during *Mass* so that those outside would be reminded of what was going on inside the church.

Matrimony. One of the seven *Sacraments*, by which two free persons take one another for husband and wife. It reflects the union of Christ with the Church as His mystical being.

mensa. *See* **altar**.

Methodism. Protestant denomination originating in the 18th-century evangelistic movement of Charles and John

Wesley. *See* **Arminianism**; **Wesleyanism**; **Whitefieldian**.

metropolitan. *Bishop* having the oversight of the bishops of a *province*. In the West the term approximates to an *archbishop*, but in the *Orthodox* Churches a metropolitan ranks above an archbishop and below a *patriarch*.

Middle Pointed. *See* **Gothic**; **tracery**.

milleniarism. The doctrine or belief in the Millennium, i.e. a thousand-year period of blessedness before or after Christ's Second Coming.

minister. General designation of a person charged with spiritual functions in the Christian Church. It came into use after the *Reformation*, but today is associated with *Evangelicals*, *Low Churchmen*, or *Nonconformists*, the term priest being used by *Anglo-Catholics*, *High Churchmen*, *Roman Catholics*, and members of the *Orthodox* Churches.

minster. **1**. Abbey or priory church, or, more usually, a large collegiate church, distinguished from a parish church or a cathedral. **2**. A monastery or its church.

misericord. Mercy-seat, subsellium, or small ledge on the underside of hinged mediæval choir-stall seats. When the seats were upright, the misericords gave some surreptitious support to a person standing during long services. It had a carved corbel-like element under the ledge, frequently representing scenes from everyday life, fables, comic episodes, and caricatures.

monstrance. Open or transparent vessel in which the *Host* is exposed or *relics* are displayed. If it displays the *Eucharistic* wafer it is an *ostensory*.

Moresque. Style derived from Islamic architecture of North Africa and the Iberian peninsula.

mortuary chapel. Free-standing building, or one attached to a church, under which is a space used for entombment by one family. Post-Reformation mortuary chapels as extensions to churches replaced pre-Reformation *chantry chapels*.

mosque. Islamic building for communal prayer, usually with at least one minaret, and often domed.

mouchette. 14th-century light (often *ogee* on at least one side) resembling a curving dagger-like form with *foils* at one end in *Second Pointed Curvilinear tracery*. It resembles a tadpole.

mourners. *See* **altar**; **tomb-chest**.

Mozarabic. Style of Spanish Christian architecture incorporating horseshoe arches and other *Moresque* elements, judiciously mixed with *Romanesque* motifs.

multifoil. Arch or arc with several *foils* and *cusps*.

muscular Gothic. Bold, strong, stern, and robust phase of the *Gothic Revival* that drew on *First Pointed* precedents from 13th-century Burgundy. It featured brickwork (often polychrome), massive cylindrical *piers*, and chunky elements.

Nativity. Representation of the newly born Christ and His family.

nave. Central clerestoreyed *aisle* of a *basilican* church, or the main body of the church, aisled or not, between the western wall and the *chancel*. Used by the laity, it was often separated from the *choir* or chancel by a screen, and from the aisles by *nave arcades*.

Neo-Baroque. Revival of Baroque architecture, or of motifs drawn from such architecture.

Neo-Byzantine. Byzantine Revival, a style incorporating certain *Byzantine* features, as in the 19th-century *Rundbogenstil*.

Neo-Classicism. Dominant style in European and American architecture in the late 18th and early 19th centuries, essentially a return to the *Classicism* of antiquity. It embraces the Greek and Egyptian Revivals, and drew on archæological-based measured drawings.

Neo-Norman. *Romanesque* Revival, especially from *c.*1820.

net-tracery. *Second Pointed Curvilinear tracery* forming net-like shapes, so said to be *reticulated*.

niche. Shallow ornamental recess in a wall, *pier*, or buttress, usually to contain a statue or other ornament. *Gothic* niches (called *tabernacles*) have gablets or canopies over them *See* **canopy**.

nimbus. *See* **aureole**.

nine altars. *Nine Choirs of Angels* are held to mediate between God and Man, nine squaring the *Trinity*. This is reflected in the design of certain *retrochoirs*.

nodding ogee. *Ogee canopy-head*, the apex of which projects beyond the springing-line of the canopy: it is an ogee in section as well as elevation.

Nonconformists. *See* **Dissenters**.

Norman. *See* **Romanesque**.

oblate. Person devoted to a monastery or to religious work, especially a member of the Roman Catholic secular *priests* of the Order of St Charles Borromeo (Oblates of St Charles).

ogee. Upright double curve, concave at the top and convex at the bottom (or the other way round). Double ogees appear in canopies, and are characteristic of the *Second Pointed* style, especially in funerary monuments, *niches*, *sedilia*, shrines, and *tracery*. They occur in the *Perpendicular* style as well. *See* **nodding ogee**.

Old English. Architectural style involving the revival of *vernacular* elements from Sussex and the Kent Weald, one of the threads of the 19th-century *Domestic Revival*, *Queen Anne* style, and the *Arts and Crafts Movement*. It was characterised by tile-hung walls, *diaper* patterns on brickwork, leaded windows of the casement type, timber framing of gables and jettied elements, fretted barge boards, rubbed-brick dressings, steep tiled roofs, and tall ornamented chimneys of moulded brick or terracotta. Certain aspects of the style are occasionally found in late Victorian church architecture.

oratorian. Father or priest of an R.C. religious society, especially of the Oratory of St Philip Neri (aka Congregation of the Fathers of the Oratory), recognised by the papacy in 1575.

oratory. **1**. Small chapel for solitary prayer, as in a private house. **2**. With a capital O, a church and buildings of the Congregation of St Philip Neri. *See* **oratorian**.

Order. **1**. *Romanesque* and *Gothic* arched opening (Order arch) consisting of several layers of arches, usually with colonnettes, each arch smaller than the layer in front. **2**. Elements in Classical architecture making up the essential expression of a columnar and trabeated structure (column with [usually] base and capital, and entablature).

Ordination. Conferment of Holy Orders, one of the seven *Sacraments*, by which a person is invested with a ministerial or sacerdotal character by the laying-on of hands or other symbolic action, and thereby admitted to the Ministry of the Christian Church.

orientation. Planning, siting, and arrangement of a building in relation to the points of the compass. Churches in Western Europe were usually orientated with the altars set at the east. Churches sited without regard to this are nevertheless described in terms of liturgical orientation.

Orthodox. Epithet of the Eastern Church, which recognises the leadership of the *Patriarch* of Constantinople, and of the various national Churches of Russia, Serbia, Romania, etc., recognising each other as of the same Communion. It is also called the Greek Church. The Eastern Church separated from the Western by the Schism of 1054, but the fall of Constantinople to the Ottoman Turks in 1453 was probably the defining event in the isolation of the Eastern from the Western Church. Intensely conservative in liturgy and ecclesiastical art, the Orthodox Churches have remained aloof from modernising tendencies in ritual and theology.

ostensory. *See* **monstrance**.

Oxford Movement. Movement concerned with sound doctrinal teaching; the defence of the *Church of England* as a divine institution and not just a department of the State; the importance of the Apostolic Succession; and the maintenance of spiritual discipline. It is generally reckoned to have begun in Oxford with John Keble's sermon on National Apostasy in 1833, triggered by the Church Temporalities (Ireland) Act, but which probably began stirring a few years earlier. It is also called *Tractarian*, after the *Tracts for the Times* issued between 1833 and 1841 in advocacy of *High Church* principles, and prompted the revival of *Catholic* doctrine and ceremonial in the *Anglican Church*.

pace. Dais. A stepped podium or plinth. *See* **gradin**.

papist. **1**. A *Roman Catholic*, Romanist, a member of the Roman Catholic Church. **2**. Advocate of papal supremacy. The term is often used pejoratively, but it also has an historical basis that has no demeaning overtones.

parclose. *Screen* defining a chapel, etc., or between a *chancel* and a *chapel* beside it, in a church.

parish church. Church of the smallest area in a division of a *diocese* under the jurisdiction of a rector or *vicar*.

pastiche. **1**. Composition made up of fragments or elements derived from various sources, e.g. parts of a building copied from earlier buildings, or influenced by them. **2**. Eclectic architecture quoting motifs from various designs, often displaying great originality, wit, and inventiveness. **3**. Term of abuse used by those who denounce as mere copyists those who employ historical references as mnemonics to trigger resonances not perceived as desirable or necessary. Neither **1** nor **2** signifies anything pejorative, save to the ignorant.

patriarch. Official title of the *bishops* of the *sees* of Constantinople, Alexandria, Antioch, and Jerusalem in the *Orthodox* Church, the Patriarch of Constantinople being the head, or Œcumenical Patriarch, of the Church.

patristic. Pertaining to the writings and doctrines of the *Fathers of the Church*.

Pax. Representation of the *Crucifixion*.

pelican. The bird is shown piercing (vulning) her breast with her beak to draw blood to feed her young. The image is symbolic of piety and of Christ's redeeming work, especially as given through the *Eucharist*.

Penance. One of the seven *Sacraments*, aka Reconciliation, a rite in which a person who has sinned, after Confession of sins and an act of interior penance, receives divine forgiveness through *Absolution* conferred through a priest.

Perpendicular. *See* **Gothic**; **tracery**.

pew. Fixed wooden seat with a back and *bench-ends* (the last often elaborately carved with *blind-tracery* and finished with *poppy-head finials*) in use in churches from around the 13th century. Box pews were enclosed with high panelled partitions and a door, and (where they have survived at all) usually date from the late 17th or 18th century.

pier. **1**. Detached mass of construction, generally acting as a support, such as the solid part of a wall between windows, or a massive element from which arches spring. **2**. Support, such as a pier in a repetitive mediæval *nave arcade* varying from sturdy, oversized *Romanesque* examples to the lighter, taller, more slender, multi-moulded *Perpendicular* types. *Piers* are generally more massive than columns. *See* **wall-pier**.

piscina (*pl.* **piscinæ**). Stone basin connected with a drainage channel for carrying away the water used in rinsing the vessels employed at *Mass* and washing the hands of the *priest*. It was usually set in a *niche* in the south wall of the *chancel* in a church to be near the *altar*, and was often given decorative treatment. Sometimes it was incorporated with the *sedilia* in a *prismatory*. Piscinæ are also found in chapels and in aisle walls where aisles were subdivided before the *Reformation*.

pix, pyx. Box, casket, shrine, or tabernacle to hold the consecrated bread in a church.

plate-tracery. *See* **tracery**.

pointed. A pointed arch may be formed by a radius equal to the width of the opening, struck from both sides of the springing-line, or by striking the radius from any point on a line projected through the springing-lines, in which case the arch can be sharply pointed. With a capital 'P', *Pointed* refers to the *Gothic* style. *See* **Gothic**; **tracery**.

polychromy. Enrichment of exteriors and interiors of buildings by means of the application of several colours. *Structural polychromy* is achieved by using differently coloured materials (e.g. bricks, stones, tiles, etc.) in the construction, rather than by applying colour using paints.

popery. **1**. Hostile term for the doctrines, practices, and ceremonial associated with the Roman Catholic Church, and especially with the Pope as its head. **2**. Anything savouring of adherence to the Roman Catholic religion.

powdered. Wall, ceiling, etc., embellished with repetitive patterns of crossed flowers, stars, etc., usually stencilled on a painted coloured background. It is found in many fine *polychrome* interiors of the *Gothic Revival*.

predella. **1**. Platform or step on which an altar stands, synonymous with *gradine*. **2**. *Gradino*, or front of a step at the top and back of an altar, supporting the *altar-piece*. It may have panels depicting events in the lives of saints, and be associated with a *triptych* or *reredos*.

presbyter. In episcopal Churches, a *priest* ranking below a *bishop* and above a *deacon*.

Presbyterianism. System of government in a *Protestant* Church in which each congregation is governed by its session, consisting of the minister and other elders, but each session is subordinate to the *presbytery*, each presbytery to the *synod*, and (in most Presbyterian Churches) the synods to the General Assembly of the Church.

presbytery. **1**. Part of a church (presbyterium) in which the *high altar* stands, at the east of the *choir*. It is used exclusively by those who minister in services and at the altar. **2**. A Church Court consisting of the minister and one elder from each church within a certain district, in the *Presbyterian* system. **3**. Priest's or minister's house.

priest. Clergyman in the second of Holy Orders, above a *deacon* and below a *bishop*, with the authority to administer the *Sacraments* and pronounce *Absolution*. In the *Anglican Church* the term would not be applied to a *minister* of *Low Church* or *Evangelical* views.

priest's door. Entrance to the *chancel* of a church, usually on the south side.

primate. *Archbishop* holding first place among all the *bishops* of a *province*. In the *Church of England*, the archbishops of York and Canterbury are both primates, but Canterbury is the Primate of All England.

prismatory. *Sedilia* in a chancel, sometimes including the *piscina*.

procession path. **1**. Line of paving for the marshalling of those participating in processions associated with church services. **2**. *Ambulatory*.

Protestant. Originally one of those who protested, i.e. made a declaration of dissent from the decision of the Diet of Speier (1529) which re-affirmed the Edict of the Diet of Worms against the *Reformation*, it is a general designation of an adherent to the reformed doctrines or Churches that repudiated papal authority: a member of a Christian Church outside the *Roman Catholic* Communion in the West. *See* **Augsburg Confession**; **Diet**.

province. District within the jurisdiction of an *archbishop* or *metropolitan*, e.g. Canterbury and York.

pulpit. Partially enclosed elevated desk of masonry or wood in a church (usually on the north-east side of the *nave*) for a preacher. Often decorated, it may have a canopy (*tester*) over it, functioning partly as a sound-reflector. The *Anglican* three-decker pulpit contains at the bottom level a clerk's stall, a reading desk above, and at the top a pulpit proper, designed as a whole.

pulpitum. Stone *screen* set between the *nave* and the *choir*, acting as the back of the *choir stalls*, over which is a *gallery*, *rood*, or organ.

Purbeck marble. Dark grey or grey-greenish hard limestone, called a marble, originating in the Isle of Purbeck, Dorset. Capable of taking a spectacular polish, it was used by English mediæval architects for *colonnettes*, *shafts*, monuments, *effigies*, and tombs because of its attractive properties: the dark shiny shafts set against lighter limestone contribute to the richness of *First Pointed* interiors. In the *Victorian* period, coloured marbles and granites were used to create similar effects on *piers*, etc.

Puritan. English Protestant who regarded the *Reformation* of the Church under Queen Elizabeth I as incomplete, and called for its further 'purification' from what was considered unscriptural and corrupt forms and ceremonial retained from before the Reformation. The term was later applied to those who separated from the *Established Church* on points of ritual, doctrine, or polity, holding these to be at variance with a 'pure' reading of the New Testament.

Puseyite. Name given by opponents to the theological and ecclesiastical principles and doctrine of Dr E.B. Pusey, and those with whom he was associated in the *Oxford Movement* for the revival of *Catholic* doctrine and observance in the *Church of England*, more formally (and courteously) called *Tractarian*.

pyx. *See* **pix**.

Quaker. Member of the Society of Friends, founded (1648–50) by George Fox. Quakerism is distinguished by peaceful principles, plainness of dress, unassuming manners, and gatherings of extreme simplicity in which egalitarianism prevails.

quarrel, quarry. **1**. Lozenge- or square-shaped light in *Gothic tracery*. **2**. Similarly shaped piece of glass held in the cames of leaded lights. **3**. Any floor tile, lozenge-shaped or square.

quatrefoil. *See* **foil**.

Queen Anne. The Queen Anne style or Revival evolved from the 1860s, and had only tenuous connections with the style of architecture of the reign of Queen Anne. It was an eclectic melange that included tall, small-paned sash windows, rubbed-brick arches and dressings over and around openings, terracotta embellishments, *vernacular* features such as tile-hanging, open-bed and broken pediments, steeply pitched roofs (often rising from eaves-cornices), massive chimneys, shaped and Dutch gables, and white-painted balustrades, balconies, and bay windows. Although mostly found in domestic work, the style occasionally surfaced in some ecclesiastical architecture.

radiating chapels. *See* **chevet**.

rag. *See* **Kentish rag**.

Rageur. 19th-century style of French architecture in which motifs are over-stated, over-emphatic, and outlandishly proportioned. It had parallels in a few *muscular Gothic* examples in England. *Raguer* is the French for to chafe or to irritate, so is applied to a phase of the mid-19th-century *Gothic Revival* in France characterised by perversity, discordant originality, and aggressiveness, not unlike aspects of English and American *Rogue Gothic*. *See also* **Go**.

Real Presence. Actual presence of Christ's Body and Blood in the *Sacrament* of the *Eucharist*. In the *Roman Catholic* and *Lutheran* Churches it implies the presence by means of *Transubstantiation* or *Consubstantiation* of the actual Body and Blood. A more *Protestant* view would be that the Body and Blood are present only in a 'heavenly and spiritual manner', or that the Eucharistic Elements are 'only' *allegories*. *See* **allegory**, **symbol**.

Rectilinear style. *See* **Gothic**.

recusant. One who refused to attend services of the *Established Anglican Church* or conform (*see* **Conformity**) to its beliefs and practices. The term became synonymous with *Roman Catholics* even though it could theoretically be applied to *Dissenters*.

Reformation. The 16th-century religious movement that led to the establishment of various *Reformed* and *Protestant* Churches of Central and North-western Europe which broke with the Roman Catholic Church.

relic. Some object, such as a bone fragment, skull, or part of the body or clothing, or any article, remaining as a memorial of a *saint*, martyr, etc., carefully preserved and venerated.

reliquary. Container holding *relics*.

reredos. Ornamental facing or *screen* behind an *altar* in a church, free-standing or forming part of the *retable*. It is often enriched with statues in *niches*, pinnacles, etc., but could take the form of a *triptych*. In larger churches the *reredos* separates the *choir* from the *retrochoir* and other parts to the liturgical east.

Reservation of the Sacrament. Practice of reserving part of the *Eucharistic* Elements for the Communion of the sick. The presence of such Elements is usually signified by a *sanctuary lamp*.

Resurrection. **1**. The Rising of Christ after His Death and Burial. **2**. Commemoration of this event at Easter. *See* **Easter sepulchre**.

retable. **1**. *Screen* to the rear of an *altar*, rising up behind it. Often richly decorated, and including the *reredos*. **2**. Shelf or setting for ornamental panels or pictures behind an altar. **3**. Frame around the paintings or decorative panels of a reredos.

reticulated. **1**. Arranged to resemble a net, with the repetition of the same figure all over the surface or plane, e.g. in a *screen* or lattice, or in a wall made of ragstone. **2**. With a capital R (*Reticulated*), the term refers to a type of *Curvilinear Gothic tracery* consisting of a net-like mesh of interweaving *ogees*. *See* **Gothic**; **tracery**.

retrochoir. Portion of a large church behind the *retable* or *reredos* of the *high altar*, essentially the volume bounded by the *sanctuary* and the *chapels* to the east. In apsidal arrangements the retrochoir would include parts of the north and south chancel aisles as well as the area to the east and the *radiating chapels*.

riddel. In a church, the curtains suspended around an *altar*, sometimes from rods fixed into the wall behind, but more often from some means of hanging that spans between riddel posts: there were normally four of the last, polygonal on plan, coloured and gilded, and crowned by angels, often supporting candelabra. Arrangements of riddels behind and around altars seem to have been not uncommon in England and Flanders towards the end of the Middle Ages, and were revived during the late flowering of the *Gothic Revival*, especially by Ninian Comper and Temple Moore, and popularised by Percy Dearmer. *See* **English altar**.

Ritualism. The study, practice, or system of ritual observances and ceremonial revived in the *Anglican Church*. It had a profound effect on the planning and detail of many Victorian Anglican churches, and was essentially connected with those later identified with Anglo-Catholicism who began the enrichment of the Church of England's liturgy. Early Tractarians, however, had little or no interest in so-called 'advanced' ritual, and in the case of Pusey felt that, whatever its benefits, it was also causing unnecessary conflict with Church authorities.

Rogue. *Gothic Revival* architecture unmarked by scholarship, serenity, or tact. It was characterised by repetitive notchings and chamferings of woodwork and *arcades*, frantic roof structures, saw-toothed arrises, scissor-shaped trusses, and harsh, barbaric, *polychrome* decorations (much of them structural). Debauched 'acrobatic Gothic' and elephantine compositions earned opprobrium from *Ecclesiologists*. *Rogue Goths* tended to be in the *Evangelical* camp. *See* **Go** and **Rageur**.

Roman Catholic. Adherent of the Roman Catholic Church recognising the spiritual supremacy of the Pope and accepting the doctrines and teachings of that Church.

Romanesque. Dominant architectural style in Romanised Western Europe, from the mid-11th to the end of the 12th century, having certain characteristics similar to those in *Early Christian*, late *Roman*, and *Byzantine* work, notably semicircular-headed arches set in massive walls, and *basilican* form for churches. The style enjoyed a 19th-century revival connected with a general trend towards *Historicism*, and it was merged with Early Christian and Byzantine elements in the *Rundbogenstil*.

rood. **1**. Cross. **2**. Large *Crucifixion* set above the entrance to the *chancel* of a church, sometimes suspended, sometimes supported on a rood beam spanning from wall to wall, and sometimes rising from a rood loft over a rood screen. The Crucifixion group often includes the figures of the Blessed Virgin Mary and St John on either side of the Cross. A rood altar is one under a rood, or an altar physically attached to a rood screen, facing the nave.

rose. Type of *Gothic* window, circular, subdivided by complex *tracery* radiating from the centre to form a stylised floral design of great beauty. It should be distinguished from a *Catherine-wheel*, *marigold*, or *wheel window*.

rubric. Direction for the conduct of Divine Service in liturgical books, properly printed in red to distinguish it from the text proper.

Rundbogenstil. German for 'round-arched style', meaning an eclectic mix of *Byzantine*, *Early Christian*, Italian *Romanesque*, and Florentine Renaissance elements. It found favour in England under the ægis of Prince Albert and his artistic adviser, Ludwig Grüner.

Sabbatarianism. *Protestant* principle of prohibiting any recreation on Sundays, and attempts to apply the Fourth Commandment relating to the keeping of the Jewish Sabbath to the Christian Sunday.

Sacrament. Religious rite regarded as a channel to and from God, or as an efficacious sign of Grace. The *Roman Catholic* and *Orthodox* Churches (and some *Anglicans*) recognise seven Sacraments: *Baptism*, *Confirmation*, the *Lord's* (or *Last*) *Supper* (*Eucharist*), *Penance* (or *Reconciliation*), *Extreme Unction* (or *Anointing of the Sick*), *Matrimony*, and *Ordination* (to ordain to the Ministry). Among *Protestants* the two signs ordained by Christ (Baptism and the Lord's Supper) are recognised.

sacrarium. **1**. Part of a *chancel* or *choir* in the vicinity of the *high altar*, usually defined by altar rails (i.e. the *sanctuary*). **2**. A shrine. **3**. *Piscina*. **4**. *Sacristy*.

sacristry, sacristy. Church *vestry* near the *chancel* in which ecclesiastical garments, utensils used in services, etc., are stored.

saint. Person recognised by the Church as having, by his or her exceptional holiness of life, attained an exalted station in Heaven, and therefore entitled to veneration. A Saint's Day is the date identified with a particular saint, called a Feast: e.g. 17 March for St Patrick, and 23 April for St George.

sancte-bell. *See* **bell-cote**.

sanctuary. **1**. *Sacrarium*. **2**. *Chancel* or *presbytery*.

sanctuary lamp. Lamp (usually with coloured glass) suspended in a chapel near an altar, indicating that the consecrated *Host* or Element (Reserved Sacrament) is present.

Sarum Use *or* **Rite**. Order of Divine Service in general parish use in England from the 11th century until the *Reformation*, named after the Diocese of Salisbury. Aka Sarum Office or Rubric.

scissor-truss. Truss with braces crossing and fixed to each other, thus tying pairs of principal rafters together.

screen. Partition of metal, timber, or stone, not part of the main structure of a church, separating the *choir* from the *nave* (also called variously *chancel*, *choir*, rood screen, or *pulpitum*), *choir* from *chancel* or *choir aisle* (called *parclose* screen), or defining a *chantry* or *mortuary chapel*, etc.

Second Pointed. *See* **Gothic**.

sedile (*pl.* **sedilia**). Seat. The plural term describes the series of stone seats (usually three) set in the south wall of *chancels*, often crowned with elaborate *canopies*, used by officiating clergy. *Sedilia*, collectively known as the *prismatory*, may include the *piscina* within its series of arched niches.

see. **1**. Seat or a dais. **2**. *Diocese* or territory under the jurisdiction of a *bishop*. The See of Canterbury covers a great part of Kent with a small portion of Sussex. However, the Archbishop of Canterbury is Primate of England, and the Ecclesiastical Province of Canterbury covers England south of Cheshire and Yorkshire, with the other, northern province that of York. So there are two Anglican archbishops in England. **3**. *Cathedra*.

Separatist. Advocate of ecclesiastical separation; a *Dissenter*; a *Nonconformist*; a designation of Protestant Dissenters in general, so a member of any of the sects separated from the *Church of England*. In the 17th century the label was given to Independents who rejected all ecclesiastical authority outside the individial congregation.

seven lamps. Lamps suspended in front of an *altar*, signifying the *Sacraments*.

shaft. **1**. Body, fust, or trunk of a *colonnette* or column extending from the top of the base to the bottom of the capital. **2**. Slim, cylindrical, tall element (one of several around a *Gothic pier* and tied to it by shaft rings or bands of a shaft), often made of *Purbeck marble* or some other material (such as granite) capable of taking a high polish to contrast with the lighter stone of the pier proper. **3**. *Colonnette* set at an angle of a building, e.g. a junction of a jamb with a wall, or one of a pair framing a reveal.

side. *See* **altar**.

side chapel. Chapel to the side of an *aisle* or *choir* in a church.

Sondergotik. German late *Gothic* from *c.*1380, characterised by *hall churches* of immense height, complicated vaults, and highly complex *tracery*.

south door. **1**. *Priest's door*. **2**. Door on the south side of the nave, often associated with a porch.

Speier. *See* **Diet.**

spire-light. Gabled *lucarne*, or opening, set on the acutely sloping sides of a spire.

squint. *See* **hagioscope**.

stage. Storey of a tower, usually defined in some way, by means of buttresses, stringcourses, etc.

stall. Fixed seat, often hinged with *misericords* on the undersides, in a *chancel* or *choir*, one of a number, generally elevated, enclosed at the back and sides, arranged in rows on the north and south sides, and, in grander churches, surmounted by high *canopies* of *tabernacle-work*. In major churches the choir stalls returned at the west, parallel to the *choir screen* or *pulpitum*.

Stations of the Cross. Series of pictures or sculptures (usually 14 in number) representing successive incidents of the Passion (i.e. the narrative of the sufferings of Christ from His Judgement to the Cross and Entombment), placed in churches (or sometimes in the open).

steeple. A church tower and spire together.
stoup. Fixed basin for Holy Water in a niche, corbelled out from a pier or wall, or free-standing on a pedestal, near the entrance to a church.
structural polychromy. *See* **polychromy**.
sun. Representations of the sun are found on the heraldic right of Christ's head, with the moon on the heraldic left, in depictions of the Crucifixion: they suggest Good and Day, Evil and Night.
super-altar. **1**. Shelf above an *altar*, or to the east of it, on which are placed objects not allowed on the altar itself. **2**. Consecrated altar stone, slab, or *mensa*.
symbol. **1**. Authoritative statement of the belief of the Christian Church; a confession of faith or a creed. **2**. Representation of something sacred, such as either of the Elements of the *Eucharist*. **3**. A representation of something that it is. *See* **allegory**.
synagogue. Building for Jewish religious observances and instruction. 19th-century synagogues tended to favour a round-arched *Byzantine Romanesque* style, sometimes with *Moresque* seasoning.
tabernacle. **1**. Cupboard with doors to contain the consecrated *Host* on an *altar*. **2**. *Pix*. **3**. Canopied *niche* containing an image. **4**. Shrine or canopied tomb. **5**. *Baldacchino*, *ciborium*, or any free-standing canopy. **6**. Place of worship distinguished from a church, e.g. a meeting house for *Nonconformist Protestants*.
tabernacle-work. **1**. Ornate *Gothic* canopy over a funerary monument. *See* **canopy**. **2**. Openwork canopy over *niches*, *sedilia*, *shrines*, *choir stalls*, or a *cathedra*.
tester. Canopy (aka *abat-voix*) over a *pulpit* or tomb.
Third Pointed. *See* **Gothic**; **tracery**.
Thirty-Nine Articles. Revised 39 Articles of Religion (1576): these are historically defining statements of Doctrines and Practices of the *Church of England*, and form part of the Anglican *Book of Common Prayer*.
tithe. A tenth part of annual produce or earnings, formerly taken as a tax for the support of the Church and clergy.
tomb canopy. Canopy, often forming a grandly decorative ensemble, over an altar tomb or *tomb-chest*, as though protecting the effigies below. *See* **canopy**.
tomb-chest. Rectangular stone funerary monument above a tomb, often with effigies on top or suggested by figures incised on the top slab or cut into inserts of metal ('brasses'). The sides were often enriched with *quatrefoils*, etc., or with *niches* containing *weepers* (upright or kneeling figures).
Tory. Nickname given in 1679–85 by Whig Exclusioners to those who opposed the exclusion of James, Duke of York, from the Succession. On the accession of King George III (1760) the Tories abandoned the lost cause of the Stuarts, and from then on strenuously upheld the Establishment in Church and State, opposing concessions in the direction of greater religious liberty, and remaining antagonistic to measures intended to widen the basis of parliamentary representation or to impair the privileges of the Church as by Law Established. Tories, at least until the so-called 'Reform Bill' of 1832, were essentially Anglican landowners and Constitutional Loyalists, aware of *noblesse oblige*, and loth to countenance tinkering with the system that had prevailed since the time of William and Mary II (1689–94).
town canopy. *See* **canopy**
tracery. Arrangement by which panels, *screens*, vaults, or windows are divided into parts or lights of different shapes and sizes by means of moulded stone bars or ribs. Early *Gothic* windows with more than one light did not have bars, but had the flat stone spandrel above the main lights (usually two) pierced with a *quatrefoil*, roundel, or other figure: this type of tracery is the *First Pointed plate* variety, consisting of a thin flat panel of ashlar pierced, like simple fretwork, with lights. Starting with early 13th-century French examples, the flat plate was abandoned, the large lights were divided by moulded mullions, the section of which continued at the heads of the window openings to describe circular and other lights, leaving the spandrels open and divided into small lights of various shapes and sizes: this type of subdivision is termed bar-tracery, and it was one of the most important elements of *Gothic* architecture, with definite stylistic connotations. Simple bar-tracery formed patterns of *Middle Pointed Geometrical* tracery, which consisted of circles and foiled circles, with roughly triangular lights between the major elements. Mullions in Geometrical tracery usually had capitals from which the curved bars sprang. After late 13th-century Geometrical tracery came Intersecting tracery in which each mullion of the window branched (without capitals) into curved bars: as the window proper had a head formed of two equal curves, the forms of the Intersecting tracery were also equal. The mullions therefore continued in curved Y-shaped branches to meet the window opening, thus forming a series of lozenge-shaped lights at the top. Intersecting tracery had bars and the main window opening all described from the

same centres, but with different radii, so that such windows were subdivided into two or (usually) more main lights, each forming a pointed, lancet-shaped arch. Intersecting tracery occurred around 1300. *Curvilinear*, Flowing, or Undulating tracery of *Second Pointed* work dominated the 14th century, when *ogees* were applied to the basic arrangement of Intersecting tracery, thus creating a net-like construction of bars at the tops of windows: this type of tracery is called *Reticulated*, because it looks like a net, and was commonly found in work of the first half of the 14th century. Curvilinear or Flowing tracery then developed further and more freely, using the *ogee* curves to create *daggers*, *fish bladders*, or flame-shaped lights called *mouchettes*: such designs evolved further throughout the 15th century in Europe, and became known as *Flamboyant* because of the flame-like forms enclosed by the tracery bars. From the late 14th century, England began to develop *Perpendicular* or *Third Pointed* tracery, in which the main mullions (often joined by transoms) ran straight up to the underside of the main window arch head, with some mullions branching to form subsidiary arches: this system created panel-like lights, and so the style became known as *Rectilinear* or panel-tracery. Later still, from the end of the 14th century, but mostly 15th- and early 16th-century work, the window heads became much flatter four-centred arches, divided into panels, with crenellated transoms, and the windows filled the whole wall between buttresses. *See* **Gothic**.

Tractarianism. Tenets or principles of the *High Church Anglican* Tractarians, who maintained the doctrines and practices set forth in the *Tracts for the Times* (1833–41), a series of pamphlets on theological and ecclesiastical topics published in Oxford. Tractarianism aimed to arrest the advance of liberalism in religious thought, to oppose State interference in matters relating to Christian theology and Church order (as in Keble's Assize Sermon, protesting at the State's suppression of ten Irish bishoprics and two archdioceses), and to re-assert what its adherents held to be true Anglican Church principles. Tractarianism is intimately linked with the *Oxford Movement*, the adherents of which are called Tractarians, *Puseyites*, or even crypto-papists.

transept. Any large division of a building lying across its main axis at 90°. In a *cruciform* church the transept is often of the same section as the nave, and may have aisles: eastern transept aisles were usually subdivided into chapels. The position where the transepts branched on either side of the *crossing* was often marked by a crossing tower, a *flèche*, or a *lantern*.

transition. Denotes the merging of one style with another, especially the 12th-century transition from *Romanesque* to *Gothic*, but is sometimes applied to other styles.

Transubstantiation. Conversion, in the *Eucharist*, of the whole substance of the bread into the Body and wine into Blood of Christ, only the appearances (and other 'accidents') of bread and wine remaining. It is a doctrine of the Roman Catholic Church, as opposed to *Consubstantiation*, in which the bread and wine are held to co-exist with the Body and Blood.

Tree of Life. *See* **Jesse**.

trefoil. *See* **foil**.

tribune. **1**. Apsidal part of a *basilica*. **2**. Eastern part of a church, especially if apsidal. **3**. *Pulpitum* or *ambo*, and therefore, by extension, a *pulpit*. **4**. Gallery in a church, usually for seating, supported on columns. **5**. Raised platform or seat in a basilican church.

Tridentine. The adjective from the Œcumenical Council of the Roman Catholic Church held at Trent in the Tirol (1545–63). That Council (*Concilium Tridentinum*) defined differences between the *Roman Catholic* and *Protestant Churches*, established certain forms of worship (especially that of the *Mass*), and reconfirmed attitudes towards iconoclasm and the legitimacy of images in churches for the purpose of reinforcing faith, among other matters. It also reinforced discipline and the authority of the papacy. It follows, therefore, that the Church *in* England before the *Reformation* was pre-Tridentine, and that forms of worship and traditions differed greatly from post-Tridentine practices (which appeared very foreign to Englishmen no matter what their religious persuasion might be).

triforium. In larger *Romanesque* and *Gothic* churches, an arcaded wall passage facing on to the *nave*, above the *aisle* and *nave arcade*. Its own arcade forms an important part of the elevation of a nave interior above the nave arcade and below the *clerestorey*.

Trinitarianism. The doctrine of Trinitarians, i.e. those who accept the Father, Son, and Holy Spirit as Three in One. Trinitarian belief is in God who exists in three Persons and one Substance, i.e. the **Trinity**. *See* **Unitarianism**.

Trinity. *See* **Trinitarianism**; **Unitarianism**.

triptych. Pictures or carvings in three compartments side by side, the lateral ones usually subordinate (though connected in subject matter) and hinged to enable them to be folded over the central compartment. A triptych was often a late mediæval altarpiece, called in German a *Flügelaltar*. When closed, the part visible (i.e. the backs of the folding leaves) often displayed grisaille paintings.

trumeau. Stone mullion, *pier*, or *shaft* supporting the *tympanum* of a wide *Gothic* doorway.

Tudor. English architecture during the Tudor monarchy of Henry VII and VIII (1485–1547), primarily associated with late *Perpendicular Gothic*, very flat four-centred or Tudor arches, domestic architecture of brick with *diaper* patterns, elaborate chimneys of carved and moulded brick, and square-headed mullioned windows with hood-moulds and label-stops.

Tudor arch. Pseudo-four-centred late *Perpendicular* arch, with shanks starting as quarter-circles (with centres on the springing-lines) continuing as straight lines to the apex. It is very depressed, and often expressed as a single carved lintel.

Tudor Revival. 19th-century revival of *Tudor* architecture.

tympanum (*pl.* **tympana**). Area above a lintel over an opening contained by the arch set above it, or over two openings carried on a *trumeau* in a *Gothic* doorway.

undercroft. *Crypt* or vaulted space under a church or other building, wholly or partly underground.

Ultramontanism. An Ultramontane (literally 'beyond the mountain') was a representative of the Roman Catholic Church north of the Alps as opposed to an ecclesiastic in Italy. Ultramontanism, therefore, was the principle and practice of the Ultramontane party in the Church advocating absolute papal supremacy outside Italy.

Unitarianism. Belief in or affirmation of the unity of God. Unitarians (a *Protestant* sect) rejected the doctrine of *Trinitarianism*.

Venetian Gothic. Prompted by Street's *Brick and Marble in the Middle Ages* (1855, 1874), and Ruskin's *Stones of Venice* (1851–3), it featured *polychrome* brick and masonry, elaborately patterned arcades, and other elements taken from Italian Gothic. It was particularly associated with *structural polychromy*.

vernacular architecture. Unpretentious, simple, indigenous, traditional structures made of local materials and following well-tried forms and types, e.g. country cottages, farm buildings, etc. It provided precedents for the *Old English Domestic Revival*.

vesica piscis. 1. Light in *Second Pointed Curvilinear* or *Flowing tracery* resembling a tadpole or air-bladder of a fish. 2. Almond, *aureole*, glory, or *mandala* of the upright almond-shaped variety. *See* **Chrismon**.

vestry. 1. Room adjoining the *chancel* in a church where vestments are stored and the clergy are vested. 2. *Sacristy* where sacred vessels, books, and vestments are stored, and meetings can be held.

vicar. 1. Earthly representative of Christ, so the Pope or the Patriarch of Jerusalem. 2. Incumbent of a parish of which tithes were impropriated or appropriated, in contrast to a rector. A vicarage is the benefice or living, house or residence, or the position, office, or duties, of a vicar.

votive. Dedicated, consecrated, offered, erected, etc., in consequence of, or in fulfilment of, a vow, e.g. a church, altar, or statue.

wall-pier. Internal buttress (*Wandpfeiler*), one of several subdividing an aisle into *side chapels* or pierced to form *passage aisles*.

weeper. *See* **altar**; **tomb-chest**.

Wesleyanism. System of *Arminian* theology, the kernel of *Methodism*. *See* **Arminianism**; **Whitefieldian**.

wheel window. 1. Circular window with spoke-like *colonnettes* or bars radiating from the centre. *See* **Catherine-wheel**; **marigold**; **rose**. 2. Circular part of an early *Middle-Pointed Geometrical* window with bar-tracery.

Whig. 1. Adherent of the *Presbyterian* cause in 17th-century Scotland. 2. Extreme anti-Royalist Nonconformist. 3. Exclusioner opposed to the succession of James, Duke of York, as King James II and VII, on the ground of his being a Roman Catholic. 4. From 1689 an adherent of one of the two main political parties in England, and, eventually, in Great Britain. From around 1840 the term was superseded by Liberal.

Whitefieldian, Whitfieldian. A follower of George Whitefield, whose Calvinistic views led to a division between *Methodists*.

Worms. *See* **Diet**.

Select Bibliography

Books are sepulchres of thought;
The dead laurels of the dead
Rustle for a moment only,
Like the withered leaves in lonely
Churchyards at some passing tread.

Henry Wadsworth Longfellow (1807–82):
'The Wind over the Chimney', Stanza 8: from Flower-de-Luce
in *The Poetical Works* (London: Henry Frowde 1893), 535.

Aldrich, Megan, and Buchanan, Alexandrina (eds) (2019) *Studies in Victorian Architecture and Design* vii: *Thomas Rickman and the Victorians* (London: Victorian Society).

Allibone, Jill (1991) *The Wall Paintings at Garton-on-the-Wolds* (London: Pevsner Memorial Trust).

Atterbury, Paul (ed.) (1995) *A. W.N. Pugin: Master of the Gothic Revival* (New Haven and London: Yale University Press).

Atterbury, Paul, and Wainwright, Clive (eds) (1994) *Pugin: A Gothic Passion* (New Haven and London: Yale University Press).

Baldeschi, Giuseppe (1853) *Ceremonial According to the Roman Rite*, John Duncan Hilarius Dale (tr.) (London: Charles Dolman).

Barnwell, P.S., Tyack, Geoffrey, and Whyte, William (2014) *George Gilbert Scott, 1811–1878: An Architect and His Influence* (Donington: Shaun Tyas).

Beresford Hope, Alexander James (1861) *The English Cathedral of the Nineteenth Century* (London: John Murray).

Bishop, Rev. H.H. (1886) *Architecture in Relation to Our Parish Churches* (London: Society for Promoting Christian Knowledge).

Bloxam, John Rouse (ed.) (1842) *The Book of Fragments* (Oxford: printed by W. Baxter).

Bloxam, Matthew Holbeche (1882) *The Principles of Gothic Ecclesiastical Architecture ... etc.* (London: George Bell & Sons).

Brandwood, Geoff (2012) *The Architecture of Sharpe, Paley and Austin* (Swindon: English Heritage).

Brandwood, Geoff (2019) *The Architecture of Temple Moore* (Donington: Shaun Tyas).

Brandwood, Geoff (ed.) (2010) *Ecclesiology Today* **xlii** (June) published as *Seven Church Architects 1830–1930* (London: Ecclesiological Society).

Britton, John (1835) *Chronological History and Graphic Illustrations of Christian Architecture in England* (London: M.A. Nattali).

Brooks, Chris (1999) *The Gothic Revival* (London: Phaidon).

Brooks, Chris, and Saint, Andrew (eds) (1995) *The Victorian Church* (Manchester: Manchester University Press).

Brown, Stewart Jay, *et al* (eds) (2017) *The Oxford Handbook of the Oxford Movement* (Oxford: Oxford University Press).

Brownlee, David B. (1985) 'The First High Victorians: British Architectural Theory in the 1840s', *Architectura* **xv**, 33–46.

Cambridge Camden Society (*later* The Ecclesiological Society) (1842–68) *The Ecclesiologist.*

Chadwick, Owen (1987a) *Victorian Church: 1829–59* (London: SCM Press).
Chadwick, Owen (1987b) *Victorian Church: 1860–1901* (London: SCM Press).
Church, Richard William (1891) *The Oxford Movement: Twelve Years, 1833–1845* (London: Macmillan).
Clark, Kenneth Mackenzie (1962) *The Gothic Revival* (London: John Murray).
Clarke, Basil Fulford Lowther (1966) *Parish Churches of London* (London: Batsford).
Clarke, Basil Fulford Lowther (1969) *Church Builders of the Nineteenth Century* (Newton Abbot: David & Charles).
Close, Francis (1844) *The Restoration of Churches is the Restoration of Popery* (London: Hatchard).
Cobbett, William (1998) *Collected Social and Political Writings*, Noel Thompson and David Eastwood (eds) (London: Pickering & Chatto).
Cole, David (1980) *The Work of Sir George Gilbert Scott* (London: Architectural Press).
Colvin, Howard (2008) *A Biographical Dictionary of British Architects 1600–1840* (New Haven and London: Yale University Press for The Paul Mellon Centre for Studies in British Art).
Comper, J. Ninian (1950) *Of the Christian Altar and the Buildings which Contain it* (London: Society for Promoting Christian Knowledge).
Crook, J. Mordaunt (1981) *William Burges and the High Victorian Dream* (London: John Murray).
Crook, J. Mordaunt (1987) *The Dilemma of Style: Architectural Ideas from the Picturesque to the Post-Modern* (London: John Murray).
Crook, J. Mordaunt (1995) *John Carter and the Mind of the Gothic Revival* (London: Society of Antiquaries of London).
Cubitt, James (1870) *Church Design for Congregations* (London: Smith, Elder, & Co.).
Curl, James Stevens (1990) 'All Saints', Margaret Street' in the *Masters of Building* series, *The Architects' Journal* **cxci**/25 (20 June), 36–55.
Curl, James Stevens (2007) *Victorian Architecture: Diversity and Invention* (Reading: Spire).
Curl, James Stevens (2012) 'Henry Roberts (1803–76)' and 'Acrobatic Gothic. Freely Treated' in Webster, Christopher (ed.) *The Practice of Architecture: Eight Architects, 1830–1930* (Reading: Spire), 15–47 and 106–41.
Curl, James Stevens, and Wilson, Susan (2015, 2016) *Oxford Dictionary of Architecture* (Oxford: Oxford University Press).
Darby, Michael (1983) *John Pollard Seddon* (London: Victoria & Albert Museum).
Dearmer, Percy (1911) *The Chancel and the Altar* (London: Mowbray).
Dearmer, Percy (1931) *The Parson's Handbook* (London and New York: H. Milford).
Denison, George Anthony (1853–4) *The Real Presence* (London: Joseph Masters).
Derrick, Andrew (2020) 'Gallicans versus Romans: Squaring Medievalism with Trent' in Kirby, Mark (ed.) *Chancel Screens since the Reformation* (London: Ecclesiological Society), 149–64.
Dixon, Roger, and Muthesius, Stefan (1985) *Victorian Architecture* (London: Thames & Hudson).
Drummond, Andrew Landale (1934) *The Church Architecture of Protestantism* (Edinburgh: T. & T. Clark).
Duffy, Eamon (1992) *The Stripping of the Altars. Traditional Religion in England* c.*1400*–c.*1580* (New Haven and London: Yale University Press).
Dugdale, William, and Dodsworth, Roger (1655–73) *Monasticon Anglicanum* (London: Thomas Newcomb). *See also* the continuation (1771–3) *The History of the Ancient Abbeys, Monasteries, Hospitals, Cathedrals, and Collegiate Churches* (London: John Stevens).
Eastlake, Charles Locke (1970) *A History of the Gothic Revival* with an introduction by J. Mordaunt Crook (Leicester: Leicester University Press).
Elliott, John Patrick, and Pritchard, John (eds) (1998) *George Edmund Street: A Victorian Architect in Berkshire* (Reading: University of Reading).
Elliott, John Patrick, and Pritchard, John (2002) *Henry Woodyer, Gentleman Architect* (Reading: University of Reading).
Emmett, John Thomas (1891) *Six Essays* (London: Unwin). *See also* the 1972 reprint with an introduction by J. Mordaunt Crook (New York and London: Johnson).

Ferrey, Benjamin (1861) *Recollections of A.N. Welby Pugin, and His Father, Augustus Pugin* (London: E. Stanford).
Fisher, Michael (1995) *A Vision of Splendour: Gothic Revival in Staffordshire 1840–1890* (Stafford: Fisher).
Fisher, Michael (2012) *'Gothic For Ever': A.W.N. Pugin, Lord Shrewsbury, and the Rebuilding of Catholic England* (Reading: Spire).
Freeman, Jennifer M. (1990) *W.D. Caröe RStO FSA* (Manchester: Manchester University Press).
Goodhart-Rendel, H.S. (1949) 'Rogue Architects of the Victorian Era', *Journal of the RIBA* 3rd Series **lvi**/6, 251–9.
Goodhart-Rendel, H.S. (1989) *English Architecture Since the Regency: An Interpretation* (London: Century, first publ. Constable, 1953).
Gray, A. Stuart (1985) *Edwardian Architecture: A Biographical Dictionary* (London: Duckworth).
Hague, Graham, and Hague, Judy (1986) *The Unitarian Heritage. An Architectural Survey of Chapels and Churches ... in the British Isles* (Sheffield: P.B. Godfrey).
Hall, Michael (2000) 'What do Victorian Churches Mean? Symbolism and Sacramentalism in Anglican Church Architecture, 1850–1870', *Journal of the Society of Architectural Historians* **lix**/4, 78–95.
Hall, Michael (ed.) (2002) *Gothic Architecture and its Meanings 1550–1830* (Reading: Spire in association with the Georgian Group).
Hall, Michael (2014) *George Frederick Bodley and the Later Gothic Revival in Britain and America* (New Haven and London: Yale University Press for The Paul Mellon Centre for Studies in British Art).
Hamilton, Alec (2020) *Arts & Crafts Churches* (London: Lund Humphries).
Hersey, George Leonard (1972) *High Victorian Gothic. A Study in Associationism* (Baltimore, MD: Johns Hopkins University Press).
Hill, Rosemary (2007) *God's Architect: Pugin and the Building of Romantic Britain* (London: Allen Lane).
Hitchcock, Henry-Russell (1954) *Early Victorian Architecture in Britain* (New Haven and London: Yale University Press).
Hitchcock, Henry-Russell (1968) *Architecture: Nineteenth and Twentieth Centuries* (Harmondsworth: Penguin).
Hôpital, Winifred De L' (1919) *Westminster Cathedral and its Architect* (London: Hutchinson).
Howell, Peter (2020) *John Francis Bentley: Architect of Westminster Cathedral* (Liverpool: University Press for Historic England).
Howell, Peter, and Saint, Andrew (eds) (2017) *Studies in Victorian Architecture and Design* vi*: Butterfield Revisited* (London: Victorian Society).
Howell, Peter, and Sutton, Ian (eds) with The Victorian Society (1989) *The Faber Guide to Victorian Churches* (London: Faber & Faber).
Hubbard, Edward (1991) *The Work of John Douglas* (London: Victorian Society, repr. Huddersfield: Northern Heritage Publications, an imprint of Jeremy Mills Publishing, 2013).
Humphrey, Stephen Charles (ed.) (1991a) *Blue Guide Churches and Chapels of Northern England* (London: A.& C. Black; New York: W.W. Norton).
Humphrey, Stephen Charles (1991b) *Blue Guide Churches and Chapels of Southern England* (London: A.& C. Black; New York: W.W. Norton).
Hunter, Gill (2010) *William White: Pioneer Victorian Architect* (Reading: Spire).
Hyland, Gerard Joseph (2014) *The Architectural Works of A.W.N. Pugin: A Catalogue* (Reading: Spire).
Hyland, Gerard Joseph (2021) *The Life and Works of Edward Welby Pugin, Architect, 1834–75* (Ramsgate: Pugin Society).
Jackson, Neil (1980) 'The Un-Englishness of G. E. Street's Church of St James-the-Less', *Architectural History* **xxiii**, 86–94.

Jackson, Neil (2000) 'Christ Church, Streatham, and the Rise of Constructional Polychromy', *Architectural History* **xliii**, 219–52.
Jordan, Kate (2019) 'A Benign Paterfamilias; John Dando Sedding, his Family and Followers', *Ecclesiology Today* **lvii**, 3–20.
King, Thomas H. (1868) *The Study-Book of Mediæval Architecture and Art* (London: Henry Sotheran).
Kingsley, Charles (1908) *Alton Locke: Tailor and Poet* (London: Nelson, first publ. 1850).
Kirby, Mark (ed.) (2020) *Chancel Screens since the Reformation* (London: Ecclesiological Society).
Legg, John Wickham (ed.) (1891–7) *Missale ad Usum Ecclesie Westmonasteriensis* (London: Harrison for the Henry Bradshaw Society).
Legg, John Wickham (1916) *The Sarum Missal* (Oxford: Clarendon Press).
Martin, Christopher (2006) *A Glimpse of Heaven: Catholic Churches of England and Wales* (Swindon: English Heritage with Catholic Bishops' Conference of England and Wales).
Maskell, William (ed.) (1882) *The Ancient Liturgy of the Church of England, according to the uses of Sarum, York, Hereford, and Bangor, and the Roman Liturgy arranged in parallel columns with Preface and Notes* (Oxford: Clarendon Press, first. publ. William Pickering, 1844).
Members of the University of Oxford (1833–41) *Tracts for the Times* (London: Rivington; Oxford: J.H. Parker).
Micklethwaite, J.T. (1874) *Modern Parish Churches* (London: H.S. King).
Micklethwaite, J.T. (1908) *Occasional Notes on Church Furniture & Arrangement* (London: Incorporated Church Building Society).
Milner, John (1811) *Treatise on the Ecclesiastical Architecture of England, during the Middle Ages* (London: J. Taylor).
Mozley, Thomas (1882) *Reminiscences of Oriel College and the Oxford Movement* (London: Longmans, Green).
Muthesius, Hermann (1901) *Die neuere kirchliche Baukunst in England* (Berlin: Ernst & Sohn).
Muthesius, Stefan (1972) *The High Victorian Movement in Architecture, 1850–70* (London: Routledge & Kegan Paul).
Myles, Janet (1996) *L.N. Cottingham 1787–1847: Architect of the Gothic Revival* (London: Lund Humphries).
Newman, John Henry (1967) *Apologia Pro Vita Sua*, Martin J. Svaglic (ed.) (Oxford: Clarendon Press).
O'Reilly, Seán (1997) 'Roman *versus* Romantic: Classical Roots in the Origins of a Roman Catholic Ecclesiology', *Architectural History* **xl**, 222–40.
Palmer, William (1845) *Origines liturgicæ; or Antiquities of the English Ritual* (London: Rivington).
Parker, John Henry (1850) *A Glossary of Terms used in ... Architecture* (Oxford: J.H. Parker).
Pevsner, Nikolaus, *et al* (from 1951) *The Buildings of England* series (Harmondsworth and London: Penguin; New Haven and London: Yale University Press).
Port, Michael Harry (2006) *Six Hundred New Churches: A Study of The Church Building Commission 1818–56* (Reading: Spire).
Pugin, Augustus Welby Northmore (1841) *The True Principles of Pointed or Christian Architecture* (London: John Weale). *See also* The Pugin Society edition (2003), with introduction by Timothy Brittain-Catlin (Reading: Spire).
Pugin, Augustus Welby Northmore (1843a) *An Apology for the Revival of Christian Architecture in England* (London: John Weale).
Pugin, Augustus Welby Northmore (1843b) *The Present State of Ecclesiastical Architecture in England* (London: Charles Dolman).
Pugin, Augustus Welby Northmore (1851) *A Treatise on Chancel Screens and Rood Lofts, their Antiquity, Use and Symbolic Signification* (London: Charles Dolman).
Pugin, Augustus Welby Northmore (1973) *Contrasts: Or, a Parallel between the Noble Edifices of the Middle Ages, and Corresponding Buildings of the Present Day*, with introduction by

H.-R. Hitchcock (Leicester: Leicester University Press). Originally published London: Charles Dolman, 1841; an earlier version, with a slightly different title, was published by Pugin (1836). *See also* The Pugin Society edition (2003), with introduction by Timothy Brittain-Catlin (Reading: Spire).
Purchas, John (1866) *The Directorium Anglicanum; ... Directions for the Right Celebration of the Holy Communion, ... and for the Performance of other Rites and Ceremonies ... according to the Ancient Uses of the Church of England* (London: T. Bosworth). Originally published 1858; the second edition was revised by Frederick George Lee.
Quiney, Anthony (1979) *John Loughborough Pearson* (New Haven and London: Yale University Press).
Quiney, Anthony (1995) '"Altogether a Capital Fellow and a Serious Fellow Too": A Brief Account of the Life and Work of Henry Woodyer, 1816–1896', *Architectural History* **xxxviii**, 192–219.
Rickman, Thomas (1881) *An Attempt to Discriminate the Styles of Architecture in England, from the Conquest to the Reformation*, J.H. Parker (ed.) (Oxford and London: J.H. Parker).
Rock, Daniel (1849–53) *The Church of Our Fathers, as seen in St Osmund's Rite for the Cathedral of Salisbury* (London: Charles Dolman).
Saint, Andrew (1976) *Richard Norman Shaw* (New Haven and London: Yale University Press).
Salmon, Frank (ed.) (1998) *Gothic and the Gothic Revival* (London: Society of Architectural Historians of Great Britain).
Saunders, Matthew (1982) *The Churches of S.S. Teulon* (London: Ecclesiological Society).
Scott, George Gilbert (1850) *A Plea for the Faithful Restoration of our Ancient Churches* (London: J.H. Parker).
Scott, George Gilbert (1857) *Remarks on Secular & Domestic Architecture, Present & Future* (London: John Murray).
Scott, George Gilbert (1879) *Personal and Professional Recollections* (London: Sampson, Low, etc.). *See also* the new edition: Gavin Stamp (ed.) (1995) (Stamford: Paul Watkins Publishing).
Scott, George Gilbert, Jr. (1881) *An Essay on the History of English Church Architecture prior to the Separation of England from the Roman Obedience* (London: Simpkin, Marshall, & Co.).
Sladen, Teresa, and Saint, Andrew (eds) (2011) *Studies in Victorian Architecture and Design* iii: *Churches 1870–1914* (London: Victorian Society).
Stamp, Gavin (2002) *An Architect of Promise: George Gilbert Scott Junior (1839–1897) and the Late Gothic Revival* (Donington: Shaun Tyas).
Stamp, Gavin (2015) *Gothic for the Steam Age: An Illustrated Biography of George Gilbert Scott* (London: Aurum Press).
Stamp, Gavin, and Amery, Colin (1980) *Victorian Buildings of London 1837–1887: An Illustrated Guide* (London: Architectural Press).
Stell, Christopher (1986, 1991, 1994, 2001) *An Inventory of Nonconformist Chapels and Meeting-Houses ...* (London: Her Majesty's Stationery Office).
Street, Arthur Edmund (1888) *Memoir of George Edmund Street, R.A., 1824–1881* (London: John Murray).
Street, George Edmund (1850) 'On the Proper Characteristics of a Town Church', *The Ecclesiologist* **xi**, N.S. **viii/lxxxi** (N.S. **xlv**) (December 1850), 227–33.
Street, George Edmund (1853) *An Urgent Plea for the Revival of the True Principles of Architecture in the Public Buildings of the University of Oxford* (Oxford: J.H. Parker).
Street, George Edmund (1855) *Brick and Marble in the Middle Ages* (London: John Murray).
Symondson, Anthony (1995) 'Theology, Worship, and the Late Victorian Church' in Brooks, Chris, and Saint, Andrew (eds) *The Victorian Church* (Manchester: Manchester University Press), 192–222.
Symondson, Anthony (1997) 'Look With Your Ears: Some 20th-century Attitudes to the Late Gothic Revival' in Whittingham, Sarah (ed.) *The Victorian Society Annual 1996* (London: Victorian Society), 37–49.

Symondson, Anthony, and Bucknall, Stephen Arthur (2006) *Sir Ninian Comper: An Introduction to his Life and Work, with Complete Gazetteer* (Reading: Spire with the Ecclesiological Society).

Taylor, Richard (2004) *How to Read a Church: An Illustrated Guide to Images, Symbols and Meanings in Churches and Cathedrals* (London: Rider).

Thompson, Paul (1971) *William Butterfield* (London: Routledge & Kegan Paul; Cambridge, MA: MIT Press).

Victoria & Albert Museum (1971) *Victorian Church Art. Catalogue of an Exhibition. November 1971–January 1972*, Anthony Burton (ed.) (London: Her Majesty's Stationery Office).

Warton, Thomas, Bentham, James, Grose, Francis, and Milner, John (1800) *Essays on Gothic Architecture* (London: J. Taylor).

Watkin, David (1977) *Morality and Architecture* (Oxford: Clarendon Press). *See also* Watkin (2001) *Morality and Architecture Revisited* (London: John Murray).

Webster, Christopher (2010) *R.D. Chantrell (1793–1872) and the Architecture of a Lost Generation* (Reading: Spire).

Webster, Christopher (ed.) (2011) *Episodes in the Gothic Revival: Six Church Architects* (Reading: Spire).

Webster, Christopher (2012) *The Practice of Architecture: Eight Architects, 1830–1930* (Reading: Spire).

Webster, Christopher, and Elliott, John (eds) (2000) *'A Church as it Should Be': the Cambridge Camden Society and its Influence* (Donington: Shaun Tyas/Paul Watkins Publishing).

Webster, Christopher (2022) *Late-Georgian Churches: Anglican architecture, patronage and churchgoing in England, 1790-1840* (London: John Hudson Publishing).

Whelan, Aidan (2014) 'George Gilbert Scott: A Pioneer of Constructional Polychromy?', *Architectural History* **lvii**, 217–38.

White, James F. (1962) *The Cambridge Movement: The Ecclesiologists and the Gothic Revival* (Cambridge: Cambridge University Press).

Whittingham, Sarah (ed.) (1997) *The Victorian Society Annual 1996* (London: Victorian Society).

Whittington, George Downing (1809) *An Historical Survey of the Ecclesiastical Antiquities of France* (London: J. Taylor).

Wigley, George Jonas (tr. and ed.) (1857) *St Charles Borromeo's Instructions on Ecclesiastical Building*, tr. of *Instructiones fabricæ et supellectilis ecclesiasticæ* (1577) with illustrations by S.J. Nicholl (London: Charles Dolman).

Wiseman, Nicholas Patrick (1841) *A Series of Papers on The Oxford Controversy (1836), etc.* (London: Catholic Institute of Great Britain).

Index

... the best book in the world would owe the most to a good index, and the worst ..., if it had but a single good thought in it, might be kept alive by it ...

HORACE BINNEY (1780-1875):
Letter to SAMUEL AUSTIN ALLIBONE (1816-89) (8 April 1868)